APOCALYPSE

THE GREAT JEWISH REVOLT
AGAINST ROME
AD 66 - 73

NEIL FAULKNER

TEMPUS

For Lucy,
Tiggy & Rowena

First published 2002

PUBLISHED IN THE UNITED KINGDOM BY:
Tempus Publishing Ltd
The Mill, Brimscombe Port
Stroud, Gloucestershire GL5 2QG

PUBLISHED IN THE UNITED STATES OF AMERICA BY:
Tempus Publishing Inc.
2 Cumberland Street
Charleston, SC 29401

British Library Cataloguing in Publication Data.
A catalogue record for this book is available from the British Library.

ISBN 0 7524 1968 4

Typesetting and origination by Tempus Publishing.
Printed in Great Britain by Midway Colour Print, Wiltshire

Contents

Acknowledgements

I owe my interest in ancient history to the infectious enthusiasm of Richard Gosling (formerly a teacher at The Skinners' School in Tunbridge Wells), and my introduction to the Roman army to the excellent lectures of Mark Hassall at the Institute of Archaeology, UCL. I am deeply indebted to four very conscientious and critical readers: Gwyn Davies (Florida International University), a specialist in Roman siege warfare; Danny Phillips, who has a profound understanding of ancient Jewish history; Keith Robinson, an old friend with a keen sense of what makes for good historical writing; and Dominic Andrews, who purged the text of much stilted phraseology. I am also grateful to Vernon Trafford, Fran Smith and John Rose for other critical comments, and more generally to adult education students at The City Literary Institute and Wansfell College, with whom I have shared and debated many of the ideas presented here. I must also thank Vernon Trafford (again) for introducing me to Avishai Tal, who gave excellent advice on travel arrangements in Israel and recommended that I stay in the delightfully simple and non-commercial Church of Scotland hospices in Tiberias and Jerusalem. My greatest debt is, however, to Dominic Andrews, for he was not only a critic of my text but also the talented young artist responsible for the reconstructions in the book; in particular we worked closely together to turn new ideas about ancient combat into the two paintings of battle that are the highlights of the colour plates. Dominic in turn is indebted to John Eagle and Peter Connolly for their help with his research on ancient military equipment. Finally, of course, there is my family to thank: Lucy Harris, who has endured two years of the Jewish War; Helen Harris and Mary Faulkner, two grandmothers who have occasionally come to the rescue; and Tiggy and Rowena, two daughters of an oft-absent father.

St Albans
June 2002

A note on ancient monetary values

The coinage of the early western empire was based on a golden *aureus*, silver *denarii* (25 to the *aureus*), and base-metal *sestertii* (100), *dupondii* (200), *asses* (400), *semisses* (800), and *quadrantes* (1600). But many eastern cities continued to issue their own coins using a Greek system based on minas, drachmas and obols (with various multiples and fractions of these), and the Jews employed a third system based on the shekel (also with various fractions). In each case the basic currency unit tended to be a silver coin – *denarius*, drachma/tetradrachma or shekel – but the weights of these could vary quite a lot (4.5g was about average for the *denarius*), and the actual silver content much more so (from 90 per cent to perhaps as little as 20 per cent). Larger amounts of money might, however, be expressed in terms of talents – though these were never coined – one talent being 26kg of silver and therefore 6,000 *denarii* (or drachmae, or tetradrachmae, or shekels, depending on weight and silver content).

It is notoriously difficult to convert ancient monetary values into modern equivalents, especially since it is relative purchasing power, not nominal equivalents, that we are really interested in. A key question is: what constituted a living wage? Agricultural labourers received one *denarius* for a day's work, and it has been estimated that a typical peasant family of six would have needed about 180 *denarii* a year for basic subsistence. The annual pay of Roman soldiers was 225 *denarii* for a legionary, 150 for an auxiliary cavalryman, and 75 for an auxiliary infantryman. Deductions may have been made for food, fodder, clothes, equipment, and the regimental burial club, but on the other hand soldiers had free accommodation, generous bonuses, and did not pay tax.

Richard Reece proposes a modern British equivalent of about £25 ($37) for a *denarius*, which would give £4,500 ($6,570) as the minimum peasant family income, £5,625 ($8,213) for legionary pay, £3,750 ($5,475) for auxiliary cavalry, and £1,875 ($2,738) for auxiliary infantry. These figures should not, of course, be compared with income levels in modern western societies, where the average standard of living is high; the ancient world was a pre-industrial society with much lower levels of material culture.

In the light of all this, I have chosen to express monetary values in the text in terms of *denarii*, i.e. in units valued at approximately £25 ($37) of purchasing power, on the understanding that this was a relatively more significant sum in antiquity than it is today.

Introduction

This is a book about revolution and war. The great Greek historian Thucydides wrote that these were the only real subjects of history. There is a sense in which this is true. History turns on its great events. The whole history of the twentieth century could be written, more or less, in terms of four great events: the First World War, the Russian Revolution, the Second World War, and the Cold War. It is difficult to think of anything of consequence that happened between 1914 and 1989 that could be properly understood without reference to at least one of them. Another great historian of revolution and war, Leon Trotsky, argued that one day of revolution had the same significance in human affairs as a whole year of normal life, and, moreover, that in revolution the inner workings of entire epochs stood revealed. The subject of this book was an event of that kind. The great Jewish revolt against Rome in AD 66–73 pitted an army of peasant guerrillas against the most powerful empire and war machine of antiquity. When we study the struggle, we see a global system of robbery with violence, a society racked by class conflict, and a battle of ideas in which radical visions of a world transformed competed with decades of deference and despair.

The story is not an easy one to write. True, the sources are fuller than for any other comparable event in antiquity. But that is not saying much: they are still sparse and problematic – the self-justifying chronicle of a conservative aristocrat, religious texts in which reference to contemporary politics is heavily coded, and archaeological evidence whose relation to historically recorded events is incapable of proof. Making sense of such difficult material – turning it into coherent narrative – is no simple matter. No scholar is ideally suited to the task, since none is a specialist in all the relevant disciplines – the classical languages, the Dead Sea Scrolls, biblical studies, the archaeology of Palestine, military history, social theory, and the historiography of revolution. Despite the difficulties, though, the subject has created a huge literature – much of it highly tendentious. To discuss Palestine in the first century AD is to enter an academic, religious and political minefield, for it is a subject with implications for modern Christianity, rabbinical Judaism, the ideology of Zionism, and the present crisis in the Middle East.

How have I approached the task? What are the distinguishing features of this history? I have treated the evidence, and the commentaries of specialist scholars upon it, as the raw material from which a history must be fashioned. It is important not to confuse the two – evidence and history – especially when the principal primary source is a work like Josephus' *Jewish War*. This is a contemporary history written by a leading participant, and some scholars have relied far too heavily on its highly prejudiced judgements. Josephus was a man of his class and time, and his role in the war was a seriously compromised one. A combination of class hatred for the revolutionaries, ignorance of the dynamics of class struggle, a personal need for self-justification, and the expectations of his Roman patrons make much of his analysis worthless. His *descriptions* of what happened are indispensable (albeit with many inaccuracies), but his *explanations* lack objectivity and sophistication; often they are little more than personal abuse. Scholars who have relied upon Josephus' *judgements* have fallen down heavily.

In a sense, what Josephus lacks, and we must supply, is what R.G. Collingwood called 'historical imagination' – an ability to use general understanding of human motives to explain decisions and make sense of social action. Collingwood's point was that because events do not speak for themselves (bare narrative explains nothing), and because the accounts given by participants are often prejudiced, self-justifying and of limited perspective, the historian's main job is to reconstruct the thinking behind past actions. This has to be done, however, in the context of specific historical situations: people make their own history, but not in circumstances of their own choosing. The historian, in other words, must reconstruct not only the thought processes which give rise to decisions, but also the framework of constraints and possibilities within which decisions are made. And when it comes to mass events like revolution and war, it is the thoughts and circumstances of the many that must be reconstructed. No one, as far as I am aware, has really tried to do this for the Jewish War.

In making the attempt, I have been deeply influenced by three historical traditions. First, there is what is sometimes called 'history from below'. Historians involved in this tradition have consciously rejected what they see as an almost exclusive focus on political élites, insisting instead on the need to study the material circumstances, thought-worlds and collective actions of ordinary men and women. Edward Thompson's *The Making of the English Working Class* is a classic study of this type, one in which the embryonic proletariat ceases to be a submerged and invisible victim, and becomes a class of real men and women actively creating their own history. In relation to my work on the Roman Empire, however, I owe a special debt to Geoffrey de Ste Croix's *The Class Struggle in the Ancient Greek World*; the author's vigorous insistence on the indispensability of Marxist class analysis for making sense of ancient history has been a profound influence. Closely entwined with history from below is the second tradition: the historiography of revolutions. Of particular value – to me anyway – has been the work of Christopher Hill and Brian Manning on the English Revolution, that of Georges Lefebvre, Albert Soboul and Daniel Guérin on the French, and that of Leon Trotsky on the Russian. We know a great deal about these revolutions, and their study offers rich insights into the dynamics of revolutionary change. It is hard to take seriously would-be historians of the Jewish War who neglect them. My third tradition – let me call it 'the new military history' – is a wholly separate development, but one whose preoccupations sometimes parallel those of history from below. John Keegan, a military historian of extraordinary originality and intelligence, is its founding father, but his work has inspired much new research into the realities of ancient battlefield experience by classical scholars like Victor Davis Hanson (on the Greek hoplite phalanx) and Adrian Goldsworthy (on the Roman legion). What drives this research is Keegan's insistence that battles are decided – and the course of history thereby determined – as much by the decisions and actions of soldiers in combat as by the directives of generals.

I have used these traditions to organise the evidence – Josephus, the Bible, the Dead Sea Scrolls, the archaeology of first-century Palestine – into a 'grand narrative'. I have set out both to tell the story and to explain it. My conclusions will offer little comfort to some. Flag-waving patriots will look in vain for any evidence that imperialism can be a force for peace and progress. Catholic cardinals and fundamentalist Christians may not recognise my version of Jesus of Nazareth. Zionist supporters of Israel will be disconcerted to discover that the Jewish rebels of the first century bear more similarity to the Palestinian fighters of Hamas than they do to the soldiers of the Israeli Defence Force. In particular, this account will disappoint those seeking a contribution to some specifically 'Jewish history', for in truth there has never been a single 'Jewish people', nor an unchanging 'Jewish tradition', and only nationalist myth can link Simon bar Giora and Ariel Sharon across 2,000 years. Throughout history there have been Jewish exploiters and Jewish resistance-fighters, Jews who were profiteers and warmongers, and Jews who struggled against oppression and violence. This was the case in the Jewish War of the first century AD – just as it is today – for the war was, in its essence, a colossal confrontation between the haves and have-nots of the Roman Empire, a struggle which ranged landlords, tax-collectors and soldiers against the peasants on whose backs empire and 'civilisation' rested. The story told here is, then, part of the history of ordinary men and women – whether Jews or Gentiles – fighting back against the evils of class domination and empire building.

1 Nero's Empire

> . . . I saw in the visions by night a fourth beast, terrifying and dreadful and exceedingly strong. It had great iron teeth and was devouring, breaking in pieces, and stamping what was left with its feet. . . . it had ten horns. . . . There were eyes like human eyes . . . and a mouth speaking arrogantly.
>
> *(Daniel, 7.7-8)*

The Great Beast

Rhandeia, near the Armenian border, summer AD 63

Gnaeus Domitius Corbulo was the most powerful general in the Roman Empire. Reappointed to supreme command in the long-running Armenian War, he held *maius imperium* ('overriding authority') throughout the East: every provincial governor and client-king from the Black Sea to the Nile Delta was required to obey his orders (**1**). Marching into Armenia in the summer of AD 63, he was at the head of about 50,000 men, one of the largest field armies Rome had ever assembled on the eastern front. He had four full legions and detachments from several others, bringing the total of citizen heavy infantry to perhaps 25,000, and these were supported by numerous auxiliaries and troops supplied by the client-kings. Corbulo also commanded the Syrian army 200 miles to the south, where another three legions and their auxiliary supports guarded the Euphrates river crossings. It was a massive concentration of military power: more than a quarter of the entire Roman imperial army – enough to block completely the direct approach into Syria and the Levant from the north and east, yet still leave Corbulo with overwhelming force in the main theatre of war, the Armenian mountains.

As the Roman army marched in, Corbulo unleashed 'fire and sword' on the territories of Armenian chiefs who resisted. Men were cut down, their women raped, and any survivors enslaved; villages were demolished, crops torched, animals driven off; and those who escaped became refugees in the hilltops, enfeebled by cold and hunger. Tiridates, King of Armenia, sought peace by offering conciliation and proposing a conference – to be held at Rhandeia, he suggested, in the western borderlands of his kingdom, where, as it happened, only the year before, his Parthian kinsmen had inflicted a humiliating defeat on the Romans.

The invasion of AD 62 had indeed been a sorry affair. Corbulo's role on that occasion had been restricted to the defence of Syria, and the invasion itself had been led by a new commander, Lucius Caesennius Paetus, charged by his government

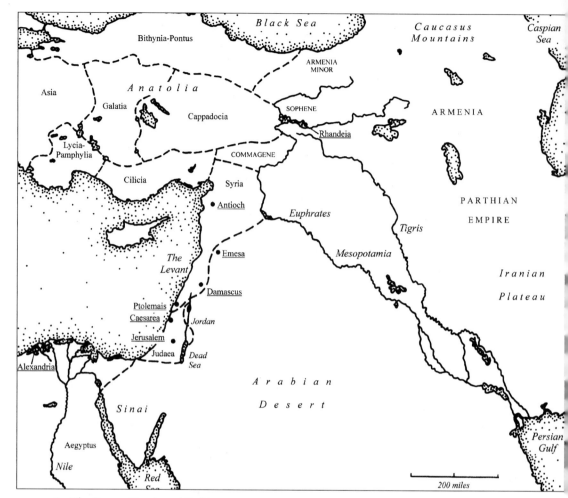

1 *The Roman East in c.AD 64*

with restoring prestige after the flight of Rome's candidate for the Armenian throne and the withdrawal of its army from the kingdom. The view had been that the Parthians needed a sharp reminder of Roman power – but it had not turned out that way. Paetus, with just two legions, had found himself up against the entire Parthian army under the personal leadership of King Vologases, who had intervened to prop up his brother's throne by invading the mountain kingdom in force. The heavily outnumbered Romans were soon besieged in an unfinished camp with inadequate supplies in the middle of winter. The Parthians had eventually let them go, but in their panic-stricken rush to get home, fearing their victorious enemies might yet cut them down, they had abandoned their wounded comrades in the freezing mountains. Paetus' expedition had been a disaster: the commander had lost his sense, the soldiers their military virtue, and the state its frontier security – leaving the Parthian Empire in control of Armenia.

The matter could not have been left to rest there. The Kingdom of Armenia was the Poland of the ancient East, a lynchpin territory around which the world strategies of two superpowers revolved. It was a great expanse of mountains, stretching 300 miles from the Caucasus in the north to Mesopotamia in the south, and 500 from the eastern edge of the Anatolian plateau to the Caspian Sea. Almost the whole of it was 2,000ft high, much of it was above 6,000, and the greatest peaks reached 10,000. The mountain tribes were scattered and isolated. The land was hard and yielded a poor living. Routeways were few and often difficult. The winters were long and bitter. Corbulo had taken his men up into this wilderness to toughen them up for the coming campaign at the start of the Armenian War. 'The whole army was kept under canvas through a winter so severe that ice had to be removed and the ground excavated before tents could be pitched,' wrote the Roman historian Tacitus. 'Frostbite caused many losses of limbs. Sentries were frozen to death. A soldier was seen carrying a bundle of firewood with hands so frozen that they fell off, fastened to their load.'

However desolate, Armenia mattered. To the south-east lay the Parthian Empire. Its vast sprawl stretched from Afghanistan to the borders of Syria, and its two centres of gravity were the ancient urban civilisation of Mesopotamia (modern Iraq), from which it drew wealth, and the great steppe-land of south-western Asia (modern Iran), where it recruited the feudal heavy cavalry and horse-archers which formed its armies. This was the only state with military power comparable to her own that Rome faced on any frontier. Rome's empire, of course, stretched back westwards and was centred on the Mediterranean (*mare nostrum*, 'our sea', the Romans called it), where hundreds of great cities were strung like shining beads around its rim (**2**). Between these two imperial systems, a great tongue of impassable wilderness projected northwards: the Arabian Desert. No army could cross this waste; nomadic raiders were the worst it could harbour. Superpower rivalry – the rivalry of great armies – was funnelled along the diagonal corridor formed by Upper Mesopotamia. As the Parthians saw it, coming from the south-east, this corridor split into three routes. One headed directly eastwards, across the Euphrates and straight into Syria, heart of Rome's eastern empire: here, as it were, was the heavily guarded main gate. The other two routes went north, one up the Tigris towards the middle of Armenia, the other up the Euphrates skirting the kingdom's western borderlands: the way into the Roman East was less direct here, but these rear gates were often badly guarded. Rome's invasion routes into Parthia flowed, naturally enough, in the opposite direction.

So 'the Great Game' – the endless jostling for strategic advantage – was played out between Rome and Parthia mainly among the hapless mountain people of Armenia. Here the great powers intrigued, plotted and manoeuvred, directing embassies and ultimatums at one another, buying and selling kings, trading the territories of border tribes, sometimes sending in a 'peace-keeping' force, sometimes fuelling a vicious little proxy war, occasionally launching a full-scale invasion. There was little chance of any final resolution. The struggle was all to do with keeping a balance of power. Parthia's vast spaces, the great distance to her heartlands, the invin-

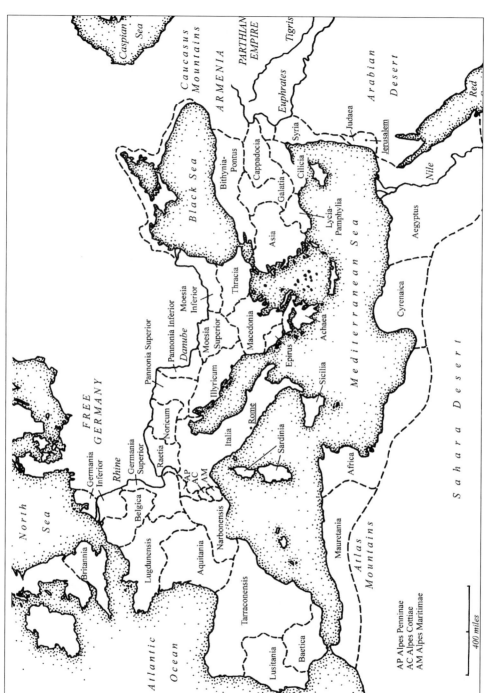

2 *The Roman Empire in c.AD 64*

cibility of her armoured cavalry and horse-archers on the open steppe, these things made a Roman conquest of the Orient impossibly ambitious. But the rootedness of Graeco-Roman civilisation in the East, the solidity of the Roman legions in its defence, and the fractious instability of their huge domains were equally effective constraints on the ambitions of the Parthian kings. Roman emperors occasionally dreamed of emulating Alexander and marching to India; the Parthians sometimes made claim to the old empire of Cyrus, which had stretched to the Aegean. It was bluster in both cases. The superpowers were at an impasse. Neither could overthrow the other. The Great Game could only continue – endlessly.

In this struggle to maintain a balance of power, prestige was all. Each side had to inspire fear and confidence in equal amounts – fear to deter the enemy, confidence to inspire one's allies. Achieving this was essentially a matter of prestige – a matter, that is, of an *appearance* of power. Prestige fell and danger threatened mainly when others perceived a shift in the balance, a weakening of one side's power, a reduction in its ability to strike back effectively when challenged. Carefully constructed networks of frontier defence – of brigades and regiments, forts and garrison towns, buffer states and petty kings – could then unravel. Corbulo's earlier campaigns in AD 58-60 had been Rome's effort to restore prestige and security after the Armenian throne had been seized by the Parthian king's brother Tiridates. Roman success had enabled them to place their own puppet on the throne, but Tigranes had then slipped the leash and attacked the neighbouring Kingdom of Adiabene, which was a Parthian ally. King Vologases had been forced to respond by the combined pressure of his exiled brother, a violated ally, and the indignant Parthian nobility. Was Vologases a proper king or not? 'Passivity does not deserve great empires,' he was told. 'That needs fighting – with warriors and weapons. When stakes are highest, might is right. A private person can maintain prestige by keeping hold of what's his; a king can do so only by grabbing the property of others.' The scene is 'faction': the words are really those of Tacitus, the Roman historian; but he displays here his understanding of ancient empire, its driving forces and transmission belts, the demands on its rulers for decision, action and ruthlessness. To prevent his empire's north-west frontier from unravelling, Vologases had been compelled to strike back hard. So in AD 61 he had invaded Armenia to oust Tigranes and reinstate Tiridates. And when Rome had retaliated the following year, he had crushed Paetus' army and sent it headlong in flight from the mountain kingdom.

Yet the aim was neither all-out war nor outright conquest; it was to redress the balance, to restore an equality of prestige and deterrence. Vologases had let Paetus' army go. 'I have sufficiently demonstrated my power,' he declared, 'and I have also given proof of my clemency.' Force had re-established the *status quo*, and now it was necessary to secure it through conciliation and compromise. He offered almost enough: Tiridates would lay down his diadem and take it up again before 'the emperor's standards and statues'; he would allow himself to be crowned again 'before the Roman army'; he would, in short, pay homage to Nero as his lord. He would be an Armenian ruler who was both brother of the Parthian king and vassal of the Roman emperor: a compromise peace for a stalemated war in a superpower impasse.

It was not quite enough. Rome's rulers, too, had met in gloomy conference. 'The ironical character of the orientals' request for what they had already seized was clear. Nero consulted his council: was it to be a hazardous war or a humiliating peace? The unhesitating decision was for war.'

The Roman setback in AD 61, followed by outright defeat in AD 62, had given too much hope to the Parthians, their allies and every would-be rebel in the Roman East. Rome's friends needed reassurance, especially the client-kings, the puppet rulers of various small buffer states along the border, whose soldiers had fought beside the legions in the Armenian mountains – Sohaemus of Sophene, Aristobulus of Armenia Minor, Antiochus Epiphanes of Commagene, and Herod Agrippa, the Jewish ruler of a string of territories in and around Palestine. These men needed to know they had not backed a loser; that their property, power and privilege were safe with Rome. Vologases' offer was too little to expunge the memory of defeat and retreat. Nero needed a demonstration of strength in the East. So Corbulo's great army found itself marching to a rendezvous at Rhandeia in the summer of AD 63 – the eleventh year of the war.

But it was meant for show. Both sides wanted peace, and the gap between them was small. Nero demanded homage from Tiridates in person, and Vologases, his own prestige restored by the campaigns of AD 61-2, would not fight a war over this trifle: Tiridates was ordered to comply. In due course the Parthian prince would go to Rome to 'receive' his crown from his overlord, and in the meantime he removed the royal diadem and laid it before the emperor's statue. A deal had been struck. A few days later there was a grand military tattoo in which a Parthian cavalry army paraded alongside the legions of Rome.

So it ended. The opposing armies had advanced and retreated many times, and each time fortune swung against them, they had raised the stakes and brought yet greater force to bear – until a balance of fear was finally restored. The defence of empire required that each opponent should match blow for blow. Parthia and Rome were battling rams locked head-to-head. To give way was to risk a potentially disastrous collapse of prestige. Whether it was open war or armed truce, each state was driven by the existence of the other always to be preparing and threatening war. Nor was it different on Rome's other frontiers. Twenty more legions guarded Egypt (where two were stationed), Africa (one), Spain (one), Britain (three or four), the Rhineland (six or seven), and the long line of the Danube through Central and Eastern Europe (another six or seven). No single enemy elsewhere was as powerful as the Parthian Empire; but collectively the many different enemies that Rome faced locked her inescapably into a struggle for existence mediated by war and preparations for war. Ancient civilisation was a world system of military competition between opposing states. The Great Beast of Judaeo-Christian apocalyptic literature was, in its essence, an imperial war machine – and its heart was the ancient city of Rome (**3**).

3 *Engraving of the Forum at the centre of ancient Rome. Though highly conjectural, it probably gives a good overall impression of the grandeur of public architecture. Rome was an imperial city built from the spoils of a Mediterranean-wide dominion*

The New Babylon

Rome, autumn AD 64

In July AD 64 a huge fire had swept through Rome destroying three of the city's fourteen districts completely, devastating seven others, and leaving only four entirely untouched. Thousands died, trapped in narrow backstreets amid blazing tenement-blocks as the fire ripped through timber superstructures dried out by the Roman summer. Tens of thousands, homeless and destitute, were left camping out in public buildings and parks. From then until the end of Nero's reign four years later, Rome seemed like a single vast building-site. Debris was cleared away, shipped down the Tiber, and dumped in coastal marshland. New wide boulevards were laid out, and low-rise, stone-built courtyard houses replaced the rickety tenements of old Rome. But the grandest of the new building projects was something quite different. The fire had cut a swathe of destruction through some of the best real-estate in the city, and the imperial court seized the opportunity to link together existing properties on neighbouring hills and create a vast palace and park complex in the centre of Rome (**4**).

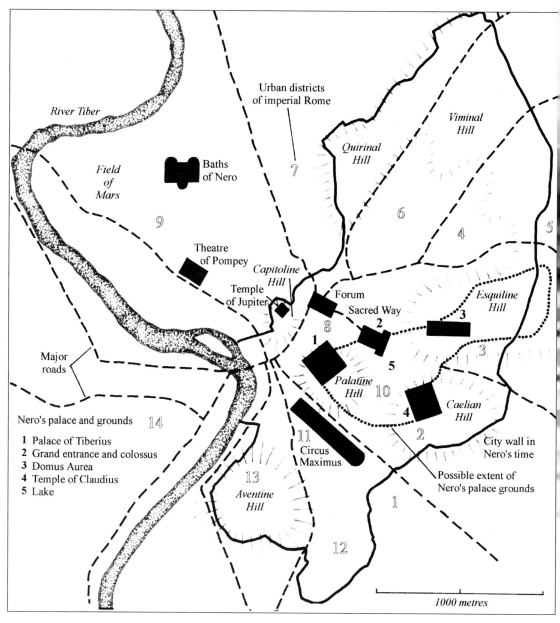

River Tiber

Urban districts
of imperial Rome

Viminal
Hill

Field
of
Mars

Baths
of Nero

Quirinal
Hill

7

6

4

5

9

Theatre
of Pompey

Capitoline
Hill

Temple
of Jupiter

Forum

Sacred Way

Esquiline
Hill

3

8

2

3

1

Major
roads

5

Palatine
Hill

10

Caelian
Hill

Nero's palace and grounds

14

4

2

City wall in
Nero's time

11

Circus
Maximus

1 Palace of Tiberius
2 Grand entrance and colossus
3 Domus Aurea
4 Temple of Claudius
5 Lake

13

Aventine
Hill

1

Possible extent of
Nero's palace grounds

12

1000 metres

4 *Plan of early imperial Rome showing Nero's palace and the possible extent of its grounds*

The grounds were between 125 and 200 acres (50-80ha) in extent – two, three, perhaps four times the size of the present Vatican. 'One house,' exclaimed the Roman poet Martial, 'took up the whole of Rome.' A great landscaped park was laid out, with lawns, woods, lakes, porticoes and grand vistas – 'a faked rusticity' as Tacitus sneeringly put it – and this provided the setting for various monumental buildings, including the fabulous 'Golden House' (*Domus Aurea*). This was Nero's new palace, a spectacular display of grandeur, art and luxury. The architecture was revolutionary, the mosaics and frescoes superb, and the numerous sculptures were an array of Greek masterpieces. The little of it that remains today can only hint at its former richness and confirm the testimony of Nero's ancient biographer.

> Parts of the house were overlaid with gold and studded with precious stones and mother-of-pearl. All the dining-rooms had ceilings of fretted ivory, the panels of which could slide back and let a rain of flowers or perfume from hidden sprinklers shower upon the guests. The main dining-room was circular, and its roof revolved slowly, day and night, in time with the sky. Sea-water or sulphur water was always on tap in the baths. When the palace had been decorated throughout in this lavish style, Nero dedicated it, condescending to remark, 'Good, now at last I can begin to live like a human being!'
>
> (Suetonius, *Nero*, 31)

Nero, though, if not actually claiming to be a god, hardly considered himself an ordinary mortal. Between the Palatine and Esquiline Hills, another great edifice, the *Domus Transitoria*, formed a monumental entrance to the imperial park, and here, in a central colonnaded courtyard looking down the Sacred Way to the Roman Forum below, stood a 35m-high bronze statue of the emperor in the guise of the Sun-god Apollo.

Nero in life was rather less impressive (**5**). The ancient writers record him as short-sighted, paunchy and prone to spots and body odour. He was also idle, hedonistic and, above all, vain. Wearing brilliantly coloured Greek costumes, Nero loved to perform in public in the hope of winning praise and prizes. He would sing, play the lyre, present his own poetry, dance, act on the tragic stage, or race chariots in the circus. To guarantee the plaudits he craved, Nero formed a claque of aristocratic fops and perfumed youths; eventually 5,000 strong, organised into sections under section-leaders, their job was to provide loud rhythmic applause at the emperor's performances, the 'bees' buzzing their approval, the 'hollow-tiles' clapping with cupped hands, the 'flat-tiles' with straightened ones. Until AD 64 these appearances as artist and sportsman had been before private audiences; now, for the first time, he participated in public games in the mainly Greek city of Naples; the following year he would appear in Rome itself, performing in his own 'Neronian Games', where a recitation from a Trojan War epic of his own composition provoked raucous demands for an encore from courtiers, guardsmen and the claque – so that he could 'display all his accomplishments'.

5 *Coin portrait of Nero, c.AD 65, when he was 27. The image accurately depicts some of the emperor's physical characteristics, notably the flabbiness recorded in contemporary descriptions*

An entourage of place-seekers gathered around the whimsical dictator. Some were impeccably aristocratic. There was the empress Poppaea Sabina. Rich, beautiful and aloof, she used sex as a political weapon to strike down enemies and advance herself to the pinnacle of power: '. . . married or bachelor bed-fellows were alike: she was indifferent to her reputation, insensible to men's love, and herself unloving – advantage alone dictated the bestowal of her favours' (Tacitus). Beauty, then, was for her the means to power, and she tended it assiduously – with face-creams of her own invention, and by bathing in milk from a private herd of 500 she-donkeys. When she died – kicked while pregnant and mortally wounded in a domestic spat (or so it is said) – Nero's devotion and remorse were such that he had the corpse mummified.

Another close associate of top rank was Aulus Vitellius, destined briefly to be emperor in the turbulent year of AD 69. He was, according to Suetonius, renowned for his gambling, gluttony and addiction to the games. He banqueted three or four times a day, often at the expense of unwilling hosts; an alcoholic flush, huge belly and much loud belching proclaimed his good fortune. Flattery, it seems, was the key to his patron's favour. As president of the Neronian Games in AD 65 he had scurried after a seemingly diffident Nero urging him to grace everyone with a personal performance.

The senators – the class to which Nero, Poppaea and Vitellius belonged – were a tiny group of around 600 millionaire families, some of them blue-blooded aristocrats who could trace their descent back hundreds of years, others recently ennobled 'aris-tocrats-of-office' whose fathers and grandfathers had risen through service as governors and generals under the Caesars. The equestrian order formed the second tier of the Roman aristocracy, the most ambitious of whom, like the new senatorial families, sought advancement through imperial service. These men aspired to be procurators (governors of small provinces or finance officers in larger ones), often with service as military tribunes in the army (senior officers below the rank of general) as important rungs on the career ladder. The peak of an equestrian career might be one of the two prefectures of the Praetorian Guard (the élite bodyguard troops of the emperor in Rome), a rank which often earned a top position at court and admission to the highest councils of government. Such a man was Gaius Ofonius Tigellinus. Having made his fortune as a landowner and breeder of circus horses, he became known to Nero, who made him first Rome's chief of police, then Prefect of the Praetorian Guard; this brought him into Nero's informal cabinet (*consilium*) and made him part of the inner court clique. The enormous political power accumulated by 'upstart' equestrian officers like Tigellinus evoked the wrath of senatorial conservatives – for Tacitus, looking back on these events two generations later, he was 'a notorious criminal' whose 'unending immoralities and evil reputation' the emperor found fascinating.

Resented even more by men of Tacitus' standing were the *liberti* of the imperial household. All great Roman lords had former slaves (or 'freedmen' as they were known) serving them as secretaries, accountants and stewards. The emperor – whose personal estate was vastly in excess of anyone else's, and whose private 'household' affairs were inextricably enmeshed with the business of the state – relied heavily on his own staff of freedman. This provided extraordinary opportunities for advancement to men of humble status. Men like Phaon, the imperial chancellor-of-the-exchequer (*a rationibus*), Doryphorus, who handled relations between Rome and the cities and provinces of the Empire (*a libellis*); Anicetus, the former tutor who became an admiral of the fleet and an accomplice in the murder of Nero's irritating mother; and Polyclitus, a senior minister who led a high-level commission of enquiry to Britain in AD 61, and who would later serve as one of two imperial viceroys governing Rome during Nero's year-long absence in Greece in AD 67-8. These men and women – senators, equestrians and freedmen of the court – formed the pinnacle of the imperial system. Their aims were retaining power, amassing wealth and pursuing pleasure. The state, for them, was a junket.

> The most prodigal and notorious banquet was given by Tigellinus [early in AD 64]. . . . The entertainment took place on a raft constructed on Marcus Agrippa's lake. It was towed about by other vessels with gold and ivory fittings. The rowers were degenerates, assorted according to age and vice. Tigellinus had collected birds and animals from remote countries, and even the products of the ocean. On the quays were brothels stocked with high-ranking ladies. Opposite them could be seen naked prostitutes, indecently posturing and gesturing. At nightfall the woods and houses nearby echoed with singing and blazed with lights.
>
> (Tacitus, *Annals*, 15)

Such displays, we are assured, were typical. And the conspicuous consumption of the court – in monumental building, in works of art, in carousing and indulgence – served as a model for the imperial aristocracy as a whole. Tacitus records that one Titus Petronius Niger was admitted into the small circle of Nero's intimates as 'Arbiter of Good Taste', having qualified for this role as 'a refined voluptuary' who 'spent his days sleeping and his nights working and enjoying himself'. He may well be the author of our earliest surviving Latin novel, the *Satyricon*, which includes a bizarre satire on the *nouveaux riches* freedmen of the day, the famous 'Dinner of Trimalchio'. Satire relies for its effect on merely distorting – not supplanting – a widely perceived reality. Petronius depicts a world which, allowing for exaggeration, must actually have existed. Archaeology, moreover, confirms this life of ostentatious luxury. The *Satyricon* is set in the Greek-dominated south of Italy; Trimalchio's dinner might have taken place at Pompeii, Herculaneum or Stabiae, in one of the many grand town houses or suburban villas found there with floors of cut marble or figured mosaic, fresco-covered walls and ceilings, and formal gardens ornamented with colonnades, statues and fountains (**6**). We can imagine it taking place, for example, in the *triclinium* (dining room) of Pompeii's House of the Vettii, the host, resplendent in scarlet cloak, tasselled bib, gilt ring, and gold and ivory bangle, explaining to his assembled guests, while conspicuously holding a silver toothpick, that the household gods whose images they see before them are Gain, Luck and Profit. Trimalchio's dinner was a vulgar display of wealth and largesse in which a grubby entrepreneur, by virtue of newly acquired wealth, could begin to play the role of great lord, a beneficent patron able to shower gifts on dependants and accumulate in return debts of gratitude, honour and loyalty. Petronius was depicting a central feature of Roman life: the network of patron-client relationships which bound society together through a million vertical ties. At the top of this pyramid – a pyramid of gifts, favours, obligations and services – stood the emperor himself, the richest and most powerful of Roman nobles, and thus the greatest patron of all. Nero's grip on power depended, in part, on the success with which he played his role as 'father of his country' (*pater patriae*) – Rome's patron-in-chief.

The soldiers were his most important and demanding clients: regular pay, comfortable conditions, occasional donatives and a generous retirement package were the essential prerequisites of army loyalty. (The army, it should be noted, probably accounted for between half and two-thirds of total state expenditure.) In Rome the army was represented by the Praetorian Guard, and their lead in politics was usually followed by the legions on the frontiers. The Guard, therefore, was both the key to power in the capital and a litmus test for power in the empire as a whole. When Claudius died in AD 54 and Nero's minders made their move to secure the succession for their boy-candidate, it was to the barracks they took him first. 'There, after saying a few words appropriate to the occasion – and promising gifts on the generous standard set by his father – he [Nero] was hailed as emperor,' relates Tacitus. 'The army's decision was followed by senatorial decrees. The provinces, too, showed no hesitation.' The order of events reflected the realities of power.

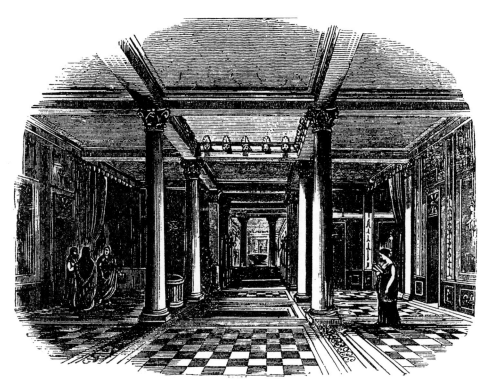

6 *Engraving depicting the* atrium *(front hall) of a Pompeian-style house. The image reflects the grandeur of many of the private residences excavated on Vesuvian sites in the Bay of Naples – residences which seem to provide a setting for Petronius'* Satyricon, *an early-imperial work which satirises the manners of the rich*

The personal bond between emperor and soldiers was the central support of the political system founded by Augustus almost a century before – though it had its roots in the armies of late Republican warlords like Marius, Sulla, Pompey and Caesar. The soldiers swore allegiance to the emperor himself, they were commanded by generals he had appointed, and it was from him they received their payments and rewards. The stability of the throne and the welfare of the soldiers were inextricably linked. This patronage was inflationary. Roman soldiers were both highly privileged and immensely powerful – in a position, that is, to ratchet up the price of loyalty. Caligula had paid 500 *denarii* per man to secure the support of the Praetorian Guard at his succession in AD 37. Claudius had increased the rate massively to 3,750 or 5,000 *denarii* in AD 41, and his successors felt obliged to meet this new standard. Nero paid the same as Claudius in AD 54, and later, in the crisis of AD 69, the Guard would be offered as much as 7,500 per man for their allegiance.

The common citizens of Rome were also important imperial clients. Though corrupted by bribes and petty prejudice, the mob could still sometimes turn on the government. There was often booing, catcalling and chanting in the safe anonymity of crowds at the theatre, the amphitheatre or the circus. There were occasional disturbances in city markets – Claudius had been pelted with stale bread in the Forum and had had to scurry to safety through a side door into the palace. Now and again protests escalated into riots and street battles. When Nero divorced his first wife Octavia to marry Poppaea, demonstrators overturned Poppaea's statues, carried Octavia's shoulder-high, and were clubbed by the Guard when they invaded the palace. These popular outbreaks – often misdirected, usually short-lived, rarely involving more than a minority, but with the potential to turn into something more dangerous – had their origins in the misery of the plebeian quarters. In this vast city of a million people, life for most was hard. In the backstreets, where jerry-built tenements blocked out the sun and stinking sewage rotted in the road, poor citizens lived cheek-by-jowl with freedmen, slaves and foreigners. Here there were men and women who clung to citizen status as to a lifebelt. It was a meal ticket, a free pass to the games, and an ID that proved you were not quite trash. Its guarantor, of course, was the emperor.

When the satirical poet Juvenal wrote later of 'bread and circuses' (*panem et circenses*), he knew something of how the system held together. To be tolerable, the world of palaces, banquets and 'taste' had to share a little of its bounty and glamour. It was the price of social peace. Around 200,000 citizens were kept alive only by state-subsidised grain distributions. The rest relied on a regular supply of grain being shipped in to the city markets from Sicily, Africa and Egypt. It was the emperor's personal responsibility to ensure these things. So Rome's rulers maintained fleets of grain-ships, built huge dockside granaries, dug out new harbours, and planned great canals. Nero cancelled a trip to Greece in AD 64 because of popular fears about the grain supply: his physical presence was needed to maintain confidence and calm.

What of circuses? Under Augustus there had been 66 days of public games every year. Nero increased the total by several days and made the spectacles more elaborate. A new wooden amphitheatre was built in the Field of Mars. An arena yawned open to reveal a magic wood filled with exotic animals. An artificial lake was created to display aquatic beasts. Bears and hippopotamuses appeared. Senators, equestrians and guardsmen battled wild beasts in the arena. A naval battle was staged, Athenians against Persians. Gladiators were carried off in amber-studded coffins. Four-camel chariots raced in the circus. Actors playing Daedalus and Icarus flew across the stage – and one crashed to earth, spattering Nero with blood. Food-parcels were distributed to spectators, and vouchers to claim corn, clothes, gold, silver, precious stones, pearls, paintings, slaves, oxen and mules, wild beasts, even whole farms, tenement-blocks or merchant-ships. Such spectacle and largesse, like other forms of patronage, was inflationary. Each show, each handout, if it was not to flop, had to be greater than the one before, the body count of beasts and men higher, the expenditure on equipment, stage props, machinery and buildings more lavish, the amount and variety of the gifts more generous. At the centre of it all was Nero – Nero the Magnificent, father of his country, patron of his people, a fountain of benefaction. Thus was Rome controlled. Free circuses, like free bread, bought stability.

The ancient city of Rome was, then, a parasite. Its own hinterland – Latium – could not begin to support it. Instead, it fed off its conquests, its subject provinces, sucking out their wealth in taxes, rent, interest and bribes. From this succour it grew stronger: its soldiers were loyal, its army victorious, its frontiers secure; and the court, the nobility, the gentry and the merchants became rich. Greed was good, in the eyes of many at least, and the greedy felt unrestrained about lavish displays of *luxuria*. And because some of the 'spoils of empire' dribbled downwards through the intricate networks of patronage which bound the citizen body together, the social order of the city and the political supremacy of the Caesars held firm. Rome, by the first century AD, was the New Babylon: 'the mother of whores and every obscenity', a black hole of corruption at the centre of the world.

A fiery trial

Rome, autumn AD 64

Sometimes largesse – bread and circuses – was not enough. The gulf between rich and poor was vast. 'We live in a city,' wrote Juvenal in the early second century,

> for the most part shored up with gimcrack stays and props: that's how
> our landlords arrest the collapse of their property, papering over great
> cracks in the ramshackle fabric, reassuring their tenants they can sleep
> secure, when all the time the building is poised like a pack of cards. . . .
> If the alarm goes at ground level, the last to fry will be the attic tenant,
> way up among the nesting pigeons with nothing but tiles between
> himself and the weather. What did friend Cordus own? One truckle
> bed, too short for even a midget nympho; one marble-topped sideboard
> on which stood six little mugs; beneath it a pitcher and an up-ended
> bust of Chiron; one ancient settle crammed with Greek books . . .
> What little the poor man had, he lost. Today the final straw on his load
> of woes (clothes worn to tatters, reduced to begging for crusts) is that
> no one will offer him lodging or shelter, nor even stand him a decent
> meal. But if some millionaire's mansion is gutted, women rend their
> garments, top people put on mourning, the courts go into recess: then
> you hear endless complaints about the hazards of city life, these
> deplorable outbreaks of fire; then contributions pour in while the shell
> is still ash-hot . . .
>
> (*Satires*, 3)

In the excavated remains of Herculaneum, the House of Opus Craticium confirms the crudeness of much plebeian accommodation. It comprised a skeleton of brick pilasters and wooden frames infilled with mortared rubble and covered over with plaster – exterior walling of the flimsiest kind. Small apartments, each formed of tiny rooms, were ranged on two storeys round a gloomy little courtyard with a communal well. Access corridors and stairways were narrow. Light came only from the courtyard. In these lodgings, excavators found humble belongings: wooden bedsteads against the walls, a cupboard with a few utensils, a marble table, a dining couch, a little wooden shrine, simple images of the household gods – testimony to a way of life far removed from that of Rome's great lords.

In autumn AD 64, thousands of poor Romans, people like Juvenal's friend Cordus, people of the House-of-Opus-Craticium class, had been burnt out of their homes and were camped in Rome's open spaces with whatever meagre possessions they had managed to salvage. The talk there was of arson. For now, in place of homes, a park was being laid out. Amid the privation, a palace arose. There were rumours that the fire had been deliberate; that men acting under orders had hurled torches into buildings; that others had threatened those who attempted to fight the blaze; that the conflagration had died down and then been restarted. The popular mood was turning ugly – and the government felt threatened.

Relief measures were stepped up. Elaborate plans for rebuilding were announced. Holy books were consulted and prayers offered to wrathful deities. But blame still attached itself to the regime, and the leadership sought a scapegoat: someone who could be held responsible for the fire and against whom popular anger could be redirected. The chosen victims belonged to a small religious sect most of whose members were socially marginal – foreigners, freedmen, women, slaves. Its practices were somewhat secretive, and its beliefs, so far as they were known, appeared rather odd. It was also essentially Jewish and oriental with a thin veneer of Hellenism, and attacks upon it could therefore draw on deep-rooted prejudices against the East, the Greeks and the Semites. Members of the sect were, for Tacitus, 'the detested of the human race': the people known as 'Christians'. Poor and powerless, without influence or protection, they were the 'bogus asylum-seekers' of their age: victims pure and simple, common people who could be blamed and demonised, attacked and destroyed, with no hope of redress. Onto them the full repressive might of the imperial state now fell. Rome was not ruled by bread alone, nor even by bread and circuses both; under pressure, Rome's rulers also employed the salutary spectacle of the witch-hunt and the lynch mob.

The city was deeply racist. 'For years now,' exclaimed Juvenal, 'the Syrian Orontes has poured its sewage into our native Tiber – its lingo and manners, its flutes, its outlandish harps with their transverse strings, its native tambourines, and the whores who hang out round the race-course.' Here, in Juvenal's third satire, the objects of abuse were Greeks, many of whom, living in Rome, were slaves, freedmen or the descendants thereof, and thus doubly contemptible. But Greeks were Greeks. Most Romans admired Greek culture and were therefore, at worst, no more than ambivalent in their attitude to the real Greeks they came across; many, indeed, were positively enthusiastic, not least Nero himself, who was among the most philhellene of Rome's emperors. Far worse, in the opinion of most Romans, were the people of the true East, the barbaric Orient: Syrians, Egyptians, Persians, Arabs, Indians – and, of course, Jews. 'He had Egyptians and the whole strength of the East even to most distant Bactria,' wrote Virgil of Mark Antony's forces at the legendary battle of Actium a hundred years before.

On his side was the wealth of the Orient and arms of varied design, and he
came victoriously from the nations of the Dawn and the Red Sea's shore,
followed – the shame of it! – by an Egyptian wife. . . . The queen in the
centre called up her columns by sounding the tambourine of her land . . .
Her gods, monstrous shapes of every species, even to the barking Anubis,
levelled weapons against Neptune, Venus and Minerva herself. . . . every
Egyptian, the Indians, every Arab, and all the host of Sheba were on the
point of turning in flight.

(*Aeneid*, 8)

This, for contemporary Romans, was a nightmare image of 'the Yellow Peril'
sweeping in from the East to destroy culture and *libertas* and reduce all to gloomy
despotism. The Jews belonged to this world: a world of despots and slaves. 'Syrians
were born slaves,' announced Cicero, 'like Jews.' 'The customs of that most criminal
nation,' declared Seneca, detecting a sinister spread of Jewish influence, 'have gained
such strength that they have now been received in all lands: the conquered have given
laws to the conquerors.' Whether caricatured as slaves or manipulators – or both at
once (racist discourse is never rational) – the Jews were easy targets because they were
noticeably different and stood out from the crowd. They had long hair and beards –
for Romans of the time indicative of effeteness, decadence and barbarism – and they
wore skull-caps, head-scarves and prayer-shawls. There were strange food regula-
tions, like not eating pork, a habit which had especially irritated the deranged
emperor Caligula. A more serious charge was that Jews were idle, refusing to work
on the Sabbath, every seventh day, and indeed treating the whole of every seventh
year as a period of rest: a tithe of time offered up to their god Yahweh. Strange (and
arrogant) religious beliefs seemed to many the root of the problem: the notion that
there was only one god, *their* god, and everyone else's gods were wooden idols and
lumps of stone. Some aspects of Jewish 'otherness' seemed positively chilling: the
circumcision of Jewish males was a practice which would so offend the neurotic
emperor Hadrian that he would try to ban it. So strict, in fact, were the Laws of
Yahweh that many Jews considered the uncircumcised – 'Gentiles' – a source of
pollution, people who were ritually 'unclean': Romans, it seemed, were not even fit
to eat with. The more credulous believed worse still: that in honour of the Jewish
god, the most vile ritual was regularly performed in the Temple at Jerusalem, when
a captive Greek was fattened up, slaughtered for sacrifice, and then cut up and eaten
by the assembled worshippers. To many of Rome's backstreet racists, the Jews seemed
especially alien and malevolent.

For Rome's rulers, race hatred was a handy tool – part of a wider system of petty
privilege and discrimination by which the Roman masses were fragmented and
controlled. Roman society involved a cascade of contempt, which descended from
the wealthiest blue-blooded senator to the most degraded barbarian slave. Senators
were greater than equestrians, equestrians greater than decurions, but all belonged
to the governing class and looked down on the mob beneath. Land and war were

honourable, commerce less so, while manual labour was definitely undignified, though it was worse if you laboured for wages in the service of another. Clients did homage to their patrons, who were themselves the clients of greater patrons – and so on up the social tree until you got to the members of the court, who were the most powerful patrons of all, except that they of course were still mere clients of the emperor. Roman citizens were privileged as against non-citizens. The free-born were more honourable than the 'freed' (those who had once been slaves), but a 'freedman' was still better than someone who had remained a slave. Townsmen were sophisticated, countrymen yokels. Romans were better than Greeks, but Greeks were better than Jews. And so on. It has all been catalogued in a wonderful book called *Romans and Aliens* by the late J.P.V.D. Balsdon, who describes a world fragmented by class, status and power, where personal encounters were governed by snobbery, prejudice and contempt.

But there was always the danger that these divisions might break down. In the backstreets, cutting across differences of race and religion, a camaraderie of poverty could develop based on common experience. There had been a nasty moment for the government in AD 61. The City Prefect, Lucius Pedanius Secundus, was murdered by a slave. The law required that all Pedanius' household slaves should die. There were 400 of them. A demonstration formed outside the Senate House to protest against the impending atrocity. The senator Gaius Cassius Longinus spoke in favour of the full severity of the law. Our ancestors distrusted their slaves, he is supposed to have said, but the danger was much greater now when households contained people of 'every alien religion'. His conclusion? 'Only intimidation will keep down this scum.' But when the Senate voted for the mass execution to go ahead, huge crowds armed with stones and torches gathered to prevent it, and Nero had to order troops to line the whole route as the forlorn procession of the innocent – men, women and children – passed by on the way to execution. There were, then, dangerous reserves of compassion and solidarity in the backstreets. Rome's ruling class had to work constantly to stifle discontent and prise open the divisions – not only to fill bellies and provide spectacles, but also to create a pecking order of petty privilege, separating free from slave, Roman from Greek, citizen from alien, Gentile from Jew, 'one of us' from 'one of them'.

The Jews were sometimes the main target. There could be sudden bursts of official anti-semitism. The Jews had been expelled from Italy under Tiberius in AD 19, when many were also conscripted into the army. Claudius had first shut down the synagogues, and then he too, in AD 48, had expelled the Jews from Italy. But indiscriminate attacks such as this were problematic. There were perhaps seven or eight million Jews living in the empire, around 6–9 per cent of the population. In the eastern provinces, where most Jews lived, the proportion may have risen to 20 per cent overall, and here they were often highly concentrated – in the home territories of Palestine, in the ghettoes of Diaspora cities, and in many sizeable rural pockets where there had been mass conversions among the peasantry. Action against the Jews in Rome could mean disturbances in Alexandria, Antioch or Jerusalem. Many Jewish communities were large, organised and proactive, well able to defend themselves when challenged. Rome, moreover, was firmly aligned with upper-class Jews, looking to them to help maintain order in the eastern provinces, not least to the great Jewish client-king Herod Agrippa II. A ten-year confrontation with Parthia had just been successfully ended and the eastern frontier secured. Fresh disturbances in the region would hardly have been welcome. The Jews, anyway, had powerful friends at court, including no less a person, it is said, than the empress Poppaea Sabina herself. Indiscriminate anti-semitism, in short, could misfire badly and provoke unnecessary trouble.

Narrow the aim, then: a far safer target was Rome's Christian community. Though to outsiders they must still have looked much like other Jews, they were a tiny sectarian group regarded by their own people as apostates and heretics. Too weak to defend themselves, they could expect little help in a crisis from the wider Jewish community. Some, indeed, were not Jews at all, but Gentiles. Christianity had already split into a 'Judaic' wing which remained, in some sense, part of Judaism and prose-lytised only among fellow-Jews, and a 'Catholic' wing which aimed to build a universal church without distinction between Jew and Gentile. It is possible that the leaders of both factions were present in Rome in AD 64 – and may even have been martyred at this time. Peter, the Galilean fisherman-apostle who had known Christ personally, led the Judaeo-Christians, while Paul, a Hellenised Jewish businessman from a Diaspora city who had been converted some years after Christ's death, led the Catholics. But these splits hardly mattered now to the beleaguered little community in Rome. They were being blamed for the fire which had destroyed half the city. They were small, rather mysterious, and there was much ignorance about them. They were oriental and outlandish, and prejudice could feed on that. They predicted an apocalyptic End of Days, to be inaugurated, Peter had said, by 'a fiery trial'. So had they perhaps welcomed the great fire, indeed revelled in it, a bunch of eastern weirdoes celebrating as Rome burnt and Rome's own citizens suffered desolation? Why, therefore, should it not be true that they had helped it along a bit, even started the whole thing?

So under Nero, in the autumn of AD 64, in pursuit of a scapegoat, the Roman government carried out its first great anti-Christian pogrom. Known Christians were arrested and tortured for the names of others. The condemned were then grotesquely executed as a public spectacle in the Circus Maximus and the imperial park: bound naked and torn apart by starving dogs; set on fire as human torches in the night; or hammered onto wooden crosses to hang until they perished. Tacitus thought it well deserved, for this Christian cult was merely one among 'all the degraded and shameful practices which collect and flourish in the capital'. Although he reports that the victims were pitied by some, we hear nothing of any popular protests, whether in defence of the Christians, or to put blame on the regime for the fire and its effects. Many probably accepted the government line, while others were intimidated by the pogrom and the repressive atmosphere surrounding it.

Bread and circuses, petty privilege and prejudice, violence and terror: these were the instruments of Roman imperial rule at home. The government's scapegoat politics easily quelled the opposition, for the mob was corrupt, the Christians weak, and the equation of forces had favoured the regime. The Great Beast – the Roman imperial war-machine and the ruling class that directed it – was secure in the New Babylon it had built for itself. Very soon, however, it was to face a far more testing 'fiery trial', something much closer to the Apocalypse of Judaeo-Christian prophecy than the fire and the pogrom of AD 64. In the East, in Palestine, the anger of the Jews was approaching critical mass. A colossal revolutionary struggle from below was about to begin.

2 Insurrection

. . . the *Kittim* . . . are swift and valiant in battle . . . a source of fear and
terror to all the nations . . . from afar they come . . . to devour all the
nations like the eagle . . . they gather up their riches, with all the fruit of
their plundering, as the fish of the sea . . . they divide their yoke and their
taxes, which are their food, amongst all the peoples year by year, laying
waste many countries . . .

(The Habbakuk Commentary, DSS, Qumran)

The Procurator of Judaea

Jerusalem, holy city of the Jews, at the Feast of Passover, April AD 65
Cestius Gallus was among the most powerful men in the Roman Empire. As
Governor of Syria he commanded one of Rome's biggest armies and had chief
responsibility for frontier security and internal order throughout the East. The small
turbulent Province of Judaea was one of many preoccupations. In the spring of AD
65, departing his capital at Antioch, he set out to visit the province, reaching
Jerusalem in time for the Feast of Passover (or Unleavened Bread), one of those
occasions in the year when the city was packed with devout country Jews.
Traditionally these were opportunities for airing and sharing grievances, for
complaints and petitions, and sometimes for demonstrations, even riots. It was always
a bit tense in Jerusalem at festival time, and Gallus, fearing trouble, may have timed
his visit accordingly. The new procurator, Gessius Florus, who had taken office the
previous year, was not popular. Roman procurators of Judaea rarely were, but Florus
seemed especially disliked. Predictably enough, a great crowd gathered before Gallus'
tribunal in Jerusalem to denounce Florus as 'the bane of the country'. Josephus, our
principal source, paints the darkest picture of the procurator, portraying him as
arrogant and pompous in relations with provincials, sly and scheming with superiors,
and chiefly concerned with advancing himself and amassing a fortune through
bribery and extortion. Josephus probably exaggerates. He was pro-Roman, and like
other contemporary pro-Roman writers, like Tacitus for example, he blamed individuals, not the system as a whole, when revolts broke out. The Roman Empire was
essentially sound, the argument went, but the corruption of a few could sometimes
have disastrous consequences – a version of the 'bad apple' interpretation of history.
In fact, though Florus may have been a nasty piece of work, he was probably no
worse than many other Roman imperial governors at the time.

The character of empire and that of its agents cannot be disentangled as easily as writers like Josephus and Tacitus would have us believe. Systems make people, and people systems; the arrogance, ambition and avarice of imperial officials were deeply rooted features of Roman rule. Success in a political career required enormous financial resources, and, since governorships were simply rungs on the ladder, most appointees aimed to make as much money as possible in their foreign postings. This was done largely through personal contacts. The ancient world revolved around reciprocal exchanges of influence and favour among men of rank, men who met and bargained face-to-face. Roman imperial governors were especially powerful players, patrons able to attract many rich clients in the provinces they ruled, and their opportunities for self-enrichment were therefore considerable. The line between 'legitimate' and 'corrupt' gain was hazy, and those with wealth enough already, or wishing to live up to some philosophical ideal of 'good government', found it difficult going in this jungle of greed. Even the morally fastidious Cicero, briefly Governor of Cilicia in 51–50 BC, found it 'hard to be good' when torn between the self-serving demands of Roman friends, businessmen and officials on the one hand, and the interests of the native population on the other.

Florus was a notably successful product of this system of patronage and peculation. He was a Greek from the city of Clazomenae on the west coast of Asia Minor (modern Turkey). His wife, Cleopatra, had become a friend of the Empress Poppaea Sabina, and it was through her influence that Florus had obtained the Judaean procuratorship. This was a heady ascent: for a provincial noble and Asian Greek to become an intimate of the court, a member of the equestrian order and an imperial governor was achievement indeed. Florus may well have arrived in Judaea a little anxious about his elevated place in the world – about his relative lack of wealth, the modesty of his origins, and the demands of this difficult posting. Cestius Gallus, though also a product of the patronage system, was probably more confident. He belonged to the top senatorial class, the millionaire aristocrats who held almost all the most senior posts, men who believed themselves born to rule. From within this class, he had risen to the highest summits – the consulship, Rome's supreme magistracy, and, in the dangerous frontier crisis following Paetus' defeat in Armenia, the much sought-after and highly prestigious governorship of Syria. As he listened to the Jews' complaints against Florus, this great Roman lord can have had little sympathy with the grasping provincial Greek beside him. If things blew up, the Syrian army would have to be sent in to restore order, compromising security on the Parthian frontier, and Gallus would share the blame for not keeping Florus under tight enough control and allowing him to antagonise the Jews. Everyone knew the Jewish situation was delicate.

Relations had been tense between Romans and Jews since the legions' first intervention almost 130 years before. In his campaigns of 66–63 BC, Pompey the Great had destroyed the system of Hellenistic states ruled by Alexander's successors and created a huge power vacuum in the East. His 'eastern settlement' of 63 BC had been an attempt to fill it, creating a new Roman supremacy designed to keep the Parthians out and permit efficient exploitation of new conquests. Pompey's system centred on

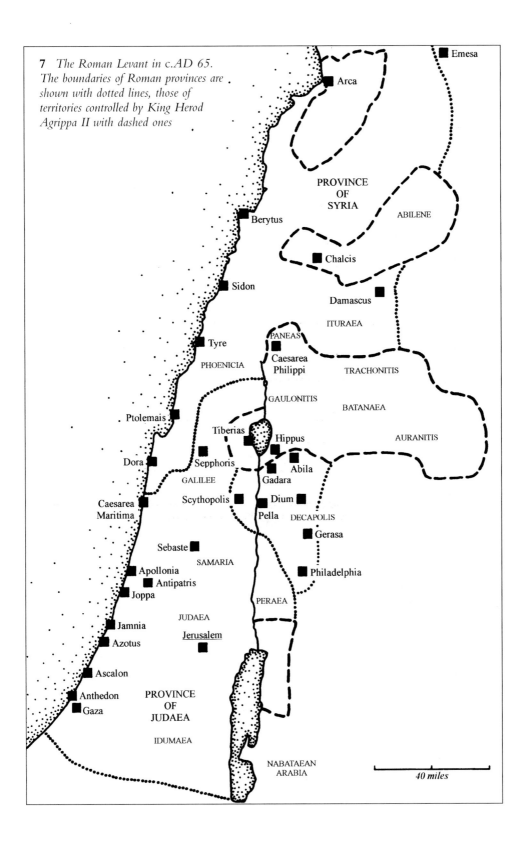

7 *The Roman Levant in c.AD 65. The boundaries of Roman provinces are shown with dotted lines, those of territories controlled by King Herod Agrippa II with dashed ones*

Emesa

Arca

PROVINCE
OF
SYRIA

ABILENE

Berytus

Chalcis

Damascus

Sidon

ITURAEA

Tyre

PANEAS

Caesarea
Philippi

TRACHONITIS

PHOENICIA

GAULONITIS

BATANAEA

Ptolemais

Tiberias

Hippus

AURANITIS

Dora

Sepphoris

Abila

Caesarea
Maritima

GALILEE

Gadara

Scythopolis

Dium

Pella

DECAPOLIS

Sebaste

SAMARIA

Gerasa

Apollonia

Antipatris

Joppa

Philadelphia

PERAEA

JUDAEA

Jamnia

Jerusalem

Azotus

Ascalon

Anthedon

PROVINCE
OF
JUDAEA

Gaza

IDUMAEA

NABATAEAN
ARABIA

40 miles

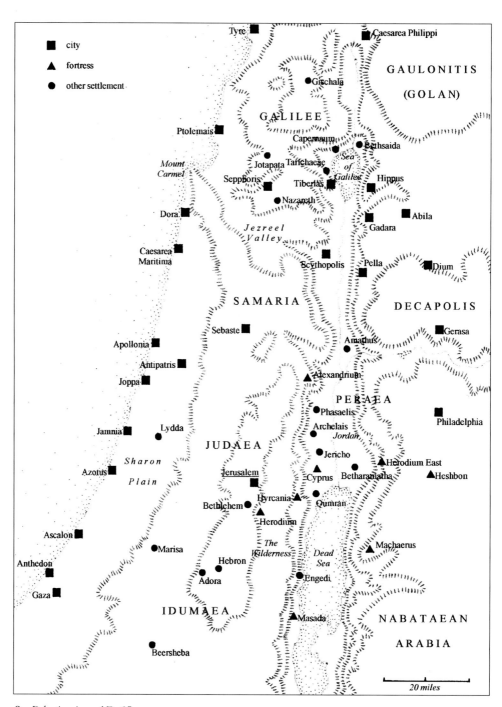

■ city

▲ fortress

● other settlement

Tyre

Caesarea Philippi

GAULONITIS

(GOLAN)

Gischala

GALILEE

Ptolemais

Capernaum

Bethsaida

Mount
Carmel

Jotapata Tarichaeae
Sea
of
Galilee

Sepphoris

Tiberias

Hippus

Nazareth

Dora

Abila

Jezreel
Valley

Gadara

Caesarea
Maritima

Scythopolis

Pella

Dium

SAMARIA

DECAPOLIS

Sebaste

Gerasa

Apollonia

Amathus

Antipatris

Alexandrium

Joppa

PERAEA

Phasaelis

Philadelphia

Jamnia

Lydda

Archelais

Jordan

JUDAEA

Jericho

Sharon

Jerusalem

Herodium East

Azotus

Plain

Cyprus Betharamatha

Heshbon

Hyrcania

Qumran

Bethlehem

Herodium

Ascalon

Marisa

The
Wilderness

Dead
Sea

Machaerus

Anthedon

Hebron

Engedi

Adora

Gaza

IDUMAEA

Masada

NABATAEAN

ARABIA

Beersheba

20 miles

8 *Palestine in c.AD 65*

the rich and heavily garrisoned Province of Syria, which was annexed at the outset and remained thereafter under direct rule. Ranged around it was a penumbra of smaller provinces and client states, whose borders and ruling authorities – even very existence – altered with each geopolitical reassessment by the imperial power. The fate of Armenia (discussed above) is a good example, but it was somewhat anomalous in being a disputed border territory. More typical was Palestine. Firmly within the Roman sphere from 63 BC, no nationalist opposition was henceforward tolerated. When the Hasmonaean king Aristobulus II challenged Pompey's settlement, the Roman army was unleashed on Jerusalem. After a lengthy siege and the capture of the city, the legionaries stormed into the Temple, cutting down soldiers, civilians and priests indiscriminately, and their leader then violated religious taboo by entering the Holy of Holies and profaning it, in Jewish eyes at least, with his 'unclean' Gentile presence. The experience was seared onto the Jewish psyche – the worst of many incidents which inflamed local opinion against the Romans and their Jewish fellow-travellers in the years from 63 BC to AD 66.

In the early part of this period, however, immediate authority had been left in the hands of client rulers – principally, in succession, High Priest John Hyrcanus II (63-40 BC), and then King Herod the Great (37-4 BC). Latterly, from AD 6 onwards, except for the brief rule of King Herod Agrippa I (AD 41-4), Palestine was divided between the Province of Judaea under direct Roman control, and various small satellite territories still governed by one or more client rulers. This was the situation in AD 65. Herod Agrippa II (AD 50-93), son of Herod Agrippa I, great-grandson of Herod the Great, ruled a kingdom of scattered northern and eastern territories with part-Jewish populations: Arca, Chalcis, Abilene, Paneas, Gaulonitis, Batanaea, Trachonitis, Auranitis, eastern Galilee, and southern Peraea (**7** & **8**). Another swathe of territory was controlled by the oligarchic governments of the 'Decapolis' (or 'Ten Cities'), a loose grouping of Greek cities – not a formal confederacy – immediately south of (and overlapping with) Herod Agrippa's territories in eastern Galilee and the Golan Heights. The ancient sources are in conflict about which cities comprised the 'Ten' (18 candidates in all are recorded), but the list certainly included, from north to south, Hippus, Abila, Gadara, Dium, Scythopolis (Beth Shean), Pella, Gerasa (Jerash), and Philadelphia (Amman). The rest of Palestine was under direct Roman control. A strip of coast in the north, including the important harbour city of Ptolemais (Acre), formed a southerly extension of the Province of Syria. But the Sharon Plain along the coast further south, the hills of northern and western Galilee, the Jezreel Valley (sometimes known as the Plain of Esdraelon), the great upland massif of Samaria, Judaea and Idumaea, and the wastes of the Judaean Desert to the south-east, all this constituted the procuratorial Province of Judaea.

These administrative divisions were not the result of a unified plan but of several decades of geopolitical fix. The boundaries sometimes followed, sometimes cut across divisions formed by culture and geography. The patchwork of mini-states and petty jurisdictions in the first century AD was underlain by much older patterns of settlement and allegiance, the result of folk movements and the wars of kings centuries before. And all these patterns, old and new, were superimposed on a diverse landscape, where rocks, soil, rainfall and what the land could be made to yield varied greatly from place to place. 'A good land, a land with flowing streams, with springs and underground waters welling up in valleys and hills, a land of wheat and barley, of vines and fig-trees and pomegranates, a land of olive trees and honey, a land where you may eat bread without scarcity': that had been the Lord's promise to his people. Certainly 'the Land of Canaan' was far preferable to the desert wilderness from which the wandering Israelites had come, and much of it was, by any standards, good land. In the Sharon Plain on the coast there was rich, red, alluvial soil, well watered by numerous small rivers. There was a belt of rolling, fertile plains running north-west to south-east across the country from Mount Carmel to the River Jordan: the Jezreel Valley (**colour plate 2**). Then there were the hills of northern Samaria to the south of it, those of Lower Galilee to the north, and the shores of the Sea of Galilee and the banks of the River Jordan (**colour plates 1 & 3**): in all these places the land was low-lying and either gently sloping or level, the soil deep and fertile, and the rainfall adequate. Josephus wrote of Galilee's abundant orchards, of northern Samaria's high-yield dairy cattle, and of the Jordan Valley's luxurious date-palms. Much, then, of the Promised Land was as Yahweh had described it. But not all.

The centre of Palestine comprised an extensive upland massif. Samaria, in the north, was mainly low hills with good rainfall and heavy tree growth. But Judaea, in the central region, was higher and harsher land: a broken plateau of steeply sloping hills, where soils were often thin, stony and eroded. Here was the core of the old Jewish kingdom, an area about the size of an English county around the holy city of Jerusalem. There was, for sure, enough of the stuff of life – earth and water – to provide a living, but you needed a good-sized patch of ground to prosper. Few, it seems, had this. Most Judaeans struggled against stones, thorns and dust on plots that were too small, growing vines and olives on hillside terraces, sometimes grain on occasional bits of flatter ground, and raising sheep and goats on the rough scrub higher up (**colour plate 4**). Jesus knew the problem: when the sower went out to sow, some seeds fell on stony ground and were scorched by the sun, while others fell among thorns and were choked by them – yet in better places, in good soil, the yield could be 30, 60, even 100-fold. South of Judaea, the agriculture was more limited still. The uplands of Idumaea were desiccated, and the region near the Dead Sea was actual desert, a life-hating land of sweat and thirst, from which men and women shrank back to huddle around occasional pools and winter streams (**colour plate 5**).

The good land, then, was limited, and hunger for land has been the thing above all others which has divided people in this region throughout its history. Palestine is one of the bloodiest places on earth. Partly, in antiquity anyway, this was because it lay beside the main routeway between two great centres of civilisation – Egypt and Syria. But also it was because the people of Palestine frequently fought each other, a fact of life in the place that was of great assistance to the empires that set out to rule it. Amid the poverty of villages short of land, there was a festering of communal hatreds, and the fracture lines along which people divided were traditional ones inherited from the past; they were lines which had long ago solidified into distinct and opposing cultural identities. Judaea itself had been almost entirely Jewish for centuries, but other parts of Palestine with a mainly Jewish population in the first century AD – Galilee, Peraea and Idumaea – had undergone conversion more recently, in some cases as late as Hasmonaean times (164-37 BC). Here was food for prejudice: some Judaeans looked down on Galileans as uncouth, lawless and irreligious, while Idumaeans could be caricatured as half-castes, nomads and bandits. A far deeper gulf, however, separated mainstream Jews as a whole from the 'heretic' Samaritans, the people who occupied a large block of territory between Galilee and Judaea in a geographical accident of history which caused endless trouble. While the Samaritans themselves worshipped at a local sanctuary on Mount Gerizim, devout Galileans who wished to go on pilgrimage to the Temple at Jerusalem had to pass through Samaria. So bad were relations between the two groups that a local woman had been amazed when a thirsty Galilean had asked her for a drink at Jacob's Well. This same Galilean, Jesus of Nazareth, told a famous parable which hinged on the fact that a Samaritan was the last person from whom a Jew in need would expect help. Twenty years later, in AD 52, the tension exploded in communal violence in villages along the Judaea-Samaria border when a pilgrim was killed on the road. Equally fraught were the Jews' relations with Greeks, Syrians and Arabs in areas of more mixed settlement on the edges of the Judaic heartland: the Sharon Plain, the Golan Heights, and the southern border regions of Peraea and Idumaea.

The cup of bitterness was full in the land-starved villages of ancient Palestine, and sometimes the cup overflowed in murderous attacks on neighbours who worshipped at a different temple. But not everyone joined in. Jesus knew that Samaritan peasants were not the enemy: in the gospels he does not attack 'foreigners' and 'heretics'; his fire is directed at the rich. The Samaritan of the parable was a good man because he helped the victim of a mugging after two Jewish priests had walked by. 'Beware of the scribes, who like to walk around in long robes, and to be greeted with respect in the market-places, and to have the best seats in the synagogue and places of honour at banquets; they devour widows' houses and for the sake of appearance say long prayers.' Jesus, as we shall see, was part of a vibrant tradition, one of many Jewish prophets and sectarian leaders at the time who attacked the corruption of the élite and the oppression of the poor. There was, moreover, a long history in Palestine of uniting to fight the foreign enemies of the people. Two centuries before, the Jews of the Maccabaean Revolt had driven out a hated foreign overlord. It could happen again. The Jews were numerous, concentrated and organised. Judaeans, Galileans, Idumaeans, even Samaritans, had much in common and might easily put aside petty differences in a greater cause. They had reason enough, and several times in the recent past there had been mass protests, these becoming bigger and more frequent in the 50s and early 60s AD.

The *Kittim* (as Jewish radicals called the Romans) were certainly on edge. Sitting on the tribunal in Jerusalem at the Feast of Passover in April AD 65, Cestius Gallus knew the situation was tense and that the man next to him, Gessius Florus, the small-town politician made good in imperial service, was something of a liability. His answer to the Jewish leaders' complaints about their procurator was conciliatory: he would see to it that Florus in future treated them more moderately. Gallus then left Jerusalem, first to go to Caesarea in company with Florus, then to continue back to his own headquarters at Antioch, leaving the problems of Judaea behind him for the time being – though not, as it turned out, for long.

The Greeks of Caesarea

Caesarea Maritima, provincial capital of the Province of Judaea, May AD 66
The Jewish synagogue at Caesarea Maritima, the provincial capital on the coast, had been built on land owned by a Greek. The owner had refused many generous offers to buy the property, and he had now turned the district around the synagogue into a building site, with access restricted to a narrow and difficult passage. There had been arguments between Jewish youths and the workmen, and, in an effort to defuse the situation, a rich Jewish financier had offered the Roman procurator a large bribe to block further building work. But Florus had taken the money and then done nothing, and, as tension mounted, he had left Caesarea on a visit to Sebaste in Samaria. The day after was the Sabbath, and as the Jews of Caesarea arrived to worship at their synagogue, they found a Greek mob assembled, one of whom began publicly sacrificing birds over an upturned pot. Nothing could have been more offensive. By this act, the Torah had been violated (i.e. the Law as set out in the canonical books of the Bible), the synagogue and the Sabbath profaned, and the Jews themselves labelled, in effect, 'plague-ridden', since *Leviticus* specified this particular ritual for the cure of leprosy. Fighting broke out in front of the synagogue, and soon Roman cavalry were on the scene trying to restore order. The officer in charge carried off the offending pot, and the crowds eventually dispersed. But the Jews feared there was worse to come – perhaps a full-blown pogrom – and many, taking with them their copy of the Torah, fled for safety to a village seven miles distant. Thirteen of their leaders travelled on to Sebaste to appeal again to Florus for protection – tactfully reminding him of the payment he had received. They were promptly arrested and imprisoned – on a charge of having removed the Torah from Caesarea!

The incident was not untypical; no Jew can have been all that surprised. In disputes between Greek citizens and Jewish residents in the cities of the East, Roman governors usually backed the Greeks. This was neither mere whimsy nor simply a matter of cultural racism – though there is little doubt that most Romans, especially of the upper classes, regarded the Greek minority as 'civilised' and in some sense 'like us', in contrast to Semites and other orientals, who, on the whole, were not. But there was something more substantial at issue. Rome's imperial bureaucracy was small, and effective local government depended not on appointed officials but on the services of local magnates. The empire was run by a class of 'decurions' (though the actual term used varied from place to place), a group defined by wealth and made up principally of landed gentry, whose role it was to provide the magistrates and councillors in each locality who maintained law and order, collected the taxes, and organised public works. In return, their property and position were guaranteed by the power of the imperial state; Rome, in other words, in its own interest, sustained a class of municipal oligarchs, and thus, to a large degree, preserved the local social hierarchies inherited by the empire as it expanded. Also, in addition to the élite proper, which was fairly small in number, there were various other client groups who, because they too benefited from the *Pax Romana*, tended to be pro-Roman in outlook. Predominantly these were urban groups like traders, artisans, transport-workers, minor officials, soldiers, and others who depended for their living, directly or indirectly, on the army, the bureaucracy or the pro-Roman élite. These people's livelihoods were inextricably bound up with the success of the imperial system in extracting surpluses from rural peasants. Agricultural rents, state taxes, temple tithes, labour-power mobilised by *corvée*, these and other levies on the countryside provided the resources to maintain an infrastructure of empire and 'civilisation' – military supplies, forts, roads, towns, aqueducts, monumental architecture, grand houses, luxury goods, 'the world of taste'. This was the economic realm of the Greeks of Caesarea. Some were the propertied oligarchs who wielded real power. Many others formed a prosperous urban petty-bourgeoisie. Both groups depended, in the last analysis, on Roman imperial control over rural land and labour. The Greek towns, in short, were parasitic on native agriculture. The anti-semitic mob which gathered outside the Caesarea synagogue in May AD 66 was composed, in effect, of Roman imperial clients.

But what were they doing here at all, these Greeks in Palestine? Greek traders had been present in the East for centuries, but a flood of immigrants had arrived in the wake of Alexander's victories and the founding of many new Hellenic cities from the late fourth century BC onwards. The original settlers had been veterans, officials, traders and mercenaries, but their descendants solidified into a privileged caste of Greek urbanites, jealously guarding citizenship rights and cut off by barriers of language and lifestyle from countryside and peasantry. Citizenship was crucial. It was not that Greek cities were any longer democracies. The Romans backed the oligarchs. They turned city councils into permanent bodies not subject to periodic re-election, and they required all magistrates and councillors to belong to the property-owning class. But these gentlemen-politicians still had to compete for popular support. Magistrates were elected from among the councillors by the votes of common citizens – and most 'backbenchers' sought the honour of 'ministerial' office. So they courted the electorate with the usual mix of favours and promises. Election notices on the walls of contemporary Pompeii capture something of the atmosphere. The common citizens intervened as blocks of clients, often in the form of guilds or clubs (the fruit-dealers, the goldsmiths, the muleteers, the worshippers of Isis, the ball-players, and so on), each one enthusiastically canvassing support for its own patron. In return, they expected their patrons to be generous private benefactors and effective political string-pullers. Individually a worthy client might look for help getting a job or a business contract, and collectively citizens expected a range of perks like free bathing, cheap bread, and occasional spectacles. Just as in Rome, patron-client networks were tied together by mutual self-interest. But only citizens could benefit, since only they had votes – patrons had little interest in currying favour with the disenfranchised. Citizenship was a political privilege tied to material advantage.

Just as important was legal protection. While the citizen could seek redress through the courts, the non-citizen could only appeal to the powerful for help – who, since the appellant lacked political weight, had no real incentive to provide it. The case of St Paul – though it concerns the advantages of specifically *Roman* citizenship – is instructive: it shows the degree to which membership of (or exclusion from) a legally incorporated urban community defined relationships with authority and entitlements to protection. When Paul was arrested *c.*AD 58 during a commotion at the Temple, the Roman garrison commander in Jerusalem ordered him flogged – a routine preliminary designed to terrorise suspects before interrogation. Paul revealed his Roman citizenship and thereby established immunity from physical abuse. Shortly afterwards, when he appeared before the Jewish Council to answer charges and became the focus of a fresh disturbance (including threats of assassination), Paul was first whisked away to the Roman barracks, and then sent under escort to the relative safety of Caesarea. His citizenship had entitled him to Roman military protection from a lynch mob. Later again he successfully 'appealed unto Caesar' and won the right to be sent to Rome for trial, sparing him the risk of a local trial before a hostile crowd. There is a striking contrast with the treatment of Jesus. The circumstances were similar: a religious radical had entered Jerusalem, stirred things up, and provoked an angry reaction. But Jesus had not been a citizen – so he had been executed there and then.

Citizenship mattered, then. It was highly valued and much sought-after. Some years before, while Paul was in custody in the city, Greeks and Jews had clashed violently in the streets of Caesarea over precisely this issue. It is not clear whether the Jews lacked citizenship rights altogether, or merely faced discrimination and were, literally, 'second-class citizens'. Either way, they demanded equal rights now, and when attacked by Greek mobs, they fought back. Unfortunately for the Jewish cause, the Roman procurator at the time, Marcus Antonius Felix, was a Greek, as were many of his auxiliary soldiers, and when the troops were sent in they acted in a highly partisan way, attacking the Jewish crowd and plundering Jewish property. When this failed to curb the disturbances, both sides were ordered to send delegations to Rome to argue the case before Nero. For the Jews this was a less than promising prospect. The Neronian court was philhellene. The emperor, as we have seen, was addicted to art, poetry and the games, and in AD 67 he would tour Greece, participate in the Olympic, Delphic, Isthmian and Nemean Games (the four main festivals), and then magnanimously announce 'the freedom of the Greek cities' with exemption from imperial taxation. Greeks were prominent among Nero's courtiers, and they included the imperial freedman Pallas, brother of the Judaean procurator and the man who had got him the job in the first place, and Beryllus, whom Josephus specifically says used his influence to block the Jews' petition for citizenship rights. Nero probably needed little persuading: he liked Greeks. The news came back to Caesarea some time before the anti-semitic demonstration of May AD 66 that Felix had not been prosecuted, the Greeks were to keep control of the city, and the Jews were to remain (or now become) disenfranchised.

The citizenship dispute had deep and complex roots. The Jews had argued for citizenship rights on the grounds that Caesarea had been re-founded by a Jewish king – Herod the Great – some two generations before. The Greeks had replied that it had previously been purely Hellenic in character, and that Herod anyway had been a Helleniser intent on preserving – indeed enhancing – the city's traditional character. There was force in the Greek argument. For 400 years, ever since Alexander's conquests, the Jewish ruling class had been entranced by Greek culture. To read Greek literature, to appreciate Greek art, to build in a Greek style, to enjoy Greek games, these things had come to denote sophistication and good taste. The Hellenised élite considered itself part of a cosmopolitan Mediterranean 'jet-set' – compared with which, the strict Judaism of the common people and their priests appeared boorish and parochial. Herod had epitomised this spirit within the Jewish upper classes. He had reconstructed Caesarea as a showcase of Hellenic culture – and of the pro-Roman political allegiance now closely associated with it. The fashionable face of power, wealth and status was nowadays to be found in classical architecture, Hellenic art and pagan ritual; and Herodian Caesarea was in the forefront of the new fashion.

The city of Strato's Tower (as it was then known) had come to Herod as part of a massive land grant which had roughly doubled the size of his kingdom in 30 BC. When yet more land was added in 20 BC, Herod became one of the greatest kings in Jewish history. He lavished huge sums on monumental building projects designed to glorify his regime and empire. Strato's Tower was especially embellished. It was given a large Mediterranean port, a full *ensemble* of Hellenic civic buildings, and a great monument to Herod's patron, the Roman emperor Caesar Augustus, in whose honour the city was renamed and a new games festival inaugurated. Much of this can still be seen. The huge moles of Herod's outer harbour lie just beneath the surface of the sea, the southern one 600m long and 60m wide, a structure built of colossal concrete blocks measuring 400 cubic metres each. There was also a middle harbour, somewhat similar in size and shape to the one that still exists today, and a small inner harbour, now largely silted up. Around these harbours ran broad quaysides, barrel-vaulted warehouses, and colonnaded walkways (**9**). Towering over all, high on its podium, was the Temple of Rome and Augustus (**10**). This edifice, 50m in length by 30m in width, housed colossal pagan cult-images modelled on the greatest in the world at the time. South of the port, Herod built a games complex – a theatre for plays, poetry and pantomimes, and a circus (or hippodrome) 300m long and 50m wide for horse and chariot races (**colour plate 6**). There was also a royal summer pavilion built on a rocky promontory: it comprised a monumental entrance, a colonnaded garden on an upper terrace, and a range of three rooms overlooking an ornamental pool on a lower one (**colour plate 7**).

Herod's Caesarea was a monument to power and paganism. Its architecture and ambience provided the perfect setting for a new four-yearly games festival in honour of Augustus – Caesar's Games. The inaugural celebration was held at the formal opening of the new city and its harbour in 12 BC. Huge numbers of distinguished guests and common spectators were accommodated and fed at public expense; there

9 *Classical grandeur at Herodian Caesarea. A row of fallen columns marks the line of the northern mole of the middle harbour. The outer harbour extended several hundred metres beyond this*

10 *Pagan cult at Herodian Caesarea. The waters of the inner harbour filled the space where the lawn now grows in the foreground of this picture. Beyond it can be seen the quayside (with steps and mooring posts) and warehouses (including a surviving barrel-vault on the right). These harbour works provided an elevated podium (centre of the picture) for a temple dedicated to Rome and Augustus (of which nothing now remains)*

were spectacular decorations and furnishing; and the games continued for many days, with musical and athletic competitions, horse and chariot races, beast hunts and gladiatorial combats. To many Jews all this was highly offensive: a pagan festival in a Greek city for a foreign overlord. The graven images, the nakedness of competitors and the blood-letting in the arena were 'no better than a dissolution of greatly venerated customs' and 'an instance of barefaced impiety' (Josephus). But this, in a sense, was the point. Hellenisation challenged 'backwardness'. Palestine's rulers wanted to reform their country by making it philhellenic and pro-Roman. Pagan festivals and imperial loyalty were *de rigueur* in the new Mediterranean world of the Caesars, which it was intended the Jewish people should join. But at the same time, these rulers created islands of privilege for themselves and their favourites, from which ordinary Jews were excluded. The 'modernisers' were rich, snobbish and self-serving. Herodian Caesarea symbolised both the new political allegiance demanded of everyone under the Roman *imperium*, and the exclusive, fashionable, Hellenic culture of the east-Mediterranean upper classes. Symbols, after all, have meaning and potency only by virtue of contrast; what they are not is as important as what they are – difference is all. The alien 'other' – against which 'the beautiful people' of Graeco-Roman Palestine measured themselves – was the countryside, the poor, traditional

11 *This fragmentary inscription found at Caesarea Maritima in 1961 refers in the second line to* [Pon]tius Pilatus *and in the third to his rank of* [Praef]ectus

Judaism, and the world of the Jewish masses. Because of this – and because privilege, property and power rallied around the symbols of Rome – native Jewish culture came to express the class antagonism of the excluded and the dispossessed. Because their rulers demanded obedience and loyalty, yet denied most Jews entry to the gilt-edged citizen commonwealth of Greeks and Romans, the people would often flare into wild anger defending the symbols of their faith. The coming revolution announced itself in fierce clashes over cultural tokens.

Shortly after his arrival in AD 26, for example, the new prefect (as Roman governors were titled at that time), Pontius Pilate, decided to impose a form of emperor-worship on the Jews (**11**). It was 20 years since the foundation of the province, and some officials felt it was high time that it conformed to general practice in the empire and showed loyalty to Rome by honouring its rulers. So Pilate ordered Roman military standards decorated with busts of the emperor to be displayed in Jerusalem. These were graven images of a pagan deity in the holy city – a clear violation of the Torah. A protest movement formed and quickly gained momentum, with large hostile crowds following Pilate back to Caesarea, where he was besieged by demonstrators in his official residence (perhaps Herod's old summer pavilion). For five days and nights the protestors engaged in mass civil disobedience, lying on the ground and refusing to move until the offensive emblems were taken down – a tactic they repeated when addressed by Pilate in the circus and threatened with attack by his soldiers if they did not disperse. The prefect, fearing the consequences of a massacre, relented and had the military standards withdrawn.

It was merely one of many such incidents. Palestine under the Romans seemed often on the brink of some terrible conflagration, and yet, until AD 66, things did not spiral out of control. Sometimes the rulers backed off, as Pilate had done over the military standards. Sometimes the troops went in, and the militants, battered and intimidated and lacking wider support, were driven off the streets. But in May AD 66, when popular anger was ready to boil over across the whole of Palestine, the authorities did not back off. The blows began to fall in quick succession, and each protest was met with bloody repression. The news from Caesarea reached Jerusalem quickly – it was only 60 miles away. Several years before it had been the citizenship riots, the Roman attack on Jewish demonstrators, and the dispatch of delegations to Nero. Some time later it was Nero's perverse judgement denying citizenship to the Jews in the city. Recently it was an anti-semitic outrage, fresh clashes in the streets, the threat of a pogrom, and a mass exodus of Caesarea Jews to the countryside. Finally there was Florus' arrest of 13 high-ranking Jewish delegates on the most absurd of charges. But even at this late hour, though the popular mood in the volatile holy city was restive, things remained outwardly calm. What transformed the situation was the extraordinary announcement from Florus that he wanted 102,000 *denarii* from the Temple treasury 'for Caesar's needs' – and that he was coming to the city to get it. 'He marched rapidly on Jerusalem with an army of horse and foot, determined to impose his will by force of Roman arms, and by terror and threat to bring the city to heel' (Josephus). It was a show of Roman military power designed to cow an increasingly disorderly province – but its effect was to detonate revolution.

The May Days

Jerusalem, mid-May AD 66

Why did Florus demand a large sum of money from the Temple? This was not a matter of routine extortion; it was exceptional and outrageous, and there was every possibility it would provoke serious trouble. It was probably a response to a shortfall in tax revenues, perhaps even an organised tax strike. Josephus has the client-king Herod Agrippa II say to a gathering of Jewish rebels a little later: 'You have not paid the tribute which is due to Caesar.' Any such failure would be blamed on the local authorities, and any Roman administrator might be expected to take direct action to make good the losses. Probably, in Judaea, it was up to the high priests and the Sanhedrin (or Jewish Council) to organise the levy, with much of the practical work contracted out to tax-farmers (*publicani*) on a commission basis. *The New Testament* makes frequent disparaging reference to the *publicani*. Jesus could be vilified by his enemies as 'a glutton, a drunkard, and a friend of tax-collectors and sinners'. Jesus' advice to tax-collectors who sought salvation was to 'collect no more than the amount prescribed'; presumably they commonly extorted more. The popular view was that *publicani* were corrupt and on a moral level with prostitutes and sinners. It is not difficult to fathom why.

43

Work on the land was hard, with inadequate plots, modest yields, and most peasant families only just getting by. Taxes to Rome came on top of rents and tithes: the landlord, the priest and the emperor all came for their cut. The main state levy was the land tax (*tributum soli*), which would have been paid annually at harvest time, and was probably between 10 and 12.5 per cent of the crop (though much higher rates are sometimes recorded in ancient sources). There was also the poll tax (*tributum capitis*), which might be levied on movable property if there was some, but otherwise, in the case of the poor, on bodies and the capacity to labour – on existence itself, that is. The annual rate may have been a *denarius* for everyone of 14 or over in the household; if so, a typical peasant family might have been paying two or three per cent of income. Thirdly, there were various indirect levies – tolls, salt taxes, customs dues – though the overall amount of these is likely to have been modest, and the impact on the peasant less than that on town-dwellers. Many other exactions also existed, though their incidence and net effect are impossible to quantify. These included official impositions like the occasional billeting of troops, extraordinary requisitioning of supplies, forced sales at fixed prices, and civilian labour *corvées*; and such unofficial levies as resulted from the straightforward corruption, bribery, bullying, arbitrary pillage and random violence to which the ancient sources sometimes allude. Overall it is likely that Jewish peasants paid not less than 15 per cent of their annual income to the Romans, but it may in fact have been rather more, even a lot more, and in addition they must have lived with the fear that at any time a sudden and unexpected new demand could descend upon them. For many, grappling with the poverty and insecurity of rural life, Roman levies must have consumed whatever small reserves they managed to accumulate. Taxation, in consequence, was a burning political issue.

'Render unto Caesar the things that are Caesar's, and to God the things that are God's.' Thus did Jesus sidestep his enemies' attempt to implicate him in rebellion against Rome. But whatever the incident tells us about Jesus' own attitudes, the implication seems to be that tax strikes – a refusal to 'render unto Caesar the things that are Caesar's' – were practical politics and something that a popular leader like Jesus might be expected to advocate. When, in AD 6, the client state of Judaea had been dissolved and direct Roman rule imposed, the new provincial prefect, backed by the Governor of Syria, had ordered a census of people and property for tax purposes. The gospels have made the event famous (though they misuse it to construct a birth myth), and Josephus records that it was the occasion of an attempted tax strike. One Judas the Galilean, supported by Zaddok the Pharisee, 'called on his countrymen to revolt, and said they were cowards if they would bear to pay a tax to the Romans, and would, after God, submit to mortal men as their lords'. In the event, the high priest opposed the call and most Jews were persuaded to co-operate with the Roman authorities. Nonetheless, the evidence relating to both Judas and Jesus reveals that the tax strike was a recognised form of mass resistance, and one which could be justified in religious terms. The question therefore arises: was Florus' extraordinary demand for 102,000 *denarii* of Temple money a response to a shortfall in tax receipts caused by widespread refusal to pay? Josephus certainly implies this – in the words of the speech he attributes to King Herod Agrippa – and there is, in fact, much evidence in the 60s AD of over-taxation and consequent rebelliousness in the empire generally.

Nero's government was profligate and avaricious. As we have seen, the emperor spent lavishly on buildings, shows and largesse. He was a young emperor, without political or military distinction when he came to power, and he compensated through generosity and grandeur. His style was, in his biographer Miriam Griffin's phrase, that of 'the Magnificent Monarch' – one who proved his right to rule by elevating himself far above the common herd, from which height he could be seen generously showering the world with gifts, favours and benedictions. Nor was this just a matter of style: largesse bought loyalty – especially that of the Praetorian Guard and the Roman mob. The cost of Nero's accession donative to the soldiers was probably around 45 million *denarii*, and there were further special payments in AD 59 and AD 65. The state visit to Rome of the Armenian king Tiridates in AD 66 (marking the formal end of war in the East) cost 200,000 *denarii* a day – and, including the journeys there and back, it lasted nine months. The cost of the finishing touches – these alone – to the Golden House were estimated at 12.5 million. And Nero is recorded once spending a cool million on a single bowl. Vespasian, emperor from late AD 69, surveying the financial wreckage he inherited, concluded that a billion *denarii* would be needed to restore the treasuries.

The empire was plundered to make up the shortfall between regular income and actual expenditure. In AD 61, in Britain, it was the seizure of their estates by imperial finance officers acting on behalf of the emperor that had driven Boudicca and the Icenian nobles to revolt. In AD 68, Gauls, Spaniards and Africans were also in revolt against Nero, and there is strong evidence that increased state exactions were the principal cause. Dio Cassius talks of heavier taxes and forced levies in Gaul and Britain. Plutarch claims that Galba, briefly emperor in AD 68-9, had sympathised with the plight of the Spanish provincials in his charge, and Tacitus quotes him later attributing the downfall of Nero to 'his own monstrousness and extravagance'. Pliny the Elder records that Nero had six African landowners put to death so that he could expropriate their estates, these amounting to 'half the province'. The rapacious Procurator of Judaea, then, appears to have been part of an empire-wide drive to raise the rate of exploitation in the provinces – and the Jewish response part of an equally widespread mood of anger and resistance.

In Judaea, however, the crisis acquired special piquancy from the intended attack on the Temple at Jerusalem, the pre-eminent focus of Jewish national and religious sentiment. All Jews paid a tithe to the Temple, and hundreds of thousands packed the city for its three great annual festivals. The holiness of the site was rooted in a millennium of myth and history. This, supposedly, was where King David had founded a city in the tenth century BC, and where his immediate successor, King Solomon, had built the First Temple. This was where, at the end of the sixth century, the exiles who had returned from Babylonian captivity, an event remembered as a miraculous national rebirth, had built the Second Temple. The legendary history of the Jews depicted them struggling to survive amid the storm and strife of centuries, and the Temple had come to be seen as a towering symbol of their solidarity, defiance and right to exist.

For this reason, the enemies of the Jews hated the Temple, and ever since Pompey the Great had first defiled it with his unclean presence in 63 BC, it had been the focus of numerous clashes between Roman and Jew. The governor of Asia tried to stop Jewish communities in his province sending their annual tithe to the Temple in 59 BC. The general Marcus Crassus plundered the Temple on his way to fight the Parthians in 53 BC. The display of a gilt-bronze eagle – a graven image and symbol of Rome – over the main gate of the Temple by King Herod led to rioting by students and their teachers in 4 BC. The same year, when Herod died, violent anti-Roman protests erupted across the country, and amid the chaos Roman troops looted the Temple treasury and were then besieged in the Royal Palace by a furious crowd. When direct rule was imposed in AD 6, the first Roman prefect took custody of the high-priestly vestments used in Temple ritual (thus profaning them), and had troops in battle-gear posted around the Temple porticoes during festivals. Pontius Pilate, prefect from AD 26 to 36, caused offence repeatedly – first (as noted above) by displaying military standards with imperial images in the holy city, then by using Temple treasure to fund an aqueduct, and finally by having shields erected, again in the holy city, with inscribed dedications to the emperor Tiberius. When a colossal gilt statue of Caligula in the guise of Jupiter was made for the Temple in AD 40 – so that the Roman emperor might be worshipped alongside Yahweh – the scale of local protests against attempts to install it brought Palestine close to war. At the Feast of Passover in AD 48, when the Temple Mount was packed with pilgrims, a Roman auxiliary soldier on duty there provoked a riot by deliberately exposing his backside and farting at the crowd. The Temple, then, was a symbol of Jewish independence, of a distinctive Jewish culture, and of a barely concealed yearning to be free of Greeks and Romans – free, that is, of foreign tax-collectors and their pagan idols. Which is why the Romans repeatedly attacked it, and the Jews always rallied to its defence.

When Florus demanded 102,000 *denarii* from the Temple funds, he knew that he risked igniting a conflagration. So he came in force, entering Jerusalem with a small army, determined, as the Jews saw it, to enrich the Roman emperor by stealing from God the offerings made to him by his people. A centurion was sent ahead with 50 horsemen to clear a way through the crowds which had assembled to meet the procurator on his arrival. Florus then entered the city and took up residence in the Royal Palace (**16** & **63**). The following day he set up his open-air tribunal, called before him all the leading Jews, and demanded that they arrest and hand over the radicals who had been denouncing him in the streets. The story was that a group of them had gone around with a collecting basket for Florus, as if raising money for charity, on the grounds he was 'destitute of possessions and in a miserable condition'. The Jewish leaders were in no position to comply. Even had they been able to identify the culprits – or at least agree on which of the known militants to round up – it would have been impossible to carry out arrests without provoking riots and universal opprobrium. Instead, knowing how tense was the situation in the city, they urged Florus to drop his demand for Temple funds and withdraw the troops. The Jewish leaders' position was an unenviable one: they were the local notables responsible to Rome for the maintenance of order and efficient tax-collection, but the native population in their charge was now on the very brink of revolution. Their traditional role was that of mediation between imperial power and subject people, but on this occasion the gulf between the two was unbridgeable unless, as so many of his predecessors had done in moments of crisis, Florus was willing to back down. But this he would not do; instead the troops were sent in to reimpose imperial authority by force, and in the three days of street-fighting that followed the Romans lost control of the city.

Florus had brought with him at least two auxiliary units, perhaps 1,000 men in all, and to punish the rebellious city these were now ordered into the Upper Market area to kill and plunder at will. The result was mayhem. Many were cut down in the streets, and others who fled to their homes for safety were killed when the troops smashed their way in. Some were arrested, hauled before Florus' tribunal, and then condemned, flogged and crucified.

The Upper Market massacre threw the Jewish leadership into deep crisis. Some of its own number had been swept away in the killing: Josephus reports that among the crucified were Roman citizens of equestrian status – high-ranking Jews, presumably. The rest of the leadership was treated with contempt. When the princess Berenike, sister of King Herod Agrippa, a devout Jew who was in the city at the time to perform a vow, stood shaven-headed and barefoot before Florus' tribunal to appeal for an end to the massacre, she was ignored. Though unable to make any impression on Florus, who had in effect unleashed a war on the city, the leadership still struggled with their own people to suppress the street protests. They could hardly have done otherwise: as men of property and power, men who thrived under the *Pax Romana*, they stood in desperate fear of a movement from below getting out of control. What security would there be for wealth and rank if it came to popular revolution and large-scale Roman military intervention? So, as the Upper Market filled again with furious crowds protesting the massacre, 'the men of power, together with the high priests, rent their garments, and fell down before each man, pleading with them to desist and not, after all they had suffered already, to provoke Florus to some irrevocable measure.' They had some success: perhaps responding to another demand by Florus for a token of submission, the high priests persuaded many of their followers to join an unarmed procession to welcome the arrival of two more Roman cohorts from Caesarea. These 1,000 or so men, as they approached the city, were confronted by a strange gathering of humble penitents led by priests in torn garments and a covering of dust. It is impossible to know precisely what happened, but the fragile peace of the first moments was quickly shattered. The soldiers charged into the crowd and the mass of people fled in panic back towards the gates of the city. Here there was a terrible press of bodies, and, in addition to those cut down by the soldiers, many collapsed and were suffocated or crushed to death beneath the stampede; some corpses, it is said, were mashed to pulp and could not be recognised.

In the wake of this second massacre, the Jewish leaders' authority collapsed and the common people of the city rose against the Romans *en masse*. Opinion was already polarised between appeasers and militants, and many Jews had ignored their leaders' call to welcome the new cohorts – 'the seditious part,' Josephus calls them, 'those who were boldest for action' – and even some who did join the procession had shouted denunciations of Florus when the troops first appeared. Opinion now swung overwhelmingly in favour of resistance and the people began to fight back in tens of thousands. As the new cohorts broke into the city and advanced through the Bezetha district, and as Florus led out the existing garrison to join them, both heading for the Antonia Fortress which dominated the Temple, the Jews filled the narrow streets, blocking them off with improvised barricades, and lined the flat rooftops above. The troops found themselves hedged in and assailed by a hail of spears, stones and tiles, and their commanders quickly abandoned the attempt to march through the city and pulled their men back to the Palace on the western hill. As they did so, Jewish militants, fearing that the Romans might yet gain control of the Antonia, broke down the colonnades linking it with the Temple.

They need not have bothered. Their victory in the street-fighting had been greater than they realised. Florus, massively outnumbered by the insurrection he had done so much to bring about, had no stomach for a second attempt to reach the Antonia. He summoned the high priests and councillors to the Palace to tell them that he was leaving Jerusalem with most of his troops. When he departed, he left only a single cohort of 500 men as a token of imperial power. These men remained beleaguered in the Palace on the western edge of the city, unable to venture forth into streets now controlled by a mass revolutionary movement. In the language of the Dead Sea Scrolls – which, as we shall see, was the language of the popular militants – 'the Company of Belial' was in retreat, and 'the Sons of Righteousness' were shining forth.

3 Collaborators and compromisers

The princes of Judah . . . are all of them rebels, for they have not turned from the way of traitors, but have wallowed in the ways of whoredom and wicked wealth. They have taken revenge and borne malice . . . every man has sinned against his near kin, and been guilty of incest, and has acted arrogantly for the sake of riches and gain. . . . they have wilfully rebelled by walking in the ways of the wicked, of whom God said, 'Their wine is the venom of serpents, the cruel poison of asps.'

(*The Damascus Document*, DSS, Qumran)

King Herod Agrippa II

Jerusalem, late May or early June AD 66
A short time after the mid-May disturbances, two top-ranking figures met at the Palestinian coastal port of Jamnia to discuss the crisis. One had come from the north, the Roman military tribune Neopolitanus, dispatched by the Governor of Syria, Cestius Gallus, to make an on-the-spot assessment and report back. The other was King Herod Agrippa II, the most powerful Jewish ruler in the region, who was on his way home from a diplomatic visit to Alexandria in Egypt. Though his territories did not include Judaea, he was a dominant figure in Jerusalem, for he held the important rights of supervising the Temple, guarding its treasures, and appointing the high priests. It was to him, therefore, that a delegation of dignitaries from Jerusalem now came, men desperate to distance themselves from the rioting and win support for their efforts to restore order. Encouraged by this, Herod Agrippa and Neopolitanus made the journey to the holy city. There, however, though the streets were outwardly calm, they found the popular mood angry and volatile. A radical minority were demanding independence. Many of the young men seemed ready for a fight. Large crowds were backing the demand for an embassy to Rome to denounce Florus and gain redress for the massacres. But there was also fear of Roman retribution: a slave had struck his master and entered a world of frightening uncertainties; should he beg forgiveness or stand defiant? Sensing that the mood might yet swing back in favour of order, when Neopolitanus departed for Antioch to make his report, Herod Agrippa remained in Jerusalem determined to try to rally the peace party. He called a mass meeting in the Gymnasium, and there, packed into the great open courtyard and the colonnades around it, tens of thousands assembled to hear him. In

full view above them, on the roof of the Hasmonaean Palace, stood the king's sister, the Princess Berenike, a beautiful woman still popular with the crowd after her abortive intercession with Florus during the massacres.

We cannot know for sure what Herod Agrippa said. Josephus reports a six-page speech, and, given that he may have been present in person, and also that he later came to know the king well, it is possible that he gives us, if not the actual words spoken, then at least the gist of them. On the other hand, they may simply be the words Josephus himself would have spoken had he been in Herod Agrippa's place; in which case they are a direct reflection of his own views on the power of Rome and the futility of resistance. But whichever it is, we learn something from the speech about the opinions of upper-class Jews who favoured peace. Florus alone – the king is supposed to have said – was to blame for recent atrocities, and it would be both wrong and foolish to revolt against the whole Roman Empire because of them. Jewish liberty was lost long ago, and the world has moved on too far to try to reclaim it now. The Romans control vast territories and resources. Their span extends from the Atlantic to the Euphrates, from the Danube to the Sahara. Wealth flows to them from every quarter. Alexandria alone pays more than ten times the tribute of Jerusalem, and her grain-ships provide one-third of Rome's annual needs. Great warrior peoples have been crushed and now live at peace under the empire – Hannibal's Carthaginians, Alexander's Macedonians, and the fierce tribesmen of Spain, Gaul, Germany and the Balkans. What hope, then, could there be for a small and impoverished people like the Jews, fighting without allies, against the might of Imperial Rome? Even God would forsake them – for how else could the Romans have built their empire but with his support, and how else could the Jews fight except by violating his laws? To rise against Rome is to doom the Jewish people to defeat, death and desolation:

> . . . when the Romans have won . . . they will make an example of you to other nations by burning down your holy city and destroying your entire race. . . . not even if you survive will you find a place of refuge, since every people recognises the lordship of Rome or fears that it will have to do so. Again, the danger threatens not only ourselves here but also those who live in other cities – for there is not a region of the world without its Jewish colony. All these, if you go to war, will be massacred by your opponents, and through the folly of a few men every city will run with Jewish blood. . . . Pity your wives and children, or at least pity your mother city and its sacred precincts. Spare the Temple and preserve for your use the sanctuary and its sacred treasures. . . . If you make the right decision, you will share with me the blessings of peace, but if you are carried away by your passions, you will go without me to your doom.
>
> (Josephus, *JW*, 2.397-401)

To choose to fight Rome was indeed to face a terrible ordeal. The odds were stacked high against the rebel. But for many ordinary Jews – long oppressed by taxes, corruption and brutality – the time had now come when not to fight seemed worse still. It was quite different for Herod Agrippa and the Jewish aristocracy. They were men of property, privilege and power, men who enjoyed Roman protection. Revolution threatened everything they had: it meant 'mob rule' and social levelling, the destitute marching on the mansions, followed by war and retribution, the indiscriminate looting and killing of an enemy army unleashed on the homeland. The nightmare of revolt from below – shared in some form by all ruling classes – was especially vivid for the Jewish élite in AD 66. Most of these men were thoroughbred creatures of Rome, a new Herodian nobility formed by purges and promotions in the 130 years since Pompey's invasion first brought the legions to Palestine. Under Roman governors and Jewish client-kings, the old nationalist nobility had been all but liquidated, its estates parcelled out to 'new men' of the victorious faction, creating a Jewish ruling class of Hellenised and pro-Roman gentlemen with little in common with their fellow-countrymen. They were, therefore, frightened men in May AD 66, and they looked eagerly to Herod Agrippa, their natural leader, to find a way back from the abyss.

The king was the great-grandson of Herod the Great, known as 'King of the Jews' and 'Friend of the Romans', that archetype of the client-king who had ruled Palestine from 37 to 4 BC. Seventy years later, Herod's former kingdom, though now divided between a lesser Jewish king, a Roman governor and semi-autonomous Greek cities, still retained much of his heavy imprint. Before Pompey's invasion, Palestine had been ruled for a hundred years by Hasmonaean kings and high priests as an independent Jewish state. After 63 BC, the ruling dynasty had been irrevocably split into pro- and anti-Roman factions. Herod's father, Antipater, had risen to power as head of the pro-Roman faction and chief minister to the Hasmonaean high priest John Hyrcanus II (76-67 and 63-40 BC), and when the father was assassinated by a nationalist opponent, his son had assumed his mantle. These ambitious politicians, father and son, were new men, aristocrats-of-office on the make, unscrupulous and opportunistic in their own advancement, and much hated by the blue-blooded establishment they threatened to displace. Not only did they lack connections with the Jerusalem nobility, but Antipater was an Idumaean, his wife a Nabataean Arab, and his son could barely count himself a 'half-Jew'. Herod, then, was an upstart who could not hope to win power by conventional means, and his policy was at all costs to retain the backing of Rome in his struggles against the Hasmonaean establishment. This he managed consistently, though only with much fast footwork in the shifting sands of civil war – switching allegiance rapidly from Pompey, to Caesar, to Cassius, to Antony, and finally to Octavian-Augustus, as the needs of the moment demanded. He proved his value especially in the great crisis of 40-37 BC, when the Parthians swept across the East and installed a Hasmonaean nationalist on the Jewish throne. When the exiled Herod appealed to the Romans for support, they made him King of Judaea, for, in the words of Peter Robinson, a recent biographer, 'he had been tried in the fires of eastern politics and not been found wanting by his political masters'. He fought his way back to power, destroyed the Hasmonaean regime, and built a new Herodian monarchy in its place. Later, having made his peace with Octavian-Augustus after Actium, his new patron rewarded continuing loyalty and service with steady increments of territory, until, by 20 BC, Herod had become the greatest Jewish king since Solomon.

What was the deal with Rome? Client-kings like Herod offered imperial domination at a discount. These men ruled their own states and paid the costs of government from their own resources – there was no need for Roman funding, infrastructure and soldiers. But they deferred to Rome in everything that mattered, and stood firmly on its side as policeman of internal order, buffer against foreign aggression, and ready source of troops and tribute in times of trouble. The Herodian state was a Roman construct, built and sustained by Roman power, put in place to protect Roman interests against three connected dangers – the militant nationalism of the Jewish people, the cantankerous character of the Hasmonaean dynasty, and the ever-present danger of Parthian intervention. It was in the struggle against these threats that Herod emerged as Rome's loyal guard-dog in the East.

There was, though, a price to pay in political popularity. Like all collaborators, Herod was tainted by his dependence on a foreign power, especially when, through him, Rome plundered Jewish resources to support its wars. Though curbed, the nationalist opposition persisted, drawing on the social discontent simmering in the Palestinian countryside, and Herod could never relax his guard. The tension between ruler and ruled shaped every aspect of the state he and his Roman patrons created. Even the composition of the kingdom seemed designed to contain and control its festering Jewish kernel. To the original territories of Judaea, Idumaea, Peraea and Galilee, all mainly Jewish, were soon added Samaria, the cities of the Sharon Plain, and the north-eastern (Transjordanian) territories of Paneas, Gaulonitis, Batanaea, Trachonitis and Auranitis, thereby incorporating large numbers of Samaritans, Greeks, Syrians and Arabs (**7**). The result was a kingdom less cohesive and nationalist, and one therefore more easily controlled by a skilful mixture of divide and rule.

The Jewish ruling class was largely reconstituted. The hawkish wing of the Hasmonaean faction was destroyed by civil war and subsequent purges. The main holocaust – though by no means the last of the killings – was in 37 BC, when, after three years of war, Herod finally mounted a blood-spattered throne: King Antigonus and 45 of the 70 sitting members of the Sanhedrin were immediately executed. With the more tractable elements of the old order Herod at first formed an uneasy alliance, principally through his marriage to Mariamme, a blue-blooded princess in the direct line of Hasmonaean descent, a device designed to offset the king's glaring disadvantages as a new man, an Idumaean 'half-Jew', and a quisling of the Roman emperor. It ended miserably – Mariamme and most of her family would eventually be consumed in Herod's successive purges – but by then the Hasmonaean alliance had served its purpose in allowing Herod a breathing-space to tighten his grip. Usurper he might be, but he had by now constructed a powerful Hellenistic-type state machine, well able to crush the broken fragments of nationalist opposition that remained. He had taken control of the Temple at the outset, arrogating to himself the right to appoint the high priest, and choosing a succession of relatively obscure men of whose loyalty he felt confident (though he did not hesitate to sack them promptly when they lost his favour). This ensured that the aristocracy, which was traditionally recruited from high-priestly families, was reinforced by an influx of Herodians. The vacant seats in the Sanhedrin were filled, and its political balance shifted sharply in Herod's favour.

This reconstruction of the aristocracy was underwritten by wholesale land redistribution. Herod had inherited from the Hasmonaeans the vast royal estate amassed by the Hellenistic rulers of Palestine in the third and second centuries BC, and he added to this land confiscated from his defeated political opponents. We do not know the precise extent of the royal estate, and our fragmentary picture has been pieced together from diverse evidence – scattered literary references, surviving inscriptions, and the results of archaeological survey. But the picture is consistent: the king owned much of the best land across Palestine, usually in large blocks, much of it organised in specialised farms producing high-value commodities for the market. Several ancient writers refer to the royal estate at Jericho, famous for its date-palms and balsam plantations, which stretched unbroken for 11 miles, with further detached estates at Phasaelis to the north and at the Dead Sea oasis of Engedi to the south (**8**). A Seleucid stone inscription indicates a royal estate in the rich Jezreel Valley, and Josephus implies that Herod's descendants owned land there at the time of the revolt. Place-name evidence, a Ptolemaic papyrus and further references in Josephus indicate another royal estate in a region of western Samaria where archaeological field-survey has revealed the existence of almost 1,000 small towers, all built in a short period of time to a fairly standard design, as if part of a single project. We have passing references to other royal estates in Batanaea, Gaulonitis and Trachonitis in northern Transjordan, at Lydda, Azotus and Jamnia on the coast, in Peraea in southern Transjordan, and, as is to be expected, in the Herodian homeland of Idumaea.

This royal estate was a source of immense patronage and power. Herod used grants of land to reward and ennoble his own supporters, while revenue from the holdings he retained helped fund his programme of largesse, benefactions and public works. The king was a fountain of generosity to the leading members of his entourage, mainly family and friends, people who formed an inner circle of (usually) loyal lieutenants: what a Roman might have called his *amici* ('friends') or *comites* ('companions'). Not all were Jewish, or even native to Palestine. Herod was networked into a cosmopolitan Mediterranean élite. Never at ease in Jerusalem society, craving the company of sophisticates, eager to 'reform' and 'modernise' his kingdom, he filled his court with foreigners, some Roman, most Greek. The Herodian court was, in fact, thoroughly Hellenised: Greek was much spoken, Greek names and titles were commonly used, and many leading officials were either actually Greek or at least Greek-educated – men like Nicolaus of Damascus, who was Herod's tutor, secretary, royal councillor, special ambassador and close friend. This new Herodian ruling class – a landowning aristocracy-of-office comprising army commanders, administrators and priests, Hellenised Jews mixed with Greeks and a sprinkling of Romans – was essential to the stability of the state.

The essence of that state – as of any state – was its army: the military force it deployed in defence of the monarchy, the ruling class and the territory of the kingdom against enemies at home and abroad. The Jews – most of them – were not to be trusted with arms, so Herod and his successors recruited a hotchpotch army of professional soldiers, men whose allegiance depended on pay not principle. Many came from Idumaea in the south of the kingdom, the Herodian homeland where

12 *An armoured horse-archer. He wears a conical iron helmet and body-armour of scales stitched to a leather tunic. His equipment includes a wooden shield, a composite bow (shown unstrung), a long slashing sword, and a dagger. Soldiers of this type were probably very common in the armies of the ancient East, including those of the client-kings allied to Rome, though some men probably deserted to the rebels in AD 66*

there were reserves of family loyalists, and some also from Batanaea and perhaps other parts of the far north-east beyond the Jordan. Others came from still further afield: there were Germans and Thracians, Babylonian Jewish horse-archers, and Galatian Gauls from Asia Minor inherited from Cleopatra and organised as a royal bodyguard. There was also a special regiment of Greeks (or Hellenised Syrians) recruited from the two new Herodian cities of Caesarea and Sebaste. We hear of battalion-sized units of 400 or 500 men, and we can guess that the total strength of the standing army was around 10,000. Though we have no contemporary images, it is probably safe to imagine Herod's soldiers, like those of neighbouring client-kingdoms, as fighting in an eastern Hellenistic style. The merging of Macedonian and Persian military traditions in the region had created armies which combined the mobility of cavalry, massed missile shooting, and heavy shock action: the armoured horse-archer was the epitome of this system (**12**). Officers, on the other hand, were often Greek or Roman – we hear of men called Gratus, Rufus and Volumnius commanding royal troops under Herod – and these 'western military advisors' must have influenced organisation, training and equipment, modifying the local tradition in line with their own experience, much as the British officer 'Glubb Pasha' helped shape the modern Jordanian army.

On retirement, many of these soldiers were settled in veteran colonies. This was common practice in the ancient world – not least among the Romans – and had clear advantages for the state: a good retirement package ensured loyal soldiers, the colonists acted as a military reserve, and the settlements eventually provided new recruits for the army. We know from Josephus of several such colonies – one for Babylonian Jews in northern Transjordan, another for demobilised cavalry in the Jezreel Valley, a third at Sebaste for no less than 6,000 men (if we can believe the figure), a fourth at Heshbon in Peraea close to the Nabataean border, and a string of fortified villages in southern Idumaea, where veterans formed a local militia guarding the desert frontier. These military colonies constituted a web of strongpoints across Palestine, which also included regular fortresses manned by serving soldiers. At Caesarea, Sebaste and Jerusalem, Herod built or restored the city walls, and troops may have been permanently stationed at all three. He also built or improved about a dozen fortresses. Jerusalem itself was guarded by two, the Antonia Fortress over-looking the Temple in the east of the city, and the Royal Palace with its three defensive towers, Hippicus, Phasael and Mariamme, in the west (**63** & **colour plate 21**). Others stood alone, often in bleak wilderness locations, like Machaerus in the Transjordanian hill-country near the Nabataean border, Masada deep within the

13 *The interior of the palace-fortress of Upper Herodium looking east. In the centre of the picture is the rectangular colonnaded courtyard of the mini-palace, with the remains of the eastern citadel behind it. The summer dining-room (triclinium) was to the right of the steps, the bath-house to the left, and the casemate walls can be seen curving round on either side of the tower. Originally both tower and walls were very much higher, and the palace would have been pleasantly shaded and cool for much of the day*

Judaean Desert on the west side of the Dead Sea (**79** & **colour plate 22**), and Hyrcania and Herodium, each a short distance south-east of Jerusalem on the desert fringe. We know of others at Alexandrium, Cyprus and Herodium East. Though these fortresses were concentrated in the south-east of the country – opposite the principal foreign threat in Nabataean Arabia – few were in the border zone itself: they were as much defences against Jews as Arabs. Some quickly acquired a sinister reputation as places where 'enemies of the state' were incarcerated, tortured and murdered – it was in a dungeon of the Machaerus that John the Baptist was later beheaded on the orders of Herod Antipas. Many were also palaces – notably Herodium, Masada and the Royal Palace in Jerusalem – for Herod felt the need of numerous fortified residences in which he could take refuge.

Upper Herodium is especially well preserved. Visible from miles around, it has the appearance of a volcanic cone rising out of the yellow-brown desert fringe (**colour plate 8**). Herod's engineers cut off the top of the hill to create a level platform and there built a cylindrical stone fortress with casemate walls, three round projecting towers arranged symmetrically to the north, west and south, and a high round citadel on the east. Massive quantities of earth and stone were dumped against the outer walls to create a steep approach, and access was via an underground flight of 200 steps leading up from the bottom of the hill. Also buried in the cone were cisterns and storerooms, and above them, enclosed by the fortress walls, was a royal pleasure palace. A rectangular colonnaded courtyard open to the sky occupied the eastern half of the enclosure, and giving onto it from the west were a summer dining-room, a suite of

14 *However elegant the palace at Upper Herodium, it was part of a fortified refuge and space was limited. The main palace complex – Lower Herodium – was laid out extensively on a series of terraces at the base of the hill. This view shows part of the huge colonnaded courtyard on the third terrace*

15 *The famous Wailing Wall illustrates well the massiveness of the Herodian reconstruction of the Temple Mount. The lower part of the wall, where it is formed of huge square blocks, is Herodian in date. Note that, towards the right at the base of the wall and part-shaded by the gateway structure, there is a single huge block*

bedrooms, and a bath-house – the whole *ensemble* forming a grand private residence in the Graeco-Roman style (**13**). But it was cramped: a luxury apartment squeezed inside a fortress in case of troubled times. At the bottom of the hill lay the sprawling complex of Lower Herodium, much of it today a tumble of ruins yet to be fully explored (**14**). It comprised several monumental elements, including a large palace built on an elevated barrel-vaulted terrace, a 350m-long track which may have been a private circus for horse and chariot races, and a huge colonnaded courtyard of 2.5 acres (1ha), whose centrepiece was an ornamental pool with a round colonnaded shrine (*tholos*) perched on an island in the middle. Herodium was, then, both the fortified refuge of a hated autocrat and the palace of a Hellenising king.

Herod's building programme extended also to civic monuments. Among many other towns, Caesarea (as we have seen) attracted particular attention, as did Sebaste, that other splendid classical city rebuilt by Herod in honour of his patron. But his greatest efforts were in Jerusalem itself, the Jewish holy city and capital of the kingdom, where the Temple, the centre of world Judaism, was completely rebuilt. The new Sanctuary or Outer Court measured 480m by 300m, and constructing this involved a massive extension of the Temple Mount platform, which was supported by a 5m-thick containing wall up to 45m high; some of the individual blocks of stone used were over 10m long (**15**). The Sanctuary was surrounded by colonnades formed of twin marble columns 11m high, and these framed the reconstructed Inner Court and Temple in the middle of the concourse, a huge and glittering complex of stone, white marble, bronze and gold (**16** & **68**). Herod's Jewish piety in this and other respects has caused much confusion. It has led revisionist scholars to question his portrayal as a single-minded Helleniser wholly at odds with traditional Judaism. But this is to erect a false dichotomy: Hellenism and Judaism were never simple alternatives. Nor was Hellenisation mere whimsy, an aristocratic fad, a senseless provocation to traditional belief. Herod's aim was precisely to Hellenise Judaism as a way of depoliticising it: to purge it of its popular, militant and nationalist aspects, and to reform and 'modernise' it – in a sense, to 'civilise' it – so that it could assume a comfortable place within a Roman-dominated world. Herod's struggle was at root political, not religious or cultural. It was not Judaism as such that had to go, but an uncompromising traditional Judaism which encouraged militancy, even fanaticism, in a futile and dangerous struggle for Jewish national liberation. Hellenisation was a programme to defeat the very idea of revolution – and make Palestine safe for privilege, property and Roman power.

Hence Herodism – Jewish client-kingship – was, as a political tradition, contradictory and unstable. Representing Greek cities, Jewish landlords and Roman tax-collectors, inhabiting a world of palaces, games and banquets, presenting to their enemies a mailed fist of mercenaries and prisons, the Herodians were hated by the peasants. It was this chasm between ruler and ruled that ensured obloquy for the cultural tokens of Hellenism, failure for the modernisation programme, and the slow disintegration of Herodism after the great king's death in 4 BC. Augustus, disillusioned by vicious factionalism within Herod's family in the closing years of his reign, and unimpressed by the calibre of the late king's surviving sons, declined to maintain a unified kingdom. Palestine was at first divided into three segments ruled by three sons – Archelaus, Philip and Herod Antipas – but the former failed miserably, and after ten years, in AD 6, direct Roman rule was imposed on Judaea, Samaria and Idumaea. Philip and Herod Antipas continued to rule their territories for as long as they lived, however, and after their deaths (in AD 34 and 39 respectively) a role was found for Herod the Great's grandson, Herod Agrippa I, who became successively king over the former territories of Philip (in AD 37), and then over a reunited kingdom of all Palestine (in AD 41-4). This experiment in the wholesale restoration of client rule was cut short by the king's premature death, and the reconstituted Roman province of Judaea was extended to include Galilee, Peraea and northern Transjordan. Only somewhat later, when he reached manhood and demonstrated reliability, did Herod Agrippa's son have territory allocated to him, a little at first in AD 50, much more in AD 53, and a final grant in AD 54 (**7**). Thus, Herod Agrippa II (AD 50-93), great-grandson and successor to Herod the Great, stood before the crowd in the Gymnasium at Jerusalem in late May or early June AD 66 as the most powerful Jew in the world – king of numerous scattered part-Jewish territories in the north and east of Greater Palestine, including northern Transjordan, eastern Galilee, and Peraea.

The crowd, though, was not easily impressed. Revolutionary crowds are not the fickle monsters that some historians imagine them to be; they do not simply lurch

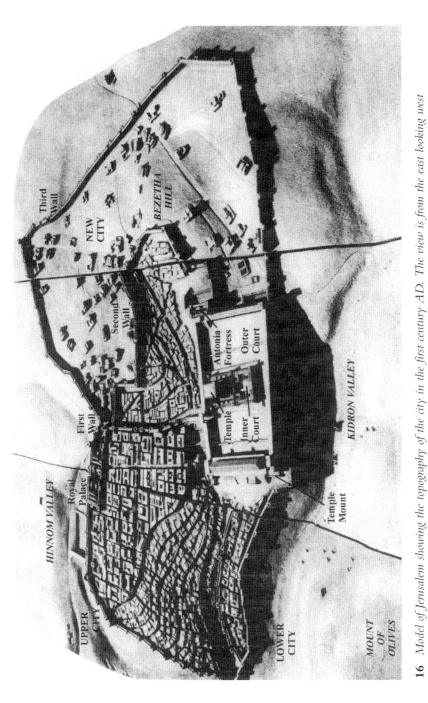

16 *Model of Jerusalem showing the topography of the city in the first century AD. The view is from the east looking west*

from one contrary opinion to another on mere whims of the moment. They embody collective opinions arrived at through experience and debate, and each time they gather they tend to have clearer vision, more definite demands, and heightened aspirations. In May the crowd had approached Florus as humble petitioners and there had been a massacre. That event could not be erased from consciousness: the crowd would never trust Florus again. But there was still much fear and uncertainty. Especially there was fear of Rome's military power and uncertainty about whether the Jews could and should challenge that power in all-out war. All knew that Florus was a butcher and none would tolerate his return; but many still hoped that the business could be ended there. This was Herod Agrippa's opportunity, and his speech in the Gymnasium won a short reprieve: the Temple porticoes pulled down during the May fighting would be rebuilt, and the unpaid tribute collected and handed over – the imperial power was to be appeased and Jerusalem's rebellion restricted to a dispute with the procurator. But then, growing in confidence, the king overreached himself, arguing that even Florus should be obeyed until a replacement was sent. This amounted to complete capitulation, and things had gone too far for that: the crowd rounded on Herod Agrippa, hurling abuse and stones, and he and his entourage fled the city. The Herodians had exposed themselves as a faction of pro-Roman collaborators for whom no atrocity was too awful to merit breaking their allegiance. Indeed, they were worse than that, for when they next intervened in the politics of the capital, in the late summer of AD 66, they came as a counter-revolutionary army.

The Herodian coup

Jerusalem, early August to early September AD 66
Herod Agrippa's flight split the Jewish ruling class irrevocably. A minority sided openly with the revolution and attempted to place themselves at the head of it. This group was led by Eleazar ben Ananias, a man of high-priestly family who held the post of Temple Captain in charge of administration and security. He persuaded the Temple priests to refuse gifts and sacrifices from foreigners, which meant abolishing the imperial cult at Jerusalem and signalling a clear breach with Rome. The pro-Herodian majority group were led by the former high priest Ananias, Eleazar's father, along with other leading priests. (Though strictly there was only one high priest at any one time, he was assisted by various other senior priests, and the top position tended to circulate within a small group of aristocratic families; thus, collectively, 'the high priests' formed the top echelon of the Jewish ruling class, much as 'proconsulars' – men who had held the consulship – did in the Roman system.) The Herodians immediately attempted to get the imperial cult restored, and when their advice was rejected at a mass meeting held in the colonnaded Court of Women in front of the Temple, they began preparing a counter-revolutionary coup. One delegation was sent to Caesarea to confer with Florus, another to Transjordan to obtain armed support from Herod Agrippa. The king sent 2,000 cavalry, probably including armoured horse-archers, and with this reinforcement the

Herodians seized control of the Upper City. It was here, on the western hill over-looking the Temple Mount and the Tyropoeon Valley, that the royal palaces and élite residences were located; this was the geographical centre of the Jewish aristocracy (**16** & **63**). The coup was a property-owners' revolt: the leadership and upper ranks were drawn from the families and descendants of high priests, client-kings and old nobles; the lower ranks were a mixture of young bloods, tax-collectors, minor officials, and the dependants of élite households; all those, in short, who lived off temple tithes, royal patronage, government salaries or contracts, and the income from great estates. It was, quite simply, a revolt of those who lived, directly or indi-rectly, off the exploitation of the Jewish peasantry.

All Jews, wherever they lived, in Palestine or the Diaspora – all pious ones at least – paid an annual half-shekel tax to the Temple. But in addition to this, temple tithes were levied on farms in Palestine – in keeping with the biblical injunction that 'the children of Israel' should give to their priests, the descendants of Aaron and the Levites, 'the first-fruits of all that is in their land', including the best of the grain, oil and wine. This was a good deal for the priests; so good, indeed, that we can be sure it was the priests who drew up the contract – fraudulently, since it probably dates to the eighth century BC or later, and certainly not to the time of Moses, as was claimed. The tithe may have amounted to a tenth of the harvest – as the Bible said it should – but later rabbinical sources (of the second century AD onwards) consid-ered a thirtieth or a fortieth sufficient, so we cannot be sure about the situation in the first century. Either way, substantial amounts of wealth were involved, enough for the tithe to have become the focus of a vicious three-cornered conflict. The Hasmonaean kings had centralised tithe collection and given control over receipts to the priest-nobles of Jerusalem, making village priests, who relied on local tithes for their subsistence, dependent on their superiors for handouts. The peasants resented paying tithes at all, but especially they resented paying them to a distant aristocracy, and as the social cohesion of the old order began to break down in the 50s AD, the flow of tithes to the capital was often disrupted. The high priests responded by sending armed squads into the countryside at harvest time to collect the tithes; they went 'onto the threshing-floors to take away tithes that were due to the priests, such that some of the poorer priests starved to death' (Josephus).

Rulers levied taxes, priests collected their half-shekels and first-fruits. But both also drew income from their ownership of large private estates. Extensive tracts of land, as we noted above, were organised as royal estates in Hellenistic, Hasmonaean and Herodian times. Though much of this remained either in the ownership of King Herod Agrippa and his family, or in that of the Roman emperor, much had also passed into the possession of other big landowners. The Jewish kings had used grants of land to build a political base by ennobling their supporters, and it is likely that a mix of old Hasmonaean estates and new Herodian ones, especially in Judaea itself, formed the economic foundation of the Jerusalem nobility. Archaeological field-survey has revealed the remains of 42 possible Roman-style villas in northern Judaea and western Samaria, while literary sources – *The New Testament*, the *Talmud* (the collected rabbinical writings of the second to fifth centuries AD), and Josephus – all record the existence of rich landowners in Palestine during the first century. The rabbis may exaggerate when they tell us that three landowners were rich enough between them to supply the whole of Jerusalem with all its wheat, barley, oil, wine and wood; but we can at least conclude from this that some estates were very large. The parables of Jesus confirm this. In these stories we meet with absentee landlords, rich creditors, and bailiffs whose job it was to hire labour and collect debts. Though we cannot assess the relative proportions of large, medium and small landholdings, it is clear that Jesus' world was one that included men rich enough not to work themselves, men who lived off the labour of others and could afford to 'relax, eat, drink and be merry'. *The New Testament* tells us also of the tensions in this world (and to this we shall return in the next chapter), as does the *Talmud*, which preserves this Jewish lament for its oppressiveness – naming some of the culprits, the old Herodian high-priestly families who owned so many of the biggest estates:

> Woe is me because of the House of Boethus, woe is me because of their staves!
> Woe is me because of the House of Hanin, woe is me because of their whisperings!
> Woe is me because of the House of Kathros, woe is me because of their pens!
> Woe is me because of the House of Ishmael, the son of Phiabi, woe is me because of their fists!
> For they are high priests, and their sons are temple treasurers, and their sons-in-law are trustees, and their servants beat the people with staves!

If we allow that many of the richest landowners were absentees, where did they in fact reside? Rescue excavations after 1967 in the Jewish Quarter of the Old City of Jerusalem may provide the answer. Many of the excavation trenches were located on the eastern scarp of the Upper City, from which, in ancient times, one could have looked east over Tyropoeon Valley to the Temple Mount, and south-east to the Lower City ranged on the slopes of the Ophel Hill. Here the archaeological preservation was often superb, for the area had caught the full blast of the Roman torching of the city in AD 70, and beneath a mass of soot-blackened debris were found ancient Jewish houses with walls still metres high, furniture *in situ*, and the bric-a-brac of everyday life strewn about. The character of first-century occupation was clear. 'Construction in the Upper City was dense,' wrote Nahman Avigad, the director of excavations,

> with the houses built quite close together; but the individual dwelling units were extensive, and inner courtyards lent them the character of luxury villas. These homes were richly ornamented with frescoes, stucco work and mosaic floors, and were equipped with complex bathing facilities, as well as containing the luxury goods and artistic objects which signify a high standard of living. This, then, was an upper class quarter,

where the noble families of Jerusalem lived, with the High Priest at their head. Here they built their homes in accordance with the dominant fashion of the Hellenistic-Roman period.

(1984, 83)

In one case, indeed, a brief inscription on an artefact appeared to provide a direct link with the Herodian aristocracy of the first century AD: a stone weight with the words *bar Kathros* on one side – meaning '(of) bar Kathros' or '(of) the son of Kathros' – a reference to one of the high-priestly families listed in the *Talmud* lament quoted above.

One house – the 'Palatial Mansion' – especially stood out, both for its ancient grandeur and state of preservation (**17**). Although only one in a row of similar buildings, it was, at 600 square metres, large for a private house in a city as densely built-up as ancient Jerusalem. It was constructed on two terraces against the side of the hill. Stairs indicated the former presence of an upper storey. On the higher terrace there was a paved central courtyard open to the sky with an extensive enclosed suite of rooms to the west. The latter included: an entrance vestibule with a rosette-pattern mosaic on the floor; a large room with Pompeian-style frescoes imitating stone-panels, windows and architectural features; a magnificent hall, 11m long by 6.5m wide, whose walls and ceiling were decorated all over with white moulded stucco; and a row of three rooms, perhaps bedrooms, where a later layer of white plaster concealed old frescoes beneath. On the eastern side of the main courtyard only one room survived at the upper level, a small bathroom decorated with a compass-formed rosette mosaic, but there were steps down from here to the lower terrace. This comprised a small courtyard, service and storage rooms, and vaulted water-cisterns, pools and ritual baths; the decoration was again, in places, of a high order.

Also recovered, both at the Palatial Mansion and at other contemporary houses nearby, were some of the artefacts in use at the time. There were small rectangular stone tables standing on single legs, or round ones with three wooden legs, often orna-mented with carved floral and geometric designs. Drinks had been served in delicate coloured-glass vessels decorated with concentric rings or splayed ribs, and food presented on superior ceramic tableware, either red glossy-surfaced bowls imported from Greece, or wafer-thin plates painted with sprigs and wreaths of foliage from local workshops. For the more conscientious, there were stoneware vessels made on lathes – ritually pure because non-absorbent – including jars, bowls, dishes, trays, goblets and cups. And in the service areas there was a clutter of rough pottery containers and cooking pots, some attesting the arrival of imported luxuries like Italian wine.

We learn, then, that these Jerusalem nobles were both Hellenised – with their taste for Graeco-Roman mosaics, frescoes, pottery and wine – but also in a real sense Jewish – symbolised by their ritual baths, stoneware vessels, and the avoidance of figurative art. We learn a little more about them from Josephus' brief descrip-tions of the Sadducees. He distinguished this group sharply from the other main religious sect at the time, the Pharisees, who operated mainly as local teachers and spiritual leaders, and who treated the Torah as a living tradition in need of constant development – the original rabbis. The Sadducees, by contrast, accepted only the

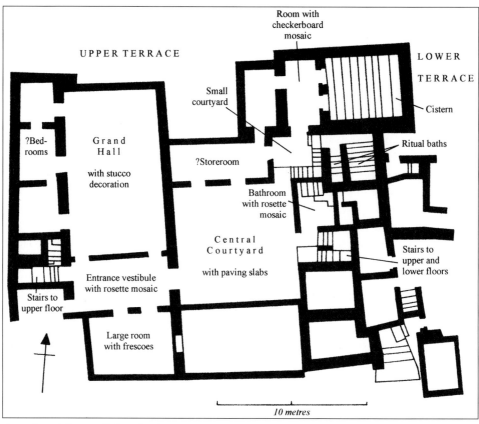

17 *Plan of the so-called 'Palatial Mansion' excavated in the Jewish Quarter of Old Jerusalem in the late 1960s. One of many Hellenised grand residences in the Upper City at the time of the revolt, it was terraced into the hillside and built on two levels with up to three storeys in parts. To the west of the central courtyard are the grand reception rooms and bedrooms, while to the east is the bathing, service and storage area*

biblical written law, and they were mainly concerned with correct performance of ancient ceremonial. They also denied the immortality of the soul, the existence of heaven and hell, and the promise of a messiah's advent. God, for them, was an impersonal force with little interest in human affairs, and once appeased by ritual and sacrifice, people could get on with their lives pretty much as they wished, enjoying the 'free will' to make their own decisions, for good or ill. Quite alien was the idea that God intervened actively to shape the future, that history had divine purpose and direction, and that those who submitted to him were certain to be on the winning side and to receive rich rewards in the afterlife. The cult of the Sadducees, a desiccated religion of empty ritual, appealed to high priests, courtiers and big landowners, people who were comfortable, conservative and smug. Josephus states that the Sadducees were a rich minority without popular support; and it is significant that on the half dozen or so occasions they crop up in *The New Testament*, the setting, with only one exception, is Jerusalem.

The two linked power-bases of the Sadducean nobility were the Temple and the Sanhedrin. The Temple priests were almost always Sadducees, and it was they and their families who dominated the Sanhedrin, the Jewish Council of Elders, which seems to have combined the roles of a senate, a high court and a holy inquisition (**18**). Though marginalised by the royal absolutism of Herod the Great, the Sanhedrin had achieved renewed importance under the procurators as the institution favoured by the Romans to head the local administration. We catch glimpses of it at work in the pages of Josephus, the gospels and *The Acts of the Apostles*, and what we see is not attractive: the Sanhedrin represented a client ruling class, and the Sadducean majority within it formed a self-interested clique whose policy was reactionary, repressive and pro-Roman, their aim being to safeguard their own property and position by giving loyal service to the imperial power and firmly suppressing popular opposition. When Jesus of Nazareth entered Jerusalem and began preaching sedition to the festival crowds, it was the high priest Caiaphas and other leading members of the Sanhedrin that had him arrested and handed over to Pontius Pilate. It was the Sanhedrin also which, in the years after Jesus' death, threw Peter and John into prison, had Stephen and James stoned to death, and were instrumental in the arrest and deportation of Paul.

Now, in the summer of AD 66, the Sanhedrin and the Sadducean ruling class, facing a far graver challenge than ever before, launched an armed counter-revolution against their own insurgent people. Royal troops and an aristocratic militia had seized the Upper City. The revolutionaries still held the Lower City to the east and south, a predominantly plebeian residential district, as well as the Temple itself, which was now, in a period of civil war, converted into a citadel. For seven days the two sides faced each other along improvised lines formed of walls, rooftops and street barricades. Mostly they watched and waited, guarding their positions, but sometimes missiles were hurled across the open ground – stones, slingshot, darts, anything that came to hand – and occasionally there were concerted rushes and brief flurries of close-quarters fighting somewhere along the line. Several times Herod Agrippa's armoured professionals advanced in force and attempted to fight their way through to the Temple, but each time they were driven back. In seven days the lines hardly moved. The Herodians continued to hold the Upper City but gained no ground beyond it, and their attempted counter-revolution became a stalemate.

Then, on 14 August, the revolutionaries in the city were reinforced by pilgrims from the countryside, including contingents of the militants known as 'Sicarians' or 'Zealots'. The Herodians, already weakened by casualties, defections, physical exhaustion and collapsing morale, now found themselves heavily outnumbered in renewed attacks led by determined revolutionaries and men fresh to the fight. The resistance of the royal troops disintegrated and they fled west towards the Royal Palace. The Jewish nobles fled with them, or else disappeared into the network of underground sewers, and the revolutionaries surged through the streets of the Upper City. The houses of high priest Ananias, Herod Agrippa and Berenike were put to the torch. So, too, was the public record office, where official copies of the contracts which recorded debtors' obligations to their creditors were held. (Debt was one of

18 *Engraving of a Jewish high priest wearing the holy garments prescribed in* Exodus *39*

the principal mechanisms by which the rich exploited the poor, and the demand for cancellation of debts was a traditional rallying cry of radicals in the ancient world.) As the Herodian nobles and defeated royalist soldiers – along with the 500 Roman auxiliaries left behind by the procurator in May – watched from the relative safety of the Royal Palace, the panorama of victorious revolution before them must have confirmed their worst fears about the course the crisis might take: an armed people in control of the streets, the houses of the rich under attack, and property deeds consumed by fire.

The following day, 15 August, the revolutionaries attacked the Antonia Fortress, a great mass of defensive masonry by the north-west corner of the Temple Mount, from whose walls the garrison could look down into the Sanctuary. It fell after two days and the small garrison there was put to the sword. After this, only the Royal Palace remained in the hands of counter-revolutionaries. Here, though, the garrison was far stronger, and, with the first assaults beaten off, the struggle became a regular siege. The assailants were strengthened by the arrival of a further contingent of Zealots under the veteran revolutionary Menahem, son of Judas the Galilean, who had led a revolt against the Roman tax-collectors 60 years before. The Zealots had been at Masada, where they had infiltrated the fortress, overwhelmed the garrison, broken open the armoury, and equipped themselves with the weapons stored there. These were hardcore militants who knew how to organise and fight, and Menahem especially was accorded respect, for Josephus tells us that, shortly after his arrival in

Jerusalem, he was granted control over the stalled attack on the Royal Palace. Vigour was restored and the defenders' morale broken. Menahem had a mine dug beneath one of the towers along the outer wall, and when the props were fired the structure collapsed. The defenders had detected the device and built a new wall behind the tower – so there was no breach – but their confidence was fatally shaken. They lacked the numbers and energy to sally forth; they had no hope of immediate relief from the outside; they were tired, hungry and frightened; and their assailants had convinced them that it was only a matter of time before the Palace was taken in assault. On 6 September the Herodians sought terms and the king's troops and any other Jewish defenders were permitted to surrender and depart. No terms, though, were offered to the Romans, who retreated for safety into the three towers on the northern side of the Palace, which were soon put under tight siege (**colour plate 21**). They must have been desperate men, caught by a rising tide of revolution that had left them holding little more than the ground on which they stood.

Nearby, the high priest Ananias, leader of the Herodian faction in Jerusalem, had already been caught by that tide. Found hiding in an aqueduct, he was brought forth and summarily executed. With his death, the counter-revolution which he had helped to launch precisely a month before was definitively crushed.

The first aristocratic government

Jerusalem, September to October AD 66

Each great leap forward in revolution creates a new crisis of political adjustment. The month-long struggle against counter-revolution had radicalised Jerusalem. People were fast learning lessons from the events in which they were embroiled. They now knew that the state was not all-powerful: its soldiers could be defeated in street-fighting. Also that the old leaders and most of the rich were not to be trusted: the Herodian faction had fought alongside the Romans against the Jewish national cause. And further that the best fighters on the ground were the popular radicals: the Zealots who had led the attacks on the Upper City and the Royal Palace. But even in revolution, though ideas change more rapidly than in ordinary times, the learning process is still a gradual one. It was one thing to follow the radicals in the excitement of a street-battle, quite another to entrust them with state power. That the people of Jerusalem had ejected King Herod Agrippa did not mean they were immediately ready to give unconditional allegiance to Menahem the Zealot. Some of Jerusalem's traditional leaders – men who were well known, 'respectable' and politically moderate – had sided with the revolution, and these were to be preferred over obscure 'extremists' given to apocalyptic visions, wild speeches and militant 'excesses'.

Nonetheless, the struggle against the Herodian counter-revolution had shifted politics sharply to the left, and Menahem's Zealots appeared menacing to the aristocratic nationalists under Eleazar who had taken power in May. This provisional revolutionary government was anti-Roman, indeed anti-Herodian, but it was also a government of property-owners who feared the 'many-headed hydra' of popular revolt. A strike against Roman taxes could so easily be extended to the rents and debts owed to landlords. If the emperor's property were to be seized, why not great estates generally and a redistribution of land to the poor? It was, after all, the property of Jewish nobles, not Roman officers, that had been torched during the recent fighting in the Upper City. The fear was that nationalist revolt to win independence could easily spill over into social revolution to cast down the rich. The property-owners in the government therefore made nervous revolutionaries, and, having used Menahem to defend their regime against the Herodian coup, they now set out to destroy him. Having struck successfully at the right, now, to restore a balance and enable the centre to hold, they were obliged to strike at the left. They were agreed, Josephus tells us, 'that it was absurd to revolt from Rome for love of freedom and then hand over that freedom to . . . a master who, even if not violent, was certainly inferior to themselves'. The blow was carefully prepared and seems to have taken Menahem by surprise. He and his group were attacked in force on the Temple Mount, and their attempt at defence was quickly overwhelmed. Some were killed there and then; others escaped and were hunted down later in the city; a few got away altogether, some back to Masada, some to other refuges, but Menahem himself was tracked down, pulled from his hiding-place and tortured to death. The aristocratic coup was therefore a complete success: the Zealot party in the capital was crushed, the popular movement effectively decapitated, and the new regime, victorious over enemies on both right and left, was secure in power for the time being at least.

There was a long tradition of aristocratic nationalism among the Jews. The Maccabaean Revolt against the Seleucids in 167-142 BC was regarded by Jews 200 years later as one of the most important events in their history. The Hellenistic system of states which had dominated the East since Alexander had been disintegrating at the time, the military threat of Rome forcing already weak regimes to impose heavy burdens on their subject peoples. King Antiochus Epiphanes IV had attempted to impose conformity and obedience on the Jews by banning their religion and replacing it with the cult of Zeus. An elderly priest called Mattathias Maccabaeus had refused to carry out pagan sacrifice, killed an apostate Jew, taken to the hills with his three sons, and there launched a revolt which eventually won for the Jews an independent state ruled by Hasmonaean high priests and kings. People looked back on the Maccabaean Revolt as a great national liberation struggle, one which had pitted native people against foreign overlord, Jew against Greek, poor against rich.

Maccabaean success had owed much to the weakness of the Seleucids, the oppressiveness of their rule, and backing from the Romans in the struggle against them. But there had been something else. The Jewish nationalism of the Maccabaeans had belonged to a much older tradition, one which had reached a more or less finished form in the sixth century BC. Yahwism was an 'imperial' religion, one concerned with war, conquest and domination; the long-maturing fruit of centuries of struggle between states and peoples (**19**). After the death of Solomon in the late tenth century, the Jewish state had split into the 'Divided Kingdoms' of Israel in the north and Judah in the south (*c*.926-722 BC). Subsequently, both kingdoms had fallen to foreign conquest, the Northern Kingdom to the Assyrians in 722 BC, the Southern to the

Babylonians in 587 BC. The Assyrians 'ethnically cleansed' parts of Israel and settled it with non-Jews (thus creating the basis on which a distinctive 'Samaritan' culture would in due course develop). The Babylonian conquest of the south was less disruptive at the time, but its political consequences were far greater. Only the nobility was transplanted, and during the 50-year 'Babylonian Exile' they settled down in Mesopotamia, where most of their descendants doubtless decided to stay, forming the Babylonian Jewish communities known in Roman times and later. But not quite all. After his conquest of Babylonia, the new Persian ruler Cyrus the Great granted the Jews permission to return to Palestine, and some (we do not know how many) took this option (537 BC). The king had his reasons, of course: a new empire to consolidate, a need to build support for it, and a special regard in this matter for his enemies' enemies. Thus, some of the exiles returned to build a small Jewish state in Palestine under the authority and patronage of the Persian king. It even survived the Macedonian conquest of 332 BC without major upset, retaining its local autonomy as one remote ruler simply replaced another.

With them in 537 BC the returning exiles had brought back to Palestine something special, something pregnant with world-shaking potential: forged in centuries of disunity, defeat and dispersal, and recently refined by contact with Mesopotamian religion, it was a new brand of steel-hard Judaism. Solomon and the kings of Israel and Judah had never been monotheists: for them, Yahweh, however important, had been one of a pantheon of deities. Against such pluralism the prophets had for long railed in vain. God's Law was defied and the Holy Covenant broken, cried Hosea, and false idols were worshipped on mountaintops and in the shade of the forest. 'Hear the word of the Lord, O people of Israel, for the Lord has an indictment against the inhabitants of the land: there is no faithfulness or loyalty, and no knowledge of God in the land.' But they did not hear. The prophets were in a minority. They stood fast against the stream but could not turn it back. Only when the disasters of 722 and 587 BC threw Judaism into ideological crisis did the teachings of the prophets come into their own. For many, of course, the defeats of the Jews were defeats for Yahweh, who thus lost the power to inspire his weaker brethren, many of whom fell away to worship alternative, apparently more effective gods. Others, though, especially those who experienced exile as a humiliation and longed to return home, heeded the advice of the prophets. If the people had lost God's favour and succumbed to their enemies, the road to recovery was via a 'return' to the Law and the Covenant. The traditionalists were a minority of a minority – a fraction of the outcast nobility who clung through the long years of exile to the hope of restoration. To sustain them – to preserve their 'Jewish' identity, to keep alive the flame of hope, to steel men for battles to come – their Yahwism hardened into an intolerant and inflexible monotheism. Strict ritual defined the Jews as different, as pure and godly, as a 'chosen people' who could be confident of God's favour. The frustrated nationalism of the exiles found perverse expression in Yahweh's claim to worldwide dominion. If, instead of a pantheon of warring deities, there was but one all-powerful god, then history moved to a single divine purpose, and those chosen for God's special favour, as long as they remained loyal and obedient, were bound to win out in the end. The myth of Moses,

69

19 *Engraving of David with the head of Goliath based on a painting by Guido. The myths and legends recounted in the Hebrew Bible constituted a 'nationalist' epic which substantiated Jewish claims to independence from foreign rule*

in short – at least in the finished form in which we have it – was a sixth-century construct. The 'Mosaic' religion was the belligerent response of hardcore nationalists to their own weakness and fragmentation, and the whole of Jewish history up to that date was now substantially rewritten in the light of new religious 'truths'. But this, as yet, was the work of a sect, a small exile group whose restorationist ambition took the form of religious fantasy. Alone they could have done nothing but hope and pray. It was the intervention of Cyrus the Great that saved them: it was he who planted the New Judaism back in Palestine, where in time it prospered greatly.

Why was this? The New Jews, at first, must have been a very small minority. No doubt they quickly rallied the Judaean peasantry left behind at the beginning of the Exile. But later there would be mass conversions in Galilee, Idumaea and further afield, and by Roman times the Jews of Palestine and the Diaspora numbered many millions. There seems little doubt that Judaism became a proselytising and crusading cult, one actively seeking converts, whether by persuasion or by force, and having a real appeal to the downtrodden and discontented. Probably, in individual minds, it tapped deep psychic wells with its message of father-worship, the washing away of sin and guilt, and personal redemption through obedience and service. Certainly, it inspired great confidence, courage and endurance when it argued that God intervened directly in human affairs, that there was divine purpose in events, and that history was meaningful, progressive and promised hope for the future. Nor, despite Mosaic Law, was this Judaism the rigid fossil it later became, unable to adapt to changing conditions, and increasingly irrelevant to the problems of real life. On the contrary, holy scripture was not standardised, many different texts circulated, and these were read, interpreted and debated. There were Scribes who created copies of the texts and were learned in scripture. There were Pharisees who lived among the people as readers and teachers. There were synagogues where ordinary men (and perhaps women) could meet to hear scripture read, to consider the commentaries of rabbis, and to thrash out a 'truth' relevant to their own world. *The New Testament* records both Jesus and Paul intervening in just such debates; the Dead Sea Scrolls lay down rules of procedure for them at Qumran; and Josephus attests the Essenes' devotion to scripture and discussion. 'Jesus grew up among people who had texts but no Bible, and whose predicament is still familiar,' argues Robin Lane Fox.

> The authority of their main texts, the books of the law, was unquestioned, but what exactly did they and all the others mean? There were laws that contradicted each other and did not cover obvious problems; there were apparent contradictions in the narratives, and there were masses of prophecies whose original reference had long passed or been forgotten. . . . . The laws . . . told people what to do and were thought to tell them what would happen, but they did not exhaust these subjects. They were obscure and often contradictory, and as a result they could accommodate life's changes and improvements. They set a framework which exercised the curious, but left room for people to find what they wanted.
>
> (1991, 114–16)

The holy texts comprised 'a jungle with gaps and holes', within which it was open to each and every group to map out its own path to God. Thus, without a canon, the national struggle and the class war would resolve themselves into fierce sectarian strife over the meaning contained in scrolls of papyrus. Judaism could, therefore, be highly innovatory in response to changing conditions. The great anti-Seleucid war of the 160s BC had, for instance, spawned the apocalyptical *Book of Daniel*. The legendary Daniel had fathered on him various past prophecies now known to be true – namely, the overthrow of the Babylonians by the Persians, and then of the Persians by the Greeks – and these were linked with a new prediction that the Hellenistic kingdoms would also fall (**20**). This was resistance literature: it was all part of God's long-laid plan, apparently, that the enemies of the Maccabees should be defeated. Also, as there was a cost in martyrdom and it was hard to accept that war heroes went to oblivion, the author of *Daniel* argued – though this idea was new to Judaism – that eternal life in heaven awaited those who died in the holy war.

It is clear from Josephus – both from his descriptions of the sect and his accounts of conflicts involving them – that the Pharisees of the first century AD were continuators of this vibrant, flexible and subversive kind of Judaism. The sect had its origins in the early Hasmonaean period, when it may have developed principally as a reaction to backsliding by the new Jewish rulers – in contrast to the Sadducees, who were upper-class loyalists. There was especially bitter conflict in the reign of Alexander Jannaeus (103-76 BC), whose programme was to build an empire abroad and a centralised state at home, symbolised by his determination to unite the kingship and high priesthood in his own person. This shift from a revolutionary 'kingdom of the saints' to an earthly kingdom built on modern (i.e. Hellenistic) lines was unavoidable if the Jewish entity was to survive in a world of warring states. But herein lay a contradiction basic to the whole Hasmonaean project, and a deep split opened between 'fundamentalists' and 'modernisers'. A furious revolt provoked furious repression, and hundreds of Pharisees and other rebels were crucified in a grotesque public spectacle at which the victims' wives and children were murdered before their dying eyes.

By AD 66, repeatedly recharged by upsurges of nationalist struggle against Greeks, Hellenising kings and Roman governors, the cult of the Pharisees was at full vigour. The group probably comprised full-time local priests, professional scribes and notaries, and lay preachers with other occupations – a 'middle class' group united by its commitment to Judaism and a distinct Jewish identity and way of life. Some were missionaries eager to make converts. Some were radicals who favoured political independence and social reform. Many were more conservative – including, no doubt, those with seats in the Sanhedrin – and we should think of the Pharisees as a broad trend of opinion, not as an ideologically uniform sect. Nonetheless, as Josephus makes clear, there was an irreducible core of common ideas, and these, it seems, were those that now formed the mainstream of popular Judaism. The Pharisees advocated an austere and sober lifestyle, strict obedience to the Law, careful study of holy scripture, and an intelligent, thoughtful, 'rationalist' approach to the world. Though they believed that God controlled the course of events, they also held that men could

20 *Engraving depicting Daniel interpreting the famous 'writing on the wall' in the Babylonian court. The Jewish prophets were popular leaders who led opposition to both corrupt Jewish kings and oppressive foreign overlords; their prophecies of eventual victory for the righteous gave confidence to the resistance.* The Book of Daniel, *in particular, was a resistance text of the Maccabaean Revolt against the Seleucids in the mid-second century BC*

choose between good and evil, and, since the soul was immortal, that the choices they made would determine their eternal fate. These were popular ideas – in contrast to the empty formalism of the Sadducees – and many local village priests were Pharisees. It is for this reason that Jesus was preoccupied with the opposition of 'Scribes and Pharisees', not that of Sadducees; as a popular preacher, it was the former he encountered as competitors.

There were, then, in Palestine during the first century AD, strong traditions of Pharisaic traditionalism and Jewish nationalism. But these essentially upper-class perspectives were contradictory and fractious, and their histories had been chequered. To preserve an independent Jewish kingdom within a Balkanised region contested by the great powers, the Hasmonaean rulers had been driven towards centralised administration, a professional army and imperial expansion, policies which imposed heavy burdens on the population and provoked strong opposition. Direct Roman intervention then drove deep wedges into the fractures, splitting the Hasmonaean royal house into pro- and anti-Roman factions. For 30 years (67-37 BC) the strife continued, erupting thrice into full-scale war (63, 57 and 40-37 BC) as Hasmonaean nationalist claimants to the throne attempted to drive out the

Romans and their Jewish clients. (This, of course, was the conflict that raised Herod the Great to power, first as the pro-Roman Hasmonaean faction's leading lieutenant, then later in his own right.) Though weakened by defeat, defections and purges, aristocratic nationalism survived as an oppositional current – poisoning the Herodian court with its plotting, using the Sanhedrin as a platform for populism, and seeking to exploit mass protests when they arose. Now, in AD 66, the aristocratic nationalists were in power again, and – even without direct testimony in the ancient sources – we can guess that the aim was to construct an independent state on the Hasmonaean model. Past experience suggested that this was a pipedream – that the project would be torn apart by internal dissension and superpower intervention. To this, though, was now added the nationalist aristocracy's paralysing fear of their own people – paralysing because defending the revolution meant mobilising the masses, and mobilising the masses meant empowering the dispossessed. The nationalists had needed the Zealots to defeat the counter-revolution; but then, in fear for their property and position, they had destroyed them. Though this had purchased a breathing-space, the aristocratic regime remained narrowly based, riddled with contradiction, and highly unstable. It was, moreover, about to face a far sterner challenge than that of the Herodian counter-revolution. Cestius Gallus, Governor of Syria, leading Roman general in the East, was on the march to restore order and authority in the troublesome little province of Judaea. The legions were coming.

4 The revolutionary movement

[There] shall be a time of salvation for the people of God, an age of dominion for all the members of His company, and of everlasting destruction for all the company of Belial. . . . The dominion of the *Kittim* shall come to an end and iniquity shall be vanquished, leaving no remnant; for the Sons of Darkness there shall be no escape. The Sons of Righteousness shall shine over all the ends of the earth; they shall go on shining until all the seasons of darkness are consumed, and, at the season appointed by God, His exalted greatness shall shine eternally to the peace, blessing, glory, joy and long life of all the Sons of Light.

(The War Scroll, DSS, Qumran)

Fire and sword

The towns and villages of Palestine, September to October AD 66
The news from Jerusalem ignited Palestine and much of the East. The Greeks – bastions of reaction under Hellenistic kings and Roman emperors – turned on the Jewish ghettoes in the classical cities. A privileged and protected minority in their urban enclaves, the Greeks' attitude to their Jewish neighbours was a colonial one, a potent mixture of disdain and fear. They were haunted by the spectre of Jewish revolution, and now that Jerusalem had risen against Rome the Greeks turned on the Jews in their midst and destroyed them in a hateful explosion of pre-emptive violence. There were communal massacres at Caesarea, Scythopolis, Ascalon, Ptolemais, Tyre, Hippus and Gadara (**7**).

The violence of the pogroms moved Josephus to the uncharacteristic comment that 'the war of the Jews against the Romans was not so much a matter of choice as necessity'. So great was the danger of massacre, he implied, that many Jews were forced to take up arms in self-defence. In the small towns of the hinterland and in villages across Palestine, in places where they found themselves outnumbered, it was the Greeks who were killed or chased out and their property looted. Some who tried to stand against the trend – moderates opposed to war, or people too bewildered to decide – were swept away. The Jews of Scythopolis at first stood with the Greeks in defence of the city, only to be massacred by their allies once the danger from the countryside had passed. Everywhere the logic of communal violence destroyed the middle ground. Everyone, Greek or Jew, was at risk from militants on the other side.

Everyone was forced to find protection among people 'of their own kind'. Soon whole areas had been 'ethnically cleansed' and Palestine split in two. Most of the big cities of the coast and the Decapolis remained Greek. Some of them – chiefly Ptolemais, Caesarea and Scythopolis – would soon provide Roman generals with the military bases they needed to wage war against the rebels. Jerusalem, the Herodian fortresses, and most of the small towns and villages of Galilee, Judaea, Peraea and Idumaea were held by Jews. Across these battle-lines, drawn in blood by the violence of September and October, the Jewish national revolution would now confront the Roman counter-attack massing in the north.

Cestius Gallus, Governor of Syria, had already marched out of Antioch at the head of 30,000 men. They included the entire Twelfth Legion plus 2,000 men from each of the other three Syrian legions: some 11,000 citizen heavy infantry in all. They were supported by 10 regular auxiliary units, at least 3,000 infantry and 2,000 cavalry, and by almost 14,000 eastern allied troops, mainly cavalry and archers, supplied by Herod Agrippa II and the client-kings of Commagene and Emesa. Arriving at Ptolemais, the initial campaign base, Gallus' army was further swelled by contingents of Greek irregulars from local cities. The pogromists had done what they could on their own; henceforward they would shelter behind Roman shields.

From Ptolemais the Romans launched a probing attack against the border town of Zebulon in north-western Galilee (**21**). The Jews could not risk a stand. They lacked armour, sophisticated weapons, cavalry support, and the drilling and discipline that could turn large numbers of men into an efficient battle machine. Above all they lacked numbers, since the Romans moved in concentrated masses, whereas the Jews were mostly local farmers defending their own patch of soil. So the rebels abandoned Zebulon and fled into the hills, while the Romans looted and burnt the town and then fanned out across the surrounding countryside to lay it waste. Any living thing they came across – person or beast – they slaughtered on the spot or carted off as booty; anything else – trees, standing crops, wells, barns, farmhouses – they did their best to destroy. Wherever they passed, they left a desert of devastation and death. This was no wanton violence: it was the systematic policy of 'fire and sword'. Its aim was to starve and terrorise the Jewish peasants into submission – or to force their young men to come down from the hills and risk battle in defence of their farms. Roman commanders always favoured pitched battle. Let the enemy, whether barbarians or rebels, hurl themselves onto the iron front of the legions but once – and that will decide it. If not, if they will not, if they prefer to skulk in the hills while their farms burn, then they will starve in the winter. Fire and sword was the deliberate strategy of an imperialist – an intruder on someone else's land – confronted by mass defiance.

Gallus was emboldened by the attack on Zebulon. The Jews had fled from his main force; they could not countenance a serious fight; they were basically weak. So he shifted his base south, to Caesarea, and from there, dividing his forces, he sent out heavy punitive columns to strike at targets in the Sharon Plain and western Galilee. Joppa was captured, the land around Narbata near Caesarea devastated, and a substantial rebel force attacked and defeated in the hills near Sepphoris. By late October, confident that his rear would be secure and a safe supply-line remain open to the coast,

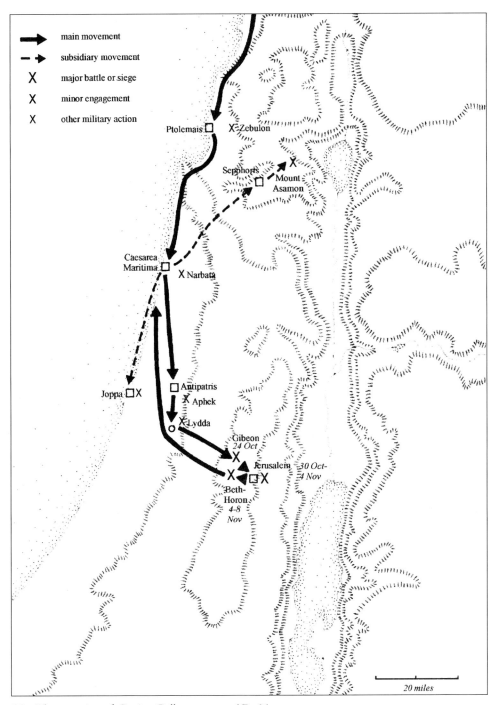

21 *The campaign of Cestius Gallus, autumn AD 66*

Legend:

→ main movement

--→ subsidiary movement

X major battle or siege

X minor engagement

X other military action

Ptolemais □ X Zebulon

Sepphoris □ → X
Mount Asamon

Caesarea Maritima □
X Narbata

Joppa □ X

□ Antipatris
X Aphek

X Lydda

Gibeon 24 Oct
X

Jerusalem 30 Oct–
X □ X 4 Nov

Beth-Horon
4–8 Nov

20 miles

Gallus marched out with his main force into the uplands of Judaea, still looting, burning and killing as he went. But resistance thickened as the holy city was approached, and there was a hard-fought battle at Gibeon, six miles out, which brought the army to a halt for three days. But then it surged forwards again, routing the Jews standing in its path, and Gallus took position on Mount Scopus, three-quarters of a mile to the north-east of the ancient walled city of Jerusalem. He waited there for three days, perhaps hoping for surrender; but none came, and so, on 30 October, he commenced a six-day attack on the city. The Romans first occupied and fired the New City or Bezetha district to the north (**16** & **63**). This brought them up against the main northern defences, and these they assaulted at various points. Finally, on the sixth day, they launched an all-out attack on the Temple at the eastern end of the line, the legionaries going in with locked shields against a hail of spears and stones from the parapets above. The Romans were winning, Josephus tells us; inside the city the rebels were in a state of panic, the peace party calling for the gates to be opened. But at that moment Gallus called off the attack, withdrew his men to their camp on Mount Scopus, and the following day commenced a retreat to Caesarea – one which would quickly degenerate into disaster. Josephus was bewildered by the decision and could offer no plausible explanation. He believed the Romans could have won the war there and then, and many later historians have followed him in this. But it is difficult to believe that Gallus was such a fool, and that he retreated without reason when on the very brink of victory. Something must have gone badly wrong.

There are many ways to fight a war. The Roman way was not the only one. Rome deployed large masses of disciplined, armoured, heavily equipped profes-sionals. In conventional battle Rome's armies at this time were the finest in the world and close to invincible. But this, the fighting of conventional battles, was not the Jewish way. Theirs was to wage people's war, pitting the slings of shepherds against the imperial Goliath, the elusiveness and resilience of guerrilla fighters against a cumbersome machine. In this way, in the Maccabaean Revolt 200 years before, they had slowly ground down and defeated the Seleucid Greeks. The rules of this kind of war were simple but effective: to avoid pitched battles in the open; to make full use of mobility and surprise; to harass the enemy with skirmishing, ambushes and hit-and-run attacks; to fight all-out only when the enemy was weak or unsuspecting – an isolated unit, an exposed flank, a retreating column; in general, to fight the enemy 'where he was not' – or at least only where he was outnumbered or unprepared; and to wear him down over time through attrition and despair (**22**). Already the Jews had delivered several object lessons in such 'asymmetrical' warfare. Most towns and villages attacked by the Romans were found deserted. All who could escaped to the hills. This always included the able-bodied, the younger men, the fighters of the Jewish resistance, who thus survived to continue the struggle. For usually, in the hills, people were safe. When the Twelfth Legion tried to attack Galilean rebels holding an upland position near Sepphoris, they were at first thrown back with heavy loss. Only when they manoeuvred to seize higher ground overlooking the rebel position could they defeat them. At Zebulon, when Gallus withdrew his main force back to Ptolemais, the rebels swooped down from the hills without warning to attack the

22 *Engraving depicting 'the eastern way of war'. It shows lightly equipped men deployed in open order, making use of cover, and skirmishing at long range. The contrast is with a 'western way of war' based on frontal collision by massed formations. To a large degree, in military terms, the Jewish War was a conflict between these two different traditions*

units left behind, including Greek irregulars busy with looting, and killed many, perhaps hundreds (Josephus says 2,000, but he always exaggerates). At Gibeon, Gallus had faced a fierce onslaught on his invading column. The Jews, attacking suddenly and in strength, smashed through the Roman line and inflicted (it is said) over 500 casualties. They then broke off and escaped back to the city as quickly as they had come. At this point, just as suddenly, a second Jewish attack struck the Roman rear, inflicted casualties, seized numbers of baggage-animals, and then also broke off and returned to the city. Gallus was unnerved by these tactics: he halted for three days in a defensive posture, with the Jews watching from the heights around. When he was ready to attack, the Jews fled, refusing battle now that the Romans were prepared, and the march was resumed.

The battles at Zebulon and Gibeon heralded a different kind of war from that favoured by Roman generals; a more dangerous kind, in which the enemy ignored the rules, dodged defeat, dragged things out, and awaited his chance. It was this, surely, that compelled Gallus to withdraw. Mostly, as the Romans advanced through Judaea, the rebels had kept clear, biding their time in the relative safety of the hills as their villages burned in the valleys below. It was this revolt in the rear, the swelling masses of the enemy closing in behind him and threatening to throttle the life out of his army, that forced Gallus to retreat – retreat, or starve in front of Jerusalem when his supply line was cut. But as he withdrew, the olive terraces above the Roman column filled with thousands of rebels – farmers with slings and javelins, set on vengeance, scenting victory, and closing in. The battle of Beth-Horon was about to begin.

Saints and scrolls

Qumran, near the north-west shore of the Dead Sea, AD 66
The 150 or so Essene monks (for such they almost certainly were) who resided at the Qumran monastery had devoted their lives to preparing for this moment. Two hundred years before, the Jews of the Maccabaean Revolt seem to have split into hostile factions, and some, disgusted by the betrayals of their leaders, had retreated into the Wilderness to escape worldly corruption and commune more closely with God. The separation had been vitriolic. The Essene leader, a 'Master of Justice' (though he was known by many titles), had denounced his main opponent as a 'Wicked Priest' and his opponent's supporters as 'scoffers spitting mud and slime', 'a community of wickedness', and 'a horde of Belial'. Trekking off into the Wilderness, the Essene minority formed itself into an ascetic sect determined to uphold Judaic piety against the backsliding and compromises of the new Jewish élite. Qumran probably became their main religious centre. Pliny the Elder, writing in his *Natural History* 200 years later, reported that 'the solitary tribe of the Essenes' – womanless and without money, but maintaining numbers thanks to 'the multitude of new recruits, who, tired of life, are led by the tide of fortune to adopt their way of life' – were to be found on the north-west shore of the Dead Sea. Archaeologists have estimated from the size of the settlement and cemetery at Qumran that the number of monks could not have much exceeded 150. There may have been other monasteries, but even so, the total number of Essene monks is unlikely to have been great. Probably, when Josephus reports there were 4,000 Essenes altogether, his estimate (it is no more than that) includes many lay followers living in the community. The Essenes, at the outbreak of the revolution, were a small minority struggling to preserve what they believed was an authentic tradition of Judaic holiness.

Qumran is a desolate spot (**colour plate 9**). It lies on the edge of the Judaean Desert – the biblical 'Wilderness' – an orange-yellow furnace of rock and sand. About a mile away, glinting through the heat haze, is the Dead Sea, a vast salt-filled depression flooded by the Jordan. It is a barren landscape – but it has just enough of the stuff of life for men content with only the basics to eke out an existence. So it was to here, in ancient times, that the Essene 'exiles of the desert' came to live. Local springs watered clumps of palm-trees and patches of subsistence cultivation – as they still do – and an aqueduct channelled water from natural reservoirs at the base of nearby limestone cliffs directly into the monastery's cisterns (**23**). This provided water for drinking, bathing, domestic chores, and the all-important ritual washing (**24**). So a community of monks, committed to the simple life, could survive here. On a high

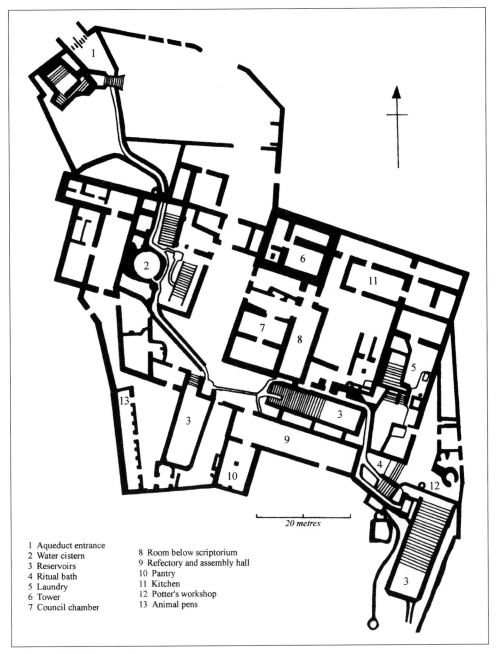

1 Aqueduct entrance
2 Water cistern
3 Reservoirs
4 Ritual bath
5 Laundry
6 Tower
7 Council chamber
8 Room below scriptorium
9 Refectory and assembly hall
10 Pantry
11 Kitchen
12 Potter's workshop
13 Animal pens

20 metres

23 *Plan of the Essene monastery at Qumran near the north-western shore of the Dead Sea*

24 *The steps down into one of several ritual baths at Qumran. The steps are divided so that the ritually unclean can descend on one side, and those who have been cleansed by the water ascend on the other. These features are a mark of the obsessive piety of the Essene monks*

white terrace, beside a wadi gouged deep by winter rains, with the cliffs of the desert behind and the rift valley below, they erected a compound of buildings out of roughly squared blocks covered in whitewashed mud. They had a kitchen, pantry, and refectory (1,000 bowls were found stacked against a wall), a laundry room, a potter's workshop, and a tanner's yard. There was a strong defensive tower guarding the main entrance. Some monks, the more senior perhaps, may have lived inside the compound, others probably in crude huts nearby, or even in caves, since both wadi and cliffs are riddled with them. The dead of the community were buried in a cemetery to the east of the settlement: 1,100 bodies were found there, placed in recesses in the walls of vertical, rock-cut shafts, apparently with minimal fuss, and little in the way of grave-goods. They are simple burials conforming to an austere and democratic lifestyle.

Communal life took place in one or more assembly halls – perhaps the refectory was used for larger meetings, and a room with low benches around each of its four walls for smaller ones (**25**). The monks were organised in a strict hierarchy, with regular routine, clearly defined duties and obligations, and severe discipline for breaches of the community code. They were ruled by a 'Master' or 'Guardian',

25 *The refectory at Qumran, looking east towards the Dead Sea. This is the largest single room in the complex, and it is likely that it doubled as a place of general assembly*

assisted by a board of three priests and 12 elders, and the brotherhood as a whole would meet under his chairmanship, each man seated according to rank – there were novices, probationers and four grades of initiate – forming a general assembly or 'Congregation of the Community'. A common daily task for the monks was the copying of holy texts. In one room of the compound, archaeologists found fragments of smashed furniture and other debris, which had fallen through the ceiling from an upper storey (**26**). There were plastered tables and benches, writing palettes, inkpots, and pens made of reed: evidence of a *scriptorium*, a monastic manuscript workshop, where monks had laboured to produce copies of holy texts. Another of the rooms in the compound must have housed the library, but we will never know which one. For, sometime before the destruction of Qumran in the summer of AD 68, perhaps two years earlier when the war first broke out, the monks cleared out the library, wrapped the scrolls in linen bindings, stuffed them into large pottery jars, and then, carrying oil-lamps to light the way, concealed them in various caves along the wadi and the cliffs near the monastery (**27-9**). Almost certainly the monks perished in the revolution – some at Qumran itself when it was destroyed, perhaps, others at Jerusalem and on battlefields elsewhere to which they had gone to fight – because the monks never came back to retrieve their library. The holy writings lay undisturbed in the caves for some 1,900 years. When they were rediscovered between 1947 and 1956, they amounted to one of the greatest archaeological finds of all time: the Dead Sea Scrolls.

The corpus is huge. From 11 caves have come a dozen complete scrolls inscribed on leather, another on copper, and tens of thousands of further fragments on leather or papyrus. The leather ones are formed of separate pieces sewn end-to-end, usually about 0.25m high, often many metres long, and they are read from right to left, the small neat writing organised in columns down the width of the scroll (**30**). About 800 documents are wholly or partially preserved, but some are duplications, so the total of distinct compositions is around 400. Most are written in Hebrew (the holy language of the time), some in Aramaic (the vernacular), and a few in Greek (recalling the existence of the Septuagint, the Alexandrian Greek version of the Bible, since the third century BC). Based on the evidence of coins and pottery found at the monastery itself, the palaeography of the texts (i.e. the character of the handwriting used), radiocarbon dates on some of the scrolls and their cloth wrappings, and the actual content of the texts (what the writers did and did not know), we can safely assume that all the documents belong to the period from *c*.250/200 BC to AD 66. The material can be divided into three broad classes of document. First, there are mainstream religious texts, versions of holy scripture which probably circulated widely in the first century AD, most of them already known as part of the Judaeo-Christian tradition. Virtually every book of the Hebrew Bible is represented, at least in fragments, plus some of the Apocrypha (which occur in the Septuagint and later Christian Bibles), and some Pseudepigrapha (texts which failed to become canonical and were not included in any version of the Bible), the last category including a

26 *The room beneath the* scriptorium *at Qumran, looking approximately south-east. Excavators found tables, benches and writing implements on the floor of this room, these apparently having fallen through the ceiling from a first-floor room when the monastery was destroyed in AD 68*

27 *The wadi beside the Qumran monastery and the cliffs above it are studded with caves, many of them artificial or deliberately enlarged. Scrolls have been recovered from 11 caves in the vicinity altogether*

number of previously unknown works. Secondly, there are sectarian religious works – texts which would not have been generally accepted among contemporary Jews and which mark the Essenes out as a distinct group. This category includes highly tendentious Bible commentaries, thanksgiving psalms and other religious poetry, wisdom literature, sectarian calendars, liturgical texts, and horoscopes. The third class of material concerns the internal organisation of the sect, its ideological perspective, and its politico-military strategy. The three principal texts of this type are *The Community Rule*, *The Damascus Document*, and *The War Scroll*.

Before the discovery of the Scrolls, we knew a little about the Essenes from contemporary classical writers: not just Josephus, but also the Roman senator and polymath Pliny the Elder, and the Hellenised Jewish philosopher Philo of Alexandria. But their information is fragmentary and biased. Now, with the Dead Sea Scrolls, we have vastly more information, and it comes from the Essenes themselves, giving authentic and intimate detail about a tradition of revolutionary millenarianism (see below) which flourished in Palestine 2,000 years ago. The Scrolls take us inside the thought-world of anti-Roman rebels in the first century AD. Nothing else like them has survived. They deserve detailed study. Let us explore what they tell us about the Jewish resistance to Rome.

The origins of the Essenes

We have noted already that Judaic nationalism was reborn in the Maccabaean Revolt against the Seleucid Empire in the mid-second century BC. Jewish victories held out the promise of a free state that would be just and holy. When the corruption – political and personal – of the Hasmonaean kings was seen to belie this promise, Judaic nationalism split into rival factions, as some, the more comfortable, came to an accommodation, while others, the disadvantaged, went into opposition. The Sadducees, we have seen, were aristocratic conservatives who backed the ruling regimes, and the Pharisees a 'middle class' of priests, scribes and teachers based in the villages and reflecting mainstream opinion. The Essenes, on the other hand, were probably direct descendants of pre-Maccabaean *Hasidim* – the Hebrew word means 'the pious ones', and *Essenoi* is probably a Hellenised Aramaic version of the same word. Later, recoiling at political betrayal by the 'Wicked Priest', they split from mainstream Judaism. Quite probably the Wicked Priest was Jonathan Maccabaeus, who, though not of Zadokite descent and therefore disqualified, accepted the post of high priest in 153-152 BC when it was offered by a Seleucid usurper seeking Jewish support. Double apostasy, this: a violation of the Law of Moses on the priestly succession, and an alliance with the Great Beast and his Hordes of Belial. But the breakaway – to form an ascetic, traditionalist sect untainted by worldly corruption – was a hard struggle.

A new prophet

Jewish myth and history were filled with prophets who came to reclaim the Israelites from backsliding and sin (**31**). Abraham had brought the first news of God's Covenant with his Chosen People and his demand for faith and obedience. Moses had condemned idol-worship, taught the Israelites God's Law, and led them out of the Wilderness. Elijah had denounced King Ahab's Baal-worship in the ninth century, and Isaiah had railed against the wickedness of an ungrateful people in the eighth. Ezekiel had drawn the lessons of defeat and exile in sixth-century Babylon, and Nehemiah and Ezra had restored the faith in the fifth. These men – and there were many others – came to the Israelites as divinely inspired prophets, as messengers of God, to forge and re-forge the Holy Covenant between deity and people. Their role was to rescue the people from sin, to restore their faith, to teach obedience to the Law. They had advance knowledge of what might otherwise happen, of God's terrible wrath, and they prophesied spine-chilling disaster if Israel did not reform. The Essene leader, the Master of Justice, had been such a man. For him, the new apostates corrupted by power, wealth and Hellenism were Hasmonaean kings, Sadducean nobles and even Pharisees, 'seekers of smooth things', who had given up strict observance for an easier life. These formed 'an assembly of worthlessness and a Congregation of Belial', a false leadership that had broken the Holy Covenant, 'interpreters full of guile who led the people astray' and 'prevented the thirsty from drinking the draught of knowledge'. God's true prophet, by contrast, was persecuted, tortured and cast out: 'I was an object of scorn to them,' the Master of Justice recalls in a thanksgiving psalm, '. . . [and] I

28 *A scroll jar from Cave 1 at Qumran. The scrolls were wrapped in linen bindings and placed in ceramic jars like this one before being deposited in the caves around the monastery, probably in AD 66 or 67. Each jar held four or five scrolls*

was driven from my country, as the bird from its nest, and all my companions and acquaintances were thrust far from me . . .' Most of the Essene psalms – over two dozen are known – concern the exiled prophet's lonely struggle against the temptations of evil, 'the snares of the Pit', his continuing persecution by the state, and his attempt to attract a following, a gathering of those 'who have joined together in Thy Covenant, and have hearkened to me, and who have walked in the way dear to Thy heart, and who have (all) set themselves (to join) Thee in the Assembly of the Saints.' He succeeded: the outcast prophet cried aloud in the Wilderness and some at least among the poor and pious heeded him. A sect – an 'Assembly of Saints' – was formed, and through it the light of truth flickered on in the darkness of corruption. Though probably eventually martyred, the Master of Justice had founded a small movement.

A living tradition

From what stuff were the revolutionary ideas of the Master made? What do we know about Jewish religious writing and teaching in the second century BC? Most books of *The Old Testament* were composed between *c.*550 and 300 BC, that is, during the Exile and after the Return, as a fiercely nationalist élite struggled to re-establish a Jewish state in Palestine. *The Old Testament* involved much re-working of earlier material – origin myths, tribal laws, popular fables, wisdom literature, prayers and psalms, royal chronicles and sagas, stories and sayings of the prophets – but in the form we have it the text is essentially a product of the New Judaism of early 'Second Temple' times. In the first century AD these holy writings had still not achieved canonical form: there were many texts which never found their way into later bibles, and many versions of all the texts were in circulation. The canon of post-AD 70 – a gradual fossilisation of Jewish holy writings by rabbis and priests – was not, as often claimed, an attempt to exclude later deviations and restore scripture to an original pristine condition. There was no original version, no common source: at the beginning there had been many versions, and the canon was a late standardisation of a much larger corpus of earlier literature. Second-Temple Judaism was a living, changing, fighting tradition. Ideas circulated and clashed in a ferment of debate. The scriptures were raw material from which to fashion ideological weapons for the battles of the present. Any attempt to impose orthodoxy and a canon soon melted in the fires of ideological struggle. As Robin Lane Fox put it, the scriptures were 'a jungle' and the Jews' 'inheritance from long years of history lived on in splendid discord'. There was, of course, a core of common belief: in Yahweh as the one and only god; in Israel as the 'Promised Land' of a 'Chosen People'; in the Temple, with its rituals, priests and festivals, as the proper focus for Jewish worship and pilgrimage; in the Torah and Mosaic Law as an infallible guide to living life in a holy way; and in various taboos whose purpose was to avoid 'pollution' and preserve ritual purity (e.g. kosher food, Sabbath observance, and male circumcision). These were the immovable foundation blocks of first-century Judaism: God, Israel, Temple, Torah, taboo. Beyond this, however, debate raged. Just as the Protestant Reformation of the sixteenth century shattered Christianity into a hundred fragments, so the Jewish Revolution of the first shattered Judaism. The common ground, which was wide, mattered less than the areas in dispute, for groups like the Essenes define themselves by their differences with others.

The Congregation of Belial

Revolutionary ideologies are always dichotomous: labour and capital; freedom and slavery; reason and superstition; the godly and the ungodly; Jehovah and Satan. The Essene mind inhabited such a dichotomous world. Forming a reactionary pole at one extreme was the Jewish aristocracy – the client-kings, the Sadducees, the Temple priests, the 'beautiful people' of Jerusalem's Hellenised upper-class districts. These were Belial's instruments in Israel, won to his service by earthly rewards, 'rebels' and 'traitors' who 'wallowed in the ways of whoredom and wicked wealth' and 'acted arrogantly for the sake of riches and gain'. Behind these Jewish renegades stood the imperial superpowers – first the Kings of *Yavan* (Greece), later the Rulers of the *Kittim* (Romans). Pagan warlords and conquerors, they came as scourges of God to punish Israel's wickedness with violence and oppression. They 'devour all the nations like the eagle', 'gather up their riches', 'lay waste many countries', and 'put many to the sword, young men, adults, old men, women and children, for they had no pity for the fruit of the womb.' So Israel's subjugation – its abandonment by God to pagan soldiers and tax-collectors – was punishment for the sins of its leaders. Romans, Greeks and Jewish nobles constituted a 'Congregation of Belial' which oppressed and desecrated Israel. But ranged against them was a small party of the righteous holding out a promise of redemption and liberation – a small party of revolutionary hope.

29 *A leather scroll from Cave 1 at Qumran. The scrolls have survived only because of the dry desert conditions in the area*

The Community of Saints

The Essenes saw themselves as a holy 'remnant' of the true Israel at a time of widespread corruption. This was not a new idea – it can be found in *Isaiah* – but, like so much else in the Scrolls, it had been updated. For the Master of Justice was the new Isaiah, a prophet to whom God had vouchsafed a message and a mission: he was to create 'a rock' of righteousness for the faithful to cling to when all about them were falling into 'the snares of the Pit'. With this group God had made a New Covenant, an agreement that, in return for obedience to his will, its members would be saved and enjoy eternal life. To preserve their holiness in such difficult times, the Essenes, after parting company with the mainstream, imposed upon themselves rules of strict separation – from Gentiles, from Temple cult, and from intimacy with unrighteous Jews. The most committed chose to live a monastic life in the Wilderness at Qumran, where they formed a 'Community of Saints' devoted to God, the Law and the study of scripture. 'The Essenes profess a severer discipline [than other sects],' reports Josephus. 'They eschew pleasure-seeking as a vice and regard temperance and mastery of the passions as a virtue.' On the other hand, this disciplined life was a choice, not an imposition, and those granted authority were chosen by their fellows and shared with them the simple communal life. 'Contemptuous of wealth, they are communists to perfection, and none will be found better off than the rest. . . . Men to supervise the community's affairs are elected by show of hands, chosen for their tasks by universal suffrage.' In this way, a small group could withstand the pressures

30 *A scroll inscribed with a copy of* The Book of Isaiah *from Cave 1 at Qumran*

to conform in a hostile world; by cutting itself off from that world, by imposing tight control over its own members, by creating in effect a self-contained micro-society in the Wilderness, it could uphold a tradition of pious Judaism against the tide of opinion. From this secure base it could set out to recruit others in a campaign for the redemption of the nation.

The battle for hearts and minds

The Essenes believed that God had created a world guided by 'two spirits', that of the 'Prince of Light' and that of the 'Angel of Darkness', one that was 'born of truth springing from a fountain of light', another that was 'born of injustice springing from a source of darkness'. These two spirits waged an eternal war for domination. The Company of Belial – the corrupt Jewish élite – abused their power to mislead the people into unrighteousness. 'Teachers of lies and seers of falsehood,' the Master of Justice had exclaimed, 'they withhold from the thirsty the drink of knowledge, and assuage their thirst with vinegar, that they may gaze on their straying, on their folly concerning feast-days, on their fall into their snares.' Into this battle for hearts and minds waded the village Essenes, those who lived not in a monastery but as organised congregations in the community, believing themselves to be God's 'elect of mankind', convinced that 'there is hope for those who turn from transgression and for those who abandon sin', and hoping that the time was fast approaching when 'all the nations shall acknowledge Thy truth, and all the people Thy glory'. This Essene mission was primarily to the poor. On one side, that of Belial, were the rich and powerful; on the other, on God's, the holy brotherhood of the prophet; and between them lay the mass of ordinary Jews, benighted and oppressed by God's enemies, but, uncorrupted as they were by the trinkets of earthly power, open to the revolutionary message of the New Covenant for Israel. For God 'hast not abandoned the fatherless or despised poor', but rather 'hast done marvels among the humble in the mire underfoot, and among those eager for righteousness, causing all the well-loved poor to rise up together from the trampling'. The poor were destined for salvation, the rich for the Pit. The split between the Company of Belial and the Assembly of Saints, between corruption and righteousness, was a class split, a split between the haves and have-nots of Roman Palestine.

The meaning of salvation

Most pagan religions were concerned mainly with worldly events and the hazards of real life; the measure of divine favour was health, prosperity and good fortune. The underworld and routes into it were ill-defined and played little part in everyday belief and ritual. The major exceptions were the increasingly popular 'eastern mystery cults' – of Dionysus, Cybele, Isis, Mithras, and others – in which initiates entered into a special relationship with a saviour-god who offered an afterlife of eternal bliss. At the extremes of the spectrum, it was the difference between official cults dominated by ritual formalities, and ecstatic religions suffused with spirituality and spontaneity. First-century Judaism also had this distinction. Josephus tells us that the Sadducees were preoccupied with correct performance of holy service, and denied outright the resurrection of souls and the existence of Heaven and Hell. The Pharisees, by contrast, while more flexible about interpreting holy writ, seem to have believed in everlasting imprisonment underground for the wicked and some sort of eventual reincarnation for the righteous. But it was the Essenes who had the clearest conception of spiritual salvation. They believed, according to Josephus, that the body was corruptible but the soul immortal, and that good souls would reside in 'a home beyond the ocean untroubled by rain, snow or heat', whereas bad ones would be consigned to 'a dark, stormy abyss full of torments without end'. The effect of such beliefs was, we are told, 'to encourage virtue and discourage vice'. Such inducements were certainly needed. The Essenes faced persecution in the present world, and they were steeling themselves for world war in an imminent future. A cosmic confrontation between the forces of light and darkness was about to begin, and a guarantee of eternal bliss for holy warriors who fell in the fighting could be expected to stiffen God's battle-line. The widespread notion that the Essenes were pacifists – based on the misunderstanding of a single ancient reference – is comprehensively refuted by the whole corpus of the Dead Sea Scrolls. The Essenes, while opposing the imperialist wars of their rulers, so far from being pacifists, lived with the expectation that they would shortly be engaged in God's great war to cleanse the world of evil.

31 *Engraving of the Jewish prophet Elisha based on a painting by de Champagne. Many of the biblical prophets are likely to have been messianic itinerant preachers like the Essene 'Master of Justice' or Jesus of Nazareth, men whose mission was to bring a distinctly revolutionary message to the poor of rural Palestine*

The Apocalypse

The Essenes believed that the Apocalypse, a cataclysmic 'End of Days', was imminent. This was not the idea of a cranky fringe, nor of a particular moment of crisis; it was deep-rooted in the Judaic tradition, resurfacing repeatedly in Jewish history, and was predicted and described in detail by many of the biblical prophets. There are apocalyptic passages in all of the following biblical books: *Isaiah, Ezekiel, Daniel, Zechariah, Malachi, Matthew, Mark, Luke, John, Baruch, 2 Esdras,* and, of course, *Revelation.* Judaism (like its Christian offshoot) was a highly teleological faith: it rejected the cyclical views of time which dominated pagan thought, seeing history instead as a linear progression, in which God's design gradually unfolded and his people were led towards a predetermined end. This end was the Apocalypse. In the Christian reworking of the myth recounted in *Revelation*, the appearance of the Four Horsemen of the Apocalypse – Conquest, Slaughter, Famine and Pestilence – heralds a period of cataclysmic disasters which will destroy the existing world. The beasts and their riders are dream-symbols for the earthly forces which would, unwittingly, do God's dreadful work of punishing the wicked and ridding the world of corruption. In the earlier version of the myth recounted in *Daniel*, the four beasts were four successive conquering kings, those of Assyria, Babylon, Persia and Greece; but as the old story was retold, the identity of the kings could change. Myths are good to think with, Lévi-Strauss once wrote; they are also good to fight with; but to be effective, for both thinking and fighting, they must be continually updated. Because Second-Temple-period Jews used their holy writ as philosophy and politics, the texts were endlessly reinterpreted. *Daniel*, as we have seen, was the work of an author writing at the time of the Maccabaean Revolt, and its purpose was to provide an Apocalypse for that time, a revolutionary message to inspire Jewish fighters against the Seleucid monarchy; the fourth, last and most dreadful of *Daniel's* beast-kings was undoubtedly intended to be Antiochus Epiphanes IV of Seleucid Syria. His tyrannical rule had prepared the ground for the final 'End of Days' struggle in which 'the people that do know their God' were to rise up in overwhelming strength to crush 'the wicked against the Covenant', to end 'the abomination that maketh desolate', and to inaugurate the Rule of the Saints. Some, it was predicted, would fall in battle, but their sleep would be short, for the dead were soon to be resurrected, 'some to everlasting life, and some to shame and everlasting contempt'. For God himself was coming to rule on earth and inaugurate a new golden age, and the living and dead would then be judged. (The Christian author of *Revelation* has Christ rule on earth for a thousand years before the Last Judgement – thus the term 'Millennium' for a period of divine rule on earth, and 'millenarian' for one who works towards this end.) 'And it shall come to pass in the Last Days,' Isaiah had predicted,

> that the mountain of the Lord's house shall be established in the top of the mountains, and shall be exalted above the hills, and all nations shall flow unto it. And many people shall go and say, 'Come ye, and let us go up to the mountain of the Lord, to the house of the God of Jacob; and he will teach us of his ways, and we will walk in his paths': for out of

> Zion shall go forth the Law, and word of the Lord from Jerusalem. And
> he shall judge among the nations, and shall rebuke many people: and they
> shall beat their swords into ploughshares, and their spears into pruning-
> hooks: nation shall not lift up sword against nation, neither shall they
> learn war any more.
>
> *(Isaiah, 2, 2-4)*

Fragments at least of this complex of myth and hope – the Apocalypse, the Millennium, the Last Judgement, the Golden Age – were present in many ancient cultures. Greeks and Romans believed that at the beginning of time Saturn had ruled and men had lived without toil, feasted in plenty, and never grown old. The Near East had its myths of a primeval Garden of Eden, enshrined by the Jews in *Genesis*. As for the end, pagan oracles predicting the fall of Rome circulated widely in the East, some purporting to date from as far back as the Trojan War. So the Jewish Apocalypse did not exist in isolation. What made it special was the conviction that a new golden age was imminent, and that the cleansing conflagration to bring it about would begin among the Jews of Palestine. The vision, stripped of its mystic elements and seen as practical politics, was of nothing less than a revolutionary insurrection of the poor to destroy the ruling regime and create a world of peace and plenty. It was a programme for the present and it concerned change on earth. It was not, as it later became, an abstract concept to do with the resurrection of the spirit in some unspecified future time. It was a powerful ideological weapon for class war and national liberation in the here and now. And this conception of the Apocalypse was the fixed centre-point of the whole Essene world-view as revealed in the Scrolls. The sectarians thought of themselves as a holy vanguard, recruiting other Jews, building up God's army, preparing for the day when they could lead the Sons of Light out into battle with the Sons of Darkness and begin the apocalyptic 'End of Days' struggle. The plan was for the 'exiles of the desert' first to defeat the 'Ungodly of the Covenant' (the Jewish élite) and the *Kittim* (the Romans) in Palestine itself, retake Jerusalem, and restore the Temple cult to a holy form. Then the war, expected to last 40 years, would expand to engulf the entire world, and into the maelstrom would descend cosmic forces: on one side 'the Prince of Darkness', Belial himself, followed by all the demons of Hell, and on the other 'the Prince of Light', the Archangel Melchizedek, leading heavenly armies of angels. It was a vision of class war in the form of global jihad.

So the Dead Sea Scrolls show the Essenes to have been a revolutionary millenarian sect whose aim was to destroy the Romano-Jewish state in Palestine as the prelude to a world war of poor against rich. It would be easy – in the light of modern ratio-nalist thought – simply to dismiss their ideas as so much mystical nonsense. But when we seek to enter the thought-world of ancient people, we have to accept the religious framework which structured ways of thinking. Nature was inexplicable and unpre-dictable. Society was oppressive and cruel. Life was ruled by the terrible tyranny of fate. God was a rock of support to cling to, and no endeavour, great or small, could be expected to succeed without his help. Throughout history, revolutionary struggles have been fought under many different banners, and the Jewish Revolution of AD

66–73 was no exception. It was decked out in the ideology of its own time and place – the ideology of ancient Jewish scripture – because this was the way in which men and women made sense of their world and organised themselves to change it. But it was no less for that a genuine struggle for national liberation and social transformation. Consequently, considered as historical documents, the Dead Sea Scrolls have something of the significance of the pamphlets of the Levellers, the speeches of Robespierre, or the newspapers of the Bolsheviks, for in them we hear the authentic voices of revolution from below 2,000 years ago.

Yet the Essenes did not lead the revolution. We know from Josephus that they were a large group, and from the Scrolls that they were revolutionary millenarians. But they did not intervene in events as a corporate body: they did not constitute a nationally directed revolutionary party. Probably this was partly because the millenarian excitement of the early years had passed with the death of the founder. The Apocalypse, after all, had not come as soon as expected, and, as the group settled down for a longer wait, with its members more resigned to everyday routine and less active in 'the struggle', the Essenes perhaps became staid. The dogmatic certainties of the young and rootless probably gave way to the caution of family men with farms and workshops. They may also have split – Josephus records the existence of two groups divided by their attitude to marriage, and Hippolytus, an early third-century Christian writer, states that the Essenes broke into four factions. Disappointment is, of course, highly divisive in politics, and different groups of Essenes may have followed different trajectories as the messianic expectations of the early years were deflated. We should think of them, then, not as an organised party, nor even a coherent sect, but as a broad millenarian tradition, an ideological stem from which activist branches could grow. The Essenes' historical role was to have transmitted through two centuries of history the ideas of apocalyptic revolution – a minority current for most of the time, dependent for its survival on modest numbers of monks and village sectarians, but capable, at certain moments in history, of inspiring tens of thousands of fighters. It should occasion no surprise at all that among a small collection of texts recovered from the Zealot occupation of Masada is a fragment of *Songs for the Holocaust of the Sabbath* – an Essene document known at Qumran. This archaeological link between monastery and fortress symbolises admirably the relationship between theological theory and political practice in ancient revolution.

Messiahs

Jerusalem, at the End of Days

Revolutionary millenarianism has been a recurring feature of protest in pre-industrial societies throughout history. Norman Cohn wrote a classic study of such movements in medieval Europe: *The Pursuit of the Millennium* (1957). He defined the millenarian sect as a group with a quite specific view of salvation: as being something collective (not personal), earth-bound (not heavenly), imminent (not distant in time), all embracing (not limited in scope), and involving supernatural intervention (not just

human action). Such sects had a particular appeal to the atomised and rootless, especially in periods when many people were left insecure and impoverished by changes
in a traditional social order. Most of the time the sects were small and isolated, but
their existence ensured that millenarian ideas survived as an undercurrent, perhaps for
centuries, within some medieval societies. At certain moments of crisis the sectarians
would attract a mass audience and revolutionary millenarianism would flare into social
revolt. But this never lasted for long: the movement might rise like a rocket, but it
would then fall like a stick. Only the message – the expectation of deliverance –
bound the disparate membership together, so the movement quickly burnt itself out
and collapsed when the Millennium did not come. So central, indeed, was the
message that millenarian movements depended heavily for success on an effective
messenger: a charismatic leader able to convince large numbers of otherwise uncon-
nected people that the Millennium really was about to happen. Millenarian
movements, in other words, were also messianic: they required a messiah to lead them.

In Jewish tradition, *the* Messiah ('the Anointed One'; in Greek, *Christos*) would
be a prophet of special type: one sent by God to warn that the End of Days was
imminent and to lead the people in their final struggle for redemption and liberation. The Messiah would not be divine, but, chosen to be God's messenger at the
most critical of times, he would perhaps be the greatest of all the prophets, the
ultimate deliverer of the people from wickedness, and also a powerful leader in war
– a prophet-king, in fact. Theologically there could be only one true Messiah (since
the end of the world came but once), but in practice many claimed the status. Old
Testament prophets like Ezekiel and Isaiah may have been messiahs in their time. The
Essene Master of Justice was certainly another. Josephus mentions several in the
century or so before the revolution, among them Simon the Royal Slave and
Athronges the Shepherd, who each placed diadems on their heads in the manner of
prophet-kings and led their followers in revolts against the Romans in the period
after Herod's death in 4 BC. 'They were cheats and charlatans,' rants Josephus about
messianic leaders in general, 'men who claimed divine inspiration and aimed at revolutionary changes by stirring the mob into a frenzy, leading them out into the
Wilderness, and persuading them that God would there show them signs of their
coming liberation.'

So, with numerous claimants, how was one to tell the true Messiah from the false?
According to some the Messiah would be chosen from the House of David, and his
coming would be heralded by signs, including a precursor prophet to prepare the
people in advance. But such clues were little help: anyone could claim descent from
David, and there were plenty of eccentrics around making messianic announcements.
An ascetic Judaic mysticism linked with millenarian ideas was a strong enough
current in the first century AD to attract even a respectable upper-class Jew like
Josephus. In his youth, before becoming a Pharisee, he dabbled with Essenism,
spending three years in the company of one Banus, who, he tells us, 'lived in the
desert, and used no other clothing than what grew upon trees, and had no other food
than what grew of its own accord, and bathed himself in cold water frequently, both
by night and by day, in order to preserve his chastity'. First-century Palestine was full

of ascetics, millenarians and would-be Messiahs – this was part of the background canvas onto which big events were superimposed. And, as Norman Cohn discovered in those areas of medieval Europe where the millenarian tradition was well established, in periods of tension, when many people had a profound need to believe, fresh outbreaks of messianic excitement around different leaders could be frequent. The true Messiah was not needed to create a movement; rather the movement – 'historical necessity', if you will – could make a would-be Messiah 'true'. At some point in the development of such groups a critical mass was achieved: enough people believing and following to make the Messiah credible and transform a fringe sect into a popular movement. The Messiah was then propelled forwards by the pressure of expectation building up behind him, acting out a series of biblical prophecies that placed him on a collision course with the ruling authorities. The climax – if matters proceeded thus far – would come at Jerusalem. If this was indeed *the* Messiah, and this truly the End of Days, then Jerusalem, royal capital and holy city of the Jews for a thousand years, was bound to fall. When the time was judged right, the Messiah had to attempt the liberation of Jerusalem – or the bubble of belief would burst. The Simon and Athronges mentioned above did not reach that stage; but several others known to us did, including, of course, the most famous Messiah of them all: Jesus 'the Christ' of Nazareth.

We cannot pursue this discussion further – our attempt to characterise the Jewish radicals in Palestine in the first century AD by analysing messianic leadership – without confronting what is perhaps the most difficult, and is certainly the most discussed, of our primary sources: *The New Testament*. It records the work of a first-century Jewish Messiah and the fate of the millenarian sect he left behind. In my view – notwithstanding some radical comment to the contrary – there is no doubt whatsoever that Jesus Christ existed, that he was a charismatic mass leader, and that *The New Testament* is an immensely rich source of information about his life, work and times. It is equally my view – notwithstanding 2,000 years of Christian tradition – that he was not God, never claimed to be God, and could not have made such a blasphemous claim before a contemporary Jewish audience without condemning himself to political oblivion. The gospels were written a generation or two after Christ's death by Greeks or Hellenised Jews of the Diaspora who had never known him – *Mark* probably in Rome in the years around AD 70, *Matthew* possibly in Alexandria, *Luke* in Antioch, both sometime between AD 70 and 100, and *John* perhaps around AD 100 at Ephesus (though the debate about time and place in each case is far from settled). The gospel-writers inhabited a milieu that was less Jewish and more Hellenised than the context of Christ's own life and mission, and, moreover, one that was overshadowed by the Roman terror against millenarian radicals in the wake of AD 66. In the period they were writing, Christianity was emerging from the wreckage of the Jewish Revolution as a universal cult of spiritual salvation which viewed Christ as a living god. This new form – essentially a religion invented by St Paul (who, like the gospel-writers, had never known Christ) – can be seen overlying an earlier tradition of revolutionary millenarianism in the gospels. The authors had transformed Christ from Jewish prophet into Hellenistic saviour-god, and had replaced down-to-earth political Judaism with a personalised dream-world. Fortunately for us they did the job messily, leaving many patches of early text unaltered and in place. After all, they were not deliberate fakers. They knew their job was to produce a standardised text out of a disorganised heap of material, much of which was obscure or contradictory, and some of which, to their minds anyway, was downright dubious. Faced with this, confident that they were about God's work and that he would guide their hands and prevent error, and knowing in their hearts that Christ was divine, that his kingdom was not of this earth, and that his message was a universal one, they produced a version of the texts which depoliticised and denationalised Jesus. They made a new Jesus for their own time and place. But that is as far as it went. The gospel-writers did not *invent* the gospels. They did not write straight fiction. They worked from primary sources in whose essential authenticity they believed, and because of this, enough of the earlier versions survive for us to try stripping away the Christian gloss to get at an underlying *historical* truth.

This is more easily done partly because we have four gospels and they do not always agree, and partly because we can distinguish elements in the texts which jar with Christian interpretation and are therefore likely to be earlier. An original text may be evident in one of two situations: first, where the gospels share a common element (which, as it happens, excludes virtually all divine, fabulous and mythological features, these tending to appear in only one of the texts); and second, where the gospels contradict, either internally or with each other, and one of the versions lacks a Christian gloss. 'Blessed be ye poor, for yours is the kingdom of God,' Luke has Jesus say in the Sermon on the Mount. 'Blessed are ye that hunger now, for ye shall be filled . . . But woe unto you that are rich, for ye have received your consolation. Woe unto you that are full, for ye shall hunger.' But it is not quite like that in *Matthew*: 'Blessed are the poor in spirit, for theirs is the kingdom of heaven . . . Blessed are they that hunger and thirst after righteousness, for they shall be filled.' For Matthew, it is not the poor as such, but the poor *in spirit* who will be saved; not a kingdom of God which might be of this world, but definitely a kingdom *of heaven*; not everyday hunger and thirst, but hunger and thirst *after righteousness*; and nothing at all about how rough it is going to be for the rich. The clarion call of class war has been transformed into a spiritual opiate.

The New Testament, then, can be read as a revolutionary millenarian text. Indeed, in my view, if it is studied not as a religious work containing universal 'truths' but as an historical source for Palestine in the 30s AD, this is the *only* way to read it, since the evidence for Jesus having been a millenarian radical is overwhelming. What can such a reading teach us? How close can we get to the 'historical' Jesus?

We know that he was a Galilean Jew from Nazareth born around the time of King Herod's death in 4 BC. He probably worked with his father as a carpenter, but he was almost certainly educated above average and may have been a Pharisee. When he was about 30, he seems to have undergone some sort of conversion experience, probably to a form of Essenism, or something closely allied: he was baptised in the Jordan by the ascetic prophet John the Baptist, becoming a sort of 'born-again' Jew, and after that he spent time in the Wilderness seeking spiritual enlight-

enment. His return coincided with the arrest of John, which may, in a sense, have
cleared the field for Jesus' own ministry, especially if John had played the role of
precursor prophet and recognised Jesus as *the* Messiah. The ministry lasted about
three years. Jesus operated as faith-healer, exorcist, preacher and prophet – all well
established roles for an itinerant holy man – mainly, but not entirely, in Galilee. His
general message appears to have been very similar to that of the Dead Sea Scrolls. It
was addressed to Jews only – 'Go not into the way of the Gentiles,' he told his
disciples – and, among Jews, to the poor of small towns and villages, to peasants
mainly, to those Jesus described as 'the salt of the earth' because their humility made
them virtuous. Before them he defended the fundamentals of Judaism – faith in
God, obedience to the Law, respect for the Prophets, purity of mind and deed –
arguing that 'righteousness' in such things was the only route to salvation. By
contrast he railed against the backsliding, hypocrisy and empty formalism of people
like the Pharisees, and, more generally, against the rich and powerful, men whose
smug corruption put them largely beyond redemption. 'Ye cannot serve God and
Mammon,' Jesus declared. The choice, it seems, was wealth or holiness, and class
hatred runs like a red thread through the gospels.

> He [Jesus] sat down opposite the treasury, and watched the crowd putting
> money into the treasury. Many rich people put in large sums. A poor widow
> came and put in two small copper coins, which are worth a penny. Then he
> called his disciples and said to them, 'Truly I tell you, this poor widow has
> put in more than all those who are contributing to the treasury. For all of
> them have contributed out of their abundance; but she out of her poverty
> has put in everything she had, all she had to live on.'
>
> (*Mark*, 12.41–4)

The people attracted to Jesus were farmers and fishermen, artisans and petty
traders, even beggars and outcasts. Essenes, Zealots and other radicals were probably
also among his audience, for Jesus never attacks these groups – in marked contrast to
Scribes, Pharisees and Sadducees. What did he offer his listeners? He was a
convincing Messiah – a caring, charismatic, powerful leader – and he was building a
mass movement to overthrow the Jerusalem ruling class and their Roman backers.
The movement had its dedicated cadre: there were the 12 disciples (one for each of
the legendary Twelve Tribes perhaps), to whom Jesus passed on his 'powers', and
who renounced their homes, families and property to go forth as itinerant preachers
and 'gather the lost sheep of Israel'; and a further 70 were later added whom 'he sent
two and two before his face into every city and place whither he himself would
come'. There were not enough of them – 'the harvest truly is plenteous, but the
labourers are few' – yet the movement still grew fast. The doubtful were impressed
by the size of the crowds, seduced by the messianic excitement, won over by the
revolutionary vision of the leader. And soon there was critical mass and a millenarian
momentum hurtling towards its essential consummation: either the Messiah would
enter Jerusalem and overthrow the Old Regime, or he was a charlatan and this was

not the Apocalypse after all. So he led his followers to the Mount of Olives and established a camp there. This was partly force of circumstance: it was festival time and
the city was full of pilgrims; accommodation was hard to get and expensive. But the
Mount had also been predicted by Zechariah to be the site of miraculous signs
heralding the Apocalypse. He then entered Jerusalem itself riding on an ass (in fulfilment of prophecy) at the head of a procession of millenarians. The pilgrim crowds
greeted him ecstatically, spreading clothes and branches in his path, and acclaiming
him 'Son of David', 'King of Israel', and 'the King that cometh in the name of the
Lord'. This was not some innocuous religious gathering. The Judaeo-Christians
quickly established themselves in effective control of the Temple Mount, where Jesus
denounced the money-lenders and traders in the precincts and had his supporters
throw them out. 'My house shall be called the house of prayer, but ye have made it
a den of thieves.' The 'righteous' were on the offensive, and the authorities appeared
to be losing control. More and more it must have seemed that the Apocalypse had
really begun. As Jesus explained it to his senior cadre:

> Ye shall hear of wars and rumours of wars . . . For nation shall rise against
> nation, and kingdom against kingdom, and there shall be famines, and
> pestilences, and earthquakes, in diverse places. All these are the beginning
> of sorrows. . . . When ye shall therefore see the abomination of desola-
> tion, spoken of by Daniel the prophet, stand in the holy place . . . Then
> let them which be in Judaea flee into the mountains . . . For then shall
> be great tribulation, such as was not since the beginning of the world to
> this time, no, nor ever shall be. . . . Immediately after the tribulation of
> those days shall the sun be darkened, and the moon shall not give her
> light, and the stars shall fall from heaven, and the powers of the heavens
> shall be shaken. And then shall appear the sign of the Son of Man in
> heaven. And then shall all the tribes of the earth mourn, and they shall
> see the Son of Man coming in clouds of heaven with power and great
> glory. And he shall send his angels with a great sound of a trumpet, and
> they shall gather together his elect from the four winds, from one end of
> heaven to the other. . . . Verily I say unto you, this generation shall not
> pass till all these things be fulfilled.
>
> (*Matthew*, 25)

We cannot at this distance judge the balance of forces and the real strength of the
messianic movement. The authorities may have been taken by surprise, or perhaps
they wished to avoid a bloody clash in the streets; either way, there was a delay, and
when they struck, they did so in secret. The millenarians camped out on the Mount
of Olives were armed and there was brief resistance, but this was quickly overpowered and Jesus was arrested and led away. He was hauled before the high priest
Caiaphas and his close associates for interrogation – it is unlikely there was a full
meeting of the Sanhedrin – but he was then passed on to the Roman procurator
Pontius Pilate for a final decision about his fate. This probably means that he was

cleared of any charge of heresy – a special responsibility of the Sanhedrin – and was condemned and executed by the civil power as a political subversive and disturber of the peace. It may be significant that the four gospels, which disagree in so many other details, concur that the Roman inscription pinned to the crucifixion cross read 'King of the Jews' – Christ, on this evidence, had been a Messiah, a prophet-king to lead the Jews in the apocalyptic struggle at the end of time. He died on the cross – like thousands of other Jews in the first century AD – not because he was a blasphemer who claimed to be god, but because he was a revolutionary who threatened the authority of Rome and its Sadducean allies.

His mass movement then collapsed, leaving a rump of confused and demoralised followers who, perhaps rather like the Essenes after the martyrdom of the Master of Justice two centuries earlier, somehow managed to hold themselves together as a group. Central to their survival, almost certainly, was their belief that Christ was not really dead and would reappear at any moment to lead them. Messianic hope was thus held in suspension. Ideologically rearmed in this way, the Judaeo-Christian cadre regained their confidence and continued preaching – apparently with great success, membership rising from 120 to over 8,000 in a few years, if we can trust the testimony of *The Acts of the Apostles.*

One way or another, millenarian and messianic ideas formed the core of revolutionary conviction among first-century Jews. There were many variants, many different Messiahs and sects claiming a monopoly on truth, and many unresolved arguments about the meaning and relevance of the numerous prophecies recorded in scripture. But the belief that a Messiah would come, the Apocalypse follow, and the Rule of the Saints result was the common currency of Jewish radicals in the first century. When Christ denounced the Pharisees, it was not simply because they denied his messianic claims; after all, many Essenes probably did so too, but they were never attacked. The problem with Pharisees was that they denied the very possibility of a Messiah. For them the Apocalypse was a delusion, an invention of fanatics and demogogues which had no basis in Torah and was bound to lead to disaster. Attitudes to the Apocalypse divided the moderate mainstream, which might not like Roman rule but were resigned to it, from the radical sectarians, who wanted to overthrow it and believed it could be done. The Apocalypse was the touchstone distinguishing compromisers from revolutionaries.

Millenarians

Jerusalem, shortly before the End of Days

'And all that believed were together, and had all things in common, and sold their possessions and goods, and parted them to all men, as every man had need': thus *The Acts of the Apostles* describes the Judaeo-Christian sect led by Peter the Apostle in Jerusalem shortly after Christ's death. 'No one's house is his own in the sense that it is not shared by all . . . and they have a single treasury and common disbursements, and their clothes are held in common, and also their food through the institution of public meals': in this case it is Philo of Alexandria describing the Essenes – not the monks of Qumran, but secular sectarians who lived in ordinary villages alongside other Jews. Quite different sources – Christian accounts of the first-century 'church', and Graeco-Roman commentaries on the Essenes – complement one another in providing a uniform picture of radical sectarian groups. Geza Vermes, a leading Dead Sea Scrolls scholar, detects a clear distinction between the 'Community' of desert monks at Qumran, the probable headquarters of the sect, and a wider 'Covenant' embracing all Essenes. The village sectarians were not celibate, lived in families, owned their own houses, and rubbed shoulders every day with non-Essene neighbours. Though they formed organised corporate bodies and perhaps lived close by each other – Josephus speaks of 'large colonies everywhere' – they were not isolated from the wider community, and all our sources agree they were actively recruiting converts; Pliny the Elder specifically states it was the only way of maintaining the celibate community at Qumran. In the case of the Judaeo-Christians, there is no doubt that they were dynamic evangelists within the community. 'The Lord,' it seems, 'added to the church daily such as should be saved.' Indeed, the sect split and split again over problems arising from its strategy of mass proselytising among the poor.

First came a division between 'Hellenists' (Greek-speaking Jews) and 'Hebrews' (Aramaic-speaking Jews) over food distributions. The result was the election of 'seven men of good standing' of the Hellenist faction to ensure these were organised fairly. Then there was a division between Peter the Apostle, at that time leader of the group, who went to Caesarea and converted a Roman centurion, and the Jerusalem brethren, who accused him of ritual defilement through contact with Gentiles. Peter claimed divine inspiration, and the brethren 'held their peace and glorified God, saying, then hath God also to the Gentiles granted repentance unto life'. The third division went far deeper. There had always been converts to Judaism. It was a pros-elytising faith which had won millions of adherents in and around the Diaspora cities of the Mediterranean. But Peter's centurion had converted to Judaism, and the followers of Christ were still a Jewish sect. Now Paul suggested that a Gentile might become a 'Christian' without becoming Jewish. The debate revolved around the various rituals and taboos which defined Jewish identity – crucially the semitic practice of male circumcision, an ordeal which put off many would-be Gentile converts. But far wider questions were implicated. Was 'Christianity' a new universal religion, or was it still a millenarian tendency within Judaism? Was it something spiritual and personal and therefore potentially open to all, or was it concerned with a revolutionary struggle against Roman oppression? Something of these concerns probably underlay the two earlier rows, but in its final form, whatever short-term patching up there may have been, the gap between Judaeo-Christians and Pauline or Catholic Christians was unbridgeable. From some time in the 50s AD, Paul's 'church', powered by mass conversion in the Diaspora cities, was on the trajectory which would lift it clear of the wreckage of the Jewish Revolution in AD 70. The Judaeo-Christians, by contrast, remained rooted in Jerusalem and, in effect, part of a national revolutionary movement. As such, they were periodically battered by persecution. Peter, the group's first leader, was jailed three times. Stephen, one of its seven 'Hellenist' deacons, was stoned to death. Later, in AD 62, James, the brother of Jesus and apparently Peter's successor as leader of the group, was also stoned to death.

Taking all the evidence together – *The New Testament*, the Dead Sea Scrolls, Josephus, and Philo of Alexandria – we have a uniquely rich corpus for reconstructing the character of a radical counter-cultural movement in antiquity. In the picture that emerges we seem to see Palestine in the first century full of sectarians – perhaps one or two in the smallest villages, but with organised groups in most of the larger ones, and many competing tendencies represented in Jerusalem itself. These groups were overwhelmingly oriented towards the peasantry and rural artisans. Jesus declared his intention to preach to the poor not the rich, he set his parables in the grain fields and vineyards of the countryside, and he castigated cities 'because they repented not'. The Essenes, according to Philo, 'live in villages and avoid the cities because of the iniquities which have become inveterate among city dwellers, for they know that their company would have a deadly effect upon their souls, like a disease brought by a pestilential atmosphere'. The poor and the countryside were pure and holy, the rich and the city mired in corruption. It is a refrain that rings down the centuries, but it was especially true in antiquity, when the city was a consumer rather than a producer, a place of monuments, luxury and 'taste', a parasite sucking wealth out of the countryside to feed its indolence.

The sectarians made a virtue of their poverty, turning it into an edifying austerity, a communal lifestyle, and a symbol of moral purity unsullied by worldly corruption. More than this: it grew into a demand for egalitarian and democratic revolution. 'They have become moneyless and landless by deliberate action,' declares Philo, 'because they judge frugality with contentment to be an abundance of wealth.' Moreover, 'not a single slave is to be found among them, but all are free, exchanging services with each other, and they denounce the owners of slaves, not merely for their injustice in outraging the law of equality, but also for their impiety in annulling the statute of Nature . . .' Jesus might have agreed – we will never know because the gospel-writers would have expunged any calls for slave liberation in deference to their Roman overlords, but, on Philo's evidence, Jesus must have heard these arguments, and abolitionism would have sat well with his oft-repeated hostility to the rich and belief that 'the poor shall inherit the earth'. Along with this austere egalitarianism went high standards of piety and probity. *Acts* portrays the Judaeo-Christians as pious Jews who attended the Temple at the regular hours of prayer and 'came together to break bread' on the Sabbath. 'Neither shouting nor disorder ever desecrates the house,' reports Josephus of the Essenes, 'and in conversation each man gives way to his neighbour in turn – to outsiders the silence seems like a dread mystery, but it is the natural result of their unfailing sobriety.' 'Their defining standards were three,' explains Philo, 'love of God, love of virtue, and love of men,' and he goes on to describe a way of life that was pious, sober, frugal, egalitarian and warm-hearted. It was also concerned with education and self-development through reading and discussion. Two key institutions were the Sabbath and the synagogue.

As for philosophy . . . they [the Essenes] retain only that part which treats philosophically of the existence of God and the creation of the universe. But the ethical part they study very industriously, taking for their trainers the Laws of their fathers . . . In these they are instructed at all times, but particularly on the seventh days. For that day has been set apart to be kept holy and on it they abstain from all other work and proceed to sacred spots which they call synagogues. There, arranged in rows according to their ages, the younger below the elder, they sit decorously as befits the occasion with attentive ears. Then one takes the books and reads aloud and another of especial proficiency comes forward and expounds what is not understood.

(Philo, *Every Good Man is Free*)

At the start of the 60s AD, the sectarians were a small but dynamic and fast-growing force in popular politics. Communities of monks, networks of preachers and synagogues, and occasional messianic outbreaks contributed to a pulsating undercurrent of revolutionary millenarianism in first-century Palestine. But the sectarians could not bring about the Apocalypse on their own. This they knew well enough. The history of the nation told in holy writ was of repeated struggle to win the majority for redemption, a renewal of the Covenant, and the restoration of Israel. Sometimes the prophet would find himself crying out in the Wilderness. Sometimes the righteous were reduced to a rump. But they always knew they could not succeed alone, that God would never favour a rebellious people, and that only when the Israelites as a whole returned to faith and obedience could they prosper. It had always been thus. The sectarians knew they had to win the battle of hearts and minds in the villages if the Congregation of Belial was to be overthrown.

Bandits

The mountain caves of Palestine, summer AD 66

What is a bandit? At the age of 16, the peasant boy Francisco Villa killed a Mexican government official who had violated his sister and was forced to take to the hills. For the next 22 years he lived as a bandit, with a price on his head both for the murder and for stealing cattle from rich estate-owners. But when the American journalist John Reed watched him enter Chihuahua City in 1914, he came as the leader of a revolutionary army and was greeted by a roaring crowd of thousands who hailed him as 'Friend of the Poor'. Pancho Villa had made the transition from mountain bandit to revolutionary leader.

The rich lump together all those who break the law – criminals – and all those who live beyond the law – robbers, brigands, outlaws. The poor are more sociologically discerning. They know what drives angry young men into the hills, and they know the difference between tax-collectors, bailiffs and soldiers who rob the poor on behalf of the rich, and bandits who take a little of it back and return some to the villages.

32 *Engraving depicting a bandit encampment. Though highly fanciful, this nineteenth-century book illustrator's reconstruction does convey the idea that banditry was a deeply rooted feature of Palestinian life in the first century AD*

Eric Hobsbawm wrote an excellent short study of 'social banditry' in the late 1960s, drawing his examples from different places and times, and spawning a host of more specialised studies by historians and social scientists since (**32**). 'The point about the social bandit,' he argued, 'is that they are peasant outlaws whom the lord and state regard as criminals, but who remain within peasant society, and are considered by their people as heroes, as champions, avengers, fighters for justice, perhaps even leaders of liberation, and in any case as men to be admired, helped and supported.' Such banditry is 'one of the most universal social phenomena known to history', a more or less invariable response of traditional peasant communities to being 'oppressed and exploited by someone else – lords, towns, governments, lawyers, or even banks'. Most of the time, as far as the authorities are concerned, the bandits exist only as a nagging irritant on the fringe of events, rarely amounting to more than one in a thousand of the rural population, the typical band numbering no more than 10 or 20. The bands are formed of the marginal, the displaced, and the pursued – impoverished crofters, unemployed labourers, escaped slaves and serfs, army deserters, fugitives from the law – and they hide out in remote and inaccessible areas beyond the reach of government authority. So what is the evidence for social banditry of this type in first-century Palestine?

Our principal source is, of course, Josephus, but as an upper class, Hellenised, pro-Roman he regarded any threat to property and privilege, whether highway robbery or social revolution, as something to be condemned equally as the work of 'brigands' and 'tyrants'. But everything we know of first-century Palestine would lead us to expect social banditry, and, if we look at the detail in Josephus, we seem to detect it in several of the incidents he describes. When in 48-47 BC, for instance, the young Herod ran down and killed the 'brigand-chief' Hezekiah and 'a great band of men' in the mountainous border region of northern Galilee, he was applauded by 'the Syrians' (probably citizens of the Greek towns), but condemned by many local Jews, some of whom took their case to Jerusalem, where 'the mothers of the men who had been murdered by Herod, every day in the Temple, kept begging the king and the people to have Herod brought for judgement before the Sanhedrin for what he had done'. Banditry continued on a large scale in Galilee over the next ten years, thriving in conditions of civil war and precipitating a second major confrontation with Herod in 38-37 BC. On this occasion the bandits were numerous enough to fight an unsuccessful pitched battle, before retreating to the Mount Arbel caves near the Sea of Galilee (**33** & **colour plate 10**). The caves were cut into the mountainsides, the entrances opened onto precipitous drops, and the only access was down long, narrow, winding tracks. Hundreds of bandits were holed up there with their families. Herod lowered his toughest fighters down in baskets from ledges above the entrances. The defenders were then yanked over the cliff-edge with hooks, the caves were stormed and fired, and the inhabitants slaughtered, taken as slaves, or driven to suicide. This action seems to have destroyed mass banditry in Galilee for at least a generation.

All this sounds very much like social banditry in Hobsbawm's sense. Many of the peasants, who were exploited by Greek townsmen, Roman generals and Jewish landlords, seem to have taken to the hills and caves of Galilee to live outside the law – beyond the reach of tax-collectors, soldiers and bailiffs. The village communities from which they sprang backed them willingly against foreign oppressors and were cheered by their robberies and escapades. But the scale of banditry Josephus describes is far from normal: it is not a matter of tens and twenties, but hundreds, perhaps even thousands, camped out in the hills and in arms against the state. This too, though, is a well-attested feature of social banditry – its potential, that is, to swell into rural insurrection in times of war, economic crisis and mass pauperisation. The simple bandit with his village roots and peasant code might then, like Pancho Villa in the Mexican Revolution, find himself a freedom fighter at the head of thousands.

> In so far as bandits have a 'programme', it is defence or restoration of the traditional order of things 'as it should be' . . . Two things may, however, turn this modest, if violent, social objective of bandits – and the peasantry to whom they belong – into genuine revolutionary movements. The first is, when it becomes the symbol, even the spearhead, of resistance by the whole of the traditional order against the forces which disrupt and destroy it . . . The second . . . is inherent in peasant society. Even those who accept

33 *A cave entrance high on the cliffs of Mount Arbel near the western shore of the Sea of Galilee*

exploitation, oppression and subjection as the norm of human life dream of a world without them: a world of equality, brotherhood and freedom, a totally new world without evil. Rarely is this more than a dream . . . Yet there are moments when the apocalypse seems imminent: when the entire structure of existing society whose total end the apocalypse symbolises and predicts, actually looks about to collapse in ruins, and a tiny light of hope turns into the light of a possible sunrise.

(Hobsbawm, 1972, 26–8)

Ordinary levels of banditry were part of the background which Josephus took for granted and would never have thought to mention. He noticed it only when it exceeded this level and became a danger to the state. We can safely assume that social bandits were as permanent a feature of Roman Palestine as messiahs and millenarians. More than that: we can see how these two currents might repeatedly fuse and reinforce one another, quickly bringing popular politics to explosive condition. The bandit offensive in Galilee in the 40s BC occurred in the context of an unsuccessful Jewish national struggle against growing Roman domination. The bandits and the nationalists were defeated and a puppet dictator raised himself onto the throne in 37 BC. But when Herod died in 4 BC another great upsurge began. With the Roman-backed usurper out of the way, hopes ran high again for national redemption. Herod, though, had planned differently, intending that Palestine after his death should be divided into three, each part to be ruled by one of his sons as a Roman client-king, an arrangement later confirmed by the emperor Augustus. The Jews rose in revolt. Jerusalem was captured by the crowd after fierce street-battles against Herodian troops and Roman legionaries, and the insurrection then spread through Judaea and Galilee. It was at this time that Simon the Royal Slave and Athronges the Shepherd launched their claims to messianic status. Simon, we are told by Josephus, operated mainly in Peraea, where 'he went around with a band of brigands and burnt down the palace at Jericho and many magnificent country residences, securing easy plunder for himself out of the flames'. At the same time Athronges put each of his four brothers in charge of an armed raiding party, and 'they harassed all Judaea with their brigandage'. Simon and Athronges appear, then, to have been not only messiahs (as we noted above), but also bandit-chiefs. Meanwhile, at the Galilean city of Sepphoris, 'one Judas, son of the brigand-chief Hezekiah, who had previously overrun the country and been crushed by King Herod, got a large crowd together, broke into the royal armoury, equipped his followers, and attacked other rivals in the struggle for power'. The insurrection was eventually crushed by the Governor of Syria, who invaded with two legions, devastated Galilee and Judaea, and then stormed into Jerusalem, where captured rebels were crucified *en masse*. There seems little doubt that it was a fusion of urban riots, millenarian excitement and swelling social banditry that had produced this failed revolution.

Nor was the movement entirely broken. Ten years later, in AD 6, the national struggle flared up again when Archelaus was deposed and Judaea turned into a Roman province under the rule of a prefect. Judas the Galilean, son of Hezekiah, again raised the banner of revolt, supported this time by a radical Pharisee called Zaddok. They called on fellow Jews to boycott the census and refuse to pay taxes. Though the revolt seems to have made little headway, Josephus credits Judas with founding an ideology and a sect – the so-called 'Fourth Philosophy' (to distinguish it from that of, respectively, Sadducees, Pharisees and Essenes). 'These men,' he explains, 'have an inviolable attachment to liberty, and say that God is to be their only ruler and lord.' Judas' sons and other kinsmen continued the struggle later in the first century, among them James and Simon, who organised a revolt in the late 40s AD, Menahem, whom we have already met in relation to events in AD 66, and Eleazar ben Yair, who was destined to lead the last stand of the rebels at Masada in AD 73 or 74.

These descendants of Hezekiah and Judas are sometimes described as 'Zealots' or 'Sicarians', and it seems clear – though Josephus does not explicitly state this – that Zealotism is what he had in mind when he described Judas as the founder of a new politico-religious tendency. The family of Judas the Galilean thus provides a clear link between revolutionary activism and social banditry. But it does more than this: as with the careers of Simon and Athronges, it seems to link activism and banditry with millenarian expectation, for the behaviour of at least one of the Zealot leaders clearly implies messianic claims on his part. When Menahem entered Jerusalem in August AD 66, he is said to have done so 'like a king', and after his victory over the Herodians he went up to the Temple to worship 'in pomp, decked out in kingly robes, and followed by a retinue of armed Zealots'. Was not Menahem, then, an aspiring messiah? And were not his father, Judas the tax-dodger, and his grandfather, Hezekiah the brigand-chief, perhaps also aspiring messiahs in their time? We do not know, but it seems possible. What this and other evidence seems to point to is an absence of clear lines between different strands of resistance. Social banditry, revolutionary activism and millenarian expectation were forms of resistance that intersected – so much so that a prominent resistance-fighter might be at once social bandit, Zealot leader and messianic prophet.

Some historians have tried to identify distinct organisations pursuing different strategies behind terms like 'Essene', 'Zealot' and 'Sicarian'. This project seems doomed, not only because the sources are hopelessly inadequate to the task, but also because no real movement for change can ever be reduced to a handful of sharply defined groups. Palestine in the middle of the first century AD was a society on the brink of revolution, and the rising mass movement was a constantly changing ferment of leaders, factions and programmes, a ferment continually fed by new drafts of sectarians, bandits and protestors. Diversity and fluidity were dominant characteristics, since the movement in its very essence was a political *process*, not a static entity. But all those who formed it – and their numbers were increasing rapidly in the 50s and 60s AD – were headed in roughly the same direction: towards the Apocalypse, the revolutionary overthrow of Rome, and a passage into 'the light of a possible sunrise'.

Peasants and preachers

The villages of Galilee and Judaea, AD 66

The village of Capernaum on the north-east shore of the Sea of Galilee was the place where Jesus lived during his ministry. He preached in the synagogue there and is supposed to have performed miracles. The main site was bought by Franciscan monks in 1894, and they have been assiduous about excavating the remains and publishing their results. Five blocks of houses (or *insulae*) have been uncovered, each comprising a series of one-room family houses ranged around a central shared courtyard (**34**). Each house was built of crude basalt blocks grouted with a mud and pebble mix and covered with plaster. Mostly they were single storey, but they had internal stairways leading to flat roofs formed of palm branches, reeds and plaster, and some may have had rooftop shelters. Each house-room was small – the largest excavated was 7 x 6.5m, but most were only half or a third this size. Domestic artefacts were numerous and mainly homemade: peasant families may have lacked cash to buy things, but not the labour to make them. On excavated sites at Capernaum and elsewhere, finds of everyday items have been abundant: storage jars, cooking pots, tableware and oil-lamps in plain ceramic; querns, mortars and pestles

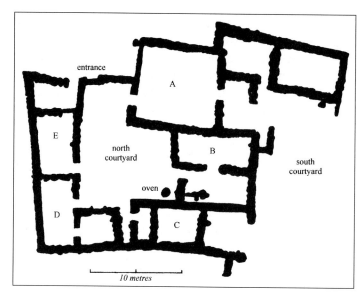

34 *Plan of the building known as 'St Peter's House' at Capernaum on the Sea of Galilee. It is typical of peasant compounds in Palestinian villages of the first century AD. Probably five family units (A, B, C, D and E) shared use of communal facilities in the north courtyard*

made of volcanic stone; pots, pans and jugs of bronze; stone mugs and bowls; beads, earrings, finger-rings, brooches, mirrors, toilet instruments, mixing palettes for cosmetics, and delicate glass perfume bottles. And from the dry desert conditions of Masada and the Engedi caves have come rare fragments of items made from organic materials which do not normally survive: cloaks and tunics of homespun wool; brightly coloured rugs with tasselled ends; a child's linen shirt; mats and bags made of rush; baskets of willow withies; a wallet, a purse and sandals in leather; wooden boxes, bowls and combs; even a hair-net. If we add in some simple furniture (though very little has been found in excavation on low-status sites), and if we allow that a typical peasant family comprised six people, we can imagine the house-rooms of Capernaum cluttered and claustrophobic. Whenever possible, and certainly through the summer, the life of each household must have spilled out into the communal courtyard and onto the rooftops.

Most courtyards were between 5m and 10m square, sometimes with flagstone paving, otherwise packed dirt, and each was shared by two or more households. Here water was stored in cisterns, grain in underground silos, and there was space for ovens, corn-mills, olive-presses, and a range of domestic activities. Around the courtyard, in addition to houses, there were various ancillary buildings – animal byres, sheds for carts and tools, and storerooms for food, straw and wood. Some courtyards probably contained a single extended family, but many scholars believe this traditional pattern – based on the ownership of large peasant farms – was breaking down in the Graeco-Roman period, in which case many courtyards may have comprised separate nuclear-family units. Courtyards in turn were grouped by alleyways or streets; later rabbinical sources often refer to five courtyards per alley, as if this were average, giving us at least 10 households, or 60-plus people, for each one. Sometimes an entire settlement was no larger than this, but the norm was for Jewish peasants to live in much larger villages, even small towns, ranging in population from a few hundred up to one or two thousand people. Even the largest of these, however, lacked the defining features of the Graeco-Roman city: the street system was unplanned; there were few public buildings – none that were monumentally constructed – and few élite residences; there might be craftsmen – potters, blacksmiths, carpenters, tailors, shoemakers – but the luxury trades were absent. These were traditional working communities made up of people bound to the fields, olive-groves, vineyards and pastures of a small locality; bound also to the agricultural cycle and the eternal routines of labour on the land; and bound to one another in intimate, exclusive, inescapable solidarities.

These features of ancient peasant life must be stressed, for they are so different from the atomised social experience of so many today. The family dominated each individual's existence, since the household was not only a unit of consumption but also of property and production. One worked as a member of the family, within a family-based division of labour, and drew one's sustenance from the family pool. Because of this, major life decisions were always family decisions, and the individual was subsumed within the family and accepted its authority. Beyond the family there were other links to kin and close neighbours, other solidarities among people who lived out their whole lives together in the same courtyard or alleyway. Familiarity was reinforced by interdependence, the landless looking to the landed for wage-work at harvest time, the poor in land to the better-off for the loan of a field, a plough or a cart. Among such people, the largest unit that really mattered was the village (**colour plate 11**). Modern studies of traditional peasant communities have revealed intense village solidarities, manifested in hostility to neighbouring villages and indifference to authority outside the village. This was, of course, quite rational: the household was largely self-sufficient, the village entirely so; the peasants had no need of anyone or anything beyond. Absentee landlords, kings and high priests, tax-collectors and soldiers: who were these to the villager but so many robbers? Towards them, the village, with its shared experience and intense relationships, presented a solid and hostile front – for here ran the deepest fracture-line of class conflict in the ancient world.

If the life of the peasant was a life of land and labour, of family and village, of traditional routine and the eternal cycle of the seasons, it was also a life of exploitation and oppression – of some mixture of tax, tithe, rent, forced labour, low wages, high prices, and debt – sometimes so severe that small plots were abandoned, households disintegrated and villages sank into slump. 'Civilisation has made the peasantry its pack-animal,' Trotsky once remarked. So what do we know about the rate of peasant exploitation in Palestine in the mid-first century AD – about, that is, what must have been the revolution's deepest roots?

All traditional peasant classes are internally differentiated. There are rich peasants who hire labour, produce a surplus, and dominate their villages. There are middle peasants who produce enough for their subsistence, but no more. There are poor peasants, families without sufficient land for their support, who eke out their living by selling their labour seasonally or working part-time as potters, carpenters, tanners or whatever. Then there is the underclass of landless poor – labourers, migrants, bandits, beggars, prostitutes, lepers and others struggling on the margins of existence. These groups always exist, but the proportions vary, and crucial to this – the balance within the peasantry between the viable rich and middle and the marginal poor and landless – is the overall rate of exploitation imposed on villages by the ruling class. All the evidence we have points towards intensified exploitation and impoverishment of the Jewish peasantry in the Graeco-Roman period.

Overall the population of Palestine appears to have been growing under the procurators. Surface surveys have revealed higher settlement densities in AD 6-66 than those at any other time before the Byzantine period. This must have resulted in a subdivision of family plots and an increase in the proportion of poor and landless peasants. This in turn would have reduced peasant surpluses and made peasant farms more vulnerable in bad years. Small farmers had no margin of safety: drought, blight, war, anything that destroyed the crop, forced them to borrow from the rich at high rates of interest. When they could not repay, they lost their land and were forced to seek a tenancy, search for work as labourers, or become debt-bondsmen – serfs in effect – to their creditors. This outcome – control over land and labour by the rich – was undoubtedly the main incentive in lending to the poor. Other methods may also have been used to seize peasant land – like fraudulent contracts, illegal movement of boundary stones, and straightforward threats and violence. The poor could not afford legal redress, and the rich anyway controlled the courts. But debt was probably the principal mechanism of land accumulation; the Parable of the Unjust Steward makes it seem as commonplace as taxes and rents. The great estates of Graeco-Roman Palestine – those of the emperor, the Herodian royal family, the high priests and other Sadducees – were probably composed largely of land which had once belonged to peasants. The decline of the city-states under Macedonian and Roman suzerainty had empowered oligarchs everywhere and left small citizen-farmers defenceless before them. The city-state had periodically cancelled debts and redistributed land; far less often did Macedonian kings and Roman emperors provide relief. The inexorable long-term tendency of wealth and poverty to polarise had been left to take its course; without collective action, the rich got richer, the poor poorer.

Tenancies could be tough. Some paid a set rent, which could be crippling in bad years. Others paid a percentage of the crop, but this would be high, usually at least a quarter, sometimes a third, often half, even two-thirds in some recorded cases. There was little that tenants could do but accept these gruelling terms. Not only was there shortage of land, but the poor tenant often needed his lord to supply seed, tools, draft-animals, even bread to feed his family in times of hardship. Debt tightened the screws of dependence. Bailiffs might come with armed force to ensure payment. In the Parable of the Wicked Husbandmen, Jesus has the tenants of an absentee landlord murder a succession of bailiffs sent to collect the rent on a vineyard; clearly he and his audience believed violence possible in such encounters. Much more common than attempted resistance, no doubt, was the bitter resignation of men struggling on marginal plots to keep ahead of rent, debt and the legalised thuggery of landlords. And somewhere along the spectrum, impoverished free tenancy graded into the utter hopelessness of debt-bondage, where a man was tied to a lord and a plot, compelled to work off his debts as a serf. Yet others were slaves pure and simple – perhaps the ultimate fate of the debtor or the debtor's children. *The New Testament* refers in passing to slaves working in the fields, monitoring weed growth, collecting rents from tenants, and killing the fatted calf for a party – so they seem to have been part of the scene.

Other peasants worked for the landlords as day labourers – ploughing, weeding, harvesting, threshing, manure-gathering, fruit-picking, reed-cutting, wood-carrying, or serving as watchmen guarding animals or crops. These hirelings might be landless men or poor tenants whose plots were too small for subsistence. Either way, with no control over the land they worked or the tools they used, and with an abundance of surplus labour seeking employment, terms and conditions were often severe. The Parable of the Labourers implies there was casual labour available for hire in local villages at any time of day. Skeletal evidence has revealed that some faced a crippling burden of physical work. Examples from the cemetery at Qumran – to which some peasants perhaps fled as a refuge – include a 22-year-old man whose bones already bore the scars of years of heavy labour from an early age, and a 65-year-old with a permanently deformed bone structure after carrying great weights on his shoulders for much of his life. There is good evidence also that day labourers were frequently defrauded. Rabbinical sources report landlords paying below the seasonal rate, paying late, and paying in a form different from that agreed. Even when proper payment was made, standard rates were desperately low. The average daily wage of a labourer was probably one *denarius*, but allowing for seasonal unemployment, bad weather, illness, the Sabbath and festivals, a man would be lucky to work 200 days in a year. Two hundred *denarii* were, it seems, a subsistence minimum (below which one qualified for poor relief), and scholars have estimated that this amount would have been just enough to put bread in the mouths of a typical family of six. With nothing left over for anything else – shelter, clothing, other foods – most families of labourers must have hovered on the very margins of survival.

What all peasants wanted was a piece of freehold land big enough to provide a sufficiency of all essentials in bad years as well as good – perhaps 15 or 20 acres (6-8ha), including a grain field, a vineyard, an olive grove, a vegetable patch, and some pasture for a few sheep and goats. How many were in this fortunate position? Very few on the evidence of surface surveys. The ruined village of Hirbet Buraq in Samaria was surrounded by 445 acres (180ha) of land divided into plots for 70 households: 6 acres each. In Galilee, while the range was commonly 1 to 15 acres (0.4-6ha), the norm was about 4 (1.6ha). In Judaea the situation was no better. Scholars argue about the minimum needed to support a family at basic subsistence, but the lowest estimates are 6-8 acres (2.4-3.2ha), and this means that most first-century Jewish peasants were poor in the absolute sense defined above: their plots could not support their families and they were forced to supplement their incomes in other ways. But when they sought to do this, they found themselves competing for work on the big estates with many others: poor freeholders like themselves, poor tenants threatened by debt, landless day labourers, and the serfs and slaves of landed masters. For the great majority there can have been no margin of safety, and debt must have poisoned the lives of most freehold farmers – an observation that brings us full circle, back to the rise of the great estates and the impoverishment of the peasantry, the two dominant trends in the

Palestinian countryside of Graeco-Roman times. It is against this background that we must judge the impact of the many impositions on the peasantry discussed at various points above. Tenants paid rents of between a quarter and two-thirds of the crop. Freeholders paid a land tax of probably 12.5 per cent. Everyone paid a poll tax: perhaps one per cent on property if they owned some, or a *denarius* per head for everyone over 14 if they did not. Most – though we are not sure exactly who – paid tithes to the priests of anything between a tenth and a sixtieth of the harvest. Then there were various indirect levies – tolls, salt taxes, customs dues – and a wide range of extraordinary impositions like the billeting of troops, requisitioning of supplies, forced sales at fixed prices, and labour *corvées*. Many, of course, also had debts to pay, and interest rates in the ancient world could be heartbreakingly high; there was often a legal limit of 12 per cent, but we sometimes hear of much higher rates, even 48 per cent; and what help could the law be to a peasant in debt to his lord?

We should consider how peasants must have perceived their own predicament. The best land was on the great estates, owned by absentee landlords who lived in the cities. Peasants struggled against thorns and stones on tiny plots. After their families had toiled for months – ploughing, sowing, weeding, harvesting, threshing – people came out from the cities to take their cut: people who did not work, people who lived off the work of others, people who were never seen save when they came to take what they had not earned – the bailiff, the tax-farmer, the creditor, the priest, the soldier. And they took it to the city, this wealth stolen from peasants, where they built mansions and monuments, aped the manners of the pagans, fawned on foreign overlords, and scorned God, the Law and the Prophets. That is how the ancient peasant experienced the city, 'civilisation', and 'The Grandeur That Was Rome': as so many parasites leaching off his labour to feed their corruption. It is easy to understand why some became bandits. The Parable of the Wicked Husbandmen – who killed the landlord's bailiffs – was plausible to Jesus of Nazareth's audience. Josephus tells us that when the high priests levied tithes in Judaean villages, they needed armed thugs to do it. Truly was the peasantry the pack-animal of civilisation.

Even when villagers did fight back – as a crowd or as bandits – resistance was usually local. The peasant's life was ruled primarily by his own household and its land, and to a lesser extent by a network of interdependent kin and neighbours in his village. He had few organic links with a wider world, and, in the ordinary course of things, little knowledge of such a world. The peasant economy was self-sufficient and 'embedded' in village society, and peasant resistance was mostly a matter of occasional scuffles confined to particular villages. The peasantry was a class of individualists dispersed across the countryside, a collection of households too independent to fuse together readily into a revolutionary force. This political weakness was exacerbated by the conservatism of village authorities. A headman, judges and a council of elders were appointed for each village by the Roman authorities and charged with keeping order. They were drawn mainly from among better-off peasants and small traders, and, along with the priests and scribes, formed an ageing 'middle class' establishment. At best their loyalties were divided; at worst they were stooges. Either way, they were the crucial mediators and moderators of peasant life – in disputes within the village, between neighbouring villages, and, crucially, in relation to external authority. The more politically volatile elements in the village were certainly in the majority: this included most middle peasants, all the poor peasants, the landless labourers, the young in general, and any other marginal people with nothing to lose. But the revolutionary potential of these groups was contained by the deep-rooted parochialism of household and village, by the economic dependence of the poor on the better-off, and by the conservatism of village power structures. What was it, then, that in the summer of AD 66 made it possible to realise this potential and turn a thousand villages into centres of revolution?

Those who ruled the peasants fostered an ideology based on Sadducean formalism, Hellenic culture and Roman authority, but this had little impact in the villages, where an older Judaic folk-tradition survived. Two institutions were central to this: holy scripture and the synagogue. The former was not the literary fossil it has since become, but a developing body of writings packed with ideas for making sense of the contemporary world. Ancient religion, especially Judaism, was a language for discussing ancient society. The synagogue was also a young and vigorous institution. There has been some debate about how many there were in the first century AD, but this seems misplaced. Though the earliest synagogues were in the Diaspora, where distance from the Temple made the need greater, they probably spread through Palestine in late Hellenistic times. One is mentioned in *Ecclesiasticus*, an apocryphal text of the early second century BC, and *The New Testament* makes several references to either Jesus or St Paul preaching in synagogues – something that Christian authors in the late first century AD would have had no wish to invent. Josephus also refers to them, notably in his discussion of the communal riots in Caesarea in May AD 66, and the *Talmud* records that Vespasian destroyed 480 synagogues in Jerusalem (though it must in fact have been Titus, and the number is no doubt exaggerated). Most first-century synagogues are probably archaeologically invisible. Purpose-built structures would not have been necessary, and the majority may have been ordinary rooms, often in private houses, or even certain open spaces out of doors. At Qumran, for instance, where no 'synagogue' can be recognised, religious meetings were probably held in either the council chamber or the assembly hall (**23**). Even so, four probable first-century synagogues have in fact been excavated – at Herodium and Masada in the Judaean Desert, and at Magdala (ancient Taricheae) and Gamala near the Sea of Galilee (**35**). That at Magdala was 8 x 7m in size, had columns and aisles on three sides, five stepped rows of stone benches on the fourth, and an open flagstone floor in the middle. The basic design was the same elsewhere, except that the synagogues at the fortresses and at Gamala were somewhat larger and had their benches on all four sides, leaving a gap only for the single entranceway. The design, it must be said, is a democratic one: a square room with seating round the walls tends to foster discussion within a group. That this indeed happened is the impression we get from literary sources. Men and women would gather at the local synagogue each Sabbath, a copy of the Torah would be taken from the ark (a special cupboard for its safe keeping), and there would be readings and commentaries by selected members of the congregation, perhaps followed by general

35 *The reconstructed synagogue at Gamala, a fortified hilltop town in western Gaulonitis (Golan), a few miles east of the Sea of Galilee. The roof was supported on pillars and the congregants sat facing one another on the benches around the walls — an essentially democratic design which encouraged discussion. In the synagogues, radical ideas like those of the Essenes could connect with a mass audience of village peasants*

discussion. There would also be prayers for Israel and the singing of psalms. Later Jewish sources describe synagogues as 'houses of gathering', 'houses of prayer' and 'houses of exegesis [scriptural commentary]'. No doubt this is also how they functioned in the first century, when they were the focus of activity for numerous priests, scribes, Pharisees, itinerant preachers, prophets and would-be messiahs, all debating scripture's meaning for the present in a battle for Jewish hearts and minds (**36**). It was in the synagogues that Judaism lived as a peasant religion under Roman rule.

Something of this religion we can perhaps reconstruct. Peasant ideas must have clashed with the claims and behaviour of the élite at many points. Scripture, after all, stated clearly that the land was a gift of God to the people of Israel – not to Greeks or Romans. It was given for distribution in small plots for the subsistence of all – not to be divided into great estates to make a few men rich. Was not the original assignment by lot (*Num.* 26.55)? Did not the Law enjoin that every seventh year should be a Sabbath Year when all debts would be cancelled and all bondsmen made free (*Deut.* 15.1-18)? Did it not also say that every fiftieth year should be a Year of Jubilee when all land would be restored to its former owners (*Lev.* 25.8-17)? Between times was there not to be a tithe for the poor every third year (*Deut.* 15. 28-9)? Were not the gleanings of the fields to be left to the poor (*Lev.* 19.9-10)? Might not the passer-by satisfy his hunger from the field (*Deut.* 22.25)? In the traditional view, God had bestowed the land on Israel as a sacred trust for the benefit of the whole people, and his Law for the trust was violated when the land was seized by a few at the expense of the many.

Scripture, in fact, was describing a tribal society in which each plot of land had been intended as the inalienable patrimony of an extended family. It envisaged a stable community of comfortable and secure peasant proprietors, and it proposed a practical programme of reform to restore that community when it was undermined by growing inequalities – tithes for the poor, cancellation of debt, release of bondsmen, and redistribution of land. We cannot be sure when exactly this traditional Israelite society existed – nor how successfully it lived up to the biblical ideal – but what is certain is that it no longer existed in the first century AD. Now only the concept existed, providing a yardstick against which to compare present reality – part of the Judaic religious language for talking about the world and what was wrong with it. Describing so clearly how things ought to have been – how God wanted them to be – was, of course, to question the fundamentals of the actual Graeco-Roman social order in contemporary Palestine. Against the reality of great estates and desperate poverty could be set this image of a land filled with prosperous, independent, respectable peasant proprietors, unburdened, of course, by landlords, tax-collectors and press-gangs. And that which centuries before may have been a matter of practical reformism – regular minor adjustments to maintain an essentially egalitarian set-up – now, in the context of the present age, amounted to a set of far-reaching revolutionary demands. This brought about a merging of the traditional egalitarian Judaism of the peasants with the revolutionary millenarian politics of the sects. The existing order could not celebrate a Year of Jubilee, for to cancel debts, free bondsmen and redistribute land would be to destroy the wealth and power of the ruling class. The time-honoured social aspirations of the peasantry could not be realised without revolution. The Year of Jubilee had to become the Apocalypse.

There is no question that this link had been made. It is there in *Isaiah*: the prophet heralds not only an apocalyptic End of Days and the reign of God on earth, but also a restoration of traditional freedom and equality to the land of Israel. Interestingly, after his 'born-again' conversion – involving baptism in the Jordan and a soul-searching sojourn in the Wilderness – Jesus began his mission by quoting the relevant passage and identifying himself with its message.

> When he came to Nazareth, where he had been brought up, he went to the synagogue on the Sabbath, as was his custom. He stood up to read, and the scroll of the prophet Isaiah was given to him. He unrolled the scroll and found the place where it was written: 'The Spirit of the Lord is upon me, because he has anointed me to bring good news to the poor. He has sent me to proclaim release to the captives, and recovery of sight to the blind, to let the oppressed go free, to proclaim the year of the Lord's favour.' And he rolled up the scroll, gave it back to the attendant, and sat down. The eyes of all in the synagogue were fixed on him. Then he began to say to them, 'Today this scripture has been fulfilled in your hearing.'
>
> (*Luke*, 4.14-21)

36 *Engraving of an ordinary priest wearing a prayer shawl (talit) and reading from the Torah, probably a common scene in Jewish villages in the first century AD*

The connection between Apocalypse and Jubilee is made explicit also in an Essene bible commentary from Qumran. The badly damaged text concerns the mysterious figure of Melchizedek – in *Genesis* the Canaanite priest-king of Salem (or Jerusalem), but later, in Essene and Judaeo-Christian texts, an archangel and heavenly saviour.

> . . . And concerning that which He said, *In* [*this*] *Year of Jubilee* [*each of you shall return to his property* (Lev. 25.13); and likewise, *And this is the manner of release:*] *every creditor shall release that which he has lent* [*to his neighbour. He shall not exact it of his neighbour and his brother,*] *for God's release* [*has been proclaimed*] (Deut. 15.2). [And it will be proclaimed at] the End of Days concerning the captives as [He said, *To proclaim liberty to the captives* (Isa. 61.1). Its interpretation is that He] will assign them to the Sons of Heaven and to the inheritance of Melchizedek; [for He will cast] their [lot] amid the [portions of Melchizedek], who will return them there and will proclaim to them liberty, forgiving them [the wrong-doings] of all their iniquities.
>
> (*The Heavenly Prince Melchizedek*, DSS)

It seems clear, then, that in the minds of first-century radicals the Jubilee and the Apocalypse had fused into a single event. Through the village synagogues, moreover, messiahs and millenarians could bring this conception to a receptive mass audience, connecting popular notions about justice which survived in the heart of the peasant with revolutionary ideas about an apocalyptic war to destroy the unrighteous. The End of Days preached by messiahs and sectarians came to mean also the Jubilee of the peasant. Through this vision, the peasant could transcend the household and the village. He could connect not just with the preachers who came to the local synagogue, but with peasants in other villages who also heard and believed. He could join with others anywhere so long as they too were righteous. Scripture, faith and a shared vision of a better world could bind together hundreds of thousands in common struggle. So the Apocalypse was not just the hoped-for end of corruption and injustice; it was also a way of organising to achieve it, a way of turning a class of farmers and villagers into a revolutionary force for overturning the state and building heaven on earth. By the 60s AD, all the currents of anger and protest at the base of society – land hunger, social banditry, messianic movements, urban riots, sectarian agitation – were flowing in the same direction: towards their ultimate consummation in an apocalyptic confrontation with The Great Beast.

The rising tide

Palestine, AD 44-66

Revolutions appear to be sudden events, but often this is because the smaller protests that precede them have fallen beneath the gaze of history. Josephus is quite excep-tional among ancient historians in providing a detailed catalogue of the clashes between Roman and Jew in the generation before AD 66. We can therefore chart the rising tide of revolution in these years.

In AD 40, when Caligula attempted to inaugurate the worship of his own godhead alongside that of Yahweh on the Temple Mount, mass protests had threatened Roman rule. On that occasion the authorities had backed off, and after Caligula's assassination a few months later, his successor, Claudius, had offered further conciliation by ending direct rule and making Herod Agrippa I client-king of Judaea. It was but a momentary respite, for the king died prematurely in AD 44. The Greeks of Caesarea and Sebaste, including many Roman auxiliary soldiers, joined in riotous celebrations of Herod Agrippa's death. Wearing garlands they feasted and drank in the streets, pouring libations to Charon, the ferryman of the dead, and removing statues of the king's daughters to the town brothels. On the other side of the country, at Philadelphia in Peraea, Greeks and Jews clashed violently over a disputed border, and in Idumaea in the south there was an outbreak of social banditry and raiding led by a man called Tholomaeus. Soon afterwards a new messiah arose, called Theudas, who led a party of 400 followers to the Jordan, claiming he could divide the river to allow safe passage across. Claudius had by now decided to restore direct rule over an enlarged province of Judaea, appointing Cuspius Fadus (AD 44-6) as his procurator. Pro-Greek in sympathy, his response to the crisis was repression of the Jews: Hannibal, leader of the rebels in Peraea, was arrested and executed, as was Tholomaeus, the Idumaean bandit, while the millenarians at the Jordan were dispersed by Roman cavalry, with many killed, including Theudas himself, whose head was cut off and carried back to Jerusalem.

Fadus fell foul of the Jerusalem élite, however, when he sought Roman guardianship over the Temple through possession of the high-priestly vestments. He was replaced by Tiberius Alexander (AD 46-8), a former Jew and a conciliator, but famine stalked the countryside in these years, and a revolt by James and Simon, the sons of Judas the Galilean who had led the resistance to Roman taxation in AD 6, ended with their crucifixion. More serious clashes followed under Alexander's successor, Ventidius Cumanus (AD 48-52), each time involving embittered confrontations between the procurator's local Greek auxiliaries and the Jewish neighbours they hated. First, one of the soldiers on duty in the Temple during the Feast of Passover made an obscene gesture and provoked a riot among the thousands of pilgrims gathered there. When Cumanus rushed in reinforcements, the crowd panicked and many were trampled to death in the narrow exits. A year or two later, when bandits attacked one of the emperor's slaves and seized his baggage on a road through the hills a few miles from Jerusalem, Cumanus sent troops into the region to make summary arrests of village leaders. This time a soldier provoked anger by tearing up a copy of the Torah and casting the pieces into a fire. As news of the outrage spread, thousands descended on Caesarea and compelled the procurator to have the offender executed. Next, a Galilean pilgrim was murdered in Samaria on his way to Jerusalem. When Cumanus did nothing, the veteran bandit Eleazar ben Dinai led an angry mob out of the city into nearby Samaritan villages to exact vengeance. Thereafter communal violence between Jews and Samaritans spread across central Palestine. Again the troops were sent in, many Jews were killed, and others were imprisoned and later crucified or beheaded.

Claudius was not impressed by his procurator's performance: his job was above all to maintain order, not to provoke riots by naked partisanship and heavy-handed repression, so Cumanus was exiled, three leading Samaritans were executed, and a senior Roman officer guilty of atrocities was delivered to the Jews for torture and beheading. Moreover, during the next two years, most of Transjordan was cut away from the Roman province to create a new client-kingdom for Herod Agrippa II, while the reduced territory under direct rule was assigned to the care of Marcus Antonius Felix (AD 52-60), a most senior and well-connected figure whose appointment as procurator was a clear mark of the regime's concern about the deteriorating political situation in Judaea. Felix had close ties to the imperial household: his brother was a leading minister, the freedman Pallas, and his first wife was Mark Antony's grand-daughter. He also had, again by marriage, impeccable Jewish connections: his second wife was the sister of Herod Agrippa II. The anti-semitic and hawkish administration of Cumanus had been a disaster. Could the situation be retrieved again, as it had been in AD 41, by more moderate government of the Jews?

Men do not lightly take up arms as rebels, but many Jews had already, in AD 52, passed the point of no return. Some, unable to survive on tiny plots, lacking work as labourers, outraged by the abuse and violence of anti-semitic soldiery, had taken to the hills as bandits. One of Felix's first acts as procurator was an attempt to stamp out such banditry: Eleazar ben Dinai and his associates were captured and sent to Rome for trial, while many lesser bandits were crucified at home. Other Jews threw themselves into overtly revolutionary activity, becoming terrorist assassins who mixed with the Jerusalem pilgrim crowds, concealing short curved knives under their clothing, with the aim of striking down prominent political figures. (These were the original 'Sicarians' – though the term came to be used for revolutionaries in general – since *sica* is a Latin word meaning 'dagger', and *sicarii* were therefore 'daggermen'.) The first victim, early in Felix's procuratorship, was the ex-high priest Jonathan – but there were to be many others, and, for leading members of the ruling class, fear of sudden death in a crowded public place was to become a feature of everyday life. Yet other Jews kept watch for the long-awaited deliverer: there was a rash of would-be messiahs, men who, according to Josephus, linked claims of divine inspiration with plans to overturn the state. The most serious attempt was led by an 'Egyptian false prophet' who brought his people (4,000 of them according to *Acts*) out of the Wilderness to an encampment on the Mount of Olives, 'and from there was ready to force an entry into Jerusalem, overwhelm the Roman garrison, and seize supreme power with his followers as an armed retinue'. This, like other messianic attempts, Felix destroyed by sending in the troops. The deployment of troops on the streets – almost unknown in most parts of the empire – had, in fact, become routine in Roman Palestine. Felix used them again to rescue the heretical St Paul from a Jerusalem lynch mob, and yet again against Jewish rioters after communal clashes in Caesarea. This repeated intervention of soldiers in civil affairs shows that order was breaking down and repression becoming ineffective as the growing activity of bandits, terrorists, millenarians and rioters merged into a single opposition movement. This was a development noted by Josephus in his commentaries on the successive procuratorships of Felix, Porcius Festus (AD 60-2) and Clodius Albinus (AD 62-4):

The religious charlatans and bandit-chiefs joined forces and drove numbers to revolt, inciting them to strike a blow for freedom . . . Then, splitting up into groups, they ranged over the countryside, plundering the houses of the well-to-do, killing the occupants, and setting fire to the villages, till their rampaging madness penetrated every corner of Judaea. Day by day the fighting blazed more fiercely.

(*JW*, 2.264-5)

. . . the country was afflicted by bandits and all the villages were being set on fire and plundered by them. It was then that the *sicarii* (as they were called), who were bandits, grew numerous. . . . they slew a great many people by mingling with the crowds at festivals . . . They also came frequently upon the villages belonging to their enemies, with their weapons, and plundered them and set them on fire. Festus sent troops, both cavalry and infantry, to fall upon those who had been seduced by a certain impostor who promised deliverance and freedom from the miseries they were under to those who would follow him into the Wilderness.

(*JA*, 20.185-8)

The strength of the movement was displayed when the newly arrived Clodius Albinus carried out mass arrests of suspected terrorists. The Sicarians responded by kidnapping prominent aristocrats and using them as hostages for the release of detainees, including the principal secretary to the Temple Captain. The tactic was successful: Albinus was forced to release ten terrorists to secure the secretary's return. The assassinations, the kidnappings, the negotiations with the government, and the inability of the authorities to root out the terrorist cells suggest that the Sicarian underground was a large and well-organised urban guerrilla movement. Albinus was castigated by Josephus for corruption and incompetence, but the slide into deeper disorder can hardly have been a deliberate choice. Other evidence suggests that the mounting pressure from below was giving rise to increasing demoralisation and disarray at the top. Herod Agrippa was repeatedly at loggerheads with the Sadducees – over an extension to one of the royal palaces in Jerusalem, over royal gifts to the pagan Greek city of Berytus (Beirut), and over the dress code to be followed in Temple ritual. The king retaliated by exploiting his power to hire and fire high priests, and what little prestige the office had retained from its glorious past was now quickly destroyed when six high priests succeeded one another in just three years between AD 61 and 64. The high priesthood was degenerating into naked greed: bands of thugs were dispatched to seize grain tithes from the peasants and prevent them being given to village priests. Factionalism was rampant: bribes were traded for the top post, and at one point rival supporters of three candidates battled each other in the streets. There was erratic but vicious repression of popular radicals: James, the leader of the Judaeo-Christians, was arrested with some of his associates, condemned by the Sanhedrin, and stoned to death – but, as further evidence of the disarray among Palestine's rulers, the high priest responsible was then sacked by Herod Agrippa with the backing of Albinus.

Thus, when Gessius Florus arrived in AD 64 to succeed Albinus as procurator, the land of the Jews was already on the brink of revolution. The ruling class was divided and vacillating. Sporadic repression was mixed with half-hearted concessions. Large parts of the countryside were controlled by bandits. There was urban guerrilla warfare in the city. The regime's officials were threatened by violent street protests. The events of Florus' procuratorship are therefore easily understood. Florus was a redneck who believed in the mailed fist. Conciliation had failed, he figured; the province was out of control. Order must now be restored in the only way possible. So the cavalry attacked Jewish demonstrators in Caesarea and their leaders were incarcerated. Jerusalem was ordered to hand over Temple funds for the procurator's use. Protests were met again by troops, first in bloody clashes in the streets of the holy city, then outside the gates as reinforcements were called up. It was at this moment that the anger finally boiled over, and, as the masses came out to confront the troops in unprecedented numbers, protest turned into insurrection. In the street-fighting that followed, Florus' auxiliaries were defeated and the bulk of his army was withdrawn from the city. That was in May. The following August, Jewish counter-revolutionaries backed by units of King Herod Agrippa's army were also defeated. Then, in early November, as revolutionary Jerusalem resisted a third assault, this time by Cestius Gallus' legions from Syria, the countryside rose in revolt around him. The holy city had launched a revolution to free the poor, and now the poor came to the rescue of the holy city.

The battle of Beth-Horon

The road from Jerusalem to Beth-Horon, 4-8 November AD 66
The task facing Cestius Gallus in early November AD 66 was one of the most difficult in war: to execute a retreat under enemy attack. His predicament was unfortunate in that until now he had done only what any competent Roman commander would have done: faced with an armed challenge to imperial power, he had not hesitated to strike back aggressively with whatever force was to hand. Nine times out of ten this worked. The idea was to terrorise the opposition before it could get a grip. A swift, brutal, devastating attack was usually effective in restoring the impression of military invincibility on which the empire's security largely depended. Nor could he be blamed for taking inadequate force: his army of 30,000 men was twice the size of that which had defeated Boudicca's massive rebellion in Britain a few years before – 30,000 well-equipped professional soldiers against a mob of farmers, shopkeepers and deserters. But the fact is that he had miscalculated. The revolutionary city had resisted his onslaught, and the Judaean hill-country had risen around him. His communications with the coast were cut and, as winter approached, he doubted his ability to feed his tens of thousands of soldiers, servants, grooms, drivers, traders and camp-followers, and his many thousands of horses, mules and draught-animals. To save his army, Gallus had somehow to march it through the midst of tens of thousands of fighters and back to the coast – and an army on the march, especially in retreat,

is perilously vulnerable. Adversity, of course, is the real test of military leadership, and a confident and skilful commander might have extricated his army successfully – perhaps by launching a punitive attack, seizing the high ground above the road, and then marching fast to the coast before the enemy had time to recover. Gallus, however, was no Caesar. The best he could manage was to form a ponderous column and to begin trudging heavily and slowly back the way he had come.

The Romans could not adopt a standard marching formation, for the army would then have been strung out along many miles of road, the rear elements only setting out hours after those at the front. For security, they had to be much more compact, perhaps moving in 'squared column' (*agmen quadratum*), a short, wide formation that enabled units to turn or wheel into battle-line facing any direction at short notice. It had the further advantage that the slowest and most vulnerable part of the column – the train of pack-animals and ox-carts which carried the army's heavy equipment and baggage – was protected by a box of soldiers. Command and control was also easier in a tight formation. A retreating column under attack could quickly disintegrate into rout if not kept well in hand. Gallus' tribunes and centurions would need to be moving up and down the ranks continually to prevent straggling, keep the men fully alert, maintain morale, and improvise hasty responses to enemy attacks. Men anyway felt safer in a compact formation with a secure rear: fear and panic were kept in check by the proximity of comrades. But there was a big drawback: advancing on such a wide front slowed the army's progress to a crawl, especially over difficult terrain, such as the steep hills and olive terraces around Beth-Horon (**colour plate 12**). The men marching on the road itself would continually have to halt and wait while the columns either side of them stumbled across broken ground. But there was no alternative: mobility had to be sacrificed for security. Progress would be slowed further by attacks from the hills, which would force parts of the column to halt and deploy into line. This involved turning or wheeling towards the enemy, closing up and dressing ranks, and then presenting weapons. And then back into column again to continue the march. It would all take time.

The first attacks were launched from the city itself on the rearguard of the column as it marched out on 4 November. Many of these attackers were probably well equipped and prepared to fight at close-quarters. There must have been deserters from Herod Agrippa's army, veteran bandits, fighters from established guerrilla forces, and many who had joined one or other of the fast-growing popular militias that had emerged in the last few months. But they were a minority among those who assailed the column over the next four days. As Gallus continued his retreat on the following day, having spent the night camped on Mount Scopus a mere mile or so from the city, he was assailed from the hills by hordes of Jewish irregulars (**37**). These men were lightly equipped, with only a shield for protection, and they fought with stones, slings and javelins in a loose formation, hanging on the flanks and rear of the column to pelt it with missiles, but scurrying away up the hillsides when threatened, avoiding a close-quarters clash at all costs. Their weapons were home-made or improvised: slings made from strips of leather; pebbles or baked-clay slugs as slingshot; javelins with iron heads hammered out in village forges; rocks hurled by hand. The sling had many advantages. It was cheap and easy to make, required virtually no maintenance, and there was always ammunition to hand (though proper lead shot was much more effective than stones scavenged on a hillside). It was a traditional weapon of the Jewish peasantry, so many men were skilled in its use, and, in ideal conditions, an experienced slinger could probably put several stones in the air inside a minute, each aimed with the precision of a trained archer. Effective range was perhaps 100m or so (though more with proper shot). Javelins had much shorter effective ranges – perhaps 35m – but their metal points and greater weight made them more destructive. Javelins, like slings, were low-tech weapons easy to produce in quantity, and, since they could be handled readily by inexperienced fighters, many men came to Beth-Horon armed with a bundle; when they had thrown these, they could continue with weapons salvaged from the battlefield, or with hand-hurled rocks, effective at a similar range. Scattered among the thousands of irregular slingers and javelinmen on the slopes, there were probably also some hundreds of army deserters equipped with the composite bow, the professional long-range missile weapon of the East, effective at up to 150-200m.

Ancient armies protected themselves against missiles in one of two ways: by deploying their own screens of skirmishers, or by mounting charges to disperse the enemy's. Gallus' army must have contained many hundreds, perhaps thousands, of archers and slingers, some of them regular auxiliaries, many more supplied by the client-kings. Had these been able to engage effectively, they would have afforded the Roman column good protection. Recent studies of men in combat have revealed that many do not use their weapons against the enemy at all, and those that do usually deploy weapons randomly and without precision. Combat is terrifying and the dominating concern is personal safety. Few men have the courage to expose themselves unnecessarily, so most, given the chance, will tend to hover at extreme ranges, or, closer in, cower behind their shields or any natural cover they can find. It is likely that light infantry especially behaved in this way. They were not trained and steeled for close-quarters combat and high casualties; they expected to fight at a distance, making use of available cover and vantage points, and benefiting from their open, loose formation to scatter in front of enemy attacks and to dodge incoming missiles or knock them aside with their shields. Officers had limited control over their men in this sort of tentative skirmishing, particularly when, like most of the Jews at Beth-Horon, they were irregular volunteers not subject to normal military discipline.

Combat of this kind might continue for hours with very light casualties. Studies of massed musketry in the age of gunpowder have shown that, in optimum battle conditions, 20 per cent of shots fired scored hits at ranges of 25m or less, but only 3-5 per cent at ranges of 100-200m, while there were so few hits at longer ranges (the extreme maximum was around 300m) that expenditure of ammunition was not justified. Ancient weapons were less effective still, as the velocity of missiles was limited by the physical strength of the soldier, making their trajectories erratic and reducing the force with which they struck targets, many of which were protected by armour and shields. Moreover, ideal conditions for the use of missiles rarely occurred

37 *Reconstruction drawing of Jewish irregular light infantry of the first century AD. Though later in the war some men acquired armour and engaged at close-quarters, most Jews fought as lightly equipped guerrillas and skirmishers, relying on missile weapons like the sling and the javelin. Employing this 'eastern way of war', the Jews defeated 30,000 Romans at Beth-Horon and won their greatest victory for 200 years*

in practice; it is estimated that the *actual* battlefield performance of gunpowder weapons was on average only about a third of the theoretical optimum. Numerous 'inefficiencies of the battlefield' intervened to reduce the effectiveness of shooting. The target was often moving, or making use of cover, or obscured by an intervening obstruction. Clouds of dust would swirl across summer battlegrounds (or black smoke in the age of gunpowder). Weapons could malfunction, or ammunition run short, or men mishandle a shot. Physical exhaustion would quickly set in, especially in the case of muscle-powered weapons; perhaps after two or three dozen vigorous sling-casts or draws on a composite bow, the soldier would begin to tire, bringing a steady reduction in the rate and velocity of successive shots. But the greatest restriction of all was battle stress and the often paralysing fear of men in combat that they could be killed or horribly injured. The amount of fear, and its effect on weapon handling, was related to the danger faced – in the case of light infantry exchanges, mainly to the threat posed by incoming missiles. This is the concept of 'covering' or 'suppressing fire', which, if successful, involves delivering a weight of shot sufficient to destroy the ability of the enemy to use his weapons. Under effective suppressing fire, men are killed, driven into flight, forced under cover, or left cowering in fear;

in military terms, 'neutralised'. More usually, in ancient battle, neither skirmish line could achieve this, but each tried to maintain a screen protecting their own army's heavy formations from the enemy's missile shooters. This was the struggle the Romans failed to win on the second day of their retreat.

The rearguard was again attacked, but so too were the flanks. With the Jews on three sides, any skirmish line the Romans formed risked being surrounded, while detachments of cavalry who attempted localised sorties up the slopes were in danger of being cut off and destroyed. Stragglers who fell behind the column – the exhausted, the wounded, or those who were just careless – were quickly dispatched by their enemies. Fear of this fate kept every man stumbling forwards. So there was no concerted defence of the column – little suppressing fire and few sorties – and the Jews gained in confidence, approaching closer to the column, taking careful aim with each cast, and bringing the dense mass of close-order infantry, heavy cavalry and the baggage-train under effective missile attack. This target was far more promising than a skirmish line: not only was it crowded, but most men were hurrying forwards and unable to protect themselves efficiently – unlike a battle-line, in which men crouched down behind their shields and watched for incoming missiles. A steady hail of javelins, sling-stones, arrows and rocks dropped on the men in the column from their flanks and rear. Many of these would find a target. Most injuries were not lethal – a javelin might slice into an arm or leg, a sling-stone take out an eye or smash a hand, an arrow lodge in a shoulder – but such injuries, especially if multiple, would work their effect over time, eventually bringing a man to collapse. Skeletons of men killed in medieval battles often display multiple minor injuries and one or more fatal blows to the back of the head – as if men weakened by several earlier wounds had been too slow to escape their pursuers. This must have been the fate of growing numbers in the Roman column as the hours passed. On their feet all day, weighed down by over 100lbs (50kg) of arms, armour and equipment, moving in fits and starts, hunched up against the missile storm, perhaps afflicted by hunger and thirst, men who had been hit and hit again must gradually have weakened to the point of collapse. Some may have been helped along by comrades at first, but soon there were too many, and as morale sank, the solidarity of military units began to dissolve and each man looked out for himself. Then those who could not go on were left behind to be battered and speared to death by their pursuers. To keep casualties down, senior officers struggled to keep the column moving, but as they shouted their encouragement above the roar of noise reverberating off the slopes, several were struck down in the blizzard of shot – a cavalry leader, a military tribune, and the commander of the Sixth Legion. As the situation worsened, the bulk of the baggage was abandoned. Only then did the column gain sufficient pace to reach its old camp at Gibeon before nightfall. The day had been a military disaster. And there was worse to come.

Gallus halted at Gibeon for two days, his demoralised army safe behind ditch and rampart for the time being. But many supplies had been abandoned on the road and the Romans were fast eating through what was left, while every hour brought further reinforcement to the enemy host all around the camp; delay favoured the Jews. So Gallus ordered all the pack- and draught-animals slaughtered, all except those which carried artillery and ammunition, and then set off again on the morning of 8 November. At first the road passed through relatively open country, where cavalry sorties threatened Jewish positions, and the battle remained tentative, the enemy's slingers and javelinmen keeping their distance. But then, Josephus reports, the pass narrowed towards Beth-Horon and the surrounding slopes became more precipitous. On such ground, close-order infantry found it difficult to deploy and operate without losing formation, and the cavalry in particular were unable to mount attacks. Instead, with the Jewish skirmishers edging closer, often ranged on higher ground overlooking the column, the soldiers bunched together close to the road and tried to hurry forwards: an ideal target for the massed slingers and javelinmen around them. The shooting was rarely directed at individuals; the intention was to engulf a body of men in a missile storm, and the more crowded it was, and the less able men were to protect themselves, the higher the casualties. Progress was slowed when the bolder elements among the Jews blocked the road ahead. Operating on such a narrow front, and with the enemy close on all sides, the Romans were not able to organise an attack to clear the way. The column was brought to a halt and boxed in, the enemy in control of commanding ground around it. The hail of shot and the roaring of the assailants reached a crescendo. Roman infantry cowered beneath their shields; cavalrymen lost control of their horses; a few missiles were hurled back, flying wildly; above the din could be heard the screams of those hit, the hoarse cries of frantic officers, and the bellowing of terrified animals; broken equipment lay scattered among twisted corpses; there was a stench of urine, animal dung and men's gore. 'The Jews would certainly have captured Cestius and his whole army,' Josephus believed, 'had not darkness descended, enabling the Romans to take refuge in Beth-Horon, while the Jews ringed them in and waited for them to come out.'

They came out that night, secretly, their retreat now turned to virtual rout. Gallus ordered 400 picked men to take post on the roofs of the village and shout out the watchwords of the camp-sentries to give the impression the whole army was still present. The rest he led out along the road to safety, covering three and a half miles in complete silence, and putting further distance between his own army and the enemy before dawn. The Jews, alerted in the morning to Gallus' escape, quickly overran and killed the defenders of Beth-Horon, and then set off in pursuit of the main force. But Gallus was now in headlong flight, moving as fast as he could once the sun was up, abandoning the last of his baggage-train carrying the artillery as he went, thus outpacing his pursuers. The Jews, nonetheless, had won a stunning victory. A makeshift army of farmers armed with spears and stones, with a leavening of deserters, bandits and guerrillas, had all but routed a professional army of 30,000 men, killing 5,300 infantry, 480 cavalry and at least three senior officers, as well as capturing heaps of armour and weapons, several batteries of artillery, an entire baggage-train of supplies and even, so Suetonius tells us, the eagle standard of a legion. It was the greatest Jewish victory over a foreign overlord for 200 years. The news must have sounded through the villages of Palestine like a clarion call to holy war. This, surely, was God's work. This, the beginning of the long-awaited End of Days. The world, after all, had just been turned upside down.

1 *The Sea of Galilee. A view east from Tiberias towards the Golan Heights. In the first century AD a sizeable population of farmers and fishermen lived on the shores of the sea and in the valleys of the rivers that fed into it. The relatively low, gently sloping and well-watered hills west of the sea were also heavily populated*

2 *The Jezreel Valley. A view looking south-west from Mount Tabor. Samaria and the central upland massif are visible as a range of hills in the distance. The site of Nazareth in Lower Galilee appears as a range of hills in the middle-ground on the right. In antiquity the Jezreel Valley was probably dominated by wheat production on large estates*

3 *The River Jordan. The ancient agriculture of the Jordan Valley, benefiting from high temperatures and extensive irrigation, was both abundant and exotic, but, as in the Jezreel, large estates seem to have predominated*

4 *Judaea. The central upland massif is a region of hills and stones with increasing desiccation towards the south. In antiquity much of it was organised as small terraced plots on which peasant families grew barley, cultivated vines, olives and figs, and grazed sheep and goats. The land was poor and there was not enough of it*

5 *The Wilderness. South of Jerusalem, in southern Judaea and Idumaea, the land becomes increasingly dry, merging into desert in the east and the far south. This view is taken from the hills of the Judaean Desert looking east towards the Dead Sea. The hills of southern Peraea can be seen in the distance. The south was renowned as a region of pastoralists and bandits*

6 *The Herodian circus or hippodrome at Caesarea (sometimes misleadingly called an 'amphitheatre'). This was one of the settings for pagan-style games in the city – in this case horse and chariot racing – and the plaster on the wall around the course was decorated with images of plants and animals. Both the games and the decoration were offensive to traditional Jews*

7 *Herod's promontory pavilion at Caesarea. It was built on two levels on a projecting headland: the lower terrace (just visible on the left) comprised a summer dining complex and a large ornamental pool surrounded by a colonnade; the upper terrace comprised a large colonnaded courtyard garden (shown here) and an entrance complex (just out of view on the right). The colonnaded court – or peristyle – was the basis of most Hellenistic domestic architecture*

8 *Upper Herodium, on the edge of the Judaean Desert about ten miles south of Jerusalem, was one of many fortress-palaces built by Herod the Great for defence as much against his own people as external enemies. In the Jewish War, it was one of the last rebel-held fortresses to hold out against the Romans*

9 *The Essene monastery at Qumran looking east towards the Dead Sea. The monastery sits beside a wadi on a shelf of land between the rift valley below and the Judaean hills behind. In this picture the remains lies just to the right of the trees in the centre*

10 *The Mount Arbel caves near the Sea of Galilee, where Herod the Great fought a fierce battle against a large force of bandits in 38 or 37 BC. There were cave complexes all over ancient Palestine, and these featured heavily as resistance refuges both in 'normal times' and during major revolts*

11 *The Arab shanty-village at Arganam in the West Bank. The difficulties of agriculture in the upland massif of Palestine, now as in the past, are apparent; the farming regime and the pattern of rural settlement have probably changed little in 2,000 years*

12 *The countryside around Beth-Horon, where steep, rocky slopes overlooking the ancient road provided perfect ground for Jewish irregular light infantry, armed with slings and javelins, to inflict a massive defeat on a retreating Roman army*

13 *The fortified hilltop town of Jotapata viewed from the far right of the Roman position looking south-west. The picture shows the north hill which was the lynchpin of the town's defence; the town itself lay to the south of this hill (towards the right of the picture)*

14 *The Roman position on the ridge north of Jotapata, with the site of the heaviest fighting in the foreground. The view is taken from the approximate position of the Jewish wall looking north*

15 *Vespasian's grand assault on Jotapata, 20 June AD 67. The view looks north-north-east and shows the Jewish wall in the foreground (raised and reinforced with towers), two* Roman ramp*s outside the wall, and a major breach in the defences at the end of the nearer ramp. The Roman army is formed up en masse:* there are *heavy assault columns on the ramps themselves; banks of artillery, archers and slingers*

tween the ramps; lines of men with ladders also between the ramps; and the rest of the army waiting in reserve on the hillside behind.
he defenders are shown taking cover from the missile storm, the great weight of incoming Roman shot preventing them from engaging the
ssault columns with missiles on their approach

16 *The site of the naval battle on the Sea of Galilee near Tarichaeae, where Roman rafts defeated Jewish fishing boats, probably on 7 September AD 67*

17 *The fortified hilltop town of Gamala looking west from the top of the Roman position. The eastern wall can be seen running up the slope on the left, with the northern tower in the centre of the picture. Behind the tower, the northern ridge can be seen rising to the citadel, the highest point in the town*

18 *The Muslim Quarter of the Old City of Jerusalem looking south from the Damascus Gate. It is likely that in antiquity also much of the city comprised a warren of narrow streets, small courtyards and low-rise buildings with flat roofs – ideal terrain for the mobile skirmishing tactics of the Jews*

19 *The Temple Mount and the southern walls of Jerusalem looking east-north-east, with the Mount of Olives in the background*

20 *The battle in the Outer Court of the Temple, mid-July AD 70. The view looks north-east towards the levelled Antonia Fortress (on the left) and the northern colonnade of the Sanctuary (centre and right). The Roman line is made up of centuries of legionaries formed up eight*

...anks deep, the men ranged shoulder-to-shoulder with their shields providing a protective shell against missiles. The posture of the facing Jewish ...ne is equally passive. Heavy infantry confrontation on the ancient battlefield was far more tentative and defensive than is usually imagined

21 *The Phasael Tower is the only part of the first-century Royal Palace on the western side of the Upper City to have survived. The lower two-thirds of the existing structure are Herodian*

22 *The northern face of Masada viewed from the east, with the three terraces of Herod's hanging-palace at the top, and the Dead Sea in the distance*

23 *Herodian storerooms at Masada. The rebels found these full of foodstuffs when they took over the fortress in AD 66. This view looks east towards the Dead Sea*

24 *Siege camp F viewed from the top of Masada, a Roman 'vexillation fortress' able to accommodate about 2,500 men, with the wall of circumvallation running just in front of it. The Roman siege works at Masada are among the best preserved in the world*

5 The war in Galilee

. . . the powerful men of Jerusalem, seeing that the robbers and revolutionaries had plenty of arms, feared that, lacking arms themselves, they
would find themselves overborne by their enemies – which is what eventually happened. Learning that not all of Galilee had yet revolted from
the Romans, but that some parts were still quiet, they sent me [Josephus]
. . . to persuade the ill-disposed to lay down their arms and to inform
them . . . that it had been decided that the best men should keep arms
at the ready for future action, but that they should wait and see what the
Romans would do.

(Josephus, *My Life*, 28)

The second aristocratic government

The Temple Mount, Jerusalem, mid-November AD 66
The Jewish people were now at war with the Roman Empire. As guerrillas they
could harass the avenging columns which were certain soon to descend on Palestine,
but if they did only this, homes and farms would burn and the land be made desert.
To safeguard their livelihoods, the guerrillas would have to come down from the hills
and fight a defensive war. To resist the advance of an even larger Roman army in the
new year, men and supplies would need to be concentrated in well-placed strongpoints, there would need to be centralised control over resources, and a grand
strategy would have to be thought out. The revolution, in short, had to have an
effective national government.

The victory at Beth-Horon had been a polarising event. It made the breach with
Rome irrevocable, and it confirmed the seriousness and possible longevity of the
struggle that had begun. Some Herodian aristocrats who until now had remained in
Jerusalem – no doubt keeping a low profile and hoping for a quick Roman victory
– chose this moment to flee. But the anti-Roman nobles, lifted up by a great tide of
popular insurrection but fearful of its radicalism, moved rapidly to bring the
movement under their own control. Soon after the victors returned to the city, a
great meeting was summoned on the Temple Mount to inaugurate a new government. The dominant moods must have been those of celebration, optimism and
festive unity. At such moments, early in the history of a revolution, it is relatively easy
for well-known political figures who declare for the popular cause to marginalise
obscure lower-class 'extremists'. Thus, the new government which emerged was led

by the high priest Ananus ben Ananus. He belonged to one of the top four or five high-priestly families in Jerusalem. His father and four brothers had all served as high priest, and, though his own tenure had been a brief three months in AD 62, his rapid dismissal by King Herod Agrippa and the Roman procurator at that time was no great disadvantage now. Associated with him in top government posts – they were styled 'generals' (*strategoi*) – were another high priest, a high priest's son, three other priests from noble families, two lay nobles, and four others whose social status is uncertain. Many priests and nobles also held secondary posts. One or two of the generals may have been token plebeians, and many lower-ranking positions must have gone to popular local leaders, but this presented no immediate danger to the aristocracy: on the contrary, in firm control at the top, their aim was to contain the burgeoning mass movement by turning its leaders into the army officers and admin-istrators of a new Jewish state organised on conventional Hellenistic lines.

Jerusalem itself was to remain under the direct control of Ananus and another general appointed as his colleague. Presumably they relied heavily on a circle of trusted advisors recruited from among their own families, friends and peers. They may have consulted with the rump of the Sanhedrin and were perhaps subject to pressure from some sort of popular assembly – but the evidence is unclear and there are certainly no details. What we can say is that, however it was managed constitu-tionally – and it may have been very loose – Jerusalem remained under the control of the old ruling class (Josephus' *dunatoi*, literally 'the powerful men'), or at least that part of it which had adopted an anti-Roman stance. Control of Jerusalem was decisive. The city dominated the country, dwarfing in size and strength any other urban centre held by the revolutionaries. It was of immense political and religious significance to all pious Jews, it was the seat of the Jewish aristocracy itself, and it contained huge reserves of wealth in public and temple treasuries and in collections of booty taken from the defeated Romans and their allies. From Jerusalem the high-priestly aristocracy could hope to run the country.

One of their first measures was to begin minting coins – necessary to pay soldiers and other government expenses, but also a clear symbol of political independence (**38**). There were three denominations – the shekel, half-shekel and quarter-shekel – all struck in silver to the same basic design. On the obverse was a chalice, probably the golden vessel used in Temple ritual on the second day of Passover, and on the reverse a branch with three pomegranates, a traditional symbol of fertility and abundance. The coins were inscribed 'Shekel of Israel' and 'Holy Jerusalem', and they were dated with a figure '1' – 'Year 1', that is, of the Liberation. A second key policy was to divide the country into military districts and appoint a governor to the command of each. Josephus' account seems to imply there were eight: Jerusalem itself; another in Peraea east of the Jordan; a third in Galilee in the far north; two in Idumaea in the south of the country; and three in Judaea covering the approaches to the capital, where there were separate western, eastern and northern commands (**8**). The government's main aim was to use its funds and its governors to establish centralised control over the country and weld its disparate revolutionary militias into a regular army. Nor was this simply – or even at all – a matter of military expediency.

38 *Silver shekel issued by the revolutionary government in AD 66. The obverse (above) shows a holy chalice and is inscribed 'Shekel of Israel' around the edge and 'Year 1' above the chalice. The reverse (below) shows three pomegranates and is inscribed 'Holy Jerusalem'. Coins were issued in this style for each year of the revolt until AD 70 ('Year 5')*

The many armed militias which had sprung to life under radical leadership between May and November were perceived by the government as no less of a problem than the Romans themselves. After the August-September fighting against the Herodian coup, the Zealot militia led by Menahem had been attacked and dispersed on the Temple Mount by Eleazar ben Ananias' faction. Now, in November, after the victory at Beth-Horon, the new government of Ananus ben Ananus successfully marginalised the most prominent and independent of the popular leaders – those, that is, with a large militant following. The Zealot militia under Eleazar ben Simon had been the strongest in the city – it had controlled the Temple Mount, the city's public treasury, and a huge haul of booty brought back from the victory at Beth-Horon. Yet Eleazar was denied a government post and lost control of the public funds (though his forces could not be dislodged from their occupation of the Temple Mount). Another casualty was Simon bar Giora, a formidable radical and a distinguished commander in the campaign against Cestius Gallus, who was not only denied an official post but was soon driven from his base in northern Judaea by government forces and compelled to seek safety in the Idumaean wilderness. A complementary policy was to incorporate some popular leaders – the more tractable or those with only small followings – into the government administration. The three men appointed to lead an abortive attack on the coastal city of Ascalon may be examples: they were Silas the Babylonian, a deserter from King Agrippa's army; Niger the Peraean, who had been some sort of 'governor of Idumaea' before he was superseded; and John the Essene, whose epithet speaks for itself.

The government's policy in making appointments was underwritten by its control over public funds. Militiamen willing to accept the authority of military governors would receive government pay, while new recruits were, as far as possible, enrolled in regular government units. Josephus happens to describe the composition of a detachment sent by the government from Jerusalem to Galilee in the winter of AD 66-7. It was led by the militia commander Jesus the Galilean, whose 600 men had been given three months' advance pay, but it also included 300 'civic troops' (*politai*) and 100 'regulars' (*hoplitai*) – an interesting example of how a formal army was being created by the merging of paid militiamen with the new state troops. The hope was that the military balance would gradually shift in favour of government forces and against the independent militias, forcing the latter either to accept regular army discipline or face liquidation. Thus the threat to property and power posed by so many armed and 'undisciplined' millenarians would be extinguished. But however strong the government's position appeared to be in formal terms – through its control of Jerusalem, the public funds, the new administration, and the army high command – the political and military realities in the country as a whole were much less favourable.

Between May and November, thousands of new fighters had joined one or another of a multiplicity of militias. Some of these had existed before the revolution began, but many others had been formed since on the initiative of local bandit-chiefs, sectarian militants or would-be messiahs. The peasant revolt, which was spilling out angry young men from the villages, was filling the ranks of these militias rather than those of regular government units. So it was the militias that were organising, training, equipping and directing the revolutionary energies of the insurgent population. The houses and estates of the rich or the territories of Jewish enemies were raided for supplies, and arms and armour were seized from royal fortresses, taken from deserters, or plundered from defeated enemies. The militias thus created varied greatly in size, equipment and readiness for war, and their composition was fluid, with men coming and going, some temporarily to visit families and farms, others for good because they had switched allegiance or lost heart. Many were rooted in a particular town, village or country area, while others flowed into the holy city, where they formed unstable coalitions at moments of revolutionary crisis. Each militia owed allegiance primarily to itself, its leaders, its own politico-religious aims, and other groups of similar composition and persuasion with which it chose to join. Any wider allegiance was provisional, and collectively the militias exercised an effective veto over the government, which lacked significant armed forces of its own to impose its will. In short, most parts of the capital and the country were controlled by independent armed militias, and the government existed only on sufferance: it could get its orders carried out only in so far as the militias agreed.

This is the situation the Russian revolutionary Trotsky dubbed 'dual power': where the government has formal authority but its ability to act is paralysed by a mass popular movement; and where this movement contains within itself the potential to overturn the government and rule in its place. It is, in a sense, the very essence of revolution and an explanation of the extreme complexity of revolutionary events. For dual power is not simply a matter of political authority. The highly contradictory and unstable conditions of dual power cannot be overcome simply by the government asserting itself to suppress 'anarchy' and 'restore order'. Dual power is rooted in class conflict: the rival political authorities – the actual and the potential governments, as it were – represent different and mutually antagonistic social forces. The second aristocratic government formed in late AD 66 was composed of property-owners propelled into opposition to Rome by an explosive insurrectionary movement of the Jewish people. The movement on the ground was led largely by social bandits and millenarian radicals, and the rank and file were tens of thousands of land-starved peasants and impoverished urban plebs. For them, the rise of the revolutionary militias and their victories over Herodians and Romans were electrifying events. Many could see here 'the light of a possible sunrise'. It was this, indeed, that gave the revolution its power: the best of the Jewish militiamen imagined this time to be the End of Days, and these to be the battles of the Apocalypse; they believed God would send Melchizedek and a host of angels to reinforce his saints on earth; and they anticipated a Year of Jubilee to wipe out debts, free the enslaved, and redistribute the land. It was because of this vision that tens of thousands of ordinary men were finding the courage to confront the forbidding power of Rome. The clash – as increasingly it became – between the government and the militias was at root a class conflict between aristocratic conservatives and lower-class radicals.

Yet the militias had not seized power for themselves. The most prominent leaders had been pushed aside – Menahem ben Judas, Eleazar ben Simon, Simon bar Giora – and most militiamen were prepared to tolerate instead a government of aristocrats. This too is a feature of dual power. 'Moderate' leaders who appear to have broken with the old order and given their allegiance to the popular cause are more readily trusted than unknown 'extremists'. But this trust is provisional. It depends on the fulfilment of revolutionary hopes. So whenever the government, backed by property-owners and traditional conservatives, attempts to rein in the popular movement, to prevent 'excesses' and 'outrages' against property, to impose 'discipline' on revolutionary militias, to suppress militants it deems to be 'tyrants' or 'robbers', the bond of trust is broken and a split opens between government and people. On one side are the compromisers who aim to defend property and negotiate a quick end to the revolution. On the other are radicals committed to popular measures, mass mobilisation and total victory. The compromisers' greatest fear is the revolution turning into a struggle against the property of the rich, whereas the radicals accept the need for social reform to maintain enthusiasm for the revolution and ensure its victory. It was a split of exactly this kind that divided Independents from Presbyterians in the English Revolution of 1642-9, and Jacobins from Girondins in the French Revolution of 1789-93. In one form or another, it is a feature of all great revolutions.

The festive unity at the meeting on the Temple Mount quickly passed away, and the alliance of rich nationalist and popular militiaman gradually soured. The revolution was to pass AD 67 in the grip of two titanic struggles. One was that against a huge Roman army of invasion bent upon reconquest and retribution. The other was a struggle of aristocrats and radicals – *dunatoi* and *stasiastai* – within the revolution itself; a struggle to decide between surrender on terms and all-out war to destroy the power of Rome and inaugurate the Kingdom of God on earth.

Flavius Josephus: general, historian, traitor

Joseph ben Matthias (to give him his original name) was a fairly typical member of the Jewish aristocracy (**39**). Born in AD 37 into a high-ranking family which included kings and high priests in its ancestry, he was of an intellectual bent, experimenting with different philosophies before choosing to become a Pharisee. His eminence is proved by his participation in an embassy to Rome in AD 64 at the young age of 26, when, he tells us, he gained the good favour of the Empress Poppaea Sabina and helped to secure the release of a number of Jewish priests who were under arrest. It is further shown by his appointment as military governor of Galilee under the aristocratic nationalist government in AD 66. Josephus was, in other words, a *dunatos*, 'one of the powerful men', a member of the Jewish ruling class. As such he shared the Greek culture of the eastern Mediterranean élite at the time, best represented by his Greek literacy. Language was an important status signifier, in that Greek was an aristocratic lingua franca which gave access to a world of international scholarship — whereas Jewish holy rites were conducted in Hebrew, and the peasants spoke various dialects of Aramaic. It is likely that Josephus knew all three languages well, and that later, when he lived in Rome as a historian, he perfected his Greek and also acquired Latin. Whatever the case, though an early version of his *Jewish War* was apparently written in Aramaic (now lost), his four surviving works were all in Greek and often conform closely to the conventions of Greek literary genres. On this evidence Josephus was highly Hellenised.

He was also a traitor who served his people's enemies well and was handsomely rewarded for it. Josephus' mission to Galilee was a military failure, but he secured his own life by reneging on a suicide pact with other rebels, surrendering to the victorious Romans, and insinuating his way into Vespasian's good favour, so that he was able to continue the war as an interpreter, consultant and diplomat in the Roman service, and after it become a leading propagandist and historian for the Flavian dynasty. Josephus claims that, when first brought before his captor, he predicted that Vespasian would become emperor. This reinterpretation of the well-known Jewish prophecy that a world ruler would arise in Palestine may have been made on this occasion, but, more likely, it was retrospective: part of an arrangement between the Flavian family and their Jewish client — who happened to be a high-ranking priest and seer — made only after their bid for supreme power was launched in the middle of AD 69. His own treachery and the victory of his patrons in the civil war secured Josephus' future. He was granted Roman citizenship (thus becoming 'Flavius Josephus'), taken to Rome by Titus after the fall of Jerusalem in AD 70, and set up in style with a house, estates and a pension. Though his *Jewish War* was not a commissioned 'official history', it was most certainly an 'authorised' one, encouraged and made possible by court patronage, and the author himself tells

39 *(opposite) A fanciful portrait by a nineteenth-century artist of the Jewish general and historian Flavius Josephus. In fact, though we know he was a priest, an aristocrat and a man of 30 at the time of the revolt, we have no information about his actual appearance*

us that the work was offered to Vespasian and Titus (and also to King Herod Agrippa) for their approval. Josephus was, then, a Hellenised Jewish aristocrat, a treacherous revolutionary commander, and a Roman court historian, whose active life was lived out in the contradictions of a revolutionary dynamic, and whose later writing was an attempt to explain what had happened in a way that excused his own dubious role, glorified the achievements of his patrons, and attempted to exonerate from blame the Jewish ruling class of which he was a member. It is in this context that Josephan texts must be read.

His first work, in seven books, was *Bellum Iudaicum* (*The Jewish War*), which offered a summary of 200 years of Jewish history leading up to the war, and then gave a very detailed account of both revolutionary factionalism and the struggle against the Romans, especially for Jerusalem in AD 66, Galilee in AD 67, and Jerusalem again from the winter of AD 67/8 to the fall of the city in AD 70. His second work, *Antiquitates Iudaicae* (*Jewish Antiquities*), was a complete history of the Jews from Adam to AD 66, a massive study in 20 books, much of it a re-telling of well-known bible stories, but including more detailed coverage of the pre-revolutionary years than that offered in *The Jewish War*. His last two works were both much shorter and in the manner of polemical responses to specific attacks. *Vita* (*My Life*) was not a conventional autobiography but a defence of the author's role as military governor of Galilee in AD 66-7, written in response to the allegations of his enemy, Justus of Tiberias, that he had caused the rebellion. *Contra Apionem* (*Against Apion*) comprised two books written in defence of Jewish religion, law and customs in the face of anti-semitic attacks by Alexandrian Greek scholars. All these works have something in common: they aim to justify the position of Josephus and his upper-class Jewish peers within the post-AD 70 Roman Empire. The Romans did not require complete cultural conformity of the client aristocracies who ruled locally within the wider imperial system. What they did require, however, was loyalty, obedience and effectiveness in maintaining order. On both counts the Jewish ruling class appeared unreliable. Judaism had united the Jews against the Romans and propelled them into revolt. And the Jewish *dunatoi* at the time had either failed to prevent this or, in many cases, including that of Josephus, had actively participated in the struggle. In the explanatory paradigm developed by Josephus in *The Jewish War*, *Jewish Antiquities* and *My Life*, blame for the disaster was attributed to the often wilfully malevolent misgovernment of successive Roman procurators, the self-interested rabble-rousing of popular leaders, and the sinfulness of the Jewish people as a whole. Squeezed between Roman injustice and revolutionary agitation, the Jewish *dunatoi* could not perform their essential role of mediation and containment. The procurators, instead of ruling in alliance with the local nobility, showing tact and moderation, plunged head-first into a series of bitter collisions with Jewish opinion. This gave rein to the *stasiastai* (those aiming at revolution), and Jewish society was racked by a *stasis* (a crisis of extreme social conflict and political instability) from which the best efforts of men of rank could not rescue it.

As far as it goes there is a strong element of truth in this account. The problem is that Josephus did not understand the dynamics of revolution and the complex interaction of competing social forces. Consequently, like many other ancient historians – Livy and Tacitus for example – he collapses into moralism. Procurators are repressive not because they face rising opposition but because they are bad men. Revolutionaries are not driven to fight by any sense of injustice but because they are egotistical, self-serving, vicious, sinful, and aim to make themselves 'tyrants'. This gratuitous malevolence is, for Josephus, sufficient explanation for the failure of his own class to prevent revolt. However, as Martin Goodman has pointed out, the political weakness of the Jewish *dunatoi* resulted from the shallowness of their social roots. Because the old Hasmonaean ruling class had been largely displaced by Herodian upstarts, and because the high priests had become mere puppets of the authorities, 'the rulers of Judaea were, in a sense, marginal within their own society'. Nor, as Tessa Rajak has stressed, is Josephus' treatment of the popular movement at all adequate. He clearly has a strong sense of class struggle underlying the events he describes – the word *stasis* in ancient Greek discourse usually implies this – yet there is never any systematic attempt to characterise the revolutionary movement and chart its historical development. We know of a Master of Justice from the Dead Sea Scrolls and of Jesus of Nazareth from *The New Testament*, but Josephus ignores the first completely and tells us virtually nothing about the latter. From the same sources we learn much about the revolutionary millenarianism of the poor, but Josephus hardly ever refers to the ideology of the masses. The gaps in his analysis are filled with abuse – the *stasiastai* are simply 'deceivers', 'brigands', 'tyrants'. Our difficulties with his writing are perhaps most acute in the accounts of his military governorship in Galilee. Here the obscurities caused by a limited grasp of the social dynamics at work are compounded by the tendentiousness of multiple self-justifications. As Rajak has observed, in discussing his Galilean command the author was fighting for his reputation on several fronts: he had helped organise a rebellion against Rome; he had had major conflicts with other Jewish resistance leaders; he had at one point been threatened with dismissal from his post by the revolutionary government; he had been defeated by the Romans; and he had secured his own survival by tricking fellow rebels and defecting to the enemy.

Josephus is, then, a difficult writer. Using him as an historical source for the Jewish Revolution is not simply a matter of textual scholarship, important though that is; without recourse to the theory and historiography of other, better documented revolutions, it simply is not possible to make any sense of the patchy and prejudiced account he has left us. Not least important is to realise the degree to which Josephus himself was a product of complex social conflicts, which, when he later came to write about them, he only half-understood. Let us follow him now into the maelstrom of revolutionary politics in Galilee in the winter of AD 66/7 – and see what sense we can make of what he tells us.

Dunatoi and *stasiastai* in revolutionary Galilee

Tiberias, on the western shore of the Sea of Galilee, winter AD 66/67

That Josephus was sent as military governor to Galilee with a dual mission – to fight both Romans and radicals – we have from his own testimony (see the quotation at the beginning of this chapter). His job was to bring the revolt under central control by disarming bands of irregulars, establishing a regular army, and creating an administration dominated by the local *dunatoi*. The last task was more easily accomplished than the others. He appointed a ruling council of 70 elders for Galilee as a whole, and a governor and board of seven magistrates for each town. The idea, as he explained, was 'to win the support of the powerful men by sharing authority with them' and 'that of the people in general by issuing orders through the channel of well-known local men'. Raising a regular army was more difficult. Many of the militias were unwilling to surrender either arms or independence, and, since Josephus lacked the means to force them, they continued to operate alongside the regular forces, sometimes participating in joint operations, but often embroiled in conflict with government authorities. The militia of John of Gischala in northern Galilee, for instance, is said to have numbered 400 men at the outset of the conflict. Yet Josephus clearly did succeed in raising large numbers of government troops. Some of these were loyal regulars – he mentions 4,500 trusted soldiers, plus 600 picked men who formed his personal bodyguard. The rest were conscripted militia, half raised as combatants, half for logistical support, and these seem to have been used mainly in static local defence roles. Their overall numbers are hard to assess, since Josephus' figures – totals of 60,000 infantry, 250 cavalry, and perhaps 40,000 ancillaries – seem grossly exaggerated. The army was organised on Roman lines, with 'decurions', 'centurions' and 'tribunes' as officers, and drilled to carry out elaborate battlefield manoeuvres – though the commander was forced to admit that in such a short time the Jews could not hope to match the discipline and skill of the legions. The soldiers were supplied by levies imposed on the towns, and looting was firmly discouraged.

The plan was for these men to oppose the Roman advance by holding a network of strongpoints across northern Palestine, most of them in Galilee, but with outliers in the Golan Heights to the east. The two major urban centres under Josephus' control – Sepphoris and Tiberias – were fortified, along with about 20 major villages or defensible peaks. Occasionally the work was done under local administration – as at Sepphoris, where there was a large citizen body willing to build the wall, or at Gischala, which remained in effect the private fiefdom of an independent militia – but usually the military governor took charge personally. It is difficult to judge the effectiveness of the defences built, as few datable remains have been identified, but such evidence as we have does not support the disparaging remarks of some commentators. There were about 200 villages in Galilee, but Josephus appears to have selected a small number of strategically important or naturally defensible sites and to have ensured they were properly fortified, strongly garrisoned and well supplied with food and arms. Both the archaeology of the few sites that have been explored and Josephus' own account of the lengthy resistance mounted by two of them argue for a well-executed strategy. The real criticism of the governor is not that his physical defences were wanting. This charge seems not to have been made by his enemies at the time, and his generalship was in many ways highly competent, displaying knowledge of professional Roman practice and considerable technical skill and cunning – so much so that it is difficult to believe he was entirely new to military affairs when he took up his command. The problem was that his strategy was passive. Politically the aim was to defend property and restore order – the property and order of tax-farmers, absentee landlords and debt-collectors. This policy could only sap the enthusiasm of the peasants and bring the government into conflict with popular leaders and independent militias. Militarily, instead of unleashing a revolutionary peasant war in 200 villages, Josephus planned a conventional war, in which, because his regular forces would be outnumbered and outclassed, he had little option but to concentrate them in the static defence of a handful of strongpoints. The two, politics and strategy, were inextricably linked: all-out people's war meant a revolutionary struggle for the Apocalypse and the Jubilee. This was something the military governor of an aristocratic proto-state could not contemplate. But Galilee in AD 67 lent itself to just such a struggle. Let us survey the condition of the province at this critical moment in its history.

Galilee has a higher rainfall than other parts of Palestine, and its cultivation of the Mediterranean staples – cereals, vines and olives – is therefore somewhat more reliable. But, as elsewhere, much of the best land was held by 'foreigners' and absentees, and the Jewish peasants were crowded onto inadequate plots burdened by tax, rent, tithe and debt. The best land in the area was on the coast and in the river valleys, in the Jezreel Valley, on the narrow plains around the Sea of Galilee, and in the south-western hills. Elsewhere, harder rocks and higher peaks created a rugged landscape less hospitable to farmers. This was especially so in Upper Galilee, which was traditionally a remote border territory with poor communications and scattered upland villages. Moreover, in contrast to the hill-country of the centre and north, where a traditional Jewish peasant culture largely survived, the coastal plain to the west was thoroughly Hellenised, the Plain of Jezreel to the south was semi-Hellenised, and stretching away to the south-east were the Greek cities of the Decapolis. There was, therefore, a tension between periphery and hinterland. To move from the southern rim towards the centre and the uplands was to move from a region of cities, rich estates and pagan landlords to one of peasant villages and tiny hill-farms. It was to go from a cosmopolitan society integrated into Mediterranean civilisation, one ruled firmly from above, to an isolated interior which viewed the external world as oppressor and bandit-chiefs as heroes.

The division between Hellenised élite and Jewish peasant was reflected, one way or another, in most of the local conflicts which erupted in AD 66-7 – town against town, Jew against Greek, country against town, plebs against oligarchs, radical war-party against moderate peace-party. There was at first a bewildering confusion of causes in contention – and Josephus' account can be hard-going – but the rival groups gradually crystallised out into three broad tendencies, albeit each of them beset by rows and splits. First there were the active pro-Romans. These included the urban Greeks of Tyre, Ptolemais, Scythopolis, Gadara, Hippus and elsewhere, many of them having ancient feuds with Jewish neighbours and capable of the most murderous anti-semitism. Equally pro-Roman were the royalist supporters of King Herod Agrippa. Much of his own territory had by now been engulfed by revolution (southern Peraea, eastern Galilee, and parts of western Transjordan), but the king's appeal as a symbol of order extended far beyond his own borders to the Hellenised Jewish upper classes as a whole. The pro-Romans were not united, however: many Greeks hated the Herodians as Jewish rulers who favoured 'their own', and the royalists were afflicted by court intrigue and arguments between hawks and doves. The second tendency were the moderate or reluctant supporters of the war, the Jewish *dunatoi* who had been propelled into conflict with Rome by a surging popular movement they were desperate to contain, but who, in many cases, had come to regret their decision and sought a way back into the pro-Roman camp. Rival ambitions and suspicions of treachery poisoned relations within this group, and the general policy was of vacillation over decisions, half-baked measures, and a search for compromise. The third tendency was that of the *stasiastai*, the revolutionaries committed to all-out war and radical social change, whose political base was in the independent militias and among the peasants and urban poor. The ineffectiveness and half-heartedness of many *dunatoi*, especially when this resulted in military defeat, greatly strengthened the appeal of the *stasiastai*. In revolution, as in war, decision-making is essential. Each crisis presents a choice: to move forwards by revolutionary measures, or to relapse into reaction by refusing these; to fight effectively, or not to fight at all. Revolutionary conflicts drive people to the left or the right, and the centre cannot hold. These were the substantive issues behind a personal dispute of exceptional bitterness between Josephus, the aristocratic military governor who ended up a pro-Roman traitor, and John of Gischala, an independent militia-chief from northern Galilee who would die in a Roman prison.

It is virtually impossible to arrive at a true assessment of John, for our only account of him is written by a vengeful personal enemy. A few possibilities can be surmised from a critical reading of *My Life* and *The Jewish War*. Though his origins may have been humble, John ben Levi must have become a man of substance, quite possibly a business entrepreneur and dealer in olives, since he was the dominant figure in his home town of Gischala in Upper Galilee when Josephus arrived, and there is some suggestion that he had held an official post there in the years before the revolution. As a man of wealth and power – albeit a *nouveau riche* – it is probable, as Josephus implies, that John did not choose revolutionary leadership but had it thrust upon him by local insurrection. His choice was to lead the movement or be cast aside and lose his dominance in the town. Later, as a grander stage tempted his ambition, as the self-made man and small-town politician developed into a national leader, he espoused the increasingly radical ideas each successive crisis of the revolution demanded. Perhaps – like Danton in the French Revolution – he was not a principled radical, not even a radical by choice, but an opportunist with popular instincts who moved left with the people whose leader he wished to be.

Since John was not a popular radical, Josephus may at first have hoped to win his allegiance and incorporate the Gischala militia into the 'national' army. This was perhaps the basis on which John was left alone to organise the fortification of the town. But the two men soon clashed over control of Roman grain-stocks in Upper Galilee – they may have been the property of the imperial estate or taxes collected in kind – with Josephus demanding possession and John refusing it. Local control over supplies gave independence to the militias, whereas centralised control would have made them subordinate to government orders; there may, in any case, have been suspicions already about the governor's integrity and his commitment to the revolutionary cause. As well as seizing and retaining the Roman grain, John was also accused by Josephus of 'enriching himself' from the profits of the olive trade and through the imposition of levies on the wealthy. Since he was a popular and effective revolutionary leader, it is difficult to believe that this, if true, was a matter of personal enrichment; it seems more likely that John had a policy of extraordinary requisitioning to support his forces. This seems implicit in Josephus' main charge against John, which is not that he craved wealth so much as personal power. Wealth, for John, was the means to an end, a way of supporting and enlarging the militia which was his power-base. With grossly misplaced indignation – in view of his later behaviour – Josephus reports that one of John's counter-charges against him was that he planned to betray the country to the Romans. The impression we get, reading between the lines of Josephus' account, is that the conflict arose mainly from John's advocacy of what might be termed a 'Jacobin' policy of 'public safety' – that is, he favoured mass activity to defend the revolution, the subordination of individual rights, especially property rights, to the common cause, and extreme hostility to compromising and possibly treacherous leaders. That this was indeed the issue is strongly implied by Josephus' description of events at Tiberias and Tarichaeae on the western shore of the Sea of Galilee. This area became the epicentre of the struggle between *dunatoi* and *stasiastai* over the direction of the revolution in Galilee.

Tiberias was a major centre, one of only two real towns in rebel-controlled northern Palestine. It had been founded early in the first century AD by the client-king Herod Antipas as his royal capital, and had been named in honour of his patron, the emperor Tiberius. It was again part of a Jewish client-kingdom in AD 66 – that of Herod Agrippa II. Though the inhabitants were predominantly Jewish, the town had a distinctly Hellenic flavour: municipal government was modelled on the Greek *polis*, there was much classical architecture and art to be seen, and the town had a flourishing tourist trade based on its hot springs. Now, though, the town was in ferment, as the revolution brought to life both internal social tensions and traditional city-state rivalries. The mainly royalist ruling class, struggling to maintain order, found itself threatened from below by a movement of fishermen, boatmen and other urban poor led by Jesus ben Sapphias, and from within by one Justus ben Pistus, a maverick aristocrat who was flirting with revolution, playing to the crowd, and organising raids on border villages in the territory of neighbouring Decapolis cities with which Tiberias had historic feuds. A major conflict then erupted over the future of the royal palace. Josephus claims that he had government orders to have it demolished on account of its pagan imagery, but that when he finally persuaded the Tiberias *dunatoi* to co-operate in this, they were pre-empted by Jesus ben Sapphias, whose men plundered the palace treasures, fired the building, and purged the town of its Greek and royalist inhabitants. Josephus tells us that he went to Tiberias in person, seized as much of the plunder as he could, and handed it over to local royalists for safe keeping until it could be returned to the king – a Roman client-king, it must be stressed, whose army had been fighting against revolutionary forces since the previous August. This extraordinary intervention by the governor – to protect the property of active counter-revolutionaries – shortly afterwards provoked a furious reaction in nearby Tarichaeae.

A group of local militiamen waylaid the entourage of King Herod Agrippa's chief minister as it passed through the Jezreel Valley and seized all the baggage, which included expensive garments, silver goblets and several hundred gold coins. This was then handed over to the revolutionary authorities to be put to good use. Josephus denounced the militiamen as 'robbers', secured the stolen property, and arranged for it to be returned to the king. As the news spread, a large crowd gathered in Tarichaeae, a small town on the Sea of Galilee where Josephus was staying and the treasure had been stored. Some were from the town itself, others from Tiberias, yet more from local villages. Among the crowd were John ben Levi from Gischala and Jesus ben Sapphias from Tiberias. The latter, brandishing a copy of the Torah, accused the governor of betraying both country and religion, and led a party of armed militants in an attack on the house where Josephus was staying. Deserted by many of his bodyguard, Josephus dressed himself as a supplicant, gave his enemies the slip, and went out to confront the main crowd of protestors at an open-air mass meeting in the circus. Here he succeeded first in dividing them by claiming he had reserved the money to build walls around Tarichaeae, and then he placated most of protestors from outside the town by promising that they also would have walls provided for their settlements. A militant minority, perhaps several hundred strong, were unconvinced. Some of them, returning from the siege of the governor's temporary residence, had tried to prevent him from speaking at all, but the crowd had not supported them. Now, defeated in the public meeting but certain of Josephus' guilt, they pursued him through the streets and again laid siege to the house. From the rooftop Josephus offered to negotiate, and representatives of the protestors were admitted into the house – but the governor was playing for time. At least one of the representatives was flogged, mutilated by having his hand cut off and strung around his neck, and then thrown back into the street. This act of intimidation was effective: most of the protestors must by now have drifted away, and the remnant were easily scared off by the governor's guards. If we can trust our author, it had been an ugly and dangerous clash: the governor, whose policy amounted to funding the counter-revolution, had been accused of treachery and threatened with being cut down in the street or burnt alive inside a building, and he had saved himself only through an unsavoury mixture of subterfuge and brutality. He was, on his own admission, a traitor and a liar, and it is difficult to avoid the conclusion that the *stasiastai* had been justified in wanting his death.

The underlying issues in dispute seem clear enough - a clarity which is especially significant given our source's strong motive for muddying the waters. Should the property of counter-revolutionaries be seized and used to arm the revolution? Or should property rights be upheld at all costs? Should the revolution be controlled (and contained) from above? Or should it be driven by the self-activity of the masses? A decisive battle around these questions was now fought out on the streets of Tiberias.

At about this time – the chronology of events is uncertain since *My Life* and *The Jewish War* do not always agree – four commissioners were dispatched by the aristocratic government in Jerusalem to relieve Josephus of his command. Though the conflict is treated at great length in *My Life*, the government's motives remain obscure. Josephus claims that John of Gischala was the instigator of the whole affair and the principal accomplice of the commissioners once they arrived in Galilee. On the other hand, some sort of popular vote in Jerusalem seems to have gone against Josephus, and the government may have been under strong Zealot pressure to purge a military governor denounced as treacherous by local *stasiastai*. Galilee was in the front-line. The threat of war was most immediate here. The contradiction between political conservatism and revolutionary defence would be most acute in Josephus' command. Probably the commission was not, as Josephus avers, simply a product of malice and bribes; it likely reflects the more radical politics of the revolutionary capital in relation to a conservative general. There is much in Josephus' account that points in this direction. The principal charges against him were those of incompetence, misuse of funds, and 'tyranny'. The government commission comprised two men of his own rank and two who were 'men of the people'. The commissioners' instructions were to kill the governor if he resisted arrest, and, since resistance was anticipated, they were given a large sum of money and a military escort of almost 1,000 men, while messengers were dispatched to major towns in Galilee with orders to raise extra troops and place them under John of Gischala's command. Josephus, on the other hand, rallied those 'who feared they would be at the mercy of the robbers' – code for the property-owning classes – and he mustered a strong military force from among them with which to confront the commissioners. Galilee was soon in the grip of a civil war, in which, though little actual blood was shed at first, both sides competed for the allegiance of the crowd at angry mass meetings. There were sizeable and tense confrontations between gatherings of armed opponents, and the commissioners made a series of abortive attempts to arrest Josephus by trickery. The climactic clash came at Tiberias, at which point the civil war turned bloody and decisive.

John of Gischala entered the town and attempted to rally the radical forces there for a direct challenge to the administration appointed by Josephus. Warned of the danger by his own town governor, Josephus hastened to Tiberias with his bodyguard, hoping to win over the crowd as he had done in Tarichaeae. But Tiberias was now much more hostile, and before Josephus could speak, he was attacked and forced to flee from the circus, escaping from the town by taking boat to Tarichaeae. Josephus' position was, however, a stronger one than first appeared. Tiberias was in advance of Galilee as a whole, its mood already essentially Zealot, its people ready to follow leaders like John ben Levi and Jesus ben Sapphias in attempting to overthrow Josephus. The rest of the province lagged behind: people there were not yet convinced that Josephus was in fact a traitor; most Galileans still regarded the military governor and their own *dunatoi* as reliable revolutionary leaders and accepted their characterisation of their enemies as self-interested 'robbers' and 'tyrants'. As Josephan loyalists massed against Tiberias, John's militia abandoned the town and retreated north, back to the security of Gischala. The commissioners were captured by Josephus' forces and dispatched back to Jerusalem to report the failure of their mission. The plundered property of the rich was restored. There was a witch-hunt of radicals in Lower Galilee, the governor announcing that those who did not surrender their arms would have their property confiscated and their homes burnt down.

The civil war in Galilee ended, therefore, in defeat and demoralisation for the radicals and the militia movement. The effect of this was to shift the balance of power in favour of the royalists and pro-Romans, and the governor's precarious regime was almost unbalanced by the resurgent reaction it had done so much to encourage. The folly of 'moderation' in revolution – the impossibility of steering a middle course between 'extremes' – was immediately apparent in the two key cities of Galilee. In Tiberias, the royalists seized control and invited King Herod Agrippa to send in troops to complete the destruction of the popular movement begun by Josephus' forces. The governor was at Tarichaeae when news of the coup reached him, and, lacking sufficient armed forces to hand, was compelled to improvise a desperate stratagem. He sailed a flotilla of commandeered boats down the coast, giving the false impression they were packed with armed men poised to attack, and bluffed the entire ruling council into surrendering themselves into his hands. This was, however, a short reprieve, for the Tiberias *dunatoi* made at least one further attempt to betray the city to the enemy; they remained a powerful fifth column, forcing the diversion of revolutionary troops badly needed at the front to internal security operations. But there was worse news from Sepphoris. Here the *dunatoi* invited Cestius Gallus to send in a Roman garrison to crush the popular movement and hold the city against Josephus' forces. The governor intervened before the plan could be put into effect, but he then abruptly withdrew his men 'to restrain the violence of the Galileans and preserve the city of Sepphoris'. This bizarre decision, which left a city known to be disloyal unguarded, gave the Romans a bloodless victory. The invitation to them to send in a garrison was renewed and a strong Roman force duly arrived. Josephus' attempt shortly afterwards to retake the city was easily beaten off, and Sepphoris, a large city with strong defences, was turned into an impregnable military base of the counter-revolution deep behind the Jewish front-line, a place from which 'fire and sword' could now be delivered to surrounding villages.

> . . . night and day, in retaliation for [Josephus' attempt to retake the city], the Romans ceaselessly ravaged the plains and plundered the villagers' belongings, killing everyone fit to bear arms and enslaving those who could not resist. From one end of Galilee to the other, there was an orgy of fire and bloodshed; no horror, no calamity was spared; the only safety for the fugitive inhabitants was in the towns which Josephus had fortified.
>
> (*JW*, 3.62-3)

This is of course what classical scholars call a '*topos*' – a stock theme treated in a conventional way as opposed to accurate description of a specific event. Josephus no doubt exaggerates the range of Roman devastation. But the general point stands: the fall of Sepphoris was a grievous loss, and this, together with the royalist threat at Tiberias, was a direct consequence of the governor's policy of prioritising the defence of property over that of the revolution. It was a policy which undermined popular enthusiasm and reduced the potential for mass mobilisation, while strengthening the position of a rich minority who were at best lukewarm and at worst actively hostile towards the revolutionary cause. The Jewish fighters – regulars, government militia, independent bands – who now massed in a string of fortified hilltop villages to face the onslaught of 60,000 professional soldiers did so with the odds stacked against them by their own leader.

Vespasian's army

Ptolemais, on the coast of southern Syria, spring AD 67

The emperor Nero had been on tour in Greece when he summoned Titus Flavius Vespasianus into his presence to appoint him to the special military command for Judaea created after the defeat of Cestius Gallus (**40**). Vespasian – as we know him – cannot have expected it. He had been born into a small-town aristocratic family of landowners, army officers and businessmen. His grandfather had been a commoner, his father had belonged to the second-division equestrian order, and Vespasian was thus a first-generation senator. The Flavian family was, in fact, an excellent example of the class of 'new men' from the Italian municipal aristocracy whose advancement had been such a central feature of the new imperial order founded by Augustus. The advancement of such men depended primarily upon contacts and patronage, but humble origins were often positively advantageous, since the humble, unlike established nobility, appeared unthreatening to those in power. Other requirements of a successful career were that the aspirant should be loyal, deferential and even, if the occasion demanded, sycophantic. (Talent came a rather poor second to these other qualities, though outright incompetence was undesirable for the embarrassment it could cause.) Through its processes of patronage and promotion – a sort of 'new boys' network' – the imperial system created an effective 'aristocracy of office' for the administration and defence of empire. There were indeed still some men from the old families, but increasingly the upper echelons were dominated by ambitious, upwardly mobile careerists with obscure names from out-of-the-way places. The informal selection process – for the aspiring, an awkward ascent through favour and service – functioned to weed out the rebellious, the non-conformist and the overly clever. Rome needed officers, civil servants and technocrats who could be relied upon to obey orders, follow the rules, not make a fuss, and get the job done. Rome was a machine that worked, and it needed replacement parts, not redesign. That Vespasian had just landed a top job tells us much, therefore, about the sort of man he must have been.

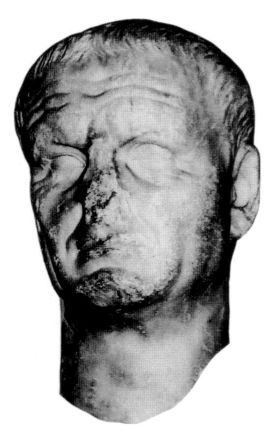

40 *Marble head of Vespasian from a statue, c.AD 70-80, found at Carthage in Tunisia. Though damaged, perhaps by Christians in late antiquity, Vespasian's rather bull-like features are evident.*
British Museum

Early in his career, after commanding a regiment in Thrace, he had held the three successive magistracies leading to the consulship – quaestor, aedile and praetor – by the end of which he seems to have entered the court, where, according to the biographer Suetonius, 'he never missed a chance of winning favour'. His flattery of the tyrannical Caligula, for instance, included the unedifying proposal that special games be held to celebrate a non-existent victory on the German frontier. Under Claudius, he was patronised by the imperial freedman Narcissus, receiving command of the Second Legion *Augusta* during the invasion of Britain, when 'he fought 30 battles, subjugated two warlike tribes, and captured more than 20 towns'. He was eventually rewarded with a consulship, Rome's supreme magistracy, in AD 51, an achievement which gave him proconsular rank and qualified him for governorship of the rich province of Africa. Thereafter, though, his career seems to have stumbled in the shifting sands of factional politics – and, as he advanced through middle age, hopes of greatness must have dimmed, finally to be snuffed out entirely when he nodded off during one of Nero's song recitals and was promptly dismissed from court. Then, at the age of 57, his moment came: appointment to the Judaean command, for which, no doubt, his humble birth, political obscurity and tireless servility were prime qualifications – coupled with the fact that he was of proven military competence and could be relied upon to conduct the forthcoming operations sensibly.

Despite his age, the general, a large, heavily built man with rugged features and a somewhat grim expression, was in perfect health. He was also relaxed and broad-minded: he had little interest in pomp and status-symbols, made would-be flatterers the targets of his active sense of humour, and lived openly with his mistress Caenis after the death of his wife. He worked hard, enjoyed life, and hated pretence. This mix of energy and ease no doubt helped to weld his senior officers into an efficient high command in war – and later, during the civil war of AD 69, into a victorious political faction. Many of these men would, in any case, have been hand-picked family and friends, men who formed a close circle of *amici* from among whom appointments to senior positions could be made with confidence. Vespasian was as much their patron as Nero his, and their future political prospects were intimately bound up with his success (or failure). The higher one's patron rose, broadly speaking, the greater his powers of reward. Especially prominent in this self-serving 'band of brothers' was Vespasian's elder son, the 25-year-old Titus, a brave, burly, flamboyant and vicious youth who was destined to succeed his father, first in the Judaean command, then as emperor.

From Greece, Vespasian dispatched Titus to Alexandria in Egypt to fetch the Fifteenth Legion, while he himself crossed the Dardanelles and went overland to Antioch in Syria. Here he assumed command of an army comprising the Fifth and Tenth Legions, plus 29 auxiliary battalions, and contingents from the armies of the client-kings Herod Agrippa, Antiochus of Commagene, Sohaemus of Emesa, and Malchus of Nabataean Arabia. Shortly afterwards, Vespasian marched his army down the coast to Ptolemais, a major harbour city at the southern tip of Syria, where he established his forward base and main supply-depot (**41**). When Titus arrived from Alexandria with the Fifteenth Legion, the concentration was complete. Already operations had begun: the pro-Roman aristocracy of Sepphoris had appealed for support, and the tribune Placidus had been sent out with a strong force to garrison the city, ravage the surrounding countryside, probe at Jewish strongpoints, and gather intelligence about enemy deployments. Now the main advance could begin. As Vespasian led his army out of Ptolemais for the invasion of Galilee, he was at the pinnacle of his career: a new man from an ordinary Italian town who was now commander-in-chief of the most powerful Roman army in the East.

Not only was it large; the army was also outstandingly professional. Rome's soldiers at this time constituted the finest army of the ancient world, a complete combined-arms force of well-paid and highly motivated volunteers, each man equipped with the best the technology of war could provide, every unit trained and drilled and disciplined to a peak of efficiency. As Vespasian's army marched out, it was headed by an advance guard of auxiliary cavalry and infantry. Their job was to scout ahead, rooting out potential ambushes, repelling any sudden attacks, and seeking intelligence about the enemy. Roman auxiliaries in this period, though recruited from non-citizens and organised in separate battalion-sized units with ethnic names, were increasingly equipped in a standardised way similar to the legions. The cavalry rode large ponies rather than horses, but these had to be tough, for they carried a heavy weight, the rider wearing flexible chainmail or scale armour and an iron helmet, carrying a large

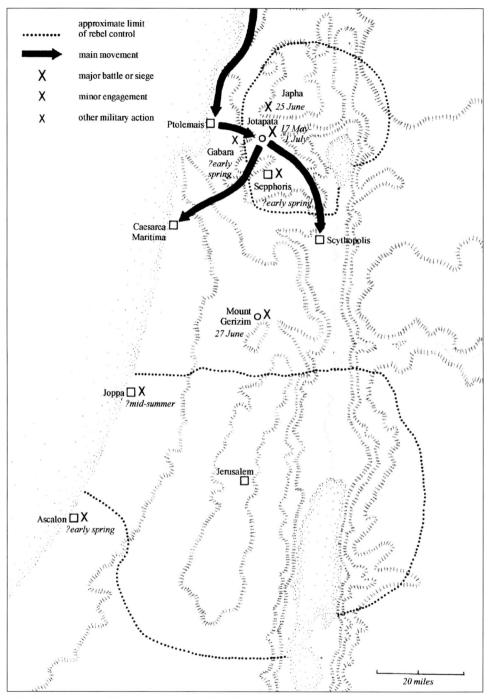

41 *The campaigns of Vespasian, spring and early summer AD 67*

Legend:

.... approximate limit of rebel control

➔ main movement

X major battle or siege

X minor engagement

X other military action

Ptolemais

Japha
X 25 June

Jotapata
X 17 May
1 July

Gabara
?early spring

Sepphoris
?early spring

Caesarea Maritima

Scythopolis

Mount Gerizim
27 June

Joppa X
?mid-summer

Jerusalem

Ascalon X
?early spring

20 miles

oval shield, and armed with lance, javelins and a long slashing sword (*spatha*) (**42**). Like horse-soldiers of other ages, Roman cavalrymen loved show, and many items of equipment were personalised and highly decorated, such as richly coloured shields with individual designs, bronze helmet facings in the style of hair or with figured scenes on the cheeks, and numerous silvered buckles, discs and pendants decorating the harness. They could fight either as skirmishers, using their mobility and missiles, or as shock troops, going in with lance and sword. This is now clear from Peter Connolly's reconstructed Roman saddle based on leather fragments recovered from waterlogged archaeological sites and images of Roman cavalrymen on relief-sculptures. Though they lacked stirrups, men were wedged in their seats by four rigid pommels which gripped their thighs and prevented them being toppled off their horses as they lunged with lances and slashed with swords. Training – on the parade-ground and in the field – was relentless: vaulting into the saddle in full armour; hurling javelins on the move; jumping ditches and walls; galloping in close order; wheeling in formation; practising spear-thrust and sword-play on horseback. They were organised into cavalry 'wings' of 480 (*alae quingenariae*) or 720 (*alae milliariae*), or into mixed cohorts of 120 horse and 480 foot (*cohortes quingenariae equitatae*), or 240 horse and 800 foot (*cohortes milliariae equitatae*). These battalions were divided into separate troops (or *turmae*) of 30 men each. A battalion was commanded by a prefect (*praefectus*) and each troop by a decurion (*decurio*). Josephus tells us there were six cavalry wings and 13 mixed cohorts in Vespasian's army, giving a theoretical maximum of 5,000 horse. Many of these now cantered ahead, hooves thudding, dust rising, arms and trinkets clattering: the advance guard and flank protectors of a huge host of armoured infantry and ox-carts backed up inside the city waiting for space on the road as the column gradually extended out of the gates.

Also probing ahead were light infantry – archers, probably slingers, and possibly javelinmen (**43**). The archers are likely to have been local recruits, since the bow was a favoured weapon of the East, and we hear of Syrian archers fighting in Romania in the early second century, and others posted to Hadrian's Wall in Britain a short time after that. Those shown on Trajan's Column in Rome wore coats of chainmail and conical iron helmets – archers, of course, lacked the protection of shields – and their weapon was the short, curving, composite bow. The basic structure was wood, but this was strengthened on the inside of the upper and lower curves with horn, which gave strength, and on the outside with animal sinew, which was elastic but tough. When strung, the ends of the bow had to be bent back and held under tension, which increased the propulsive energy stored in the bow as the archer drew back the bowstring to shoot an arrow. It is more difficult to speak with confidence about slingers. Where we have depictions – as on Trajan's Column – they appear wearing tunics and capes and carrying slings, slingshot and shields. Slingers are known to have been recruited from many parts of the ancient world – from Mediterranean islands like Crete, Rhodes and the Balearics, and from marginal mainland areas like the uplands of Greece and Thrace – and it seems likely that most armies employed locally available mercenaries. Josephus states that some at least of Vespasian's slingers were Syrians. Archaeologically, Roman slingers are close to invisible. Units may have been

42 *A Roman auxiliary cavalryman of the first century AD. He wears scale armour and an iron helmet, and carries lance, javelins, long sword and an oval body-shield. He is wedged firmly in his seat by a 'Connolly'-type saddle, and his pony has decorated harness-fittings. Many auxiliary infantrymen wore a similar weight of armour and were equipped with javelin, sword and shield*

raised on an ad hoc basis and never incorporated into the regular army. A generation later, under Trajan and Hadrian, we hear of units called *numeri*, which seem, initially at least, to have comprised barbarian irregulars; slingers may have been of this kind. Perhaps also, as some ancient sources attest, regular troops, even including legionaries, were trained in the use of the sling as a subsidiary weapon. Equally obscure are the light javelinmen who may have been present in the advance guard. Some relief-sculptures seem to depict auxiliary infantry who, though armed with spear, sword and shield, lacked armour and fought as specialist skirmishers. Most, though, wore short chainmail jerkins and were trained for close-order shock action. Josephus reports the presence of 'heavy' infantry in the advance guard, and they were probably auxiliaries such as this, men who could, in the face of a strong enemy attack, form a solid line to cover the withdrawal of cavalry and light infantry or protect the main column coming up behind. But their equipment was still lighter than that of legionaries, and they may also have been trained in skirmishing tactics. Tacitus frequently contrasts the 'heavy' legions with the 'light' auxiliaries (*leves cohortes*), and 'medium infantry' might

43 *Roman auxiliary foot-archer and slinger of the first century AD. Both were probably recruited locally, but while archers were organised in regular auxiliary units, slingers seem to have been raised on an ad hoc basis for particular campaigns*

be the best term for the more heavily equipped auxiliary foot. Like the cavalry, they were organised in various battalion-sized units commanded by prefects, either an infantry cohort of 480 (*cohors quingenaria*), or one of 800 (*cohors milliaria*), or one of the two types of mixed infantry-cavalry cohorts described above. These units (or the infantry elements of them) were subdivided into centuries of 80 men (*centuriae*), each commanded by a centurion (*centurio*). Josephus has 10 milliary cohorts and 13 mixed quingenary cohorts in Vespasian's army, giving a theoretical maximum of about 14,000 auxiliary infantry.

The archers and cavalry of the advance guard may also have included some of the men supplied by the eastern client-kings allied to Rome. Josephus does not tell us where they were placed in the column, but he reports Agrippa, Antiochus and Sohaemus each providing 2,000 foot archers and 1,000 cavalry (perhaps an equal number had been ordered from each), and Malchus, the king of Nabataean Arabia, 5,000 foot and 1,000 cavalry, again mainly archers. Our knowledge of such soldiers is hazy. Herod the Great (37-4 BC), unpopular with both Jews and Greeks living in his kingdom, had, as we saw above, depended heavily on professional mercenary soldiers to secure his power. There is clear evidence that Herod Agrippa II inherited part of this old Herodian military infrastructure. Both Idumaeans and Babylonian Jews were settled by Herod in military colonies in Transjordan, and these royalist bastions continued to supply soldiers to Herod's successors in the following century.

Roman military advisors were still present, and one unit of Herod Agrippa's army for which we have evidence from inscriptions bears the highly Romanised regimental name *cohors Augusta* ('Cohort of Augustus'). The very occasional references to unit sizes we have give 400 (for a unit of Gauls) and 500 (for the Babylonian Jewish horse-archers), and it seems sensible to assume that the armies of the client-kings conformed to the Roman cohort model in this respect. Equipment and methods of fighting may sometimes have done so too. But there was also a strong eastern tradition of war – based on cavalry, mobility, missile shooting, and skirmishing – which was different from the Graeco-Roman emphasis on heavy infantry collision. Josephus' testimony strongly suggests that, whatever the Roman influence on unit size, organisation and drill, eastern armies contained few heavy infantry and were composed largely of armoured cavalry and both horse and foot archers.

Behind the advance guard came the surveyors and engineers. Roman army surveyors had the job of seeking out a suitable campsite for the night ahead. They needed a place on clear ground that was not overlooked, in a dry and healthy location, and with good access to water, fodder, food and wood (in that order). Once chosen, they would mark out the boundaries and the lanes on the ground using the *groma* – a staff with a cross-piece on top from which dangled four plumb-bobs arranged so that the surveyor could sight in straight lines and right-angles. Then the 10 men from each century who had accompanied them for the purpose would set to work digging in, surrounding the campsite with ditch, bank and palisade to make it secure against enemy attack. Alongside them near the front of the column were the engineers, who could help with camp construction at the end of the march, but whose main job was to ensure clear passage for the army – straightening out bends in the road, levelling uneven surfaces, cutting down obstructive woods. A marching column was painfully slow and desperately vulnerable. It moved at the speed of the slowest element – the ox-drawn carts of the baggage-train – and it stretched for miles across the countryside. There are uncertainties about Josephus' estimate of 60,000 men for the entire army. Was it based on actual or theoretical unit strengths, and did it include all the drivers, servants and camp-followers? We do not know, but if Vespasian's army was this large, and if the main body of the foot marched six abreast and the horse three, it may have extended for 20 miles, so that the front of the column would have ended its day's march long before the rear had left Ptolemais – a continuous stream of men, beasts and creaking carts lumbering forwards through dust and dung. Any impediment in the road, any hold-up or bottleneck, and the whole column would concertina to a halt and be left stacked up in the middle of nowhere. It was the job of officers to stagger the departure, space the column, and, once each unit had taken its place and set off, keep the men moving forward, close to those in front. And it was the job of the engineers up near the head of the column to guarantee a clear and easy road, so the forward momentum could be maintained, and, if all went well, the whole army cover the 10 or 15 miles that would count as a good day's march.

Behind the advance guard and the surveyors and engineers came the high command and the siege train with a strong escort of auxiliary cavalry on their flanks. There were carts piled up with officers' tents, furniture, bedding and personal belongings, then Vespasian himself and his staff, protected by a bodyguard of picked men, and behind them the legionary cavalry, 120 from each of the three legions in the column. Next along was the siege train, followed by the rest of the senior officers, also with an armed escort. Six of the officers are likely to have been of senatorial rank: the three legion commanders (*legati*) and three of the 18 military tribunes (*tribuni*) who also served as legion officers. These men were not professional soldiers, but were at different stages in the mixed political and military career that had become traditional for senators. The Roman historian Tacitus records that his father-in-law, the future governor of Britain Gnaeus Julius Agricola (AD 40–93), held successively a military tribunate in Britain (when he was 21), a quaestorship in Asia (at 24), a plebeian tribunate in Rome (at 26), a praetorship in Rome (at 28), and then command of a legion in Britain (at 30). He went on to reach the summit of a senatorial career: the consulship and a top military governorship. But alongside these six politician-soldiers there were 44 fully professional officers – five military tribunes for each of the three legions, and a commanding prefect for each of the 29 auxiliary battalions. All of these were members of the lesser equestrian order, for whom the army was a career in itself, not simply a staging post to political advancement. There were also senior officers who had risen from the ranks, coming through the centurionate eventually to reach – perhaps when grizzled veterans of 20 or 30 years' service – the rank of either first centurion (*primus pilus*) or camp-prefect (*praefectus castrorum*) in their legion. This meant there were six of these generals raised from the ranks in Vespasian's army, common men who had their places alongside aristocratic legates, tribunes and prefects at councils of war – though as the great column wound its way out of Ptolemais, it is likely that they marched with the soldiers in the main column.

This came immediately behind the senior officers. Here, perhaps as much as 10 miles behind the head of the column, marched the legions, each headed by its eagle, the centurial standards, and the trumpeters. The legions were at the peak of their prowess in the first century AD. They were composed entirely of Roman citizens who had volunteered to serve. The terms were good – certainly by the standards of contemporary civilian life – with high pay, good accommodation, food and health-care, generous bonuses, and an excellent retirement package. Arms and armour were first class, drilling was relentless, and discipline severe, so that the legions achieved an unrivalled battlefield dominance that ensured high morale, strong regimental pride, and a fierce nationalist contempt for Rome's enemies and subject peoples.

Though some probably continued to wear chainmail or scale armour, many legionaries now wore the new *lorica segmentata* introduced a few decades' before (**44**). Three complete suits have been recovered from Corbridge in north Britain. They comprised overlapping and articulated strips of iron held together by leather straps and bronze hinges, hooks and buckles, thus combining the protective strength of plate-metal with the flexibility of chainmail. Each man wore a two-part casing around his torso and two large shoulder-guards. He also wore an iron helmet with a high narrow peak, wide cheek-pieces, and a projecting neck-guard. Some men – it was perhaps a matter of personal choice and expense – may also have had arm-guards and greaves. All carried the standard legionary arms: shield, javelin and sword. The

44 *A Roman legionary of the later first century AD, wearing steel helmet, segmental plate-armour (*lorica segmentata*), and optional arm-guard and greaves, and equipped with shield (*scutum*), short sword (*gladius*), and dagger (*pugio*), his javelin (*pilum*) having already been thrown*

scutum was a large, curving, rectangular shield held in a horizontal hand-grip. An example from Dura Europos in Syria shows it to have been made from strips of wood glued together to form a three-layered plywood which was then covered with hide or felt. Huddled down under missile fire, or going in low to fight hand-to-hand, a man could protect his whole body behind a *scutum*. Its strength (as a result of which it weighed 13lb or 6kg) enabled it to absorb the shock of even the most violent blows. It was also itself a weapon, the single horizontal hand-grip with a bronze boss on the outside making it possible to punch with the shield and send an opponent staggering backwards. The legionary javelin was the *pilum*, its small pyramidal head and long thin metal shaft (about 0.6m) designed to bore through shields and armour to reach the flesh behind. For close-quarters work, legionaries used the *gladius*, a relatively short (0.4-0.5m), straight-edged, sharp-pointed weapon designed more for stabbing than slashing, allowing the legionary to lunge forwards to deliver potentially lethal thrusts at his opponent without exposing his own body. Many examples of both *pila* and *gladii* – the metal parts at least – have been found. Archaeology has also recovered many fragments of other items of legionary equipment, including much that was personalised – decorated sword and dagger scabbards, engraved shield bosses, and various belt-plates and strap-ends.

Each legion comprised approximately 5,000 men: there were 10 cohorts (the basic tactical units), each divided into six centuries of 80 men each, with an additional 120 cavalry attached to the unit as a whole. Below the ranks of the senior officers – the legate, the six tribunes, the first centurion, and the camp-prefect – there were the junior officers in command of each century: a centurion, a deputy-centurion (*optio*), a standard-bearer (*signifer*), and an orderly (*tesserarius*). The military skill, gritty resolution and unswerving loyalty of the centurionate was a central feature of the Roman imperial army. The centurions were, of course, long-service veterans who had risen from the ranks, but their devotion to the army, its discipline and the imperial mission was cemented by privilege. Roman army pay differentials were extreme: auxiliary infantry received 75 *denarii* a year, auxiliary cavalry 150, legionaries 225, deputy-centurions and standard-bearers 500, but full centurions a staggering 3,750. The same huge gap is evident in the layout of Roman forts and the accommodation allocated respectively to centurions and rank-and-file soldiers: a centurion might have had 30 times as much domestic space in the officer's quarters at the end of a barrack-block as each man had in the two rooms he shared with seven other men. When mass mutinies broke out in the legions on the Rhine and Danube in AD 14, one of the soldiers' grievances was the bullying behaviour of centurions, and some were lynched before the disorders were quelled. But as long as brutal discipline and the rewards of victory and loyal service held in check the class tensions in the Roman army – as they usually did – the centurions were pivotal. They enforced the endless round of fatigues, drills, marches and inspections, and in battle, in that inferno of carnage and terror on which history so often turns, they set the example, gave the direction and inspired the fear that held the Roman line together unto victory.

Fifteen thousand crack Roman heavy infantry under 180 centurions formed the core of the army and the centre of the column marching into Galilee in spring AD 67. They probably marched in full armour as a precaution against sudden attack, perhaps carrying much of their equipment on their shoulders, a requirement that kept them tough, made them self-sufficient in a crisis, and helped lighten the baggage-train. In addition to being clothed in heavy tunic and military cloak, they bore more than 20kg (44lb) of arms and armour, and may each have humped 30kg (66lbs) of equipment, including cooking utensils, palisade stake, entrenching tool, several days' rations, water flask, and personal belongings. With the legionaries came their drivers and servants urging forward mules and carts laden with tents, millstones, other heavy gear, and the regimental artillery. Behind the cohorts of legionaries came more cohorts of auxiliaries, and behind them, finally, perhaps more than 15 miles back from the head of the column, indeed perhaps not setting out until after many thousands had already reached the new campsite, there came the rear guard, which, like the advance guard, comprised cavalry, skirmishers and medium infantry supports.

Vespasian commanded an expensive, high-tech, fully professional army. Every man was a well-equipped and thoroughly trained specialist. Losses were expensive and hard to replace. When Augustus had demobilised the civil war armies and moved his reduced standing army onto the frontiers at the end of the preceding century, he had left himself with no military reserve; pretty well every unit was in the line.

Consequently, when Varus lost three whole legions in Germany in AD 9, the frontier defences had been left so denuded that all offensive operations everywhere had been suspended. Since that time, no reserve had been created; the Augustan system, which reduced both the cost of the army and its political weight, remained in place. All Roman generals knew that the soldiers entrusted to them were highly valued – especially the citizen legionaries. Gaps in the line could not easily be made good, and any major disaster would threaten the security of the whole empire. Roman generalship was always aggressive, but now, under the emperors, aggression was tempered with caution. The aim was to accumulate sufficient power for the task in hand, to marshal it carefully to the point of decision, and only then to unleash it with maximum ferocity. Mistakes could still happen. It was not gung-ho heroics that had brought down Cestius Gallus, but his grave underestimation of the strength of the rebellion. That mistake would not be repeated. The Jewish revolutionaries were not some rioting mob or band of outlaws; they were tens of thousands of determined guerrilla fighters, many of them now well equipped and trained, defending a network of formidable strongpoints with one of the greatest fortress-cities in the world at its centre. To go straight for that centre – to repeat Gallus' rapid drive on Jerusalem – would have been extreme folly. Vespasian's strategy was to fight a long war, each move carefully staged, avoiding undue risks, reducing the rebels bit by bit through a succession of skirmishes and sieges, while destroying their infrastructure and will to fight with a ruthless application of fire and sword to villages and farmland. It was to be a terrible war of attrition and annihilation. With such a strategy, the first objective had to be the destruction of revolutionary Galilee, which would restore full communications with Herod Agrippa's territories in northern Transjordan, relieve the Decapolis cities of any Jewish threat, and secure the Roman rear for an advance through Judaea to the revolutionary capital.

The siege of Jotapata

Jotapata, western Galilee, 17 May to 4 July AD 67
At first there was panic on the Jewish side. The invading Roman army was of great size and the prospect of facing it in conventional pitched battle was too terrifying to contemplate. The main Jewish field-army, in camp a short distance from Sepphoris in south-western Galilee under Josephus' direct command, disintegrated as men deserted in droves for the safety of fortified strongpoints (**41**). Josephus himself fell back with the remnant of his army on Tiberias, apparently convinced that Galilee could not be held and determined either to broker an end to the war or at least to save himself by defecting to the enemy. Then came news of the fate of Gabara, an upland village with weak defences, which lay on the Roman army's line of march about 12 miles inland from Ptolemais. Vespasian chose Gabara to make an example. The village was stormed, its men massacred, its women raped and killed, and its buildings torched. Gabara, in a single terrible day, simply ceased to exist. The smaller settlements nearby were also destroyed and any occupants caught sold into slavery.

45 *General view of Jotapata looking south from the Roman position. The town itself lay behind the hill in the centre of the picture – the 'north hill' of Josephus' account – and was protected by deep ravines on the other three sides. Traces of the Jewish wall can be seen on the lower slope of the hill just above the larger clumps of olive trees. The boulder-strewn ground in front was where the Romans built their ramps and massed for assault*

Just as Gallus had done, Vespasian was applying the customary policy of fire and sword with deliberate purpose: either the enemy would be terrorised into immediate submission; or be forced to risk his forces in pitched battle in defence of territory; or have his logistical base systematically destroyed. It was the inescapable logic of imperialist war against a rebellious people – what great power strategists would today call 'counter-insurgency war' or 'the war against terrorism'. It is the logic of war in general driven to its ultimate extreme of victory through annihilation.

Despite the terror, however, the Jewish defence did not collapse at the first impact. The shock of the Roman invasion had scattered the waverers and stunned the more resolute, but war is full of shocks and these are followed by periods of read-justment, as men take in the news, debate its significance, and decide if and how they can fight on. The key to the defence of Galilee was the small fortified town of Jotapata (**45** & **colour plate 13**). It was located on the north-western edge of Lower Galilee, where it covered the heartland of the province against the approaching Roman army and formed the lynchpin of the ragged line of outposts strung out across the uplands. The site lay amid hills with a difficult approach along a rough track. The town had been built on a steep-sided ridge with deep ravines to the east, south and west, which precluded any attack from these directions. To the north of the town was a low round-topped hill which had been incorporated within the defences because it commanded the site. Beyond the hill and the northern defensive wall, the ground dipped before rising again to a higher peak perhaps three-quarters of a mile away (**colour plate 14**). This narrow saddle between two hills was the natural battleground for possession of Jotapata.

Josephus records that he made Jotapata the most heavily fortified and garrisoned of his strongpoints, and it was here that he decided to take his own stand (**46**). The Romans too knew the importance of the site and had already probed the defences. The tribune Placidus, sent ahead of the main army with a large force of cavalry and infantry on an armed reconnaissance, had found the garrison to be large and aggressive. The defenders had ambushed the Roman column in the hills outside the town and driven it off under a hail of long-range shot. Aware of both its strategic importance and tactical strength, Vespasian swung his main force south and marched on Jotapata, sending engineers ahead to widen and level the track. Josephus left Tiberias for the front-line, and, just before the Roman grip closed around it, slipped into the town to assume command of the defence. Soon after, Placidus' Roman cavalry set up a cordon on the hills ringing the town to prevent anyone entering or leaving. The day after, the main force arrived, setting up camp on the rising ground to the north, and interposing a solid line of infantry and cavalry around the town to establish a secure blockade. Jotapata was thereby cut off from the outside world, and the defenders, watching from the towers and battlements on the north side of the town, were trapped. From now on they would live with the stomach-sinking fear of the besieged.

Once a siege began – the defenders having foregone their chance to flee or surrender – the convention was that, if the town fell, its people would be completely destroyed. This destruction was usually accomplished in two stages. First was the frenzied sack of the city as the soldiers broke in. Men of fighting age would be cut down, sometimes along with women, children, old people and even domestic animals; women would be gang-raped; all moveable property of value would be plundered; and buildings and possessions would be ransacked and vandalised. Often the soldiers would be completely out of control – whether given licence by their officers or heedless of any attempted restraint – and in the sack would wage total war against the defenceless, operating for a few terrible hours in a moral vacuum where the old and frail might be run through with swords, women raped to death in their homes, and the heads of children smashed against walls. Then, as the frenzy of the rank and file subsided, the cold calculation of officers took over. Men of fighting age might be mutilated and cast adrift, or tortured and executed, or sold to the slave dealers. Women, children and old men would usually be enslaved, except for the decrepit, who might be executed or left to fend for themselves. The sack, then, was not simply a moment of madness and bloodlust; it involved ordered, calculated, measured terror. Its purpose was to destroy the will to resist elsewhere and to spare the conqueror the time and expense of further sieges. According to Polybius, the deliberate purpose of 'the Roman custom' of massacre and enslavement in captured cities was 'to inspire terror'. Livy calmly explains that when news spread of the sack of Agrigentum in Sicily during the Second Punic War, there was 'an immediate shift in favour of Rome', and some 60 towns were betrayed or surrendered in the

46 *Ruined walls on the lower slopes of the north hill at Jotapata. Little evidence survives on the site of the Jewish War defences*

following few weeks. Fear of such a fate must have gnawed at the nerves of every man and woman trapped inside Jotapata in May AD 67. Hatred of the oppressor had brought many to this place in arms; but now that the struggle had begun, it was with the desperation of the doomed that they would fight.

The fighting began immediately. Vespasian first tried to exploit the morale shock induced by a large Roman army's sudden appearance – not just the intimidating sight of so many armoured men with such lethal weaponry, but the machine-like way in which they marched, manoeuvred and entrenched. The men on the wall were peasants, half-trained at best, mostly without armour, clutching at weapons hammered out in local villages. A mere demonstration of military power might, in the circumstances, be enough to collapse their morale and clear the walls. Not only would this save the Romans the time and expense of a siege, but it would give their campaign a rapid forward momentum intimidating to opponents. So the day after his army's arrival at Jotapata, and for another four days after that, Vespasian ordered concentrated missile-shooting and massed assaults by heavy infantry. But Josephus countered by organising large-scale sorties which surged out through the town gateways to engage the Romans in front of the walls. Defenders have the great advantage of surprise in such operations. They can observe the enemy's conduct from the walls at leisure and plan carefully an appropriate response; they can choose the time and direction of an attack; and they can strike at men who are unprepared.

Enemy units constructing siege works, shooting at the walls or mounting an assault are always vulnerable to a sudden swoop which strikes when they are scattered, unsupported or have a flank exposed. Even so, the fighting remained tentative and fitful, with much long-range shooting, protracted stand-offs between opposing lines, and fairly light casualties – Josephus reports only 13 Romans and 17 Jews killed on the first day. Since it was hoped they might succeed more by moral force than physical struggle, the Roman assaults had been ill-prepared. When the besiegers encountered unexpectedly vigorous resistance, they faltered, their forward movement blocked by the enemy on the wall to their front and hamstrung by the threat of enemy sorties on the flanks. The Jews, on the other hand, lacking the discipline, armour and weapon-handling skill for close-quarters action, could not attempt an all-out counterattack to drive back the Roman line in front of the wall. The struggle became bogged down, and at the end of five days Vespasian called off the assaults and assembled his senior officers for a council of war.

Jotapata was too strong to be stormed and taken in direct assault. Its defences would have to be reduced, and this meant recourse to conventional siege warfare. The plan was to construct a platform of earth, stone and timber extending from the Roman lines to the Jewish wall, which would fill in the intervening dip and provide a level approach for heavy siege engines (**colour plate 15**). Vespasian divided his army into large work-details, one to cut trees from the surrounding heights to create the framework for the platform, a second to collect stones to form revetments between the timbers, a third to excavate the huge quantities of earth needed for the infill. It was in this kind of work, no less than in pitched battle, that the Roman army showed its professionalism. The construction of siege works required the services of a corps of military engineers and the presence of many skilled artisans in the ranks. It also required large investments of labour, time and logistics: thousands of men might have to toil for a fortnight to build a single platform, and all the while they consumed the army's supplies. If the estimate of 60,000 men for Vespasian's army is correct, his total supply needs – to support infantry, cavalry, non-combatants, baggage- and pack-animals – may have been around 300 tons of grain and fodder and 90,000 gallons (340,000 litres) of water each day. Meantime, the Jews mounted an aggressive defence, attempting to disrupt the siege works by missile shooting and sorties. The men engaged in the work were very vulnerable and had to be protected by others detailed for this purpose. Vespasian had some erect a row of hurdles – large protective screens made of wood – to deflect enemy missiles, and he deployed his artillery, archers, slingers and javelinmen to maintain a constant barrage against the town-wall while the work was proceeding. The weight of shot was effective in suppressing enemy shooting from the battlements, but the Jews instead launched a series of hit-and-run sorties by small units to tear down hurdles and attack the men behind, or, after the Romans had retired for the day, to break up sections of the platform and fire the timber supports. Vespasian in turn frustrated the sorties by linking the hurdles together to create a continuous screen along his front; without clear avenues of attack, it became too dangerous to approach the Roman works, and the Jews henceforward remained inside their defences.

As the Roman platform rose unhindered, the siege entered its third phase. The threat now to the defenders was that the platform would soon reach their north wall at a height level with the battlements. Roman assault forces would then be able to form up in depth and simply storm forwards over gangplanks against a thin line of defenders on the narrow parapet opposite. Josephus therefore ordered the stonemasons in the town to supervise the heightening of the existing wall, and arranged for the soldiers and townspeople carrying out this work to be protected from enemy missiles by screens of raw ox-hide. The work was done in relays, night and day, and the wall was soon raised to a height of almost 10m, with a new parapet at the top, and towers spaced at short intervals to allow enfilade fire into the flanks of attackers (**colour plate 15**). The Roman platform was now dwarfed and seemed redundant. Jewish confidence was restored and, with Roman morale depressed, the defenders went on the offensive again with a new series of surprise sorties on the enemy's lines.

Vespasian changed tactics again, abandoning active siege operations for the time being in favour of a passive blockade to weaken the defenders through hunger and thirst. Though well supplied with provisions, water was indeed a problem inside the town. There was no natural spring on either the southern ridge or the northern hill, so the defenders were entirely dependent on reserves held in numerous, large, rock-cut cisterns filled with winter rainwater (**47**). With hardly any rain to replenish supplies in May and June, and with the town population swollen by refugees and soldiers, consumption was fast emptying the cisterns. The Romans suspected a shortage. The entrances to the cisterns were located towards the top of the northern hill, and from their own position the Romans could see over the northern wall of the town to the point where the Jews queued each day to collect their water ration. So days were now passed in boredom, heat and thirst, as men on both sides watched and waited with nothing to do, except for the Roman artillerymen taking pot-shots at the water queue on the northern hill. If the siege had continued in this way, the Jews would certainly have been defeated, since their water would indeed have given out. Josephus therefore proposed that he should lead a breakout with the intention of raising a relief army in the rest of Galilee, but the idea was scotched by the opposition of townspeople who feared abandonment by their commander (whose sincerity may well have been in doubt). Instead, Josephus broke the deadlock with a ruse designed to dispel the Roman conviction that time was on their side and the town would soon die of thirst. He ordered numbers of his men to wash their outer garments and hang them out to dry on the battlements so that the walls ran with water. The ruse worked. Vespasian, who had no certain information about the amount of water left in the cisterns, was persuaded there was an ample supply, and, since he simply could not afford to become bogged down for months in the siege of a single town, he decided to resume offensive operations. Work recommenced on the old platform, which would have to be wider and taller to threaten the heightened north wall, and other platforms were built beside it, so that a multiple-approach assault would eventually be possible.

At the same time, their confidence renewed by Josephus' decision to fight on and by the success of his ruse, the Jews also resumed the offensive, mounting fresh sorties against the Roman siege works, some ranging as far as the picket lines around the

47 *The north hill at Jotapata is honeycombed with underground cisterns. This view is taken from inside one of them looking upwards at an opening sealed by a manhole cover — a view highly reminiscent of Josephus' description of his hiding-place at the end of the siege*

Roman camp on the opposite rise. These remained essentially hit-and-run raids. Success depended chiefly upon surprise, the mobility of lightly equipped men, and the élan of unconventional revolutionary fighters. The attack might come in the sleepy tedium of a hot afternoon to strike down men dispersed, tired and at ease. As alarm spread and fighting flared, the besiegers would rush to arms and engage piecemeal, forming improvised lines where they could, or embroiling themselves in chaotic running battles. Roman casualties could be relatively high in such confused fighting, and Vespasian attempted to limit the attrition by ordering his legionaries to avoid engaging enemy sorties, deploying instead strong forces of artillery and light infantry to drive off the assaults with missiles.

Slowly, under heavy guard and constant attack, the platforms grew menacingly larger, edging towards the Jewish wall. When only a short gap intervened between platforms and walls, a battering ram was pushed forwards to begin the assault, its work protected by a continuous barrage of shot from artillery, archers and slingers against the enemy battlements above. The machine comprised a timber beam with a heavy iron head suspended horizontally on ropes from the roof of an enormous wooden shed (**48**). The sloping sides were covered by heavy protective hurdles, and beneath were dozens of men who crewed the machine, manoeuvring it forwards into position, then swinging the giant beam backwards and forwards so that the iron head

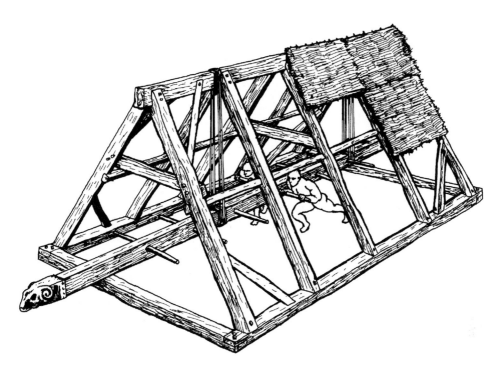

48 *A Roman battering ram, comprising a heavy timber frame, a protective covering of wattle hurdles, and the ram itself suspended from the roof and equipped with projecting spars to facilitate operation*

smashed repeatedly into the enemy wall. Because of the height of the platform on which it stood, the ram struck at the weaker upper parts of the wall, and it pounded relentlessly with great force at the same spot, gradually fracturing and dislodging the stone. The Jews tried to protect the wall by lowering sacks filled with chaff which they positioned in front of the ram to act as cushions. But this device was frustrated when the Romans deployed reaping hooks on the end of long poles to sever the ropes supporting the sacks. As the rhythmic thudding of the ram resumed, each blow sending a shudder through the stone, a major breach seemed imminent.

But the resourcefulness of the Jewish defenders was considerable. Fire, always prominent in the armoury of siege warfare, could be immensely destructive in the right conditions, but, since unpredictable and hard to control, was often a weapon of last resort. Now, if ever, was a moment to try it, but with the Romans massed close to the walls in support of the ram, only a sortie in great strength would allow a firing party to do its work. Men were deployed on the battlements to rain down missiles; Josephus recounts that one of these succeeded in breaking the head off the ram by dropping a huge stone, after which he leapt down, seized the head in his arms, climbed back onto the wall, and only then collapsed with wounds in five places. Others sallied out to attack the legionaries protecting the Roman works, in some cases breaking through gaps in the line and scattering their enemies in flight, such was the suddenness and violence of the onslaught. This gave opportunity to the firing parties. Armed with flaming mixtures of dry wood, bitumen, pitch and brimstone – carried perhaps on the ends of torches or in large pots – they rushed forth to hurl them at the timber parts of machines, hurdles and platforms. Some fires took hold and real damage was done, but, without a general conflagration, and with the besiegers hurriedly heaping earth over other exposed timbers, the battering ram and the platforms survived the attack. The Jews lacked the numbers and weight to sustain a close-quarters struggle beyond the walls once the Romans had recovered from the surprise, and they fell back inside the town to continue the battle from the ramparts. Now, as darkness fell, their own fires told against them, lighting their bodies against the sky as targets for the Roman artillery. Brave men might lean out for a moment to strike at the great machine beneath their wall, but their missiles bounced harmlessly off the hurdle roofs below, and each time they risked instant death from a high-velocity bolt or boulder. Bodies were hurtled off the parapet and smashed corpses lay in bizarre poses on the ground behind it. The artillery barrage continued through the night, allowing the ram to do its work, until, in the early hours, the wall in front of it finally gave way and collapsed into rubble.

At dawn on 20 June, after a brief rest, Vespasian marshalled his army for what he believed would be the final assault (**colour plate 15**). The breach in the wall, though it may have been only a few metres wide, was the portal through which his heavy shock troops might be expected to force a way into the town. They would have the advantage of attacking in great depth, their reserves backed up along the platform behind, while the defenders would be perched on the rubble of the collapsed wall, probably, given the height above ground level of the breach, with a considerable drop behind them. The Romans, too, would have the advantage in close-quarters fighting of their armour, superior weaponry and special training. If they could force just a small penetration, they might begin to roll up the Jewish line on either side of the breach, start a general panic among the defenders, and allow the besiegers to surge into the town along the whole front. To clear an entry through the breach, Vespasian dismounted the pick of his cavalry and deployed them in three units at the head of his assault column, each man fully armoured and with levelled lance, while rank upon rank of legionary heavy infantry were formed behind in close support. On either side of the main column, the rest of the army was drawn up, the cavalry forming a cordon to prevent any breakouts from the town, lines of archers, slingers and artillery deployed to deliver a barrage of suppressing fire, and, interspersed among these, units of heavy infantry equipped with ladders who would move forwards under the barrage to attempt to scale undamaged parts of the wall and draw defenders away from the main effort at the breach. The grand assault was to be a fully combined-arms operation – as successful siege assaults almost always were.

Suddenly the air filled with an ear-splitting roar as the trumpets of the entire army blared and thousands of men raised their battle-cry. Might not sight and sound alone crack the morale of the men in the Jewish line? Many must have been sick with fear. We know from accounts of recent combat that at such moments some men lose physical control and vomit, urinate or defecate involuntarily, and that others become demented and wander off in a daze of mental shock. Josephus knew the danger well enough. He had ordered all women to be locked inside their houses and to remain silent lest their fear panic the men in the line. And he had ordered his men to stop their ears to deaden the roar that he knew would announce the start of the missile storm and the massed assault.

The sky quickly filled with lethal flying objects, and the defenders crouched down behind their shields, avoiding exposure until the last minute, waiting for the armoured assault columns to reach the wall. What was it like for these men facing a Roman missile storm? The battle was fought on a narrow front. On either side of the neck of land on which the Roman platforms had been constructed, the ground falls away sharply, so the fighting lines were probably compressed onto a front of not much more than 250m (**45**). But because the defenders were raised up by the slope of the northern hill and their own 10m-high wall, they could be targeted by ranks of missile-men banked up to shoot over the heads of their comrades, especially where they could be deployed on rising ground to the north. Given the constraints of the ground – and the effective ranges of ancient hand-held missile weapons – it is likely that Vespasian was able to deploy only between 1,000 and 1,500 archers and slingers at any one time (**43**). There is much dispute among specialists about the ranges of ancient weapons, but a unit of archers using the composite bow could probably deliver worthwhile volleys of unaimed shots at up to 150-200m, 'effective' aimed shots at up to 75m, and armour-piercing shots at distances below this. Slingers using lead shot probably had a similar range, but without any armour-piercing potential. At Jotapata, however, as in siege operations generally, the need to shoot upwards at an enemy on a raised parapet would have reduced these ranges considerably. We discussed above the many 'inefficiencies of the battlefield' likely to impede effective missile shooting. How might these factors have affected the Romans on the day of Vespasian's grand assault? His archers and slingers were all professionals, there were reserves to provide regular relief for men in the front-line, and the weight of Roman shot seems to have suppressed any Jewish response. Overall performance is likely therefore to have been good.

Behind the archers and slingers, Vespasian deployed his artillery. Josephus reports 160 machines in all at Jotapata. This total is corroborated by other testimony which implies that each century was responsible for one machine (which would give us 180 for three legions). Josephus and other writers also attest three broad classes of ordnance. Most common were the light bolt-shooters (*scorpiones*), which were carried and operated by a couple of men, were capable of rapid fire, and could be used in close support of front-line infantry (**49**). This numerous light artillery (perhaps two-thirds of the total) was complemented by more powerful but less mobile field artillery, comprising heavy spear-shooters (*catapultae*), and even heavier stone-throwers (*ballistae*) (**50** & **51**). It is clear also – from Josephus and other historians, from surviving ancient technical treatises, and from archaeological finds of artillery parts – that there were several different calibres of each type, and that it was the smaller machines that predominated. Most probably, since they were expensive to manufacture, old machines were repaired for as long as possible, new machines

49   *A Roman light bolt-shooter (scorpio)*

acquired piecemeal, and each legion ended up with a range of ordnance. All types were powered by two springs formed by bundles of twisted sinew, hair or rope held under tension in a wooden frame. Top and bottom each spring-bundle was threaded through a round metal washer and held in place by a metal crosspiece. Since this device could be rotated in a metal counterplate fixed to the wooden frame, the spring-bundles could be twisted to tighten them and increase their stored torsion power. Between the two springs ran a central stock, comprising a fixed part, the case, and a moving part, the slider. A projecting bow-arm was gripped tightly by each spring-bundle, and the bowstring ran across the stock. The slider allowed a claw and trigger device to be brought forward to engage the bowstring, and a winch operated by hand-spikes and a ratchet-and-pawl mechanism facilitated withdrawal of the bowstring. Reconstructed machines have revealed that the maximum effective range was probably about 300m, with little variation between types and calibres, since correspondingly more powerful springs were used to shoot heavier projectiles.

Josephus reports that when Vespasian's archers, slingers and artillery began shooting the sky was darkened as it filled with missiles. Though an exaggeration, it is true that, because of the low velocity of the weaponry involved, men would have seen the missiles flying through the air, and, given the numbers shooting and their likely battle-field performance, there may at any one moment have been two or three large stones, a dozen or so bolts and spears, and two or three hundred arrows and sling-stones in motion. They would also have heard the projectiles whistling towards them, especially the larger and higher velocity artillery shot, and the sound of the impacts as they crashed down all around them. It is little wonder that Josephus had ordered his men to take cover during the barrage and not to attempt return shooting. An enormous volume of converging shot was concentrated along a front of perhaps 250m at the most, and the chances of an exposed man being hit were therefore considerable.

Arrows and sling-stones did not usually kill, but they could inflict crippling and sometimes horrifying injuries, or, perhaps more frequently, inflict several injuries in succession such that a man eventually succumbed to pain, exhaustion and blood-loss. But it was artillery that men feared most. Compared with arrows and sling-stones, the missiles shot by artillery were larger, travelled further, had greater velocity, and made much more noise. Stone projectiles might smash battlements and send splintered fragments flying like shrapnel. Or they might crush a man's chest or carry away a limb. A soldier close to Josephus on the rampart had his head knocked off. The belly and foetus of a pregnant woman were shot away by a stone that flew over the wall. Spears and bolts, on the other hand, could drive straight through a man and out the other side. Shields and armour offered little protection to such high-velocity missiles. A British hill-fort defender excavated at Maiden Castle was found to have a bolt-head lodged in his spine, a missile that had struck with such force that it had bored its way through a vertebra. Excavations at nearby Hod Hill recovered 67 bolt-heads in total, all of them small, narrow, armour-piercing points. Fatalities among those struck by such weapons in head or torso are likely to have been high.

As the defenders cowered beneath the storm of rock and metal hurled at them from the Roman lines, the armoured assault column moved down the platform towards the wall. But as it threw down its gangplanks to bridge the gap between the end of the platform and the breach, the Jewish defenders sprang up and charged forwards. Josephus may have had some hope that the Romans would be thrown into disorder and panic in the face of such aggressive defence, but the legionaries formed a solid line across the platform, shoulder to shoulder, shield against shield, many ranks deep, and the combat became for a time a classic close-quarters confrontation between opposing spear-lines. Only now are we beginning to understand the nature of such confrontations. Heavy infantry collisions rarely involved men throwing themselves onto the shield-wall and projecting spear-points of their enemies. Still less did they involve the rapid interpenetration of lines and vigorous sword-duelling commonly depicted in films. The reality was something much more tentative and protracted. Periodically men would surge forwards *en masse* to push with shields, thrust with spears, and hack and stab with swords, trying to break into the enemy line or force it backwards and start a process which might eventually bring it to collapse. But such surges were physically and mentally exhausting and could not be sustained for long, while lines were formed up many ranks deep precisely to provide the 'weight' necessary to withstand such assaults. The men in the front ranks found themselves trapped by the press of their own men behind them. To turn and run – the overwhelming instinct of any man facing the lethal danger of front-rank fighting – was impossible, and to turn without an escape route was to risk instant death at the hands of an enemy lunging forwards to strike at an unguarded back. So heavy infantry lines had great solidity, but their behaviour was instinctively defensive. Men would face the enemy at a short distance in a protective huddle. If neither side broke and ran at the first onset, or in response to an enemy surge soon after, the combat was likely to relapse into a protracted stand-off across a gap of a few yards as fear and exhaustion rendered the opposing lines increasingly inert. Reserves could then be

50 *A Roman heavy spear-shooter (*catapulta*)*

decisive. If fresh units were put into the front-line to renew the onslaught, the enemy, if unrelieved, might lack the physical and moral stamina to continue. We do not know exactly how this difficult manoeuvre of unit replacement in close proximity to the enemy was carried out, but there is no doubt that it was standard practice, and that Roman soldiers in particular were drilled to perform it. Probably it was done in a series of small stages.

In the fighting before the breach, the Jews had only limited reserves, whereas the Roman assault column was formed up in great depth along the platform. With fresh men deployed to the front, the column, in close formation, pushed forwards again up the slope towards the gangplanks and the breach. They came on in 'tortoise' formation (*testudo*), the men at the sides with their shields held vertically and locked together to form an unbroken wall, the men in the middle with shields held overhead to form a protective roof against projectiles hurled from above. Before this slow, shuffling, methodical advance, the Jews were herded backwards, and the Romans looked set to take the breach.

But as the *testudo* approached the walls, it was suddenly assailed by streams of boiling oil. The viciousness of this weapon lay in its combination of fluidity and heat retention. The oil easily penetrated the shield roof of the *testudo* and drenched the men beneath. It then ran under their armour and burnt into the imprisoned flesh. Screaming and maddened with pain, men plunged off the gangplanks into the space between wall and platform, or tried to wade through the packed ranks to their rear. But the centuries behind kept coming, their officers organising the men into another *testudo* and urging them forwards through the still-writhing wreckage of the units in front. There could only ever be a limited supply of boiling oil on hand. The centurions guessed – correctly – that the Jews had used all they had in repulsing the first assault. But they did not know that their enemies had another surprise planned. As the new line mounted the gangplanks, the Jews poured down a cold stew of fenugreek which covered the boards in a gluey slime. The second *testudo* rapidly disintegrated as men lost their footing and slithered backwards into each other, some to be trampled to death, others impaled by missiles from the Jews above. There was no third wave. From the smashed head of the armoured assault column, fear and despair now spread back down the Roman line – and Vespasian called off the attack.

Josephus and Jotapata had now held out for a month. A series of aggressive sorties and cunning ruses had severely disrupted Roman operations and brought to nothing a succession of assaults. Goliath's invincibility seemed in doubt, and among the Jews generally there was renewed confidence. The danger for Vespasian was that, with the bulk of his army tied down at Jotapata, the conflagration might flare up across the rest of Galilee. Therefore, when the nearby fortified town of Japha rose in revolt, he moved quickly to stamp it out, dispatching to the scene the commander of the Tenth Legion with a force of 2,000 infantry and 1,000 cavalry. The site was naturally strong and surrounded by two walls, but a large Jewish force sallied forth to engage the Romans in the open. Their assault was broken and they fled back through the gates of the outer wall, closely pursued by the Romans, who burst in through the gates behind them. The Jewish defenders of the inner wall, fearing the Romans might carry straight on into the town, closed the inner gates and trapped most of their comrades in the narrow space between the two walls. Here, pleading for the gates to be opened, they were butchered. With half the garrison slain and the rest demoralised, the capture of the town proved easy. Titus was sent with a reinforcement of 1,000 foot and 500 horse, and when he arrived on 25 June, assuming command, he formed up the small Roman army for an immediate assault by escalade. Surging forwards along the whole line, the legionaries placed their ladders against the wall and climbed up beneath raised shields. Attacked in strength at so many points, the defenders were overpowered and abandoned the wall, fleeing back into the town as the Romans streamed over the battlements. The resistance might have ended then – as it often did in sieges – but somehow people were rallied to carry on, and a furious street-battle continued for some hours, the Roman advance contested from barricades, windows and rooftops. But as the knots of young fighters were gradually destroyed, the killing became a massacre of the wounded, the fugitive and the noncombatant, until only a remnant of women and children were left for sale to the slave dealers. The destruction of Japha ensured that Jotapata's defiance did not inspire a fresh wave of revolt.

Meantime, at Jotapata itself, the Romans had again resorted to engineering. Work on the platforms had resumed with the intention of raising them above the height of the walls, and three towers had been built which were pushed forwards onto the platforms to protect the Roman works and command the Jewish wall (**52**). The 15m-high timber-framed towers were too heavy to be overturned, and a complete casing of metal plates rendered them fireproof. From the protection of embrasures and breastworks on the sides of the towers, Roman archers, slingers, javelinmen and light bolt-shooters could shoot down onto the Jewish battlements from above, rendering the top of the wall effectively untenable. Sorties became the defenders' only means

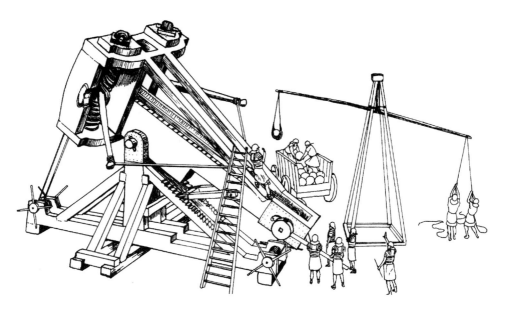

51 *A Roman stone-thrower (*ballista). *Most stone-throwers were much lighter, but ancient sources, including Josephus, do attest the existence of some ordnance as heavy as the machine depicted here*

of disrupting Roman operations, and these, especially with the towers dominating the platforms, became increasingly difficult to mount and costly in casualties. The Jews had fought with tremendous élan and each attempt to storm the town had been thrown back. But the Romans had not been deterred. Siege warfare depended mainly on engineering skill, reserves of labour, and good logistics. With these in abundance, the besiegers could apply the lessons of each repulse in tightening the squeeze on the town, gradually constraining the defence, snuffing out one by one its opportunities for riposte, and keeping up a constant pressure on the heavily outnumbered and increasingly exhausted men guarding the wall.

The end, when it came, was sudden. The attrition of siege warfare works unseen, and the moment when the defenders reach the point of collapse cannot be predicted. Ten days after the grand assault, the siege had settled down again into a predictable routine, and there seemed no immediate prospect of a Roman breakthrough. But tired men often relax their guard – a Jewish deserter from the town explained to Vespasian – especially in the hour before dawn, when few sentries remain awake. Convinced by this intelligence that an attempt to take the town by stealth was worth trying, the Roman commander ordered Titus to lead a commando-style raid on the walls. A small party of men crept silently forwards shortly before sunrise on 1 July. They remained undetected, so they climbed the wall, reached the parapet, and there dispatched the sleeping sentries they found. Josephus gives few further details about the entry, but Titus' commandos must have opened the gates and given a signal. Roman reserves were standing to – rows of silent shadows waiting in the half light – and these now surged forwards, presumably raising their battle-cry as they did so, shattering the stillness of the dawn. They quickly secured the wall and overran the northern hill; the only concerted resistance was by a handful of men defending a wall-tower, but these were easily overwhelmed. Most of the defenders, in fact, were barely awake before their fate was sealed, and as the Romans came over the crest of the hill a wave of panic swept back through the town behind. A group of soldiers gathered on the far side of the ridge on which the town stood, but, seeing no way to fight back, they committed suicide. Elsewhere there was no resistance of any kind, as men, women and children fled in terror through the streets. Though some found temporary refuge in one of the numerous underground cisterns, in the days following the capture the Romans conducted a relentless manhunt, and each hiding-place with its little complement of terrorised people was exposed and emptied (**47**). All the men were killed. Some women and children were also killed – in 1997 Israeli archaeologists uncovered a mass grave on the site which included the remains of many juveniles. Others were later sold into slavery. The town itself Vespasian ordered demolished. And the ruins were scoured for the enemy commander, without whose capture the victory would be incomplete.

Josephus had jumped into a deep pit connected on one side to a large cave that could not be seen from above. Here some 40 people had gathered with a supply of provisions for many days. Josephus came out at night to look for an escape route, but unsuccessfully, and on the third day the location of his hiding-place was betrayed to

52 *A Roman siege tower. Plated with metal as a protection against fire, towers like this were pushed close to the enemy's wall to provide shooting platforms for artillery and archers. Suppressing fire from the towers against enemy battlements and sorties gave protection to siege engineers and assault troops outside the enemy walls*

the Romans. The soldiers were eager to burn the fugitives out, but Vespasian offered Josephus his life if he surrendered voluntarily, and, after some hesitation, he was inclined to accept. What followed in the cave – if we can trust Josephus' account – was a highly charged confrontation culminating in suicide and treachery. The commander was berated by his followers for cowardice in wanting to accept the Roman offer instead of choosing death. We are not told this, but probably the safe conduct applied only to Josephus, a man Vespasian would have respected for his rank and about whom he was doubtless curious. Significantly, Vespasian had used an old friend of Josephus', a man called Nicanor, possibly one of King Herod Agrippa's officers, to conduct the negotiations: the social worlds of Roman general and Jewish aristocrat overlapped. The prospects for the others in the cave were dim by contrast. Exhausted and traumatised by the 47-day siege, they had since sat for three days in a black hole listening to the agony and grief of a dying town above. They knew that massacre or enslavement had been the fate of everyone caught so far, and fear of this must have gnawed at every nerve. That fear now flared into rage and threats of violence against the aristocratic leader for whom rank itself seemed to be an escape route. Josephus calmed the situation by appearing to relent and become party to a suicide pact. At his suggestion, the inhabitants of the cave drew lots to determine who should kill whom, and each in turn facilitated one another's death. But the lots, somehow, must have been fixed, for Josephus and one other remained at the end, and these two then gave themselves up. The Jewish commander (we are told nothing about the fate of his companion) was taken from the cave and escorted through a great crowd of soldiers to where Vespasian, Titus and the other senior officers were assembled to receive him. Though spared death, he was at first imprisoned and destined for dispatch to Rome. Later, as the value of his services became apparent, the terms of his confinement were eased. Eventually he was freed completely, having won the trust of the Flavian family, whose faithful servant he remained for the rest of his life.

He left behind a decapitated and demoralised movement. After the fall of Jotapata and the capture of the commander-in-chief, effective resistance largely collapsed in the hills of Lower Galilee, the heartland of the revolt in the north, while it was restricted to a handful of isolated strongpoints elsewhere – notably, Gischala in Upper Galilee to the north, Tarichaeae and Tiberias on the Sea of Galilee, Mount Tabor a short distance inland to the south-west, and Gamala in the Golan Heights. The Galilean revolution was disintegrating.

The fall of Galilee

Near the Sea of Galilee, September to October AD 67
It was still only the beginning of July when Jotapata fell; several months of the campaigning season remained, and these would suffice for the liquidation of the remaining pockets of resistance in Galilee. So Vespasian returned to the coast, first marching back to Ptolemais, then moving south to establish a new forward base of

operations at Caesarea (**41**). The city had many advantages: it was equally well placed for a move north-east into Galilee and the Golan or south-east to Judaea and Jerusalem; its excellent Herodian harbour meant that it was easily supplied; and it was reliably loyal – the victorious legions were fêted by the town's grandees and Greek population when they marched in – and the circus, theatre, aqueduct and other amenities which the city's Hellenising founder had provided made it an ideal troop billet. Caesarea henceforward would be the Romans' principal base. Vespasian then marched back across Galilee with part of his army to Caesarea Philippi, a minor royal city on the northern edge of Herod Agrippa's territories in the Golan, where his troops were rested for three weeks while he and his officers were entertained by the king (**53**). Serious business was also discussed, however, for the revolutionary movement was out of control in the client-kingdom, many of the king's troops were unreliable, and those he could trust were inadequate to suppress the revolt. Since his men had fought alongside Vespasian's at Jotapata, Herod Agrippa now requested Roman help in the recovery of Tarichaeae, Tiberias and Gamala.

Titus was sent back to Caesarea with orders to bring the remaining troops to the Decapolis city of Scythopolis, where Vespasian, marching south from Caesarea Philippi, would join him. From there they marched on into eastern Galilee and camped a few miles outside Tiberias. The town's internal dissensions were well known, but it was unclear how the fall of Jotapata had affected the balance of forces. Earlier in the year, Josephus had intervened successfully against both radical revolutionaries led by Jesus ben Sapphias and Herodian royalists intent on betraying the town to the Romans. The town had remained in the revolutionary alliance, but under the leadership of moderate *dunatoi* enjoying the confidence of the governor. The moderates of the political centre could not, however, withstand the shock-waves of Jotapata's fall: across Galilee generally, wherever resistance continued, the *dunatoi*, convinced that the revolution was doomed, rushed to make their peace with Rome and Herod Agrippa, while the *stasiastai* urged a strategy of guerrilla warfare and extreme measures of 'public safety' – both anathema to the upper classes – as the only way to rescue the Jewish cause. This polarisation was immediately apparent at Tiberias when Vespasian sent a junior officer to seek the town's surrender. This was a standard preliminary before attacking a town: if it submitted and relieved its enemy of the cost of a siege, it would normally be spared; but once operations began, its fate, if it fell, was sealed. A request for surrender, therefore, could be guaranteed to bring any internal dissension to crisis-point. Jesus ben Sapphias took the initiative and led his militia out of the town to attack the Roman emissary before the royalists could agree to surrender the town; but to no avail. The *dunatoi* fled to the Roman camp and made their submission, and the radicals must have lost the mass support they needed to attempt a defence of the town, for they slipped away to Tarichaeae a few miles to the north. The following day the gates were thrown open, the Roman army marched in, and Vespasian was acclaimed a liberator by a cheering crowd lining the main street. The enthusiasm was genuine: for the royalist upper classes of Tiberias it was the end of a year-long ordeal living in the shadow of popular revolution.

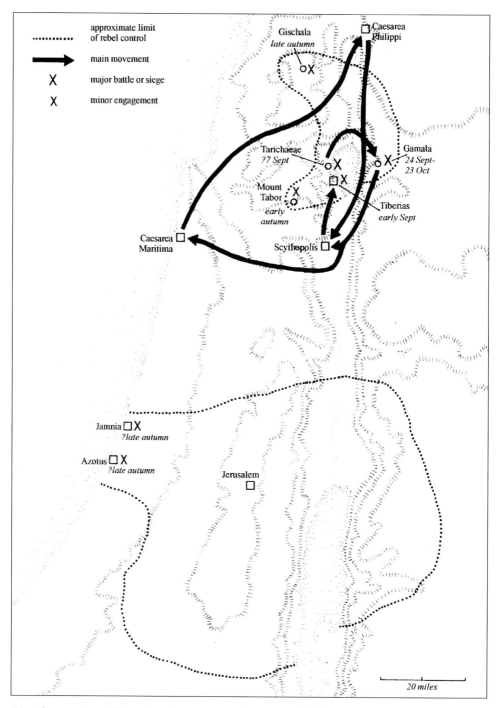

Caesarea
Philippi

Gischala
late autumn

oX

Tarichaeae
?7 Sept

oX

X

Gamala
24 Sept-
23 Oct

Mount
Tabor
o

X

X

Tiberias
early Sept

early
autumn

Caesarea
Maritima

Scythopolis

Jamnia ☐ X
?late autumn

Azotus ☐ X
?late autumn

Jerusalem
☐

20 *miles*

53 *The campaigns of Vespasian, late summer and autumn AD 67*

Meanwhile, radical militiamen were pouring into Tarichaeae, not only from Tiberias but from many other places too. The town was a good place to make a stand: it lacked the large Hellenised upper class of its close neighbour, so betrayal by a fifth column was less likely; it had been provided with a circuit of walls by Josephus, albeit of modest strength only; and on the waterfront the rebels had assembled a flotilla of commandeered boats adapted for war, giving them the possibility of mounting naval operations against the Romans, and a means of escape should their land defences fail. Vespasian moved warily: he ordered his men to construct especially stout defences around the new campsite he had chosen just south of Tarichaeae. His caution was quickly justified by the offensive spirit shown by the Jews, with an aggressive sortie on his working parties, boats being used as floating archery-platforms, and a large Jewish force massing on the plain outside the gates. In response, Vespasian stationed 2,000 archers on a hill near the town to prevent the movement of reinforcements, and deployed 1,000 cavalry under his son's command against the men on the plain. Titus formed a single line, probably about 300m across, and charged across the plain towards the Jewish force. Such crude tactics could only have worked against lightly equipped men – no cavalry could break formed heavy infantry prepared to receive them, since horses cannot be made to gallop onto a solid obstruction, especially one as lethal as a hedge of projecting spearheads. Even so, the Jews did not, as might have been expected, immediately break and run. Cavalry action was always partly bluff: for men on foot, especially those without armour or heavy spears, to stand against 1,000 armoured lancers coming at them almost knee-to-knee on charging horses required nerves of steel. But even if they did stand, without a tight formation able to exclude the enemy horse, they would be hard pushed to win the ensuing encounter. In close combat, men on horses have the enormous physical and psychological advantage of height as they lunge and swipe at men on foot. When the Roman cavalry struck, the Jewish militiaman found himself plunged into a lethal chaos of pushing and kicking horses, thrusting lances, slashing swords, and a furious jostle of men and beasts which might at any moment topple him forwards onto an enemy blade or down to the ground to be trampled. Preoccupied with dodging, ducking and trying to remain on their feet, few men can have managed any serious blows at the enemy. The cavalryman, by contrast, had an elevated vantage-point and fighting-platform, and was well protected by helmet, coat of armour and long shield. The collision was unsurprisingly brief, and soon the Jews were streaming in panic back across the plain towards the town, the cavalry among them, spearing and cutting and riding down the fugitives. Many did in fact make it back to safety – either because they had formed into a coherent knot with other men and been able to ward off attack, or simply because they had kept running and stayed lucky. But any respite was short-lived. Titus reformed his cavalry and led them through the edge of the lake so as to pass around the end of the wall. Breaking into the town amid the panic and confusion after the battle in the plain, the Roman onslaught was irresistible. Jesus and his followers fled across country, others took to the boats and pushed out into the lake, but many more were trapped in the town, some to be cut down immediately, others to be rounded up for enslavement.

The victory, even so, was yet incomplete. Without a ring of troops around the town, many rebels had been able to make their escape, so Vespasian now interposed an armed cordon and left orders that anyone who attempted to leave the town should be killed. He also had wooden rafts constructed and loaded with troops for the pursuit of the rebels who had taken to the boats. A bizarre improvised naval battle was then fought out on the western edge of the Sea of Galilee (**colour plate 16**). The Jewish vessels were probably commandeered ferry and fishing boats. In 1985-6 a severe drought caused the Sea of Galilee to shrink, revealing an ancient boat buried in deep mud a short distance offshore. Excavation, lifting and conservation – done in emergency conditions working around the clock – were immensely difficult because the wooden hull had disintegrated into a spongy material that was 80 per cent water. The boat had a single sail, plus oars, and there was space in its wide hull for several people or a fair-sized load. It has been confidently dated by associated artefacts, distinctive construction methods and radio-carbon analysis of timbers to the period between 120 BC and AD 40. Dubbed the 'Jesus Boat', it is likely to have been typical of the sorts of boats operating on the Sea of Galilee in antiquity – and therefore of the boats which formed the Jewish flotilla in early September AD 67, described by Josephus as 'small, built for piracy, and weak in comparison with the Roman rafts'. It was an unequal contest, therefore. In missile exchanges, the unarmoured men in the boats were shot down by archery, while the Romans were armoured against the slingshot of their enemies. And as the rafts closed in, the boats were sometimes crushed between them and sunk, or their crews were cut down by javelin casts, or overwhelmed as boarding parties stormed across. Men who went into the water were hacked or shot at as they struggled to save themselves from drowning. Others who stumbled ashore were cut down by waiting Roman soldiers on the beach. 'During the days that followed a horrible stench hung over the region,' recalls Josephus. 'The beaches were thick with wrecks and swollen bodies which, hot and steaming in the sun, made the air foul . . .'

Vespasian now turned his attention to the fighters trapped inside the town by his cordon of troops. A tribunal was established to separate the residents of the town from those who had arrived recently with one or other of the militias. The decision had been taken to execute or enslave all of the latter, but since Vespasian wished to avoid alienating the residents by carrying out this atrocity in the town, the doomed men were told they could depart down the road to Tiberias under safe-conduct. The several miles of road, which ran between the shore of the lake and the cliffs below Mount Arbel, were lined with Roman troops to prevent any escape. The prisoners were all herded into the circus at Tiberias, and then Vespasian had them divided into different categories: 6,000 of the strongest young men were sent to work as quarry slaves on the emperor's new Corinth canal project; the remaining able-bodied were sold to the slave dealers, either by Roman officers if they were from procuratorial territory, or by royal officials if they were subjects of the king; the remnant – those too old or disabled to be marketable, perhaps over 1,000 in number – were immediately killed.

First Jotapata, then Tarichaeae: this second great defeat destroyed most of the remaining resistance in Galilee. Only three of Josephus' strongpoints still held out in northern Palestine – Gischala, Mount Tabor and Gamala. To the last of these Vespasian now marched his army. King Herod Agrippa's forces had been conducting an ineffective siege at Gamala for seven months. Their lack of progress, and the defenders' apparent indifference to any threat, reflected the town's tremendous natural strength. It was perched on a spur of the Golan Heights which formed a steep-sided ridge shaped like a camel's back (**colour plate 17**). The ground fell away precipitously into ravines on the northern and western sides, but sloped more gently on the southern side, and it was here that the town was built, the stone houses piled one above the other on a series of mini-terraces, such that, as Josephus has it, 'the town seemed to be hung in air and on the point of tumbling on top of itself from its very steepness'. The buildings ascended to the top of the northern ridge, whose highest point was a rocky crag to the west, which could only be approached by scrambling over boulders, and from which there was a sheer drop on the far side; this served as a citadel (**57**). The only approach to the town was from the east, where the ridge of Gamala was connected by a sharply tilted saddle of land to the upland plateau of the Golan Heights. On this side, the town was defended by ditch and wall, including, at the high northern end where the defences ran up to the top of the ridge, a large round tower which dominated the approach across the saddle (**56**). Despite its appearance of strength, however, Gamala was vulnerable. The garrison was small, the town swollen with refugees, and there were shortages of water and food. Even so, there was a grim determination about the defenders, and an attempt by King Herod Agrippa to parley was greeted by sling-stones, one of which struck his elbow. Gamala was set on fighting, and, since circumvallation and blockade were impractical on such ground, and time was pressing, it now being late September and nearly the end of the campaigning season, the town would have to be stormed.

Nonetheless, chastened by his experiences at Jotapata, which had demonstrated the effectiveness of Jewish forces in defending strong fortifications, Vespasian was set on making proper preparation for an assault. He deployed the Fifteenth Legion on the north facing the tower, the Fifth in the centre, and the Tenth to the south, where the ground fell away steeply. All three legions were ordered to construct siege platforms to create level approaches. Attempts by the defenders to disrupt the siege works were unsuccessful: they were hopelessly out-shot by massed Roman artillery. The platforms were soon completed, and when battering rams were brought forward they quickly smashed breaches through the wall (**54**). At the point where the Fifth Legion attacked, archaeologists have reconstructed both a breach in the wall and the Jewish house immediately behind it (**55**). Measuring about 15 by 10m, the house comprised five ground-floor rooms and two above, the floors of the latter supported on projecting stone corbels and probably formed of timber rafters, reed-matting and beaten earth. The reconstruction underlines the fact that as the legionaries broke into the town they were immediately embroiled in dangerous house-to-house fighting. The defenders made a fighting withdrawal towards the ridge at the top of the town, moving up the narrow streets, through the backs of houses, from terrace to terrace,

54 *A breach in the town wall at Gamala, perhaps caused by a Roman battering ram, as reconstructed by archaeologists. Beyond the breach is one of the rooms of a Jewish house*

drawing the legionaries deeper into their warren. Some say this is the worst kind of fighting. Any corner, roof or opening may harbour death. The enemy may be in front, above, on either side, or at one's back. He may be lurking unseen just a few yards distant. Again and again, in house-to-house fighting, the enemy seems to threaten one's critical space, that zone of physical security around oneself whose invasion by an armed opponent represents mortal danger for it leaves no time for flight. Fighting in constricted spaces against concealed killers, nerves are stretched taut and men lash out in terror like the proverbial cornered rat. In fighting such as this there was no opportunity to deploy the disciplined armoured mass of a legion effectively. The men were broken up into small contingents, could not be properly supported, and found themselves hamstrung by hidden threats to flank and rear. The advantage was with lightly-equipped irregulars, who knew the ground, could move swiftly through it in their loose and fluid formation, and relied mainly on missile weapons discharged from concealment or a safe distance. The Jews, moreover, seem to have worked to a plan, enticing the heavy Roman formations into the heart of the town before switching suddenly from retreat to attack.

Under the stress of house-to-house fighting and then the shock of an unexpected Jewish onslaught from the heights above, the legionaries in the forward ranks panicked. But as they turned to run they found their escape blocked by the great press of their comrades in the narrow streets behind, and hundreds clambered up onto the roofs on either side in their efforts to escape. Under the weight of men, roofs collapsed and sometimes the floors beneath, burying bodies under heaps of rubble and throwing up great clouds of choking dust. The Jews pressed their attack, raining down slingshot, javelins and chunks of building debris onto the compressed mass of stampeding men. The bolder moved in to finish off the wounded pinioned in the wreckage, who were speared, hacked at, or smashed with stones. There was grim determination in the killing. The legionaries were the paid soldiers of an imperial power, and they had invaded this village, violated its private domestic spaces, and threatened its people with the horrors of the sack. Having beaten them back, the Jews – the peasants of Gamala – set about slaying those they could get their hands on with an implacable hatred. Vespasian himself was almost among the victims. He had joined the attack on the town, and, when the panic started, had found himself isolated with a small group of men near the top of the ridge. This group kept its nerve in the crisis, forming a shield wall as protection against missiles and charges from the Jews massed in front, and then withdrew step-by-step, keeping its guard up all the way back to the wall. By this time most other units had lost cohesion, and men who had got free of the carnage in the upper town were rushing for the breaches and the safety of the Roman lines. Some, blinded by panic and dust, lost their way in the maze of little streets; one small group, led by a centurion, went to ground in a house and waited for nightfall, at which point they crept out, murdered the occupants of the building, and made their way out of the town and back to camp.

Defeat on such a scale – the ignominious retreat of three legions – left Vespasian's army deeply demoralised, and there was no immediate resumption of the offensive; instead the soldiers were set to work raising the platforms higher. Despite the exhilaration of victory, however, morale was little better inside the besieged town. The Romans had not gone away and supplies were running out. Some had been driven by hunger to try escaping by climbing down the ravines or making their way along various underground passages which opened beyond the town limits. Others, fearing capture, stayed within the walls, but here they slowly starved, as the limited food available was reserved for the fighting men – though there was not enough even for them. The siege had relapsed into a blockade, and the defenders' vigilance and vigour were gradually eroded by hunger, lack of sleep and boredom. So often – as at Jotapata – it was this steady attrition of the power to resist through physical and mental exhaustion that tipped the balance against the defenders in siege warfare and made them vulnerable to a new assault.

On the night of 22 October, about a month into the siege, three legionaries crept up to the northern tower, prized out five stones, and brought about the sudden collapse of the structure, along with the sentries posted on the top (**56**). There was immediate confusion and panic among the defenders: some sentries fled from their posts on the battlements; some attempted a breakout, including Joseph, one of the two Jewish commanders, who was shot down at a gap in the southern wall; there was pandemonium on the streets as people awoke to the possibility that the Romans were inside; and Chares, the other Jewish commander, who seems to have been seriously wounded and bed-ridden, is said by Josephus to have died of shock. But the Romans were chastened enough by their earlier defeat not to want to risk a house-to-house

55 *A reconstructed town-house at Gamala. The breach in the wall appears upper left, the entrance to the street is upper centre, while the rooms in the foreground have rebates and corbels in their walls to support an upper storey. Gamala's maze of narrow streets and small houses terraced into the hillside proved to be a trap for Vespasian's legions*

fight in the dark, and there was no immediate attempt to enter the town in force. The entry, like the attack on the tower, was to be by stealth. On 23 October, Titus, who had not been present at the time of the great attack and did not share the general gloom at its failure, led forward a picked force of 200 dismounted cavalry plus some infantry and silently entered the town. The Jews were taken completely by surprise. Some men were cut down as they rushed to their posts, while others, often with women and children in tow, were killed as they tried to withdraw to the citadel on the north-eastern edge of the town. Any who offered to surrender were simply butchered. As Vespasian led the main Roman force in through the eastern wall, a great crowd of Jews, fighters and their families, gathered on the steep rocky crag that overlooked the town (**57**). The Romans surged through the streets and massed at the base of the peak. Then, as they hauled themselves up a steep slope formed of boulders, scree and scrub, their shields held overhead, the Jews hurled down stones, spears and anything else to hand. As the tide of battle edged up the slope, a fierce wind buffeted the defenders, threatening their precarious footing and sending missiles wide. As the Romans came on, the braver of the defenders lower down the slope fell back, and the circle at the top thickened into a compressed mass. All could see there was no hope: the Romans had ringed the whole lower slope and as they advanced towards the peak were slaughtering everyone in their path. While some men fought grimly on, others abandoned the struggle as enemy missiles began to drop from overhead and the air filled with the screaming of terrified women and children. Many of the people of Gamala, knowing that death was but minutes away, now plunged over the precipice into the ravine. Fear drove them over – fear of laceration by steel blades, of a lingering death, of deliberate torture, of gang-rape. So the final choice for many men, in Gamala's last terrible moments, was to throw their wives and children into the abyss and then to follow them.

The fall of Gamala brought the war in Galilee almost to an end. Mount Tabor had already fallen (**58**). A flat-topped hill over 500m high on the south-eastern edge of Lower Galilee, the summit had been walled around by Josephus, and a substantial force of rebels had taken refuge there. But Placidus, commanding 600 cavalry, had lured them down onto the plain with an offer of amnesty and then destroyed them in a single charge. Only Gischala still held out in the relatively inaccessible far north. This was the fiefdom of John ben Levi's militia, a stronghold of radicalism which, by virtue of its remoteness, Josephus had never attempted to subdue and the Romans had not yet attacked. Now, as the legions were moved into their winter quarters, the Tenth to Scythopolis, the Fifth and the Fifteenth to Caesarea, Titus was sent on a special mission with 1,000 cavalry to destroy this last rebel outpost. When he arrived, eager to avoid a siege, he offered terms and then withdrew a short distance to allow the Jews to consider his proposal and give their response after the Sabbath. In this, the young Roman general – whose intellectual gifts were modest – was outwitted by his Jewish opponent. John's position was close to hopeless. With the revolution defeated across Galilee and the Golan Heights, Gischala was isolated far beyond the reach of any help. Its defences were weak and might have been taken by storm, but

56 *The reconstructed northern tower at Gamala viewed from the Roman position*

57 *The high, rocky, windy citadel at Gamala, showing the precipice from which many of the defenders threw themselves in the closing moments of the siege*

58 *Mount Tabor, which, unlike Jotapata and Gamala, succumbed easily to a small Roman force*

if not, a winter blockade would have starved it out, and the Romans could easily have supplied the small force necessary to achieve this. Gischala, by October AD 67, had become untenable. John's plan was to evacuate the town and march his forces south to aid the defence of the holy city; and it was Titus who gave him the opportunity to do this. To plead the Sabbath as a reason for delay had been John's ruse to buy the time he needed to organise an escape, and Titus' withdrawal from the vicinity of the town and failure to place a cordon around it compounded the mistake.

During the night John's militia successfully slipped out of the town and set off for Jerusalem on a gruelling forced march, putting sufficient distance between themselves and the Romans to get most of the fighting men well away by morning. Less happy was the fate of the non-combatants who trailed along in their wake, mainly the wives and children of the militiamen. Many of these could not keep up, yet the column had to maintain its pace to out-distance pursuit. A stream of despairing stragglers was left behind as the column forged ahead, some to be cut down by pursuing Roman cavalry, others rounded up and herded back to Gischala. 'Every man for himself,' Josephus has John ben Levi shouting to his followers. 'Make for the place where you can avenge those left behind who fall into Roman hands.'

Others too were on the road to Jerusalem. As winter closed in and Galilee's year of disaster came to an end, the revolution not only still lived, but was being distilled and condensed. The half-hearted, the frightened, the easily demoralised had fallen away in the storm and strife of AD 67. The vacillating and the treacherous, men of

Josephus' class and outlook, had been tried and condemned in the great courthouse of events. The men trudging into Jerusalem from Galilee and other parts in the winter of AD 67/8 were the truly committed and the battle-hardened. They hated Romans, Greeks and Herodians. They believed in the Jubilee, the Apocalypse, and God's favour. They had faced the shocks of battle and mastered their fears. They had tasted defeat and stared down despair. They had decided to fight on with a determination to win and the conviction that victory was possible. And they had been witness to backsliding and betrayal of a kind they would not tolerate again. The revolution was becoming concentrated: geographically so as the zone of rebellion shrank to an enclave around the holy city; politically, in the grim resolution of the militiamen marching in to defend it; and militarily, in the newly forged courage and skill with which these veterans would henceforward fight. As Vespasian well knew, the greatest battles were yet to come.

6 Three revolutions

There was a young hothead called Simon bar Giora . . . he withdrew to the hill-country and there proclaimed liberty for slaves and rewards for the free, so collecting the scum of the whole district. As soon as his force was strong enough, he overran the villages in the hill-country, until the constant flow of recruits encouraged him to descend to lower levels. . . . many powerful men were led astray by his strength and continual success, so that his army no longer consisted only of slaves and bandits, but included many respectable citizens who obeyed him like a king.

(Josephus, *JW*, 4.503-10)

The Zealot revolution

Jerusalem, winter AD 67/8
War involves a rapid speeding up of events, a concentration of forces, and fierce open clashes. War is history at its most dangerous and decisive. All political structures are put under strain: leaders, parties and governments are constantly tested and failures ruthlessly punished. War is especially testing in periods of revolution, when a newly-established government without the sanction of tradition might be challenged from below by fresh upsurges of the popular movement which brought it to power in the first place.

Since its formation in November AD 66, after the victory at Beth-Horon, the second aristocratic government of high priest Ananus ben Ananus had presided over a mounting catalogue of defeats. Often enough, as a critical reading of Josephus' account of the Galilean campaign indicates, half-hearted measures, attempts at compromise and sometimes outright treachery lay behind these disasters. A year on, therefore, at the beginning of winter AD 67/8, the military pressure of Roman forces on Jerusalem was bringing to crisis-point the conflict between conservative *dunatoi* and radical *stasiastai* within the revolutionary city.

The Roman strategy continued slow but sure. The plan was still for a methodical reduction of Jewish strongpoints and armed bands, first in the north and west (Galilee, western Golan, Samaria, and the Sharon Plain), and then in the east and south (Peraea and Idumaea), so as gradually to confine the revolt to an ever smaller area of upland Judaea immediately around Jerusalem. The successive capture of Sepphoris, Japha, Jotapata, Tiberias, Tarichaeae, Mount Tabor, Gamala and Gischala in the campaign of AD 67 had secured Galilee and the Golan. By this time also both Samaria and the Sharon Plain were secure.

The Samaritans, who, like the Jews, had suffered oppression at the hands of foreign rulers and had a tradition of militant resistance, might easily have risen *en masse* and joined the revolution. The sect had its distant origins in the split between northern and southern kingdoms in the late tenth century BC. The former kingdom (Israel) had fallen to the Assyrians in 722 BC, whereas the latter (Judah) had survived as an independent state until the two Babylonian attacks of 597 and 587 BC. Samaritan and Judaic Yahwism had therefore developed differently, especially after the return of the exiles from Babylon in 537 BC and the importation of a more intolerant form of Judaism. Sectarian hostility had deepened when the Samaritans, prevented from assisting in the reconstruction of the Temple at Jerusalem, had turned Mount Gerizim into a major rival centre for the worship of Yahweh. The attempt by the Hasmonaean kings to extirpate the 'heresy' by launching an all-out war against the Samaritans in the late second century BC had made the schism irreparable, and, as we have seen, by the first century AD, Jews and Samaritans were divided by a sometimes murderous communal hatred.

Division and conflict were not, however, inevitable. In 331 BC the Samaritans had burnt alive the Macedonian governor imposed upon them by Alexander the Great, and in AD 36 an armed crowd had gathered at Mount Gerizim under a Samaritan messiah to challenge the authority of the Roman procurator. They had no less reason to resist foreign rule than their Jewish counterparts: Samaritan peasants faced the same problem of multiple impositions levied on tiny plots, and they found cause for hope in the same holy prophecies about apocalyptic deliverance. It was entirely possible that Samaritans and Jews might transcend their petty hatreds and unite against a common enemy. So when news reached Vespasian during the siege of Jotapata that the Samaritans were massing at Mount Gerizim, he was worried enough to dispatch the commander of the Fifth Legion with 3,000 foot and 600 horse to destroy them (**41**). The Samaritans were taken by surprise: they found themselves blockaded on their hill without food and water, and thirst quickly drove many to desert. On 27 June, with the defenders reduced in numbers and weakened by privation – though still defiant – the Romans ascended the hill, stormed the position, and massacred everyone they found. This swift action aborted the embryonic Samaritan revolution, and henceforward Roman control of Samaria went unchallenged.

On the Sharon Plain, too, where there were sizeable Jewish communities in urban ghettoes and many villages, the Romans fought a successful struggle in AD 67 to contain the revolutionary movement (**41 & 53**). The Greeks had terrorised the local Jews with pre-emptive massacres at Caesarea and Ascalon in the early autumn of AD 66, and shortly afterwards a Roman flying column had stormed into Joppa, killed its Jewish defenders, and burnt down the city. But the victory at Beth-Horon in November had re-ignited revolutionary hopes. The Ananus government sent an expeditionary force to Ascalon, which, though it had strong walls, was defended by only a small force, possibly a mixed quingenary cohort of 480 foot and 120 horse. The Jews force-marched to the city in an effort to take it by surprise, but, as they surged towards the walls, the Romans were ready for them. The cavalry sallied forth to meet the enemy in the plain where they could operate to advantage. 'When raw levies were confronted by veteran troops,' explains Josephus, 'infantry by cavalry, undisciplined individuals by regulars who fought as one, men with nondescript weapons by fully armed legionaries [*sic*], men guided by passion rather than by reason by men who instantly responded to every signal, the issue could never be in doubt'. The Jews were driven off with heavy loss, including two of their three commanders. A second attempt on the city a short while later was no more successful: the enterprising Roman commander laid successful ambushes in the passes on the road down into the plain, and the Jewish irregulars were again routed by Roman cavalry attacks.

Despite this setback, Joppa was reoccupied by the rebels and turned into a major base on the Sharon Plain. As the Roman grip tightened in AD 67, many local Jewish fighters sought refuge there, and, with landward communications difficult, they looked to the sea, building a sizeable fleet both to keep themselves supplied and to harass enemy shipping. Jewish pirates were soon attacking both the Syrian and Egyptian trade routes. When Vespasian reached Caesarea after the fall of Jotapata, therefore, he sent a force of horse and foot to capture the city for a second time. The walls were found to be unguarded and the Romans entered at night; the defenders had taken to their ships and were riding at anchor just off the coast. The Jews were desperately unlucky: before the night was out, a sudden gale blew up, and since there was no natural harbour at Joppa – just a beach enclosed at either end by cliffs and reefs – the Jewish ships were smashed against each other or thrown onto the rocks, and the crews crushed amid the wreckage, drowned in the sea, or cut down by Roman soldiers as they stumbled onto the beach. A Roman garrison was then planted on the site and the surrounding villages were devastated and plundered. Even after this disaster, however, the rebels still held out in parts of the central Sharon Plain, for, although we are given no details, Josephus reports that towards the end of the year, returning to Caesarea after completing the reconquest of Galilee and the Golan, Vespasian had to capture and garrison Jamnia and Azotus. This seems finally to have ended effective Jewish resistance in the Sharon Plain – and closed the long list of defeats suffered by the Ananus government in AD 67.

In the course of the year, then, all the risings by Jewish ghetto-dwellers and villagers in the Greek cities of the inner Diaspora within Palestine itself had been crushed. The implications were grim. Until now, despite recent pogroms in eastern cities like Alexandria, the possibility had existed that the revolution might spread to the millions of Jews forming the outer Diaspora beyond Palestine. That possibility was surely extinguished by the defeats at Ascalon, Joppa, Jamnia and Azotus. So too was the possibility of Samaritan support after the débâcle at Mount Gerizim. Not only that: the revolution had lost much of its core territory, principally in Galilee, an area of almost exclusively Jewish peasant settlement. Altogether, with the loss of Galilee, western Golan and the central Sharon Plain – except perhaps for small guerrilla outposts – the extent of rebel-held territory had been halved (**59**). The Jews had been reduced to Judaea, Peraea and Idumaea, and they were hemmed in by Roman forces to the north and the west – the result of an almost unbroken string of defeats since Beth-Horon a year before. Vespasian's strategy of keeping his forces concentrated and slowly destroying the revolution piecemeal seemed to be working.

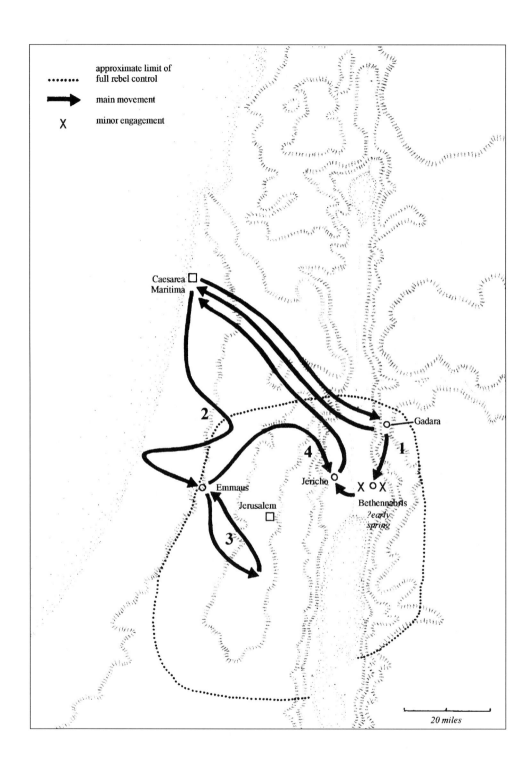

approximate limit of
full rebel control

main movement

X   minor engagement

Caesarea
Maritima

2

Gadara

1

4

Emmaus   Jericho

X ○ X

Jerusalem   Bethennabris
?early
spring

3

20 miles

Control of territory is only one measure of political vigour, however, and Vespasian's cautious strategy was itself testimony to the continuing military strength of the revolutionary forces. Jerusalem's defences were among the strongest in the ancient world, and thousands of committed fighters were falling back upon it as their positions elsewhere collapsed. An army of some tens of thousands would be needed to besiege it and operations might last for months. With the city located in difficult hill-country infested by guerrillas, keeping such a host supplied with water, food, fodder, fuel and munitions would be a massive logistical task. Moreover, to become bogged down outside the city, to suffer setbacks in the siege, might re-ignite resistance in the rear. Things could still go very badly wrong. In the holy city, then, the mood was not so much black despair as anger against the Ananus government and a growing determination to drive it out and put power in the hands of determined and proven revolutionary fighters. The military crisis at the front produced, in the winter of AD 67/8, a political crisis for the Jerusalem regime.

What brought this to a head, almost certainly, was the flood into the city of young fighters from the northern and western battlefronts. Josephus reports several examples of refugees escaping from doomed strongpoints – Gischala, Tiberias, Mount Tabor and Gamala – but these are incidental references and do not form a comprehensive list; there must have been many more. Some came as members of an organised militia under their own commander. Others arrived as individuals or in small groups and then attached themselves to whichever militia seemed most appealing. These newcomers joined themselves to an existing garrison. The latter may have included some government regulars, but no mention is made of such troops, and it seems likely that most of Jerusalem's existing garrison was also grouped in various independent militias. Though many townsmen must have been enrolled among its defenders, a majority of the city garrison had probably come from elsewhere, some from the villages of Judaea, others from more distant parts of Palestine, with a good number who were deserters from the army of Herod Agrippa, and a few who were volunteers from the Diaspora. Probably most of these fighting men had brought their families with them – women, children and old people would otherwise have been left defenceless in the villages – and the population of Jerusalem must have swollen to enormous size. Ancient statistics are notoriously unreliable and there is no proper method for deducing population levels from archaeological evidence, so any estimate of the number of people who normally lived in Jerusalem, who stayed in the city during festivals, or who crowded into it now in the winter of AD 67/8 has to be a guess. But a guess is better than nothing: perhaps the normal population was between

59 *(opposite) The campaigns of Vespasian in AD 68. 1. The capture of Gadara and victories at Bethennabris and the River Jordan gives the Romans control of northern Peraea. 2. A winding march through the Sharon Plain completes the suppression of Jewish guerrilla resistance in the area. 3. Using Emmaus as a forward base, the Romans carry out a reconnaissance in force and punitive raid deep into Idumaea. 4. Vespasian marches his army back across northern Judaea to reunite it with the force in Peraea and take Jericho. Overall, battles are few and rebel casualties light. The campaigns of AD 69 are equally inconclusive in this sense*

50 and 100,000, rising to between 250 and 500,000 at a festival or during the war. What is certain is that very large numbers of armed radical militiamen with their families and supporters were massed in the city at the end of AD 67. One principal consequence of the Roman strategy of steady advance, thorough subjugation, and fire and sword, was to drive the revolutionary fighters back on the holy city and turn them into a concentrated political force. The result, as it seems from Josephus' account, was the polarisation of opinion, a ferment of debate, and rising anti-government tension:

> . . . he [John ben Levi of Gischala] drew most of the young men into his net and whetted their appetite for war, but of the sensible, older men there was not one but saw what was coming and mourned for the city as if it had already perished. . . . First of all, in the home, family unity was disrupted by partisan bitterness; then the nearest kinsmen severed all ties of blood, and attaching themselves to men who thought as they did lined up on opposite sides. Faction reigned everywhere, the revolutionaries and warmongers with the boldness of youth silencing the old and sensible. . . . When at last the leaders of the various gangs of bandits had had enough of plundering the countryside, they came together and formed a single pack of rogues. Then they infiltrated into Jerusalem, a city without military command, where by age-old custom any of the Jewish race were admitted without scrutiny, and where at this juncture everyone thought that those who were pouring in all came out of kindness as allies. . . . Other bandits from the country slipped into the city, and joining forces with the desperadoes within gave themselves to every imaginable crime. They did not limit their insolence to theft and brigandage, but went so far as to commit murder, not by night or secretly or against the common people, but openly by day beginning with the most eminent.
>
> (*JW*, 4.128-39)

Though the account is vitiated by prejudice, Josephus was a not a deliberate liar and we can usually trust his basic factual statements. In this case, a number of things seem clear: there were political arguments among ordinary Jews, in which the young were more radicalised than the old, and families were therefore sometimes split; numerous bands of armed men, independent of government authority, were entering the city and forming alliances with other bands already present; political and military authority was being challenged, and the armed bands were taking action against prominent figures. Taken as a whole, there seems little doubt that Josephus, however ineptly, is describing a threatened seizure of power by armed popular militias.

When he picks up the story again, the authority of the Ananus government appears to have been close to collapse. Eleazar ben Simon and the Zealot militia had remained ensconced on the Temple Mount since the previous autumn, but for most of the following year the radicals had been too weak in the city as a whole to force the issue with the government. Now, though, reinforced by John ben Levi's Galileans and other newly arrived militias, and buoyed up by rising popular anger at the incompetence and treachery of the aristocratic regime, especially among the young fighters, the Zealots went on the offensive. They deposed the aristocratic high priest (Matthias ben Theophilos) and instituted a new democratic procedure for the selection of a successor. Previously high priests had been chosen by King Herod Agrippa and the Roman governors from among a small group of top Sadducean families. The new procedure involved election by lot. One of the high-priestly clans was assembled and lots were drawn among all its eligible members: the successful candidate was a commoner without high-priestly forebears (Phanias ben Samuel). What made the lot so democratic was not simply the fact that anyone could be chosen, but the fact that the rich were prevented from influencing the outcome through their control over the voting behaviour of dependants and clients. At about the same time several senior political figures associated with the Ananus regime, including members of the Herodian royal family, were arrested and charged with plotting to betray the city to the Romans. It seems likely there was an attempt to protect the conspirators by keeping them in custody rather than bringing them to trial, for a group of radicals took it upon themselves shortly afterwards to enter the prison and summarily execute them. To democratise the high priesthood and institute a policy of terror against suspected traitors was, in effect, to usurp government authority and make a direct challenge for state power. The Zealot offensive therefore provoked the government into a decisive trial of strength.

Ananus ben Ananus summoned his supporters to a rally where he denounced the Zealots and called for an armed assault to drive them from the Temple Mount. As the government forces mobilised – probably a new force raised among aristocratic youth and dependants – heavy street-fighting erupted in the Tyropoeon Valley between the plebeian Lower City and the aristocratic Upper, the area that had also been the principal battleground during the Herodian coup of August AD 66 (**63**). This time, though, the conservatives overwhelmed their opponents and the Zealots were driven back through the gates of the Sanctuary, across the broad plaza of the Outer Court, and finally into the Inner Court and the Temple itself. Here they barricaded themselves inside and remained secure from attack, but they were bottled up and cut off from the rest of the city by a ring of government soldiers holding the gates and colonnades around the Outer Court. Without a general rising of popular forces in the city, the government had been able to isolate, defeat and corral the Zealot militia.

These events, however, were merely the prologue to the radical revolution with which the city was now pregnant. The many other militias appear to have stood aside up until this point, perhaps uncertain of the issues at stake and unable to choose sides, or because the Zealots were political rivals whose power they hoped to see curtailed. Either way, they had made a grievous mistake, for Ananus used his advantage to send a delegation to Vespasian inviting him to take over the city. Had this happened, there is little doubt that the Romans, with the support of the Jewish élite, would have carried out a murderous black terror to destroy the popular movement. Josephus gives expression to the underlying issues in the speech he attributes to Ananus on the occasion of the great rally before the street-battle with the Zealots. What is the point of winning independence from Rome, Ananus asks, if the outcome is 'subservience to the scum of our own nation' and to see 'men of our own race rob and murder the nobility'. Better to have the Romans, he concludes, who spare the rich and uphold the law, than domination by 'the enemy within the city'.

The position of upper-class men like Ananus and Josephus is easy enough to understand. The revolution had split the Jewish aristocracy. A minority had remained at its head, hoping to contain the popular forces at home while winning on the battlefields a strong enough bargaining position to negotiate a compromise peace – perhaps some sort of resurrected client-kingdom under Herod Agrippa. That strategy had collapsed. The Jewish armies had been defeated and the Romans were on the rampage; the popular movement had grown enormously and armed militiamen filled the city; property and privilege were in grave danger. The choice had become a restoration of order under Roman authority or the risk of an apocalyptic war on the rich – and most men of property were in doubt which they preferred.

But as the embattled aristocratic regime moved to surrender the city to the Romans, the popular militias were galvanised into action. Josephus' text is exceptionally difficult at this point. He attributes to his arch-enemy John of Gischala a leading and thoroughly Machiavellian role in the events he describes. It is certainly possible that John continued to operate in a somewhat opportunistic manner, manoeuvring to his own best political advantage, but his power was firmly rooted in his own Galilean militia, whose allegiance he had to maintain, and could only be increased further by successful negotiation with other popular leaders and their followers. John was no free agent. He made history in the circumstances imposed upon him. He was part of a turbulent revolutionary movement comprising a plethora of leaders, militias and sects. It is only defeated and dying revolutions that spawn dictators; would-be revolutionary leaders, by contrast, must wage a constant struggle for political support. John may have played a double game, negotiating with both government and Zealots, but the rising strength of the popular movement which was his base ensured that no deal could be done with Ananus. Instead, a radical coalition was forming to destroy the aristocratic regime.

The Zealots sent an appeal for support to Idumaea. The people of this dry barren land mixed small-scale cultivation with extensive pastoralism, cross-border raiding and social banditry. The Herodians had their origins in Idumaea, the family still owned estates there, and it had in the past been a recruiting ground for the royal armies. But overall Idumaea was not a region of big estates – there was not enough good land – and landlordism was less developed here than elsewhere in Palestine. Rather, the Idumaeans had a reputation for independence and violence – Josephus thought they were 'by nature most barbarous and bloodthirsty' – and to this, in the revolutionary period, was added a fierce commitment to the struggle against Rome and the defence of the holy city. A large Idumaean force – Josephus says 20,000 strong – was quickly mobilised and led north under the command of four generals. When they reached Jerusalem, the government closed the gates against them, posted sentries on the walls, and attempted to negotiate. But with the Idumaeans unwilling to agree either to use their arms against the Zealots or to lay them aside before entering the city, the government kept the gates firmly shut and an angry stand-off ensued. The right of all Jews to enter the holy city freely was hallowed by tradition, and the government's denial of this right to men who had come to defend it against a pagan enemy could only add weight to the city radicals' claim that Ananus was bent on surrender. As night fell, the Idumaeans, forced to sleep in the open outside the city, were in an ugly mood, soon made much worse as a devastating storm broke over their heads. They sat huddled together amid thunder-claps and lightning flashes, protected from the torrential downpour by nothing more than roofs of shields, no doubt debating the implications of the day's events. 'Disaster to the human race was plainly foreshadowed by this collapse of the whole framework of things,' Josephus comments grimly, 'and no one could doubt that the omens portended a catastrophe without parallel.'

Inside the city, many government soldiers took refuge from the storm in their own homes, while those on sentry-duty sought shelter in towers, colonnades and gatehouses, where they slumbered fitfully. The Zealots, however, were active. Protected by the negligence of the sentries and the roar of the storm, a group of them left the Temple, crossed the Outer Court, sawed through the bars across the Sanctuary gates, made their way across the city to the wall opposite the Idumaean camp, and there opened the gates to admit their allies. The Idumaeans poured into the city and were guided to the Temple Mount, where, along with the jubilant Zealot militiamen they had relieved, they attacked the cordon of soldiers holding the colonnades around the Outer Court. By dawn the government's defenders had fled and the Temple Mount was under radical control, and during the following day the aristocratic quarter in the Upper City was captured. There seems to have been no further effective resistance. The other popular militias were doubtless also out on the streets, helping to guard against any rally by government forces and seeking to arrest prominent political enemies. The leadership of the fallen aristocratic regime was now destroyed by revolutionary terror. Ananus ben Ananus himself was executed first, along with another high priest and former close associate in government, Jesus ben Gamala, the man who had conducted the abortive negotiations with the Idumaeans. Subsequently, two other government leaders, Gurion ben Joseph and Niger the Peraean, were also executed. The first capital sentences seem to have been summarily imposed, but later a revolutionary tribunal was established on the Temple Mount. We hear of the public show-trial before a jury of 70 men of one Zachariah ben Baruch, a rich aristocrat charged with treason, which, if Josephus can be believed, collapsed into arbitrary violence when the accused was acquitted by the jury only to be cut down immediately by outraged militants. Nevertheless, though many suspect aristocrats were rounded up and imprisoned, few seem to have come to trial, and fewer still to have been executed. Indeed, despite Josephus' lurid description of the terror, the hard evidence of his text implies that it was small in scale. The Zachariah incident receives detailed treatment because it was an outrage; the implication is that it was exceptional, and it may have reflected the frustration of some radicals who felt embittered towards upper-class traitors, feared them as a potential fifth column, and wanted the terror to be more thorough-going. Josephus is able to name very few actual victims – either now or later – whereas he reveals the early release of some prisoners, the successful escape of a number of émigrés to the Romans, and the presence in the city, apparently at large and unmolested, of many of his aristocratic peers until the end of the siege. All the evidence is that the 'red terror' of winter AD 67/8 probably numbered its victims in handfuls, not hundreds, let alone thousands (as Josephus would have us believe). The old leadership that had wanted to betray the city had to be destroyed and the rule of the popular militias secured; the terror seems to have been measured and limited in relation to this purpose.

The countryside had rallied to the defence of the capital, bringing to it a concentrated essence of peasant revolution, and this had enabled the armed militias to destroy the aristocratic regime and empower men of their own kind – men who believed in victory and could be trusted to fight for it. Now the upsurge of radicalism in the capital flowed back into the countryside, re-energising the revolt in the villages. Every household knew a man who had joined a band of irregulars and gone up to Jerusalem. Every courtyard had discussed the bitter conflict in the capital between high priests who wanted peace and popular militants determined to fight. Every village was split between those who feared Roman retribution and those who believed that God would give victory to the Israelites. Now Jerusalem had settled that debate. A new popular insurrection in the holy city – like those of May, August/September and October/November AD 66 – had propelled the revolution forwards once more, giving confidence to militants everywhere, convincing doubters that victory was possible, and marginalising the revolution's intractable opponents. Josephus, though his surviving comments are sneering and distorted, was witness to the way in which the capital led the country.

> In all the districts of Judaea there was an upsurge of terrorism, dormant hitherto; and as in the body if the chief member is inflamed all the others are infected, so when strife and disorder broke out in the capital the scoundrels in the country could plunder with impunity, and each group after plundering their own village vanished into the wilderness. There they joined forces and organised themselves in companies, smaller than an army but bigger than an armed gang, which swooped on sanctuaries and cities. Those they attacked . . . were unable to retaliate as the raiders, like all bandits, made off as soon as they got what they wanted. In fact, every corner of Judaea was going the way of the capital.
>
> (*JW*, 4.406–9)

In one case, reporting events in eastern Idumaea, on the western shore of the Dead Sea, he is more specific. A powerful Zealot militia – Josephus consistently calls them 'Sicarians' (*sicarii*) – had been based in this area since taking over the old Herodian palace-fortress at Masada when the rebellion first broke out – except, that is, for a brief foray into Jerusalem under Menahem in August AD 66. Until now, Josephus reports, 'they had merely raided the districts nearby to procure supplies – fear prevented any further ravages; but when they heard that the Roman army was making no move, while the Jews in the capital were torn by factionalism and tyranny, they embarked on more ambitious schemes'. There was a raid on Engedi, which was taken by surprise, its defenders scattered and cut down, and supplies were looted and taken back to Masada. Then 'they proceeded to plunder all the villages around the fortress and ravage the whole area, their numbers being daily swelled by a flow of ruffians like themselves from every side'.

What are we to make of this? It is essentially a description of social banditry mixed with revolutionary expectation expanding into full-scale rural insurrection – but viewed, of course, from the distorted perspective of an aristocrat. The implication that massacre and looting were general defies all common sense. Were this so, the Sicarians could not have grown. All studies of successful social bandits have shown that they discriminate between their own actual and potential supporters and those perceived as enemies of the poor. When bandits do turn on the poor, as sometimes happens, their support in the villages collapses, their followings shrink, and they become vulnerable to betrayal and police repression. There can be little doubt that the Sicarians were building their strength by raiding the property of the rich and recruiting peasant villagers to their forces – in classic bandit style – and that they enjoyed an upsurge of support as news filtered through of the radical revolution in the capital.

In the spring of AD 68, then, Palestine was in the grip of a second Jewish revolution, and the flagging revolt against Rome was recharged with new hopes and new fighters. At the same time, by chance, the Roman state itself was torn apart by revolution – though revolution of a very different kind – an event which delayed the attack on Jerusalem and gave the new regime time to prepare its defences.

The revolt of the generals

Caesarea and Rome, March AD 68 to December AD 69
The winter revolution in Jerusalem might have been followed by a Roman attack on the city in the spring; it was partly in anticipation of this that the radicals had acted to oust the treacherous Ananus government. But the attack was postponed for a full two years. One reason was Vespasian's expectation that dissension in the city – principally among rival radical factions after the overthrow of the aristocratic regime – would weaken the defending forces. A second was the need to suppress the revolt in the countryside of Peraea, Idumaea and Judaea to ensure that the Roman rear was secure before advancing on the capital – a need made more urgent by the radical seizure of power in Jerusalem and the renewed militancy it had unleashed. Josephus has Vespasian arguing down his senior officers' clamour for an early attack on the city in favour of continuing with his preferred strategy of slow-but-sure.

> If he did march on the city at once, he would only reunite the enemy and turn their full strength against himself; if he waited, he would find their numbers reduced by internal divisions. . . . 'If anyone thinks,' he went on, 'that victory without a fight will not taste so sweet, he had

better realise that to win success by biding your time is a sounder policy than courting disaster by plunging into battle. And again, those who shine in physical combat are no more entitled to fame that those who accomplish much by self-discipline and brains.' . . . this was not the time to set their hearts on a dazzling victory. The Jews were not busy making weapons, building walls or recruiting auxiliaries – in which case postponement would injure those who granted it – but were being bled to death by dissension and civil war . . .

(JW, 4.368-75)

So for the first six months of AD 68, rather than concentrating for a direct drive on Jerusalem, the Roman forces, operating in separate columns, worked to tighten the vice around it, pressing in on the Judaean hill-country from all directions (**59**). Gadara, a fortified town in northern Peraea, was the first target. The local élite – 'partly from a longing for peace, partly to safeguard their possessions, many Gadarenes being very rich' – sent a secret embassy to Vespasian offering to betray the town in the event of a Roman advance. When the revolutionaries learned of the conspiracy – too late to prepare the town for a siege – they executed the principal traitor and fled. The Roman army entered the town without a fight on 4 March, and Vespasian then allocated Placidus 3,000 foot and 500 horse and ordered him to pursue and destroy the fugitive rebels. The chase continued for about 15 miles down the Jordan Valley, until the Jews reached Bethennabris, a fortified village on a tell a few miles north-east of the Dead Sea. Here, and on ground running down to the Jordan, a decisive battle was fought for the control of Peraea.

The fugitives from Gadara were reinforced by local villagers with improvised weapons, and together, in a manner that had become characteristic of Jewish revolutionary fighters, they sallied forth to launch an aggressive attack on the Romans outside the walls. The Romans, also characteristically, gave ground to draw the undisciplined Jewish irregulars forwards while preparing encircling counter-attacks. Once the initial advantage of surprise had dissipated, and a re-ordered Roman line began to press in and restrict the space for skirmishing tactics, the weight of heavy shock formations began to tell against the Jewish light infantry. 'As they hurled themselves on the massed Romans behind their impenetrable barrier of steel,' reports Josephus, 'they could find no chink for their missiles to enter or means of breaking the enemy ranks, while they themselves were easy targets for Roman missiles and, like the wildest of wild beasts, charged the opposing steel and perished, some struck with the sword as they faced the enemy, others scattered in flight by the cavalry.' Placidus interposed his cavalry between the Jews and the walls of Bethennabris, and many of the fugitives were shot or cut down from the flanks as they fled towards the village. Others had to fight their way through to the gates, desperate to reach them before they were barred – as they were bound to be, at the last minute, to keep the enemy out. Placidus next launched an attack on the walls themselves, and that evening the resistance of the demoralised defenders finally collapsed and the Romans broke in. As the village was destroyed – its buildings burned, its people exterminated – those who could escaped into the surrounding countryside. Here they were joined by hundreds more from nearby villages, whole communities fleeing in fear of fire and sword as news reached them of the presence nearby of vengeful Roman forces. The refugees headed for the Jordan, hoping to cross and find refuge in Jericho on the far bank, but they discovered a river swollen by winter rain and rendered impassable. So they turned to face their pursuers, the armed men forming a defensive line along the bank, the women, children and old folk behind them along with little flocks of sheep, heavily-laden donkeys and camels, and ox-carts piled up with the contents of emptied homes. Most of them were quickly destroyed, some by missiles, others by sword or spear, and many more by drowning in the bloated waters of the river. Corpses, it is said, littered the way from Bethennabris to the Jordan, and many others floated away down the river to be seen later bobbing on the surface of the Dead Sea.

Vespasian meantime had returned to Caesarea Maritima to organise the second of his two big offensives that spring. His initial task was to complete the suppression of all remaining Jewish resistance in the Sharon Plain, and this was done in a steady, winding advance southwards, destroying villages and farms as he went. Then, in the second phase of the campaign, using Emmaus as a temporary base, he thrust deep into Idumaea for what was probably intended as a combined reconnaissance in force and punitive raid. He shifted front again for his third attack, this time moving back north, marching through Samaria, and reaching Jericho on 3 June, where he effected a junction with the army from Peraea. After the massacre on the banks of the Jordan, Placidus' force had ranged widely in Peraea, destroying rebel villages, hunting down fugitive bands of fighters, and retaking the more important towns near the Dead Sea. It was now reunited with the main army perhaps in anticipation of strong resistance at Jericho. This was a desert oasis town built thousands of years before around a natural spring; in recent times it had become the centre of a royal estate based on the production of dates, balsam and honey, and the Jewish kings had built themselves winter palaces here; it was a rich prize and the revolutionaries might have chosen to mass in its defence. Vespasian perhaps hoped for this, giving him the chance to destroy another sizeable concentration of rebels; but it was not to be. Too strong a column can defeat its own purpose by discouraging guerrilla fighters from attempting a stand. Jewish forces in the Sharon Plain and Idumaea seem to have melted away in the face of Vespasian's earlier offensives that spring, and now the Romans found that Jericho also had been deserted, its would-be defenders retreating into the relative safety of the Judaean hills. All that remained for the Romans was to mop up isolated pockets of resistance in the area – Josephus reports a column of cavalry and infantry dispatched to liquidate a rebel force still holding out at Gerasa in north-eastern Judaea; while the discovery by archaeologists of Roman arrow-heads and a layer of burnt ash amid the ruins attest the violent suppression of the Essenes at Qumran.

As Vespasian again marched back to the coast with the main force, he could be confident that the Romans were in effective control of northern and western Palestine. The Sharon Plain, Galilee, Golan, Samaria, the Decapolis and northern Peraea had all now been reconquered. Judaea, the rebel heartland, was surrounded on three sides, with the Jews holding on only in the south, in Idumaea west of the

Dead Sea, and in southern Peraea to the east. A thrust now into northern Judaea by the main force – it was still only the start of summer, early in the campaigning season – could quickly have brought the Roman army to Jerusalem. But Vespasian did little more in the remaining months of AD 68.

The following year, too, Roman operations were lethargic and inconclusive. They opened strongly – if a little late – with what was perhaps intended to be a final big push towards Jerusalem. A small diversionary column was sent to ravage Upper Idumaea and distract Jewish forces from the defence of Judaea, and this succeeded in capturing three strongpoints, including ancient Hebron, which was consumed by massacre and fire. In the meantime Vespasian himself led the main column into the Judaean hill-country. He pushed in from the north-west, captured a string of fortified towns, laid waste the surrounding countryside, and installed garrisons to create a series of military outposts. The aim, once ground was taken, was to prevent reoccupation of the towns and to police the surrounding hills, denying rebel guerrillas refuge and succour, hunting down those that could be caught, and otherwise harrying them backwards into the fast-contracting Jerusalem pocket. A semi-circular band of burnt and barren land, studded with camps and criss-crossed by patrols, was edging closer to the holy city; in front of it trickled little columns of militiamen and refugees making their escape over upland tracks. When Vespasian rode ahead of the main force to reconnoitre Jerusalem itself, all looked set for the final showdown. But having espied the city from a distance, the general returned to his army and marched it back out of Judaea to the coast. The attack on the revolutionary capital had been postponed again.

Militarily the decision seems to make no sense. Jerusalem was now in the front-line and rebel territory had been reduced to areas of desert and upland in the south, including a mere handful of strongpoints, principally Machaerus east of the Dead Sea, Masada beyond its western shore, and Herodium on the edge of the Judaean Desert (**60**). Continuing resistance in these areas would be far more easily dealt with once Jerusalem itself had been taken; rebel morale would surely collapse in the south once the capital had fallen. Yet for the second summer running Jerusalem was reprieved. The reason was not military but political. Since the previous spring Vespasian had been receiving news from Rome of a gradually evolving political crisis. This had now erupted into full-blown civil war, with legion battling legion in pitched battle in the Po Valley, and the latest information was causing the most profound anxiety among the Roman generals stationed in the East. Now was not the time to begin a huge, expensive, protracted and highly risky siege. It was desperate news from home, then, that took Vespasian back to the coast early in AD 68 – and once there he was soon in urgent conclave with his most senior officers.

The crisis had gathered momentum slowly; indeed, in a sense, it had began with the fall of the Seneca government in AD 62 and the effective assumption of power by the narrow court faction presided over by Nero himself, the new empress Poppaea Sabina, and the praetorian prefect Tigellinus. With its whimsical and self-indulgent policy, and a playboy emperor who gave full rein to his philhellene enthusiasms and squandered money on court extravagance, this group had quickly lost the confidence of the Roman ruling class. Nero's real failure, however, was not his wilful refusal to

conform to the Roman model of *gravitas* (aristocratic authority, dignity and seriousness), but to induce, among many upper-class Romans, an acute sense of insecurity
– about their own safety, that of their estates, and indeed of the empire as a whole.

The root of the problem was financial. The regime was profligate and had tightened
the screws on the provinces to fill the treasury, provoking a series of revolts in different
parts of the empire in the 60s AD, of which the Jewish one was the most serious. This
mood of resistance, moreover, appears to have been on a rising scale. When, a short
while later, in the winter of AD 69/70, Roman auxiliary troops on the Rhine rose in
revolt, they would be joined by Gallic chieftains and druids predicting the imminent
collapse of the Roman Empire; without doubt, like that of the Jews, this movement,
which was briefly strong enough to establish an 'empire of the Gauls' in the western
Rhineland, drew support from people embittered by years of heavy taxation. The crux
of the crisis, then, was the fact that financial irresponsibility had compromised both
frontier security and internal stability by driving the subjects of the empire into revolt.
This crisis was compounded as political opposition to the regime crystallised and the
government responded with a policy of terror which left leading senators living in fear
of a treason charge, a death sentence, and the liquidation of ancestral estates.

The conspiracy of Piso in AD 65 was supported by a mixture of nobles from
ancient families, career politicians, army officers and intellectuals like the poet Lucan;
but it was betrayed and 19 men were forced to commit suicide. The regime was
henceforward suspicious, however, and a reign of terror began. Informers were
encouraged to come forward and a steady stream of denunciations resulted in the
enforced suicides of numerous opposition senators, like the Stoic Thrasea Paetus in
AD 66, and top generals, like the Parthian War victor Gnaeus Domitius Corbulo in
AD 67. From the time of the conspiracy onwards, Nero was openly at loggerheads
with the Roman ruling class, and all men of real standing – those with enough pull
to initiate a revolt against the regime – felt threatened. Then, in March AD 68, shortly
after Nero's return from Greece, Gaius Julius Vindex, the Governor of Gallia
Lugdunensis, declared himself in revolt against the government (**2**). His provincial
origins precluded a claim to the throne on his own behalf; instead, doubtless by prior
arrangement, he announced his support for Servius Sulpicius Galba, a 73-year-old
blue-blooded noble with an enthusiasm for discipline and traditional values, who at
the time was serving as Governor of Hispania Tarraconensis. Galba made his declara-
tion in April and was immediately supported by other top Romans in Spain, including
the Governor of Hispania Lusitania, Marcus Salvius Otho. For a while, matters were
in the balance. Vindex was defeated by loyalist forces in Gaul, but then the military
commander in Africa came out against the government. Nero himself, however, was
crippled by indecision, and this, in the face of a military revolt which enjoyed the tacit
support of most upper-class Romans, precipitated a split within the regime. One of
the two prefects of the Praetorian Guard, Nymphidius Sabinus, offered his soldiers a
huge bribe for switching their allegiance to Galba. This they did, and the Senate
legalised their decision by declaring Nero a public enemy and Galba the emperor. The
outlaw scurried out of the city in disguise and was later helped to commit suicide by
a freedman, having famously declared 'What an artist dies in me!'

Galba recovered his nerve at the news – he had retreated into the interior of his province on hearing of Vindex's defeat in Gaul – and headed for Rome. But his was to be an unstable regime criss-crossed by conflicting claims. The Roman ruling class was a band of warring brothers: though united against common enemies – whether barbarian chieftains, provincial revolutionaries, or a bloody tyrant on the purple throne – they competed fiercely among themselves for advancement within the imperial system. Always there were many more aspirants to office than places at the top; always the spoils of empire fell below the claims of aristocratic greed; and success in this murky struggle for rank and riches had come to depend, ever since the Caesars had assumed power a century before, on which faction controlled the court. The emperor was the fount of patronage, and his person became the supreme prize contended for in the dangerous political game at the top of Roman imperial society. Galba's faction was an uneasy alliance of Praetorian Guardsmen, old-school senators and career politicians from Spanish postings. What was there here for officers in the Rhine, Danubian or eastern legions? They, in fact, were as suspect to the new regime as to the old, and when Galba moved to replace some of them with his own loyalists, the seeds of new revolts were sown. First the Governor of Lower Germany was superseded, then the Governor of Upper Germany; each man had commanded around 20,000 legionaries, and in January AD 69 these soldiers, at the instigation of their senior officers, refused to renew their allegiance to Galba and hailed Aulus Vitellius emperor in his place.

News of the latest revolt brought to a head the conflicts within Galba's faction at Rome. The Praetorians had been alienated by the new emperor's refusal to pay their promised bribe. Otho and the 'Spaniards' were now also alienated by Galba's elevation of another blue-blooded senator like himself as potential successor. When Otho went to the Praetorian Barracks and offered to pay the soldiers, they proclaimed him emperor and denounced his rival as an enemy. Galba, a bald and arthritic old man, was hunted down and lynched in the forum. At his death, two rival emperors remained, each representing a powerful block of politicians and officers, one rooted in Rome, Italy and Spain, the other in the Rhineland; and only war could decide which of them would endure.

Otho, in control of Rome and given legitimacy by senatorial support, attracted the formal allegiance of most provincial governors and the practical assistance of the Danubian legions. His position appeared the stronger. But the Vitellians – though Vitellius himself was little more than a mask for the career ambitions of the Rhineland officers – controlled a large and cohesive army of veterans under skilled commanders trusted by their men. When the rival armies clashed near Cremona in northern Italy, legion against legion in a day-long battle amid the vineyards, the Othonians were defeated and their 37-year-old leader – whose fastidiously hair-plucked body was crowned by a toupee to hide his baldness – committed suicide and brought to an end his 95-day reign. As the Vitellians drove on towards Rome, the Senate and most provincial governors acknowledged the judgement of war and switched allegiance for the third time in a year, so that Vitellius was now legally installed on the purple throne. But the Vitellian revolution was in an important sense different from its immediate predecessors. The secret of empire, as Tacitus explained, was out: emperors could be made elsewhere than at Rome. Vitellius was the 'Rhineland' emperor, a creature of the generals stationed there, a ruler brought to Rome by 40,000 frontier legionaries. This was the regime of a narrow faction, and a bloody purge was needed to consolidate its power, confirming – if confirmation were needed – that other interests were now forfeit. On the other hand, only two forces were powerful enough to challenge the Rhinelanders, and one of these, the Danubian army, had shared in the Othonian defeat and the subsequent purge. That left only the eastern legions – whose leading commander at that moment was, of course, Titus Flavius Vespasianus.

The Flavian card was the joker in the pack. Vespasian cannot have thought himself in contention at the outset of the crisis. He owed his current eminence to social obscurity. Though it had quickly been established that the throne was not the prerogative of the Julio-Claudian family, Galba, Otho and Vitellius were all men from established senatorial families in Rome. Vespasian's origins were equestrian and municipal. Consequently, when the news arrived in late spring AD 68 of Nero's death and Galba's elevation, Vespasian had sent his son Titus, in the company of King Herod Agrippa, to pay homage to the new ruler and obtain fresh orders. They must have set off late in the year, for *en route* Titus received the news that Galba had been assassinated, Otho made emperor in Rome, and Vitellius acclaimed in the Rhineland. The young Flavian could only turn back for fresh consultations with his father and the eastern generals. There must have been many grim-faced councils in Caesarea that summer, much anxious waiting on the news from Italy – and little time or inclination for pressing matters with the Jewish rebels. 'In their suspense – for the Roman Empire was rocking and everything was in the melting-pot – the two commanders [Vespasian and Titus] held up operations against the Jews, feeling that while they were so anxious about things at home an invasion of a foreign country would be inopportune' (Josephus).

The news, when it came, was bad: the victory of Vitellius meant direct Rhineland control over imperial patronage and a sharp slump in the fortunes of both officers and men stationed in the East. Suetonius, for instance, reports a rumour that Vitellius was planning to switch the western and eastern legions, forcing the latter, as they would have seen it, to exchange the relative comfort and ease of their city billets for wooden forts in a cold and wet German forest. But as the Rhineland legions had shown that a Roman army could make its own emperor and impose him on Rome, why not the eastern legions also? Josephus, who was witness to the mood in Vespasian's army, conveys something of the issues at stake in words he attributes to the soldiers:

> The soldiers in Rome, living in luxury and afraid of the very word 'war', vote anyone they fancy onto the throne, and appoint emperors with one eye to the main chance. We, who have toiled and sweated and grown old in the service, let others enjoy this privilege, even when we have in our own camp a candidate with much stronger claims. . . . we have three legions and contingents from the kings, and they will be backed by all the East and as much of Europe as is safely out of Vitellius' reach, and by allies in Italy itself . . .
>
> (*JW*, 4.592–8)

Josephus avers that Vespasian was reluctant to accept the nomination. This may be so, or any reluctance shown may have been feigned to deflect charges of personal ambition. It hardly matters. Merely to be offered the poisoned chalice, whether one accepted or not, was to become a condemned man, since no reigning emperor could permit a man to live whom others had wanted in his place. The momentum towards an eastern military coup became unstoppable, and Vespasian was propelled willy-nilly into a struggle for supreme power: the prize now, an infinitely richer one than Jerusalem, was to be Rome itself.

Perhaps by prior arrangement, or perhaps through hurried last-minute negotiation, the Prefect of Egypt, Tiberius Alexander, declared for Vespasian on 1 July AD 69, reading out a letter from him to the assembled soldiers and citizens of Alexandria and calling upon them immediately to swear their allegiance. With Egypt secure, giving him control of two legions and the Nile grain-stores from which Rome was fed, Vespasian accepted the acclamation of his army in Palestine ten days later. Shortly afterwards came further declarations in his favour – from Gaius Licinius Mucianus, Governor of Syria, and from the Danubian legions, whose revolt was led by a subordinate officer named Antonius Primus. This support – the whole of the East and the Balkans, and two of the three main army groups in the empire – gave Vespasian a potentially winning hand, especially since the Flavian revolt had taken the Vitellians by surprise, and the military discipline of the Rhineland legions had broken down since their arrival in Rome. But Vespasian was ever cautious. Having visited Antioch to settle matters in Syria, instead of advancing west from there he transferred his headquarters to Alexandria, satisfying himself with cutting off the Egyptian grain-supply to Rome and sending Mucianus with 20,000 men on a slow march through Asia Minor to gather support. His dilatory strategy threatened to undo the Flavian cause, giving the Vitellians time to recover and mobilise; but it was superseded by the vigorous offensive of Antonius Primus and the Danubian legions, who, ignoring any orders they may have received from the East, crossed the Alps into the Po Valley determined to fall upon their enemies while they were still in disarray. In the late autumn the Rhineland and Danubian legions clashed again on the battlefield of Cremona – for the second time in a few months – and this time the Danubians triumphed. As the Vitellian lines broke and ran, the Flavian soldiers first massacred the fugitives and then stormed into Cremona to loot it. A second Vitellian force coming in from Gaul was defeated, and a final attempt by Vitellius to block the snow-bound Appennine passes on the approach roads to Rome disintegrated as his men deserted. The 56-year-old emperor – whose 'ruling vices were gluttony and cruelty' according to Suetonius – made a final bid to save himself by cutting a deal with Vespasian's brother, Flavius Sabinus, who was acting as the family's representative in Rome. The deal collapsed when Vitellian soldiery mutinied, stormed the Capitoline Hill, and lynched the Flavian leader. Antonius Primus' Danubians then pressed on to Rome and destroyed the Vitellian forces in fierce street-fighting. Vitellius, a big fat man, was dragged into the streets half-dressed and bloated with food and drink (Suetonius again), where he was pelted with dung and filth, tortured by little sword cuts, and finally murdered on the banks of the Tiber. Afterwards, while their senior officers installed a provisional government headed by Vespasian's younger son Domitian, the Danubian soldiers celebrated by looting the city. It was December. The empire now had its fourth emperor in a year – and Rome and the Italian towns had been twice plundered by the army that was supposed to defend them.

The bandit revolution

Jerusalem, April AD 69

In the unconquered hill-country of Judaea, Idumaea and southern Peraea, the fire of revolution had not gone out. Inspired by the defiance of the holy city, and encouraged by Rome's internal strife, tens of thousands of Jewish peasants were still in arms against the Great Beast. Around Jerusalem, resistance bristled from a hundred strongholds – hidden cave complexes, fortified upland villages, and the fortresses of Machaerus, Herodium and Masada. The Roman Empire stretched across 2,000 miles and was defended by a quarter of a million professional soldiers, but within its territory there was a redoubt 60 miles across garrisoned by peasant guerrillas where its writ did not run (**60**). Though Jerusalem was the living heart of the redoubt, the blood that flowed into it and kept it beating came from the villages. The Jewish Revolution was, in essence, a revolt of farmers, an uprising of country people whose lives had become unbearable under the rule of Jewish high priests, Greek landlords and Roman tax-collectors. This elemental challenge to the social order, a plebeian attempt to turn the world upside down, had received only distorted expression in the politics of the capital. Here, in a city filled with sectarians and rival popular leaders, the instinctive drive of the peasant to make a Jubilee – to redistribute land and free it of burdens – was often submerged. Peasant revolution is always limited. The peasant is an individualist whose ambition is restricted to his own farm; he wants to defeat his oppressors and then be left alone to work the land with his family; he has no vision of a wider social transformation involving the collective action of peasants in general. There is rarely such a thing, therefore, as a peasant state, for when peasants destroy the old state, they do not create a new one in its place – they just go home.

That is why the apocalyptic vision of the sects was so important to the revolt: it provided the unifying ideology and centralised leadership needed to overcome the parochialism of the peasants and organise them into an armed revolutionary force. But the contradiction inherent in peasant revolution could not be entirely transcended. The life and work of peasants remained tied to their farms, and the villages pulled them back into a hundred separate little worlds a few miles wide. Jerusalem, the revolutionary centre, had filled up not with peasants in general, but either with angry young fighters who had marched away from their villages, or with refugees from villages destroyed by fire and sword. This swollen population of the displaced and the desperate, of people cut adrift from the ballast of village pragmatism, gave rise to a fevered politics of rival sects and would-be messiahs. There was the danger of a decoupling of Apocalypse and Jubilee, of revolutionary vision and bread-and-

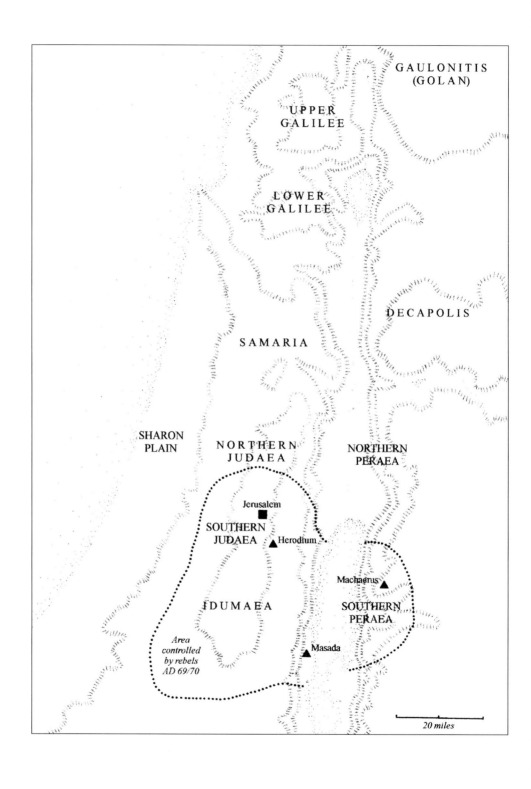

GAULONITIS
(GOLAN)

UPPER
GALILEE

LOWER
GALILEE

DECAPOLIS

SAMARIA

SHARON
PLAIN

NORTHERN
JUDAEA

NORTHERN
PERAEA

Jerusalem

SOUTHERN
JUDAEA

■ Herodium

Machaerus ▲

IDUMAEA

SOUTHERN
PERAEA

Area
controlled
by rebels
AD 69/70

▲ Masada

20 miles

butter struggle, of millenarian radicals ensconced in the capital and social bandits rooted in the villages. This contradiction gave rise to the third great struggle for the soul of the revolution.

The insurrectionary victory of October/November AD 66 had placed power in the hands of the aristocratic faction led by high priest Ananus ben Ananus. The revolution in the winter of AD 67/8 had destroyed that faction and transferred power to the radical militias headed by Eleazar the Zealot, John of Gischala, and Simon the Idumaean. The Zealots had been in the city for longest, holding the Temple since late AD 66 and successfully resisting a full-scale onslaught to drive them out in late AD 67. But, though their fighters had a formidable reputation for fanatical bravery, their numbers had remained modest – Josephus puts their military strength at 2,400 in early AD 70. Some leading Zealots were certainly priests; the name of the group implies religious enthusiasm, and throughout their occupation of the Temple – in defence of which they fought with extraordinary ferocity – the customary rituals appear to have continued through thick and thin. The impression we get is that the Zealots proper – as opposed to other determined revolutionaries to whom the term 'Zealot' may have been casually applied – were a sect of militant traditionalists, somewhat akin to modern groups like the Palestinian Hamas, the Lebanese Hizbollah, or Afghanistan's Taliban. If so – and we speculate – their religious doctrine and an obsessive concern with ritual, perhaps to the detriment of more practical concerns, may have limited their appeal. They may also have burnt out their cadre by demanding too much – in both credulity and personal sacrifice.

John of Gischala led a larger but more ideologically vague faction – Josephus puts its strength at 6,000 in early AD 70 – comprising not only his original Galileans, but many new recruits who had joined since his arrival in Jerusalem, and also some existing militias that had allied themselves with him in a loose coalition. This gave the grouping both strength and weakness: a lack of political definition will have enabled it to recruit widely, and there seems little doubt that John was, for a while after the overthrow of Ananus, the dominant political figure in Jerusalem; but without clear aims it risked degenerating into a mere vehicle for its members', and especially its leaders', self-advancement. Principle and opportunism are political alternatives.

The Idumaeans, the third sizeable armed group in the city, were even less well defined and, at least at first, took their political direction from others. They had been a hastily assembled militia responding to the call of political allies in the city, and having rescued the Zealots and helped bring down the Ananus government, the force seems to have broken up. While some remained in the city – Josephus records 5,000 under Jacob ben Sosas and Simon ben Cathlas in early AD 70 – many others returned

60 *(opposite) The 'Jewish Commune' of AD 69/70. Rebel control in this period was reduced to an area approximately 60 miles across. But the Romans faced a formidable task. The area was predominantly hill-country and desert, where keeping a large modern army supplied was difficult. It was defended by some tens of thousands of determined fighters, many of them veterans of earlier campaigns, and they held several strong fortifications. There was little chance many of them would surrender: they had overthrown their half-hearted aristocratic commanders and replaced them with popular leaders committed to all-out war* to their villages in the course of AD 68. Probably, in most such cases, they had families and farms, but the factionalised politics of the city could be disillusioning, and Josephus insists that many Idumaeans were alienated by the revolutionary 'excesses' of their erstwhile allies and helped suspects held during the terror to escape. We can only guess at how reports of events in Jerusalem might have played in Idumaean villages in AD 68, but we can be certain that it was here, and in southern Judaea, that a new revolutionary upsurge was incubating in this period. That this should be so was largely due to the political and military leadership of Simon bar Giora.

If Eleazar the Zealot represented the Apocalypse, Simon represented the Jubilee. While Eleazar was the leader of a millenarian sect, Simon was a Pancho Villa figure who embodied the struggle for peasant emancipation. He was young, strong and brave; also intelligent, dynamic and charismatic; altogether, a powerful plebeian leader in politics and war, who was, Josephus says, held in 'special awe and respect' by his men. He had joined the struggle early, raising a militia in his home territory of Acrabatene in north-eastern Judaea, and distinguishing himself as a commander in the battles to defend Jerusalem against Cestius Gallus in October and November AD 66. The new Ananus regime had distrusted him, however, and not only was he offered no government post, but he was later driven from Acrabatene by government forces and compelled to seek refuge in Idumaea. Here he formed an alliance with the Sicarians based at Masada, though he continued to recruit to his own militia, which became a mainly Idumaean force around a core of Judaean exiles. When the Ananus government was overthrown, Simon led this enlarged force back into northern Judaea with the aim of winning more recruits while waging a guerrilla war against the Romans. We do not know how long he remained here, but the area must have been rendered untenable during the campaigns of AD 68, for Simon had withdrawn south again by early AD 69. He seems then to have based himself in southern Judaea, creating a fortified strongpoint at a place called Nain. Recruits continued to flow in, perhaps including some fugitives from factional conflict in Jerusalem, and also, if we can trust Josephus, some men of rank. This seems curious, but with the collapse of organised aristocratic politics after the radical revolution, some such men may have seen Simon as a lesser evil than more familiar enemies in the city. If so, it seems they were mistaken. Simon proclaimed 'freedom for the slaves and rewards for the free' and thus collected around him 'the scum of the whole region'. This sounds, given the ancient Jewish context, like an attempt to bring about the Jubilee, and we can assume that in areas Simon controlled, slaves were freed, debts cancelled, land redistributed, and peasant farms unburdened. This would certainly explain his fast-growing strength: Josephus reports him fielding armies of 20,000 and 40,000 men (which we can take to mean ones that were 'very large'), and building fortifications, treasure-houses and grain-stores. Our source appears to be describing a classic example of social banditry ballooning into all-out peasant war.

Simon now faced counter-attack from two directions. The Jerusalem Zealots, cut off from their peasant base for three years, had failed to grow and appear to have decayed into an embittered sect mainly concerned with defending their own pre-eminence and promoting a rather unattractive brand of Judaic fundamentalism.

Instead of regarding Simon as an ally conjuring reinforcements from a rekindled peasant revolt, the Zealots saw him as a rival for power to be cut down before he overwhelmed them. They duly marched out to give battle. But they were met by Simon's forces, soundly beaten and forced to retreat back to the city. Though they later succeeded in ambushing and capturing Simon's wife, who was carried back to Jerusalem, the appearance of her husband's army outside the city and his threats of retribution were sufficient to have her returned unharmed. The second counter-attack, however, was more dangerous: an attempt by conservative forces in Idumaea to rally in defence of local property against the Judaean bandit-chief. The first clash between the two sides was an inconclusive day-long battle, after which both armies fell back to their bases. Simon renewed the war with an enlarged force, however, and, though he failed to take Herodium, the main Idumaean army was destroyed by treachery and mass desertion before battle could be joined. Its fate fits the analysis of this conflict as a class war: if the Idumaean rank-and-file perceived Simon not as an invader threatening families and farms, but as a liberator come to free the peasants, they can have had no stomach for a fight. Simon's army already contained many fellow countrymen, and later, in the factional struggle in Jerusalem, many more Idumaeans would join him. So the property-owners' army melted away, and the bandit army – Judaeans and Idumaeans united for the Jubilee – swept forwards to overrun the whole region, including ancient Hebron (changing hands again), which yielded them a rich haul of treasure and grain.

The brief civil war in Idumaea left Simon in control of the south and the most powerful leader within the revolutionary redoubt. But his army was an unstable militia of peasant volunteers held together by Simon's charismatic leadership and a vision of possible liberation. If it stood still, if it lost momentum, enthusiasm would drain away and most of the peasants would drift back to their farms. If the mirage of apocalyptic deliverance dissolved, the routine and resignation of everyday life would return to reclaim them. Simon's movement had to advance or disintegrate. If it was to advance, however, there was only one way to go – to Jerusalem, to the holy city that symbolised the Jewish struggle, to the great fortress that now stood in the front-line of the revolution. The city's resistance for three years, the fact that in that time no Roman force had dared attack it, gave it an aura of divine protection and seemed to confirm the ancient Jewish prophecy that it was to here, to Mount Zion, that God would come to His People at the End of Days. To Jerusalem, then, for the consummation of the bandit revolution – and a recharging of the centre with revolutionary energy from the villages.

Recharging was needed. Largely cut off from their mass base in the countryside, the revolutionary militias were in decay, the Zealots fossilising into a dogmatic cult, John's coalition breaking up in reaction to the leader's ambition and opportunism. The declining popularity of Eleazar and John provided conservative forces in the city – 'citizens who were trying to escape the Zealots and were anxious about their homes and property' – with their best chance of a comeback since the fall of Ananus over a year before. The Idumaean militia in Jerusalem broke with the other radicals to form an alliance with the high priests, who now called their own supporters back to arms. Together they attacked the Zealots and the Galileans and drove them from most parts of the city, forcing them to take refuge on the Temple Mount and in a royal palace on the Ophel Hill immediately to the south (**63**). However, the radicals appear to have been taken by surprise, and their conservative enemies remained very much in awe of their military strength and immediately looked around for allies to shore up their precarious position. By now, though – it was March or April AD 69 – Simon bar Giora's bandit army was camped outside the city. At first the gates were barred and it was well beyond the bandits' power to force their way in. But the high priests and the Idumaeans resolved to negotiate a deal with Simon as an insurance against the radicals bottled up within the city, and when this was done they opened the gates and the bandit army, probably about 10,000 strong, marched into Jerusalem. A fresh assault was then mounted on the Temple Mount, but this was a formidable citadel, recently further strengthened by the Zealots with the addition of four great towers, and it was defended by several thousand veterans. As the attackers approached, they came under long-range fire from numerous artillery mounted on battlements and towers, and then from archers and slingers as they got closer. Under this hail of shot from high above, attacks could make little headway. The fighting fizzled out and the opposing lines settled into a routine of desultory missile exchanges across the Tyropoeon Valley.

For the best part of a year there was a stand-off punctuated by occasional flare-ups of shooting and sorties. Cooped up on the Temple Mount and facing the frustration of a protracted siege, Zealots and Galileans fell out and came to blows, the former retreating again, as they had done in the past, to the Temple itself and the Inner Court, where they towered over the latter, who remained in control of the Outer Court and the surrounding colonnades. Jerusalem became a city semi-permanently divided into zones controlled by rival militias. Simon's men must have held a line of improvised barricades running across streets and rooftops looking out over a no-man's-land of ransacked buildings and debris-filled alleyways which dipped down into the valley to meet the base of the Temple walls on the far side. John's men would have faced Simon's from positions in the Antonia Fortress, on the roof of the Temple's western colonnade, in the newly constructed towers, and behind barricades on the Ophel Hill to the south. But to resist the Zealots they must also have improvised defences along the inside of the colonnades and around the edge of the Outer Court. A wide expanse of plaza probably separated John's lines here and the walls of the Inner Court held by the Zealots, for the latter were poised to rain down missiles from the Temple roof on any who approached across this ground. This conflict was resolved, however, shortly after the Roman siege began, when John succeeded in infiltrating armed men into the Inner Court during the Passover festival. The Zealots were taken by surprise and scattered – though the actual fighting seems to have involved little more than scuffles (Josephus refers to people being 'trampled on and savagely beaten with swords and cudgels') – and an agreement was quickly reached whereby the Galileans and the Zealots resumed their former alliance and henceforward mounted a joint defence of the Temple Mount. This incident perhaps gives a truer picture of the character of the factional struggle as a whole than the more lurid

61 *The coin on the left was issued in AD 67. The obverse (above) shows an amphora and is inscribed 'Year 2'. The reverse (below) shows a vine leaf and is inscribed 'Freedom of Zion'. The coin on the right was issued in AD 69. The obverse (above) shows a holy chalice and is inscribed 'Redemption of Zion'. The reverse (below) shows a palm branch and is inscribed 'Year 4'. 'Freedom' was a political* fait accompli; *'redemption' was an apocalyptic hope. The change in slogans may reflect the radicalisation of the revolution between AD 67 and 69*

Josephan passages with their impression of wholesale slaughter and destruction. Factionalised urban street-fighting in revolutionary situations tends to be highly tentative and desultory. Doubtless there were casualties, and perhaps some deliberate destruction of grain-supplies, but the fact is that, even though the conflict lasted for a year, the Jews at the end of it were still able to mount a fierce and protracted defence of the city against the Romans.

In AD 68 the Romans had called off their campaign mid-season and Jerusalem had been reprieved. In AD 69 they had marched through Judaea and Vespasian had come close enough to view the walls of the city in the distance, but no further. In the spring of AD 70, however, the Romans finally marched their entire army all the way to Jerusalem and prepared to fight. Inside the city, about 25,000 veteran militia (and an unknown number of citizen militia) were waiting for them. As best we can reconstruct it, they were ranged as follows. There were 10,000 Judaean and Idumaean bandits organised in units of 200 under the leadership of Simon bar Giora. Allied with them were 5,000 Idumaean militia in units of 500. These were the men who defended the New City, the Upper City and most of the Lower City. Then there were 6,000 Galileans and others in units of 300 under John of Gischala, and allied with them Eleazar's 2,400 Zealots; these holding the Antonia Fortress, the Temple Mount and the Ophel Hill. Together these 25,000 or so fighters were the cream of the Jewish Revolution. They had volunteered to leave behind homes, farms and villages to fight in defence of Jerusalem. They were now veterans, battle-hardened and grimly resolved to face the many further privations and horrors they knew must lie ahead. They were steeled to do this because they believed that God would fight with them, that they were holy warriors at the End of Days, and that victory would destroy the Great Beast and inaugurate the Kingdom of the Saints on earth. Until now the revolutionary coinage had been inscribed 'Freedom of Zion' (**61**). After Simon bar Giora's bandit revolution in April AD 69, the inscription changed to 'Redemption of Israel'. The first simply described an accomplished political fact: the Romans had indeed been thrown out of Jerusalem and Mount Zion was therefore free. The second, by contrast, announced the dawning of a mythological golden age; it announced that the Apocalypse was about to begin.

7 The siege of Jerusalem

Thou wilt kindle the downcast of spirit and they shall be a flaming torch in the straw to consume ungodliness and never to cease till iniquity is destroyed. . . . For Thou wilt deliver into the hands of the poor the enemies from all the lands, to humble the might of the peoples by the hand of those bent to the dust, to bring upon the [head of Thine enemies] the reward of the wicked . . . We will despise kings, we will mock and scorn the mighty: for our Lord is holy, and the King of Glory is with us together with the Holy Ones. . . . Smite the nations, Thine adversaries, and devour the flesh of the sinner with Thy sword! Fill Thy land with glory and Thine inheritance with blessing! Let there be a multitude of cattle in Thy fields, and in Thy palaces silver and gold and precious stones! O Zion, rejoice greatly! O Jerusalem, show thyself amidst jubilation!

(*The War Scroll*, DSS, Qumran)

The capture of the outer walls

Late April to mid-May AD 70
It was 23 April when the first elements of the Roman army appeared on the hills north of Jerusalem. It was a large body of horse – more than 500 – and they had ridden forward of the main column to reconnoitre. The rest of the army, as yet unseen, had halted to pitch camp about three miles back next to the Jewish village of Gabath Saul in the Valley of the Thorns. With the cavalry reconnaissance rode the new Roman commander-in-chief, Titus Flavius Vespasianus the Younger, the 28-year-old son of the man who was now emperor (**62**).

Titus – as we know him – was the inevitable choice to succeed Vespasian. Both men had gone to Alexandria the previous summer to establish their political headquarters for the civil war. News of the Flavian victory in Italy did not reach them before the end of the year, long past the sailing season, so Vespasian had held court at Alexandria through the early months of AD 70. Then, before departing for Rome himself, he appointed Titus the new commander in Judaea and dispatched him to capture Jerusalem and end the war that summer. Titus had the necessary formal qualifications. After spending much of his childhood years in the court of the emperor Claudius, he had first served a military apprenticeship as a tribune in Britain and Germany, and then cut his teeth in Roman politics as a lawyer and junior magistrate.

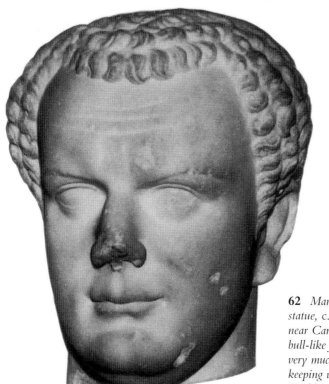

62 *Marble head of Titus from a statue, c.AD 70-80, found at Utica near Carthage in Tunisia. He has the bull-like features of his father, but this is very much the face of a young man, in keeping with Titus' image as Rome's 'Golden Boy'.* British Museum

For the last three years, of course, he had been the commander of a legion in his father's army. The soldiers, moreover, seemed to like him. Although somewhat short and paunchy-faced, his youth, muscular physique, horsemanship and skill-at-arms gave him the appearance of a soldier, while his bravery and willingness to fight in the front-line earned him the respect of the rank-and-file. His manner was relaxed and he had a reputation for generosity and a concern for the welfare of his men. His playboy and somewhat loutish image – he went in for riotous parties and was a devotee of the bloody games – no doubt also appealed to most Roman soldiers. Most important of all, though, he was his father's son at a time of acute political insecurity. The crisis of AD 69 had demonstrated that the throne was not the prerogative of a single family but could be seized by anyone with an army powerful enough to do it. Who could Vespasian trust if not his own son? It was above all dynastic politics that secured for Titus – a young man of rather modest intellect who was given to recklessness on the battlefield – the command of the largest army in the empire at the time. Fortunately, strategic and tactical brilliance were not essential. Titus presided over a well-oiled machine and was surrounded by competent operators. The war would be won – as it had been fought until now – not by brilliance but by method.

In the early spring, Titus had led his army overland from the Nile Delta, marching along the north coast of Sinai and up the Levantine coast, via Gaza, Ascalon, Jamnia and Joppa, to reach Caesarea Maritima (**1** & **8**). Here he concentrated his main force before the advance into Judaea. This had been increased from three to four legions: to the Fifth *Macedonica*, Tenth *Fretensis* and Fifteenth *Apollinaris*, the legions of Vespasian's army, was now added the Twelfth *Fulminata*, the Syrian legion defeated at Beth-Horon three-and-a-half years previously. All four legions had been brought up to full strength by detachments from other eastern units, and in all four morale was high – they had been on the winning side in the civil war, the first three had campaigned with great success in Palestine under Vespasian, and the last was eager to expunge the disgrace of defeat. Supporting the legions were 20 cohorts of auxiliary infantry and eight *alae* of cavalry, royal troops supplied by client-kings Herod Agrippa, Antiochus and Sohaemus, and, according to Tacitus, 'strong levies of Arabs, who felt for the Jews the hatred common between neighbours, and many individual adventurers from Rome and Italy, who for various reasons hoped to ingratiate themselves with an emperor whose ear might be gained'. The total was probably about 60,000 (20,000 legionaries, 20,000 auxiliaries and 20,000 allies). Many of these were already concentrated at Caesarea; others were under orders to rendezvous at Jerusalem. Even so, problems of security and supply in the Judaean hill-country prevented Titus from marching the main force in a single column. Instead he sent the Fifth via Emmaus and the Tenth via Jericho, keeping only two legions with him on the direct road to Jerusalem. The Jewish renegade Josephus marched with these. He was now a free man and prominent in the Roman general's entourage as consultant, emissary and translator. He remains, therefore, our principal source, and he has left us a description of Titus' column of march in April AD 70.

> Titus advanced into enemy country behind an advance guard formed of the royal troops and all the allied contingents. Next came the road-makers and camp-builders, then the officers' baggage with its armed escort. Behind these came the commander-in-chief with his spearmen and other picked soldiers, followed by the legionary cavalry. These marched in front of the engines, and behind them picked men commanded by tribunes and prefects of the cohorts; then the eagle, surrounded by the standards, with their trumpeters in front, and after them the main column marching six abreast. The servants belonging to each legion came next, preceded by the baggage; and last of all the mercenaries under the watchful eye of a rear guard.
>
> (*JW*, 5.47-9)

The march proceeded quickly – it was but a few days from Caesarea to Jerusalem if, as now, there was no resistance – and while his 20,000 or so men camped down just behind hills north of Jerusalem, Titus and his cavalry ranged ahead. As they topped Mount Scopus, they saw the ancient holy city of Jerusalem laid out before them, a rolling expanse of white-plastered buildings gleaming in the spring sunshine, surrounded by hills of yellow rock speckled green with olive-trees (**65**).

As ancient cities went, Jerusalem was anomalous. The land around it was parched and infertile. The main trade routes bypassed it to the west, the east and the north. Its only real advantage was that it was highly defensible. According to Jewish tradition, it had been founded as a royal fortress-city by King David in the early tenth century BC, and in the centuries after, the city's ability to withstand attack had underpinned the power of successive Jewish potentates. Here also, later in the tenth century, King Solomon was supposed to have founded a great temple to Yahweh, and, if not so early as this, certainly in the period after a new temple was built in the late sixth century, the city had become the pre-eminent focus of Jewish devotion. Tithes flowed into it from all parts of the Jewish world, and three times a year the population of the city doubled or trebled as it filled with pilgrims. They came for the Feast of the Tabernacles (Succot) in October, for the Feast of Unleavened Bread (Passover or Pesach) in April, and for the Feast of Weeks (Pentecost or Shevuot) in May. Tithes and pilgrims supported a multitude of priests, functionaries, innkeepers and traders, and the city had expanded from its original Davidic core to embrace the whole of two spurs projecting southwards from the high ground near Mount Scopus (**16** & **63**). The eastern spur comprised the Temple Mount (formerly Mount Moriah, but long since levelled and terraced to form a single huge platform) and the Ophel Hill immediately south of it (thought to be the site of the original tenth-century city). Overlooking the Temple Mount, which itself otherwise dominated the eastern spur, was the huge Antonia Fortress, abutting its north-west corner. The western spur, which terminated at Mount Zion, was altogether more substantial – longer, wider and higher – and it was here that the royal and aristocratic Upper City had developed in Hasmonaean and Herodian times. At the highest point, on the north-western edge of the Upper City, stood the Royal Palace, an immensely strong fortress build by Herod the Great. Between the two spurs ran the steep-sided Tyropoeon Valley. The Lower City, which was older and more plebeian than the other, ran from the eastern slopes of the western spur, across the intervening valley, and over the Ophel Hill – though the area actually built upon was restricted to where terracing was possible. On three sides of the city ran deep ravines – the Hinnom Valley to the west and the south, and the Kidron Valley between the Ophel Hill and the Mount of Olives to the east (**64** & **65**). The whole of the Upper and Lower cities was enclosed by a wall – known as the First Wall – but on the northern side, where the city had continued to expand, and from which it could be approached most easily by an attacker, the defences had been strengthened by two further walls. The Second Wall ran from the Antonia Fortress in the east to the Gennath Gateway in the west, the exact location of which is now unknown but is thought to have lain somewhere close to the Royal Palace. The Third Wall enclosed a much larger area to the north, where a suburb known as New City was developing on the Bezetha Hill. This wall had been started by Herod Agrippa I when he was client-king in AD 41-4, using massive stone blocks some 9m by 4.5m, but it had been left unfinished owing to Roman suspicions, and it was the revolutionaries who had recently completed it, perhaps to a height of 9m at the level of the battlemented walkway, and with a series of square towers projecting from the wall at regular intervals giving yet higher elevations.

Titus rode down from Mount Scopus, following the road which led towards the main gate through the Third Wall. Some distance short of the gate, in the vicinity of some impressive royal tomb monuments, he swung off the road to the right, aiming

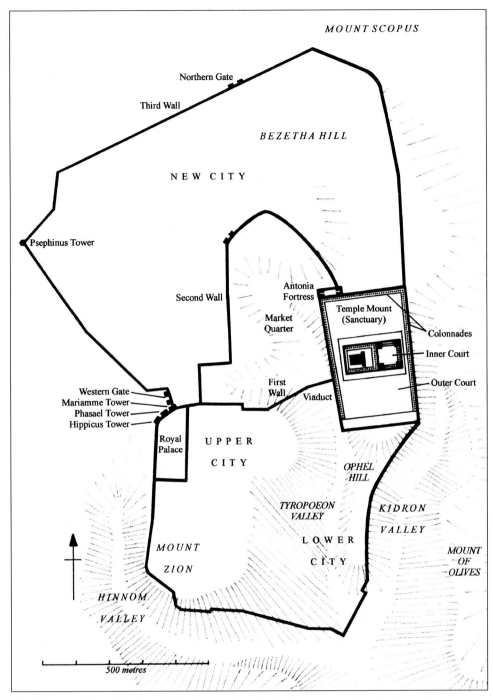

63 *The city of Jerusalem in AD 70 showing the principal features mentioned in the text*

64 *A view of the Hinnom Valley on the west side of Jerusalem looking north, with the sixteenth-century Ottoman walls of the Old City high on the right*

for the Psephinus Tower, a tall octagonal structure which guarded the north-west corner of the Third Wall (**66**). This was reckless indeed, for, close to the enemy and without support, it took him into very difficult terrain. The land around the city was in many places steeply sloping and uneven, and in others it was terraced and divided up into little gardens, orchards and olive groves by networks of ditches, hedges, fences, walls, paths and steps. There was a clutter of upstanding rocks, water-troughs, olive presses, stone shelters and tomb monuments. This was bad terrain for men trained to fight in close-ordered lines – for heavy shock infantry of Roman type – and it was worse still for cavalry, who would be slowed to a crawl and thrown into disorder as their mounts tried to negotiate a jumble of obstructions. For the Jews, on the other hand, the terrain was ideal.

The defenders were planning an aggressive defence, and the battleground as a whole afforded them ample opportunity to make good use of their military strengths. In addition to its fortifications and the broken ground all around, the built-up part of the city was a warren of narrow streets and houses, the area below ground riddled with tunnels (access passageways, water-channels and sewers). Countless gateways, small sally-ports and secret tunnel-entrances meant that sorties could emerge from virtually anywhere. Organised in small guerrilla units of between 200 and 500 men under tried and trusted leaders they had chosen themselves, the Jews mounted attacks not in tightly ordered lines but in loose fluid masses, enabling them to move easily in difficult terrain and make ready use of

65 *Engraving of Jerusalem based on a painting by Cassas. The view is from the Mount of Olives looking west over the Kidron Valley towards the Dome of the Rock (on the former Temple Mount), with the Upper City rising behind*

available cover. Generally without armour and other heavy equipment, they were highly mobile, able to rush forwards quickly and concentrate against a point of enemy weakness, and equally quickly to disengage before enemy counter-attacks could develop. Armed principally with missile weapons – some bows, but mainly slings, light javelins and hand-hurled stones – they could inflict damage without risking close-quarters action against heavier opponents; but they also had spears, swords and daggers with which they could close to contact if opportunity offered or necessity required. Above all, in their particular way of fighting, they had the skill of experienced veterans and the panache of revolutionary volunteers.

Suddenly, when only part of the Roman force had followed Titus off the road, a strong Jewish force charged out and cut the column in two. The men still on the road fled in panic, leaving Titus and the remainder struggling in the gardens and orchards into which they had strayed, their way back onto the road blocked by the Jews. Some sort of charge was improvised and the Roman cavalry burst through amid a hail of missiles to their flanks and rear. Titus had been extremely lucky. According to Josephus, he had gone out without armour, not expecting a fight, yet he, the Roman

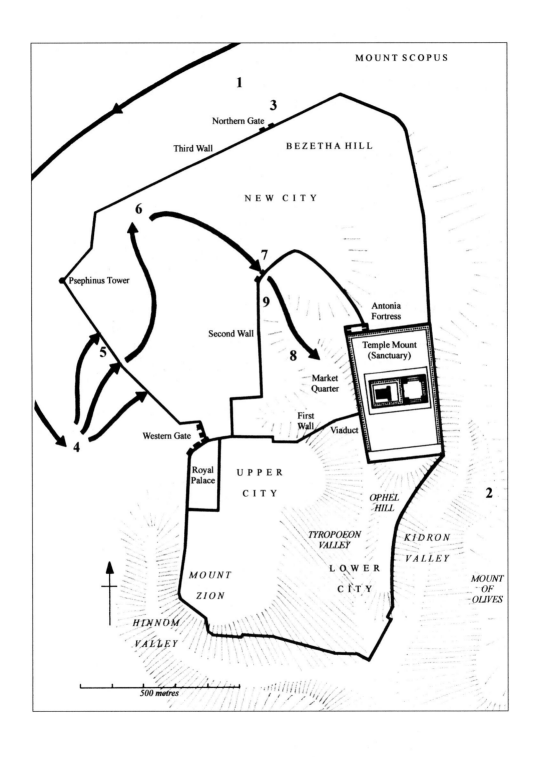

MOUNT SCOPUS

1

3

Northern Gate

Third Wall

BEZETHA HILL

NEW CITY

6

7

Psephinus Tower

9

5

Second Wall

8

Antonia
Fortress

Temple Mount
(Sanctuary)

Market
Quarter

4

Western Gate

First
Wall

Viaduct

Royal
Palace

UPPER
CITY

OPHEL
HILL

2

TYROPOEON
VALLEY

KIDRON
VALLEY

MOUNT
ZION

LOWER
CITY

MOUNT
OF
OLIVES

HINNOM
VALLEY

500 metres

commander-in-chief, had put himself in a position where he almost became the very first casualty of the siege. Even so, the lesson of this opening skirmish was not easily learnt; the very next day the Romans were to be taken by surprise again by powerful Jewish sorties, and throughout the siege Titus seems to have underestimated the bravery, cunning and skill-at-arms of his opponents.

That night and the following morning the rest of the army came up, the Fifth Legion from Emmaus, and the Tenth from Jericho. Work was begun immediately on three Roman camps, one for the Twelfth and Fifteenth on Mount Scopus about three-quarters of a mile north-north-east of the city, a second for the Fifth a short distance to the rear of this, and a third for the Tenth on the Mount of Olives, the summit of which was about three-quarters-of-a-mile east of the city on the far side of the Kidron Valley (**66** & **67**). Again the Romans were careless, and their careless-ness could be observed from the walls of Jerusalem by Jewish commanders intent on their strategy of active defence. The sortie of the previous day had been carried out by Simon bar Giora's men, since these controlled the Third Wall, but now, seeing the whole Roman army coming up and building camps, the two rival factions united their forces for a large-scale sortie against the Tenth Legion on the Mount of Olives. Most of the legionaries had grounded their arms (and may even have taken off their armour) and distributed themselves widely to dig out ditches and pile up stone revetments. Given their numbers, and the distance between the walls of the city and the campsite, they expected no attack, or at least none that came so fast as to strike them before they could form up. But surprise and speed were precisely features of Jewish warfare. A large force burst out of the eastern and southern gateways of the city, surged across the Kidron Valley, and stormed up the opposite slope of the Mount of Olives, getting among the legionaries as they rushed for their arms or fled in panic towards the summit. It is a weakness of highly-trained soldiers that they lack self-reliance and initiative. They expect to operate shoulder-to-shoulder with comrades under officers stationed only a few yards behind, moving and manoeuvring in a disciplined manner, wielding weapons in concert, fighting to a formula that has become almost instinc-tive, such that the unit seems machine-like in character. But sometimes there is no formation, none of the usual comrades around, no orders from recognised superiors. In the chaos of a surprise attack on unformed men, highly-trained soldiers sometimes go to pieces. This happened now to the legionaries of the Tenth. Each man would be assailed by the roar of an alien battle-cry echoing off the slopes. He would catch glimpses of enemies racing forwards in strength, perhaps of others already on his flank,

66 *(opposite) The siege of Jerusalem from late April to mid-May AD 70. 1. Titus' cavalry reconnaissance is ambushed by a Jewish sortie (23 April). 2. Two massed Jewish attacks on the Tenth Legion camp on the Mount of Olives are thrown back after hard fighting (24 April). 3. Romans lured to the walls by a ruse are defeated by a strong Jewish sortie (late April). 4. Titus redeploys the Fifth, Twelfth and Fifteenth Legions to two new camps west of the city (late April). 5. The Romans build three platforms, create a breach in the First Wall by ramming, and storm into the New City (7 May). 6. The Romans establish a new base at the 'Camp of the Assyrians' (7 May). 7. The Romans capture the Second Wall (11 May). 8. The Romans are attacked and driven out of the Market Quarter (mid-May). 9. The Romans regain the Second Wall and level it (mid-May)*

67 *A nineteenth-century engraving of the Mount of Olives (left), the Kidron Valley (centre) and the Temple Mount (right) looking south*

and he would see their missiles flying through the air. There would also be much that he could not see amid the olive groves and the dust clouds of battle, and his fear would be that the enemy might already have broken through to threaten him from behind. Josephus appears to capture well the essential flavour of this fight.

> Men highly organised and trained to fight according to the book and in obedience to orders are most quickly demoralised by unorthodox and enter-prising tactics. So on this occasion the Romans, having left the initiative to the Jews, gave way before the onslaught. Whenever some of them were overtaken and faced about, they held up the onrush of the Jews, and catching them off their guard in the excitement of pursuit inflicted casual-ties on them, but, as more and more Jews poured out of the city, their confusion grew, till at last they were chased from their camp.
>
> (*JW*, 5.79–80)

Titus brought reinforcements across from Mount Scopus, rallied the broken legionaries, and then led a counter-attack which drove the Jews back down the slope. Attacks by fresh units in good order are almost always successful against men exhausted and disorganised after a charge and running battle. But the Jews were adept in the tactics of evasion, and they did not regard retreat on such occasions as defeat. They raced back down the east side of the valley and then rallied for a stand on the western slope beneath the walls of the city. Here they were safe: had the Romans pursued them further, they would have found themselves attacking uphill over broken ground against determined skirmishers and within range of missiles shot from the city battlements above. There was a protracted stand-off. Then at noon, the battle seemingly over for the day, Titus thinned out the line facing the Jews across the valley and sent some of the legionaries back up the slope to resume work on the camp. An observer signalled from the battlements to a fresh force of Jews waiting at the gates and a second wave of assailants then surged forth to attack the weakened enemy line. The Romans panicked and fled without attempting resistance, and as the Jews crossed the valley and mounted the eastern slope, reinforced no doubt by the men who had carried out the first attack, the legionaries working on the camp above joined the rout. For the second day running, Titus found himself isolated with a small party of followers as the result of an unexpected, fast-moving and aggressive Jewish attack. His great personal danger may, as Josephus states, have helped the officers on the ridge to rally the fugitives and organise a counter-attack. Units were reformed and charged back down the slope. The Jews again ran for safety on the far side of the valley. And Titus re-established his defensive line, keeping it up to strength this time, so that camp building could resume without further interruption. It had not been a good day: there cannot have been many in Roman warfare on which the same legion was routed twice. But lessons had been learnt, albeit rather slowly, and over the following days, posting strong bodies of horse and foot to deter sorties, Titus ordered the soldiers to clear the ground between the Roman camps and the city by felling trees, throwing down hedges and fences, filling in ditches, and demolishing projecting rocks. The idea was to deny the guerrilla fighter a friendly environment beyond his walls; to turn the ground there into an open slope without cover or obstacle where he would be exposed to unimpeded Roman counter-attack should he venture forth; and, of course, to clear the approaches to the walls for the engines and assault columns that would soon be sent against them.

The Jews now deployed another weapon – the ruse – and not for the last time the Romans were caught in its coils. A crowd of Jews streamed out of the towers along the northern face of the Third Wall and huddled together there as if in fear. Others on the battlements shouted their support for peace and offered to open the gates, while pelting the crowd outside the walls with stones. A third party was waiting behind the walls to sally forth should the Romans fall for the ruse. Titus was convinced that the peace party inside the city was powerful, and the previous day he had sent Josephus forward to demand surrender. The defenders were playing on this idea, and, though Josephus insists that Titus was suspicious, many of his soldiers seized their weapons and charged down to the gates expecting them to be opened. They were met immediately by a hail of missiles from the men in front of the wall and on the battlements above, and by encircling attacks on both flanks as the third party surged out of the gateways on either side of them. A fierce struggle went on for some time before the Romans forced their way back to their own lines in a messy fighting retreat. The soldiers were berated by Titus for their indiscipline in attacking without orders – but the real fault was a general underestimation of the enemy throughout the Roman army at Jerusalem. This false expectation of easy victory continued for some time, producing a string of tactical reverses, and as it finally broke down under the weight of adverse experience, it was transformed into frustration, occasional despair and outbursts of vindictive savagery.

By now the Roman army concentration was complete, its initial camps constructed, and much of the ground before the walls cleared and levelled. The intelligence gathering, abortive negotiations and several brisk skirmishes of the first few days had shown that the city was not about to surrender and would in fact be defended with great vigour. So what was the Roman strategy to be? One option, given that the city was packed with militia, refugees and pilgrims, would have been to establish a blockade and attempt to starve it into submission. Roman commanders of this period hardly ever adopted such a passive strategy, however, as it had several major disadvantages: it placed huge logistical strains on the besiegers, not least in fairly barren hill-country like that around Jerusalem; it gave the enemy time to organise a relief expedition or at least to develop effective guerrilla action in the besiegers' rear; it risked igniting a wider conflict by turning the beleaguered city into a beacon of successful defiance; and it tarnished the imperial power's image of invincibility and diminished the glory of any final victory. Titus was especially eager to win military renown for the new Flavian regime and to return to Rome for an early triumph. He was, according to Tacitus, 'dreaming of Rome, wealth and pleasure'. The plan was to take Jerusalem quickly. But how? Much hope seems to have been placed on the twin strategy of treachery and terror. The Romans overestimated the relative strength of the aristocratic peace-party in the city. More than once they were tricked by Jewish rebels feigning submission, and on at least four occasions during the siege Josephus was sent up to the walls to appeal for surrender; his text reflects the frustration of his patrons at the failure of these repeated efforts to secure a cheap victory. The real basis of the appeals was of course terror – the impending horrors and privations of both siege and sack – the effect of which might have induced a popular clamour for capitulation on terms. However, though the terror eventually escalated into mass crucifixions before the besieged walls, the city was not betrayed, the rebels fought to the bitter end, and the Romans paid in blood for every position they took.

'The city occupied a commanding position,' explained Tacitus, 'and it had been reinforced by engineered works so massive that they might have rendered even a flat site impregnable.' To approach the main defences – the Antonia Fortress, the Temple Mount, the northern stretch of the First Wall, and the Royal Palace – it was all but essential first to force both the Second and Third Walls. The deep ravines of Kidron and Hinnom made the idea of attempting a direct assault on the First Wall from east, south or west too daunting to contemplate. The city could be approached on fairly level ground only from the north, and that meant driving through the two more northerly walls first. The Third Wall was strong along most of its length, but it had been completed hurriedly and there were points of weakness, especially near undeveloped areas of the New City. Even so, the wall was not to be taken by escalade, the cheapest and quickest way to storm a city. This involved large numbers of heavy infantry attacking on a broad front with scaling ladders, supported by massed missile-shooting to suppress activity on the battlements. There were two problems with this approach. The attackers coming up the ladders in single file were extremely vulnerable during the ascent, and they depended for success to a large extent on the defenders being too over-stretched to be able to man all the threatened sectors of the wall adequately. Either way, escalade often involved heavy casualties from missiles, boiling oil, dropped boulders, and the overturning of ladders. There was, in any case, a prior technical problem: the higher the walls, the longer the ladders needed, and the greater the chances they would collapse under the weight of men climbing them. The attackers had to ascend in close succession, lest the first few onto the wall be isolated and destroyed, and for walls higher than about 10m ladders strong enough simply could not be made. The height of the Third Wall was very much at this technical limit: 9m to the walkway and 11.5m to the top of the battlements. An escalade against numerous defenders on a wall this high would have been extremely hazardous; Titus did not attempt it, choosing instead the slower but safer option of using ramps and ramming.

Though Josephus' account is obscure, it seems that Titus found a place to attack somewhere on the western part of the Third Wall, that is between the Psephinus Tower and the Western Gate. He redeployed his army accordingly. Leaving the Tenth Legion in their camp on the Mount of Olives, he shifted the others to two new camps about 400m west of the city, that of the Fifth opposite the Western Gate, that of the Twelfth and Fifteenth opposite the Psephinus Tower. Given the Jews' willingness to sortie, the transfer of the baggage-train was an especially ponderous and dangerous process, necessitating the deployment of a line of men outside the north-western part of the city comprising three ranks of infantry at the front, a rank of archers, and three ranks of cavalry at the rear. The movement completed, the army was then divided into three sections and ordered to construct three earth-and-timber ramps. Wicker hurdles were erected as a protection against missiles, and archers and artillery were deployed to deter attacks. The work proceeded quickly despite artillery shooting and small-scale sorties by Simon bar Giora's men, and when the Roman engineers, by throwing lead and line, showed the distance between the end of the ramps and the wall to be within the range of a battering ram, Titus prepared to attack. The artillery was moved closer to the walls to provide covering fire, and the rams were hauled slowly up the ramps and into position. When the commanding signal was given, the rams began to swing, and as the first blows were struck, a deep, thudding, rhythmic din could be heard across the city and the surrounding hills. It was a sound resonant with terrors. It marked the formal start of a siege attack and it sealed the fate of all within the walls. Ancient writers sometimes record that a great mournful wail would arise from a besieged city at the sound of the first blows, for it was the signal that the time for surrender on terms had passed, and that the occupants now faced the horrors of the sack. Josephus reports that he heard such a wail now, as the battering of the Third Wall began, and that the shock induced by the beginning of the assault brought a final end to the factional struggle and a firm alliance between the revolutionary militias.

A furious battle now erupted around the rams. A majority of men in combat are dominated by their fears, and a yearning for safety and survival tends to suppress initiative and encourage most to huddle together defensively, especially when battle reaches one of its periodic crescendos. In a lethal chaos of aggression, noise, dust, flying projectiles and stabbing spear-points, fear and confusion can induce a paralysing inertia. For men defending walls especially, mounting an attack on the enemy – leaving the safety of the walls to fight the enemy in the open – involves a powerful psychological wrench. But in all armies there is a minority of 'natural fighters', men in whom the excitement of battle seems to suppress instinctive fears, such that they are more willing to expose themselves, to close with the enemy, and generally to take risks. Often these men become effective junior officers, but they may simply be dominant characters within the small groups of close comrades-in-arms which are the basic building-blocks of an army. In describing especially hazardous operations – like sorties or assaults on breaches – Josephus repeatedly refers to 'the bolder spirits' (Jews) or 'picked men' (Romans). It appears from this that the leading role of aggressive front-line fighters – and the way in which successful action by them could draw many other men into the fray – was both noticed by contemporary observers and formed a part of detailed tactical planning by commanders. So it was now as 'the bolder spirits sprang forward in tight groups' to attack the rams by climbing onto the roofs, tearing off the hurdles, and pelting the crews below with missiles. As they did so, firebrands were hurled down from the battlements to set the engines alight, and a hail of other missiles was directed at the archers and cavalry stationed around them. Fighting of this intensity is exhausting and cannot be sustained for long. A common pattern is for brief flare-ups to be followed by much longer lulls as the two sides recuperate and reorganise. During such a lull, when the Jewish sorties had ceased and the Roman guard was down, a sudden large-scale attack was launched by men issuing from a hidden sally-port near the Western Gate. The attack took the weary men defending the Roman works by surprise and came at them from an unexpected direction; their line gave way, and the Jews, armed with numerous firebrands, got among the engines. Some legionaries stood firm, however, and Titus counter-attacked with his cavalry, driving the Jews back into the city before they could do serious damage to the rams. They had taken a number of casualties, and one man was captured, whom Titus ordered crucified in front of the walls – the first of many such exemplary executions designed to deter sorties and encourage capitulation.

The attack on the Third Wall lasted for about a week, by the end of which the Romans had in place on each of the three platforms an iron-plated wooden tower over 20m high. Though one of these fell down in the middle of the night, causing consternation in the Roman lines, it was merely an accident, and in fact the towers were virtually invulnerable to sorties, being too heavy to overturn and fully fireproof. Almost invulnerable to missiles themselves, the artillerymen, archers and javelin-throwers inside could rake the battlements and the ground outside the walls and allow the rams a clear field in which to do their work. The defenders in this sector were exhausted by a week of 'fighting, sentry-go and night-duty far from the city', and as the weight of incoming shot forced them from the walls, the decision was taken not to contest the issue further: the First Wall was but an outwork. When 'Victor', the biggest of the Roman rams, finally punched a breach through part of the wall on 7 May, the defenders withdrew to the Second Wall, allowing a Roman storming party to enter unopposed and open the gates to the rest of the army. Titus immediately levelled part of the First Wall, occupied the whole of the New City, and built a new camp for his army in its north-western corner in an area traditionally known as the 'Camp of the Assyrians'.

The assault on the Second Wall began forthwith. This defence protected a fairly new suburb which had developed in the upper Tyropoeon Valley. The wall formed a northward projecting salient between the Antonia Fortress and somewhere near the Western Gate, but its exact line and configuration are uncertain. It may not have been very strong, since, though the fighting was heavy, after just four days one of the rams brought down 'the middle tower of the north wall' and created a breach. This, as before at the breach in the Third Wall, the Jews declined to defend, and Titus promptly led more than a thousand legionaries into the suburb. There seems then to have been a pause. Josephus reports that Titus kept his men well in hand – refusing permission to plunder in order to protect property – and again offered terms. He then retired, leaving only a small garrison to hold the towers on the Second Wall and to defend the area beyond the breach. The latter was a plebeian quarter, a warren of narrow streets, courtyards and ramshackle buildings, usually filled with wool-sellers, blacksmiths and rag-traders (**colour plate 18**). Though it seemed deserted, it is likely that many of the defenders had merely gone to ground, and now, along with others who sallied forth from gateways, they moved forwards again to infiltrate and surround the Roman position. The attack was a classic of the eastern guerrilla method: the Jews had given way before a strong assault, disappearing out of reach and suspending operations until the enemy's guard was down; now that it was, they struck back against a weak detachment in close terrain. Suddenly, for the Romans caught in the trap, it seemed that the enemy were all around them, that any corner, window or rooftop might harbour a killer in wait. Under constant missile and hit-and-run attack, the legionaries formed tight blocks behind shield-walls and fought their way back to the breach. Here many of them were pinned down. The garrison Titus had placed in the towers on the Second Wall had fled in confusion, and the Jews had since moved up close to the breach. It was no more than a narrow gap at the top of a heap of rubble; only a handful could get through at a time, and they risked being struck down by enemy missiles as they did so. Only the subsequent arrival of contingents of archers to give covering fire enabled the bulk of the legionaries to escape. The Jews then surged back onto the Second Wall, barricaded the breach, and held it through three solid days of renewed Roman assault. On the fourth day the Romans broke through again and the Jews fell back as before. This time – showing greater respect for the capacity of the enemy than he had the first time through the breach – Titus threw down the whole northern stretch of the Second Wall and posted strong garrisons in the remaining towers.

Again there was a pause. The fighting had continued with little intermission for well over two weeks. The struggle for the Second Wall had been especially severe: 'assaults, wall-fighting, sorties at unit strength went on continuously all day long,' recalls Josephus; 'dusk hardly availed to break off the battles begun at dawn, and there was no sleep for either side . . . both passed the night in arms.' Battle is physically and mentally exhausting. During the Second World War, psychiatric breakdown afflicted about ten per cent of men in the first few hours of actual combat. Though this initial shock no doubt weeded out many who were especially vulnerable, a steady stream of psychiatric casualties continued for as long as combat lasted. Different men had different tolerances, and the point at which each broke down varied, but the attrition on units kept in the line was constant. Overall, under extreme pressure, psychiatric casualties could amount to half the total. Ancient siege warfare – unlike pitched battle – must often have involved pressures of this kind, where units might be involved in intense front-line fighting for days or even weeks. Wise commanders sought periods of rest to restore strength and sanity when they could, and this may well by why Titus now suspended operations for four days. During this time he held a parade of his entire army on the Bezetha Hill. The soldiers turned out in full armour and decorative trappings to receive their regular pay, and the spectacle was viewed, as intended, by the Jewish defenders from their battlements about half a mile away. This awesome display of military power – 40,000 armoured professionals – was complemented by yet another appeal for surrender, again delivered by Josephus, who shouted the Roman offer up to the battlements from a position in front of the walls just out of range.

The rebels were in no mood to negotiate, and Josephus was greeted with the now customary abuse. The fall of the Third and Second Walls had not significantly altered the military equation. The Third Wall had been an outer ring only recently completed, defending largely open ground. The Second Wall had defended a populated area near the heart of the city, but it too was a late addition to the primary fortifications, and it comprised an oddly-shaped salient formed of mainly low-lying ground. The Jewish defence of these outworks had been skilful: missile shooting and generally well-judged sorties and counter-attacks had disrupted Roman operations and imposed casualties; yet the Jews had avoided over-commitment, withdrawing in good time when threatened, and had thus avoided taking serious losses in the defence of secondary positions. They were now massed on a much narrower front along the line of the city's main northern fortifications. John ben Levi's Galileans and Zealots held the Temple Mount and the Antonia Fortress at the eastern end of this line. In places the Temple platform rose some 45m above the surrounding ground level, and atop this, around the entire outer edge of the sanctuary, ran a 12m-high colonnade (**colour plate 19**). The Jewish defenders were deployed on the rooftop wall of the northern and western colonnades. At the junction of these, on the north-western corner of the Temple Mount, the Antonia Fortress had been built. It stood on an 11m-high rock plated with polished stone slabs. The fortress itself was a huge rectan-gular tower 18m tall, with turrets at all four corners, three of them 23m high, and one 32m (assuming, as ever, that we can trust Josephus). On the eastern, northern and western sides there were deep, wide, rock-cut ditches, which gave to the fortress even greater effective elevation. On the southern side it was connected to the Temple colonnades and there were access stairways. West of the Temple and the Fortress, Simon bar Giora's Judaeans and Idumaeans held the First Wall, which ran all the way across the city to the Royal Palace. The most notable defensive features here were the Hippicus, Phasael and Mariamme Towers at the north-western corner of the First Wall (**colour plate 21**). Built of huge marble blocks 9m by 4.5m, the towers were, respectively, 37m, 41m and 25m tall (or so we are told), and were surmounted by battlemented turrets and ramparts (**71**). The whole northern line – Temple Mount, Antonia Fortress, and First Wall – stretched for a distance of about 1200m. The Jews had 20 men for every metre of this front. Having been willing to defy the Romans at the Third and Second Walls, they could have no good reason to surrender now. The real struggle for Jerusalem was about to begin.

Into the shadow of death

Mid-May to late June AD 70
The Antonia was the key to the Lower City. From its turrets and walkways, on Jewish festival days past, the soldiers of King Herod, Pontius Pilate and Gessius Florus had looked down on the crowds of pilgrims thronging the Temple courts below. From this vantage point they had been able to watch for the first signs of trouble anywhere on the vast 480m by 300m wide concourse. The Antonia dominated the Temple Mount just as the Temple Mount dominated the Lower City. Moreover, with the fall of the First and Second Walls, the fortress constituted a bastion projecting northwards into the Roman lines and threatening operations directed elsewhere. Titus now duly launched his main effort against the Antonia (**68**).

The legions were organised into two groups, one to attack the Antonia, the other the First Wall, and each of the four was ordered to build a huge ramp. The work was done under incessant attack from missiles and sorties, the rebels' armoury including some 300 bolt-shooters and 40 stone-throwers, captured equipment in the use of which they were increasingly proficient. Despite the disruption, the ramps were completed on 29 May, just 17 days after work had commenced. The Fifth and Twelfth Legions had built theirs side-by-side 10m apart in front of the north face of the Antonia, and the Tenth and Fifteenth had ramps 15m apart against a section of the First Wall which cannot now be identified, but was probably close to the Western Gate (the modern Jaffa Gate). Jewish counter-measures appeared to have failed and all looked set for the commencement of the Roman assault. In fact, John ben Levi had long been preparing a spectacular surprise attack.

His men had been digging a mine. The area beneath the Temple platform, which was partly rock and partly terracing, included numerous underground tunnels. Some of these have been explored in recent times, but many others probably once existed and have now either collapsed and disappeared or survive but remain undis-covered. From one or more of these tunnels, John's men had been excavating a new

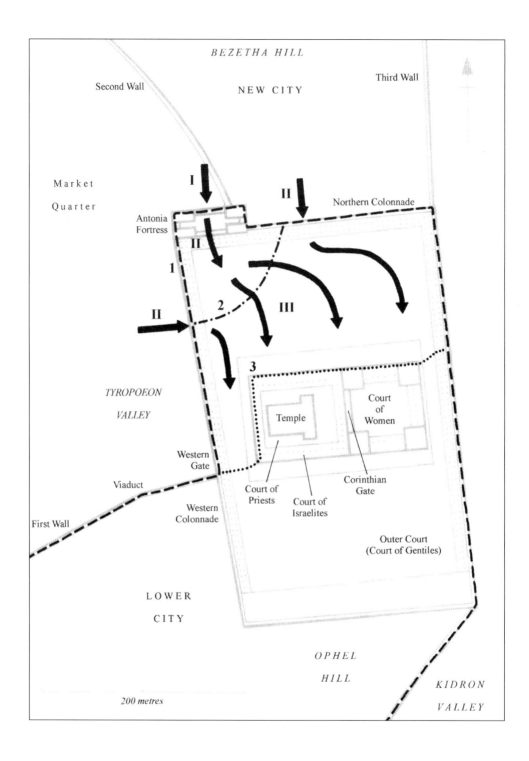

BEZETHA HILL

Third Wall

Second Wall

NEW CITY

Market

Quarter

I

II

Northern Colonnade

Antonia
Fortress

II

1

II

2

III

3

TYROPOEON

VALLEY

Temple

Court
of
Women

Western
Gate

Viaduct

Court of
Priests

Court of
Israelites

Corinthian
Gate

First Wall

Western
Colonnade

Outer Court
(Court of Gentiles)

LOWER

CITY

OPHEL

HILL

KIDRON

200 metres

VALLEY

line out past the Antonia to run beneath the Roman platforms. This was extraordinarily arduous and dangerous work. The sappers inhabited a cramped, airless, dust-filled world, where they worked to dig out spoil by the dim, flickering light of oil lamps, living every moment with the fear of an appalling death, entombed by roof collapse to perish slowly of suffocation. Nor was their work simply a matter of courage and physical toughness. Sapping was highly skilled. It involved fine judgements about the line to follow and the depth at which to work. If the mine was a few degrees off true, it could miss its target completely; if it was too shallow, it might collapse prematurely onto the sappers, or the enemy learn of it from the sounds of work beneath; but if it was too deep, its deliberate collapse might have no effect on the surface. For the idea was to drive the line directly under the enemy's works and there expand it into a wide gallery supported on wooden props. When all was ready, the props would be fired in controlled conditions, bringing down the roof and, hopefully, whatever was above it. If successful, the effects, both physical and moral, could be devastating.

The Roman machines were already on the platforms when the Jews filled the gallery beneath with faggots coated in pitch and bitumen and set fire to them. Then, no doubt, they went above to watch.

> As soon as the props were burnt away, the entire gallery collapsed, and with a thunderous crash the platforms fell into the cavity. At once there arose a dense cloud of smoke and dust as the flames were choked by the debris. Then, when the mass of timber was burnt away, a brilliant flame broke through. This sudden blow filled the Romans with consternation . . . To fight the flames seemed pointless, for even if they put them out, the platforms were already swallowed up.
>
> (*JW*, 5.470-2)

Two days later, Simon's men launched a more conventional, but no less effective, attack on the ramps and machines threatening the First Wall. Inspired perhaps by the success at Antonia, three 'natural fighters' charged out to attack the rams already in operation against the wall. Josephus identifies them. Tephthaeus was a Galilean villager, Megassarus a former royal servant, and Ceagiras, a disabled man from Adiabene, one of the 'international brigade' that had rallied to Jerusalem's defence.

68 *(opposite) The attack on the Antonia Fortress and the Temple Mount, mid-May to mid-August AD 70. The struggle fell into three main phases. For each phase, Roman attacks are indicated by roman numerals, the Jewish front-line by arabic ones. In the first phase (12 May — 2 July), the Romans built two successive sets of ramps against the Antonia Fortress wall before part of it collapsed and opened a breach (**I**, **1**, dashed line). In the second phase (3 July — early August), the Romans attempted to break into the Outer Court of the Sanctuary by building ramps, ramming, firing the colonnades, and direct assault; the Jewish forward position was eventually rendered untenable (**II**, **2**, dash-and-dot line). In the final phase (ended 10 August), the Romans brought the Inner Court under attack and Jewish resistance collapsed suddenly when fires broke out and the legionaries stormed in through open gates (**III**, **3**, dotted line)*

In the whole course of the war, the city produced no one more heroic than these three, or more terrifying. They dashed out as if towards friends, not massed enemies; they neither hesitated nor shrank back, but charged through the centre of the foe and set the engines on fire. Pelted with missiles and thrust at with swords on every side, they refused to withdraw from their perilous position until the engines were ablaze.

(JW, 5.475-7)

The sudden success of this impromptu attack quickly drew in both Roman and Jewish reinforcements, the former attempting to suppress the flames, the latter to win time for them to take proper hold. It was a battle the Jews won, and as the fires began to rage uncontrollably, platforms as well as rams were consumed. A surge of excitement carried the Jews forwards, their numbers swelled as more and more men poured out of the city, and the attack grew into a general offensive against the Roman lines. The legionaries fell back quickly through the smashed streets of the northern suburbs, and, because the Jewish tide kept growing and coming, the retreat soon became panic-stricken and chaotic. The pursuit did not end until it reached the Roman camp, where the men on guard-duty – who faced the death penalty if they withdrew in such circumstances – stood their ground and, supported by batteries of bolt-shooters hastily lifted onto the rampart, finally brought the Jewish attack to a halt. By this time Titus was on the scene and able to improvise a counter-attack against the right flank of the Jewish mass. Even so, despite disorder and exhaustion, the militiamen were exultant after the Roman rout and not yet ready to give ground; part of them turned to face the new threat, and the Jews maintained for some time a messy battle on two fronts, in which men 'blinded by dust and deafened by noise' struggled to distinguish friend from foe. The fight gradually fizzled out as the Jews retreated towards the First Wall.

By mining and fire-attack, the Jews had destroyed in two days Roman works that had taken more than two weeks to build. They had again demonstrated their enterprise, daring and courage. They had again driven Roman regulars before them in rout. Little wonder that there was despair in the Roman lines. The hills around Jerusalem had been stripped bare and timber was now in desperately short supply. Even if new supplies of wood could be found and new platforms raised, there was no guarantee that these would survive future attacks. Some, in the council of war Titus convened, argued for an immediate all-out assault by the entire army – a desperate attempt at using massed escalade and shooting to break through somewhere on an over-stretched enemy line. Such ideas were folly: the walls everywhere were high, in many places far higher than ladders could mount, and the Jewish defenders were very numerous. Others argued for starving the city into submission by putting a cordon of troops around it to stop supplies going in and people coming out. But there would be loopholes in any such blockade, the men would be spread out in small packets vulnerable to attack, and the strategy would take ages to work. There was no satisfactory alternative: the platforms would have to be rebuilt. This time, though, everything possible would be done to erode the capacity and the will of the defenders to resist – by a combination of privation and terror. Henceforward the siege was to assume an increasingly ghastly form, and the tens of thousands of human beings trapped inside Jerusalem now descended rapidly into an abyss of suffering.

Titus ordered the construction of a wall of circumvallation around the city. Nearly 8km in length, it began and ended at the Roman camp on the Bezetha Hill, otherwise following the line of hilltops which ringed the besieged city east, south and west of the Kidron and Hinnom Valleys. The wall must have been roughly built – Josephus claims it was completed in three days – but it was strengthened by 13 forts; auxiliary troops would have garrisoned these and patrolled the wall to enforce the blockade. No trace of this wall remains, but another, built a few years later at Masada and probably very similar, is exceptionally well preserved. A 2m-thick drystone wall studded with guard-towers runs for some three miles and completely encircles the base of the mountain there. Associated with it are eight siege-camps, two of them what we might now call 'vexillation forts', able to hold part of a legion plus auxiliaries (say, 2,500 men), two of them large 'auxiliary forts' (1,000 men), the other four smaller 'auxiliary forts' (500 men). The interiors are laid out in a standardised Roman way with regularly aligned streets and neat rows of tent bases. 'The Roman general,' Josephus explains, '. . . built a wall round the entire fortress, so that none of the besieged could easily escape, and he set his men to guard the several parts of it . . .' Both plan and method are probably similar to those of Titus at Jerusalem.

The blockade took rapid effect on a population that was already feeling the pinch of hunger. Bloated with militiamen, refugees and pilgrims, all of whom were now crowded into the area enclosed by the First Wall, the city had to feed perhaps a quarter of a million people or more. There were five principal sources of supply. First, on or beneath the Temple Mount were large warehouses stored with food given as tithe payments and first-fruit offerings. Second, the rebels had laid up large stockpiles of grain before the siege began, and these are likely to have been stored in royal warehouses similar to those known at Masada – though Josephus reports that much of this reserve was deliberately destroyed in the factional struggle between John and Simon. Thirdly, there were private stockpiles of food, with perhaps significant amounts in the possession of some aristocrats and merchants. Fourthly, with the incentive of grossly inflated prices, limited supplies of food continued to be smuggled into the city, at least in the early stages of the siege; a distribution of coins minted in Jerusalem in AD 70 to rural areas which traditionally supplied the city may be evidence for this trade. Fifthly, it was possible to forage for small amounts of food in the immediate vicinity of the city. Several sources – Josephus, *The New Testament*, rabbinical literature, and the results of archaeological survey – are in agreement that the slopes around Jerusalem were extensively terraced and that grain, vegetables, figs, olives, almonds and grapes were cultivated. Though it seems unlikely that much survived once the siege was at all advanced, Josephus reports that numbers of people continued to venture forth to forage beyond the walls at night. As famine got a grip, rising need must have offset diminishing returns to sustain a fairly constant level of scavenging. The aim of the new Roman strategy of tight blockade was to cut off the latter two sources of external supply – smuggling and foraging – while exacerbating the pressure on internal supplies by keeping the whole mass of fighters, refugees, pilgrims and city poor bottled up inside the walls. Central to the strategy, therefore, was the Roman policy with regard to captives and deserters.

Both sides imposed restrictions on movement between the lines, but there was never a watertight seal around the city. Each major political crisis since AD 66 had produced a wave of political refugees, most of them upper-class Jews opposed to the revolution who sought Roman protection. Until very late in the siege, these defectors were welcomed by the besiegers; the Roman leadership recognised them as men of rank who might be politically useful in the future. An anecdote related by Josephus throws light on the official attitude. Some Arab and Syrian soldiers were seizing hold of deserters and cutting them open in the belief that they had swallowed their gold to get it out of the city. The Roman generals tried to stop the practice because 'fear of this fate caused many of the deserters to return'. Lower-class Jews who escaped from the city were viewed very differently, however, especially as the famine drove increasing numbers to attempt this. In a revolt of the poor, all the poor were suspect. When the world was turned right side up again, and the poor were back in their place, it would be the men of property who mattered, not the riff-raff. Meantime, the insurrectionary poor of Jerusalem were to be bottled up in the doomed city to consume its precious food-stocks and then perish of starvation. They were to be an example to the world. To keep them bottled up – and to make the example especially memorable – those who were caught outside the walls were enslaved, mutilated or executed. Some of these were combatants too slow or unlucky in the whirlwind fighting of a sortie. Many were poor men with hungry families caught night-foraging on the slopes of Kidron or Hinnom. Others were taken trying to creep through the Roman lines and escape to safety. Certainly some hundreds of these, quite possibly thousands, were nailed onto crosses and trees around the city and left to hang until they died.

Roman crucifixion was a pageant of horror designed to terrorise those who witnessed it (**69**). First the victim was stripped naked, bound to a post and flogged with a scourge. A relief-sculpture in Rome depicting a scourge shows it with a wooden handle and two or three leather thongs threaded with small fragments of bone or metal intended to rip the flesh. A variety of other tortures might also be inflicted at this stage, and throughout the ordeal the victim faced the abuse and mockery of enemies. After these preliminaries, he was taken to a wooden cross and held against it with his arms outstretched and his legs together. In 1968 the remains of a young man crucified in the first century AD were found in the Giv'at ha-Mivtar cemetery just north of Jerusalem. This skeletal evidence, coupled with the famous description in *The New Testament*, has given us some understanding of the reality of crucifixion (though debate about details continues). Nails were hammered through the lower arms just above the wrists to pin the limbs to the cross. With knees bent and legs pushed up, a third nail, driven in sideways, was used to fix both heels in position. When the cross was raised – or, if the victim was upright when nailed, then at the time his legs were pushed up – the weight of the

69 *A Roman crucifixion. Hundreds, perhaps thousands, were crucified on the hills around the city during the siege. The reconstruction is based on limited literary and archaeological evidence*

body pulling downwards would have caused the nails in the arms to lodge firmly against the wrist-bones. Small wooden boards prevented the nail-heads burrowing through the flesh and freeing the limbs. Some crosses were provided with small wooden ledges on which the victim could sit by pulling himself up; the purpose was to prolong the agony. Provided no artery was severed by a nail, death would usually come by slow suffocation. As long as his strength lasted, the victim, despite the searing pain of his wounds, would repeatedly pull himself up to relieve the pressure on his lungs. But he would gradually weaken, his strength sapped by various factors which, depending on circumstances, might include shock, blood-loss, breathlessness, thirst, hunger, sun-stroke, blood-poisoning, exposure, and sheer exhaustion. He would then hang increasingly inert on the cross, gasping for breath with his chest extended by the weight of the body. The ordeal might last for many hours, even for a whole day and into the next. We can be sure of this, for the Jews, who had strict religious rules regarding the dead, had usually been permitted to remove bodies for burial before sunset, and it is for this reason that the bandits crucified beside Christ and the man in the Giv'at ha-Mivtar cemetery had their legs broken; unable to support themselves or lift themselves up once this was done, they would have suffocated quickly and been dead for burial before the end of the day. We do not know whether that concession was observed now, or whether the victims were left to complete their agony. Nor do we know how representative was the precise fate of Jesus Christ, the two bandits, or the Giv'at ha-Mivtar man. At Jerusalem, Josephus tells us, the soldiers vented their hatred on their victims by nailing them up in different positions ('as a grim joke'), so perhaps there were many ways to die on the cross.

The twitching bodies on crosses outside the city were one kind of horror. Another was being played out inside the walls. The defenders faced what Josephus called a 'creeping famine'. With anything up to a quarter of a million to be fed, the first shortages were felt as soon as the siege began, and the crisis developed quickly thereafter. Famine not only erodes the physical health and vigour of its victims, but, in the desperation it induces, it also destroys economic systems, social cohesion and normative frameworks. The final outcome is mass death in a moral vacuum. From the beginning, some were better able to secure food than others. The rich often had private stocks, in many cases of a commercial character, since otherwise it would be impossible to explain the black market in foodstuffs which we are assured flourished in the city during the siege – the profiteers had enough for themselves *and* a surplus to sell. Others of the rich had the resources – money or goods to exchange – to meet inflated black-market prices. The militias were also cushioned. They controlled the temple and royal warehouses, had the funds to pay over the odds for fresh supplies, and, as food became increasingly scarce, were able to organise forced requisitions of private stocks. Wealth and power, then, guaranteed access to such food supplies as the city contained; it might not be enough in the long run, but it was far more than that received by the non-combatant poor. Their predicament was near hopeless once the siege was under way. The Romans had effectively sealed escape-routes out of the city to people of their class; they did not have the money to buy food on the black market; and because of the general scarcity, the revolutionary authorities could make no provision for them. In this respect they were doomed by the relentless logic of war: soldiers had the prior claim to scarce food because it was they who manned the walls and they who had the weapons to take what they needed. The civilian poor were left rooting for themselves. Soon they were gathering weeds outside the walls, collecting stable sweepings, boiling leather from belts and shoes, and even picking bits out of cow-dung and sewage. Much of our source evidence for the famine seems to comprise literary *topoi* and apocryphal anecdote, but comparison with accounts of more recent famines suggest that most of what we are told is either possible or very likely. Starving children do have swollen bellies. Those dying of hunger do become emaciated and withered and can lose their hair; and they may stumble about in a listless daze before collapsing into terminal inertia. Families bicker over morsels and parents steal food from their children. Even cannibalism is not rare in famines. The chilling story told by Josephus is certainly not a standard *topos*, and he is at pains to refute his reader's anticipated incredulity and insist on the literal truth of it. Perhaps, therefore, even if the details are embellishments, the basic outline is true. The story goes that a woman called Mary, unable to find enough food, killed her own baby, roasted the body, ate one half, and then offered the other to a passing requisition squad attracted to her house by the smell of cooked meat.

234

What seems beyond doubt is that the famine began to kill large numbers. At first, normal burial practices continued, paid for by the authorities, who were eager to maintain ritual purity and keep up morale. But the system broke down as the death toll mounted and the survivors became too weak and demoralised to bother. Then, since corpses could not remain unburied in the city overnight without ritual defilement, they were simply dumped outside the city gates or carried to the tops of the walls and flung over. The valleys outside the walls were choked with the dead, says Josephus, and a putrid stream trickled from beneath the decomposing bodies. There we must assume they remained as long as the siege lasted, becoming part of the circumstances of battle – contorted heaps at the base of walls, rotting and stinking in the sun, gnawed by rats and swarms of flies. Nor was hunger the only killer. Though there was no great 'plague', Josephus does tell us in passing that deaths from disease were numerous, and that these in fact outnumbered those from famine in the early stages of the siege. This is only what we would expect: armies and cities have always been, until very recent times, most unhealthy environments. In the Crimean War (1854-6), cholera, typhoid, dysentery and exposure killed four times as many British soldiers as enemy fire. In the Seven Years War (1756-63), the Royal Navy lost almost three-quarters of its recruits to disease. We have no equivalent statistics for the ancient world – and not much information of any kind – but common sense tells us that disease rates must have been high in an overcrowded and starving city under siege at the height of summer. 'The real killers of antiquity were the infectious diseases,' writes Ralph Jackson, a specialist in ancient medicine, such as typhus, 'an acute disease of war, famine and catastrophe, whose infecting organism is spread by fleas, lice or ticks,' or pulmonary tuberculosis, 'a particular hazard of towns or other population aggregates if there is a high proportion of densely occupied, poorly ventilated and unhygienic housing.'

The sword and the cross. Hunger and disease. The shadow of the Grim Reaper lay over the doomed city. As the food-stocks ran lower still, the pinch of hunger, like an acid dissolving all social relations, began to erode the cohesion and commitment of the militias. There were desertions to the Romans, splits between rival militias, and, just as before when the radicals were divided and losing popularity, the peace party re-emerged and tried to capitalise on the growing mood of despair. Simon bar Giora responded to the crisis with a new terror. The high priest Matthias, who had invited Simon into the city as an ally against the radicals the previous spring, was now arrested and charged with treason along with his three sons. All four were executed and their bodies thrown over the wall. Two more of the high priestly class and 15 other aristocrats were then also executed in a second batch. The terror then struck in another direction. One of Simon's officers guarding a tower, together with ten of his men, attempted to defect to the Romans; but the mutineers were arrested, executed and their bodies thrown over the wall. Though it was probably the bloodiest red terror of the revolution, Josephus knows of no other executions. He does record that his father was kept in prison, and we can safely assume from this that there were others – quite possibly, given the circumstances, many others – but they were not executed, or Josephus would have told us so. It must be stressed, therefore, especially in view of his prejudice, that on Josephus' own evidence the revolutionary terror claimed few victims. They seem to have numbered in dozens rather than hundreds. This should be contrasted with the tens of thousands who were almost certainly killed by the Romans and their allies, not in battle, but in the destruction of villages, the sack of cities, and the mass execution of prisoners. It is counter-revolution, the reaction of the few, not revolution, the revolt of the many, that marches through history dripping blood. The Roman war against the Jews was no exception. The Roman terror had to destroy the will to resist of an entire people in arms, whereas Simon's terror in the summer of AD 70 was a measured response to the threat of betrayal and mutiny. The effect was to solve the immediate political crisis, for the peace party was decapitated, the militias did not fall apart, and the military struggle was able to continue.

In the meantime, through most of June, Roman siege engineering continued outside the walls. The blockade, the famine, the mass crucifixions, the repeated appeals for surrender, the well-fed Roman soldiers taunting the starving defenders with displays of food: all these pressures combined might, Titus hoped, cause the resistance suddenly to crack. But they could not be relied upon to secure the victory, and preparations for new assaults on the city were therefore advanced. Titus now concentrated his whole effort against the Antonia Fortress. The nearby hills having been cleared of trees, he sent his men for miles into the hinterland to cut timber – leaving 'nothing but desert and stumps of trees,' according to Josephus, 'every trace of beauty being blotted out by war' – and with these new supplies they built four massive platforms outside the fortress.

The platforms took 21 days to construct. When they were finished, there seems to have been a strange mood of fearful anticipation in both armies, as if the soldiers knew that the moment of decision was close. Or perhaps it is just that the historian knew it was close, and what follows is a literary *topos*.

> To Romans and Jews alike, the completion of the platforms brought a new terror. The Jews felt sure that unless they burnt these too the city would fall, the Romans that it would never be taken if they went the way of the others. For no more timber was available, and the soldiers' physical strength had been sapped by toil, their morale by constant reverses. Indeed, the disastrous conditions in the city proved more discouraging to the Romans than to the inhabitants: they found the fighting-men not in the least subdued by their severe reverses, while their own hopes were continuously frustrated, their platforms rendered useless by stratagems, their engines by the strength of the wall, their skill in close combat by the daring of their adversaries. Worst blow of all, they discovered that the Jews had an inner courage that rose superior to faction, famine, war and countless disasters. They began to think the onslaughts of these men irresistible, and their equanimity amidst disasters unshakeable . . . Small wonder, then, that the Romans strengthened the guards on the platforms.
>
> (*JW*, 6.9-14)

The battle for the Temple Mount

1 July to 10 August AD 70

The siege had now lasted for ten weeks. The Jewish defenders were weakened by hunger and exhausted by fighting. As they sallied out to attack the Roman platforms before the rams could be brought into action, the old vigour was not there.

> They advanced torch in hand, but before nearing the platforms lost hope completely and turned back. There seemed to be no agreed plan. They dashed out a few at a time, at intervals, with hesitation and fear – in short, unlike Jews. There was little sign of the national characteristics – boldness, dash, the massed charge, the refusal to acknowledge defeat.
>
> *(JW, 6.16-17)*

They came up against a solid wall of Roman armour protecting the platforms. Without gaps which light infantry could exploit, only here and there did groups of Jews attempt to close to sword-point, while most hung back, a weak line of faltering men, too frightened of what lay ahead to advance, not yet resigned to retreat. Then, as those who tried to press things failed, and as men in the leading ranks began to drop to the artillery bolts thudding into the line, the Jews gave way, withdrawing slowly with their guard up, still formed and defiant – but defeated.

The Romans now began an assault on the wall using battering rams and men equipped with crowbars to lever out stones at the base (**68, 70** & **71**). They worked all day, presumably in relays, protected overhead by hurdles and locked shields against the continuous bombardment of boulders, firebrands and other missiles that rained down from above. The walls seemed highly resistant to the rams, however, and by the end of the day the only discernible progress was four stones dislodged by crowbar. But something unexpected and tremendous had in fact been achieved. With the great weight of masonry, timber, earth, machines and men, and with the relentless pounding of the rams shaking the wall and the ground beneath, the tunnel which John's sappers had dug in May suddenly collapsed – and into the void tumbled the northern wall of the Antonia Fortress.

The event was a shock to both sides, but the Romans were in for another. Behind the fortress wall, John's men had already constructed a second wall in anticipation that the first would fall. A major strategic shift had taken place. The Romans had learnt from experience of the effectiveness of Jewish sorties, and security around their siege works was now much tighter. The Jews, on the other hand, in their weakened physical state, lacked the vigour to mount sorties in the old style, and their methods had perforce to become more defensive. The construction of secondary walls was a standard tactic in siege warfare, but it was a second-best to mounting sorties to destroy the enemy's works outside the walls. It involved heavy expenditure of effort, a diversion of men from actual fighting, and an acceptance that the enemy's attack on primary defences would succeed. The Jews had had little choice, however, and their strategic shift, when the evidence of it appeared, caused no less consternation

70 *The Triple Gate through the southern wall of the Temple Mount. Though much reconstructed since the first century AD, the walls today convey an impression of the strength of the Herodian fortifications which the Romans faced at Jerusalem*

to their enemies than previous surprises. The wall had been hastily assembled and was a crude work, but in front of it was a mountainous heap of rubble from the collapsed first wall, and on either side of it the corner towers of the Antonia still towered over the approaches. The thought of storming into this was terrifying. Titus assembled his best men and appealed for volunteers.

Why should anyone volunteer for such a mission? What makes men choose to fight? What brings about 'the will to combat'? There are many obvious reasons why some men choose to become soldiers and embrace the prospect of war. They may be motivated by nationalism, religion, ideology, hatred of the enemy, a cause in which they believe, a deity who protects them, or devotion to a charismatic leader. They may take pride in their professionalism, in collective discipline and individual prowess, in the traditions of their regiment; because, that is, they subscribe to some military ethos which becomes an end in itself. They may have purely personal motives; they may be 'soldiers of fortune', seeking pay, rewards, promotion, booty, women; or fugitives from a life of routine and toil, men in search of adventure and excitement, out to prove themselves by winning glory and earning the esteem of other men. Most soldiers in history who have gone to war as a choice, as volunteers, have done so for a mixture of several of these reasons. Roman soldiers did so because they believed in Rome, the emperor, and the gods of the city; because they had *esprit de corps* and idolised great generals; because they held their barbarian and rebel enemies in contempt; and because they expected to be paid and honoured and given free rein to plunder and rape in the lands they fought over. No one goes to war to die, however, and, in truth, because battle is such a harrowing experience, very few go to war to fight. Most men want to survive, and if some, the 'natural fighters', are better able than others to master their fears and risk exposure, whether in the exhilaration of battle or in the hope of special reward, there are very few willing to go to near-certain death.

Titus wanted volunteers for a mission of exceptional danger – a frontal assault on the Jewish position inside the Antonia – and it is unsurprising that only 12 responded. Led by a wiry, dark-skinned Syrian auxiliary called Sabinus, the 12 launched a commando-style attack the ferocity of which seems to have taken the Jews by surprise. Though several were struck down by missiles during the approach, Sabinus and some others succeeded in climbing the wall and scattering the defenders in front of them. They were far too few, however, and there was no support. Sabinus tripped, fell and died under a barrage of missiles as he tried to raise himself up behind his shield. Three others were battered to death with stones on top of the wall. The eight who were wounded in front of the wall were carried away by comrades. The attack had been foolhardy and irresponsible, and it left the men who had watched it with no stomach for another daylight assault.

A night assault by stealth was, however, another matter – especially against exhausted men increasingly enervated by hunger. So two days later, in the early hours of 5 July, 20 infantrymen on duty guarding the platforms, accompanied by a standard-bearer, a trumpeter and two cavalrymen, crept silently forwards and climbed into the ruins of the Antonia. The Jewish sentries were asleep. The first of these were killed

71 *A detailed view of typical Herodian masonry, which comprised large blocks of stone, often laid many courses thick. An impression of the size of the blocks is conveyed by the paperback book in the centre of the picture (an old copy of the Penguin translation of Josephus!)*

and the Romans mounted the wall. The trumpeter then blasted a signal which caused the remaining Jewish sentries to flee in panic and summoned reinforcements from the Roman lines. Titus and other senior officers led a contingent of picked men into the ruins to consolidate the Roman victory. A yet greater opportunity then seemed to beckon, for in the darkness and confusion most of the Jews had fled right back across the Sanctuary concourse to the Temple. The leading Roman elements now tried to follow them by pouring down the tunnels which John's sappers had used. For a short time the whole issue of the siege seems to have hung in the balance, with the Romans within a hair's breadth of flooding onto the wide open space of the Sanctuary, turning the flank of the Jewish positions on the northern and western colonnades, and cutting off the rebels who had taken refuge in the Temple. But contingents of both John's and Simon's militias now combined to block the Roman egress, and a desperate struggle erupted in the narrow spaces at the tunnel entrances, with vicious spear and sword combat between opposing lines pushed up against each other by the huge press of men behind them. 'Those in front must either kill or be killed – there could be no retreat – for on either side those behind pressed their own men forwards and left no space between the opposing lines.' It lasted for hours. The Romans were armoured and trained for close-quarters fighting, and they presented an impenetrable wall of shields and projecting steel to the generally more lightly clad

Jews. But we should not exaggerate the difference. Some Jews certainly wore armour – Josephus explicitly states this on several occasions (**73**). There were probably five sources of supply: deserters who came wearing their own armour; the Herodian armouries raided at the beginning of the war; the bodies of fallen enemies stripped on the battlefield; arms-dealers; and the continuing output of Jewish workshops. We do not know this, but there may have been some division between heavy and light units within the militias, with men fortunate enough to have armour grouped together for close-quarters fighting of the kind that had suddenly broken out in the Sanctuary. The Romans may, in fact, have faced a line formed at least in part of armoured men. They had other problems too. The tunnels behind limited the support that could be fed into the front-line, so they were unable to mass and form for a charge. The Jews, on the other hand, with huge reserves of men backed up across the concourse behind, were able to keep the Romans penned in at the entrances and to provide a constant stream of reliefs to their own front-line. At one point a centurion from Bithynia called Julian, a man of tremendous strength and skill, launched himself like a berserker at the Jewish line, scattered the men in front of him, and broke out towards the Temple. But no one had followed him, and when the armoured Goliath's hobnailed boots slid on the stone pavement and toppled him onto his back, he was immediately engulfed by enemies.

> The Jews crowded round him and rained blows from all directions with their spears and swords. Many heavy blows he stopped with his shield. Time after time he tried to stand up but was knocked down by the mass of his assailants. Even then, as he lay, he stabbed many with his sword, for he could not be finished off easily, as he was protected in every vital part by helmet and breastplate, and he kept his head down. But at last, when all his limbs were slashed and no one dared come to his aid, he ceased to struggle.
>
> (*JW*, 6.86-8)

Julian died because he was unsupported: the legionaries at the tunnel entrances were too few for a charge and feared they would be swallowed up in the Jewish mass. At one in the afternoon – eleven hours after the stealth attack on the Antonia – their officers pulled them back.

Again there was a lull. Titus ordered the destruction of the walls of the ruined Antonia Fortress to create a wide breach through which the army could storm the Temple Mount on a broad front. While the work proceeded, Josephus was again dispatched to appeal for surrender and encourage desertions. It was a poignant moment. On 17 July, as the Romans prepared for an all-out attack on the Temple, the priests were forced to suspend the holy rite of *Tamid*, the daily sacrifice of a lamb, the supply of fresh victims having finally given out. It seems odd that this had continued as people died of starvation, but belief in the gods, and in particular belief among the defenders of Jerusalem that their god would not allow them to be defeated, was decisive. On the other hand, if the maintenance of cult amid privation had been a mystical appeal by the Jews for divine reinforcement, the collapse of cult before any sign that divine deliverance was at hand came as a commensurate ideological shock. It is especially significant, therefore, that the deserters who responded to Josephus' offer included several of the high-priestly class and many other aristocrats – but no militiamen; on the contrary, from the latter, he tells us, there was abuse and defiance directed at himself and those among the defectors who urged that the gates be thrown open to the enemy. (Josephus was luckier this time than the last, when a well-aimed stone had knocked him unconscious.) Despite defeats, mounting losses, and a city racked by hunger, the revolutionary alliance held firm and the militia rank-and-file remained defiant. Their mettle was soon to be tested to the limit.

In the middle of July, approximately two weeks after the capture of the Antonia, much of which had now been levelled, Titus ordered a grand assault on the Temple Mount (**72**). Unable to deploy his full strength in the space available, and prevented from covering the attack adequately with artillery, archers and slingers because the Jews still held the northern and western colonnades, he resolved to put only the 30 best men from each century in the line, grouping them in 1,000-strong cohorts commanded by tribunes. The attack was to be led by Sextus Cerealis, commander of the Fifth Legion, while Titus and other senior officers occupied an elevated observation-post in one of the Antonia towers. An hour before dawn, having moved as silently as possible into line in the hope of catching the Jewish sentries asleep, the legionaries, perhaps as many as 7,200, advanced to attack. The sentries were not asleep, though, the alarm was immediately raised, and thousands of militiamen were soon rushing to find places in an improvised line (**73**). The leading Roman ranks came to a halt and the column concertinaed as the ranks behind stumbled in the darkness into those ahead. In places, confused and frightened, Romans cut down Romans. The same happened on the Jewish side, where the line was a shambles, its attacks and retreats badly controlled, the men frequently colliding into each other unexpectedly in the gloom. Then, as the sun came up, the ragged lines could be shaken out and given order.

> The two sides separated into opposing formations and began to hurl missiles in an orderly engagement. Neither side gave an inch or showed any sign of weariness. In the main the battle was stationary, the ebb and flow very slight and sudden. Flight and pursuit were alike impossible. All the time the shouts from Antonia changed with the fortunes of their own men: they were loudly cheered at every advance, and urged to stand fast at every retreat. . . . At last, after battling from before dawn to nearly midday, they broke off the fight, without either side having really budged the other from the spot where the first blow was struck, and without any decision being reached.
>
> (*JW*, 6.141-7)

This fight more closely resembles a pitched battle collision between heavy infantry than any other encounter in the Jewish War (**colour plate 20**). The fact that it continued for several hours demonstrates beyond doubt that such collisions

72 *A view across the platform of the Temple Mount today looking north-west (the Dome of the Rock is just in view on the left). The plaza is essentially unchanged since Herodian times, and we gain an impression therefore of the relatively open battleground it afforded*

were not really 'collisions' at all, but close-order 'confrontations'. Had the protagonists been duelling with lethal weapons, casualties and fatigue would have ended the combat in minutes. Instead, as Josephus makes clear, because the Roman surprise attack failed, and in the hour before dawn a Jewish line formed and steeled itself to make a stand, the legionary advance was halted, such that 'the two sides separated into opposing formations and began to hurl missiles in an orderly engagement'. This is very similar to how John Keegan pictures the clash of English and French men-at-arms at Agincourt in 1415: '. . . as movement died out of the two hosts, we can visualise them divided, at a distance of ten or fifteen feet, by a horizontal fence of waving and stabbing spear shafts, the noise of their clattering like that of a bully-off at hockey magnified several hundred times.' There is, in fact, an almost overpowering 'terror of cold steel', which ensures that a line which does not flinch in the face of an enemy charge is almost guaranteed to bring the enemy to a halt immediately in front of it. This is confirmed by the evidence of the gunpowder era: there are hardly any known cases of infantry 'crossing bayonets' on the battlefield, and bayonet wounds overall were extremely rare. What men feared when they contemplated crossing the last few yards to close fully with the enemy was not just death or injury, but steel slicing through flesh, agonising and horrific wounds, the possibility of mutilation and permanent disablement.

73 *A Jewish militiaman of AD 70. The defenders of Jerusalem were by this time veteran fighters, many of them well equipped, sometimes including armour, and prepared to engage in close-quarters combat*

Great Achilles . . . went with the spear after godlike Polydoros . . . the swift-footed brilliant Achilles hit him with a spear thrown in the middle of the back . . . The spearhead held its way straight on and came out by the navel, and he dropped, moaning, on one knee as the dark mist gathered about him, and sagged, and caught with his hands at his bowels in front of him. . . . Now Deukalion was struck in the arm, at a place in the elbow where the tendons come together. There through the arm Achilles transfixed him with the bronze spearhead, and he, arm hanging heavy, waited and looked his death in the face. Achilles struck with the sword's edge at his neck, and swept the helmed head far away, and the marrow gushed from the neckbone, and he went down to the ground at full length.

(Homer, *The Iliad*, 20.386-483)

Homer may have exaggerated the prowess of Achilles, but not the horror of close-quarters combat with edged weapons. The study of excavated human remains from a mass grave of medieval warriors killed at the battle of Towton in 1461 has confirmed the extraordinary savagery of such fighting. Many of the victims had multiple wounds to the head – a total of 113 wounds were recorded on just 27 skulls. Skeleton 25, for example, had been hacked at several times before receiving a deep cut on the left side of his head followed by a slash across the back which penetrated the brain and hurled him forwards onto the ground. He was then hit again, first by a blow that turned him over, then by another that bisected his face diagonally from left eye to upper jaw, splitting open the palette. The 38 men recovered from the Towton 'death-pit' were almost certainly killed in the rout at the end of the battle: that is, they were fleeing in terror from the very fate that overtook and destroyed them.

But in a wider sense, too, close-order combat was a traumatising experience. As the sun came up, the Roman and Jewish lines confronted each other as opposing walls of locked shields, projecting steel blades and bared-teeth aggression. Fear dominated the actions of each man, who instinctively tucked himself behind his shield and huddled close to his comrades for safety. He rarely mustered the courage to risk exposing his own body in order to lunge with his weapons at the enemy, for he found himself in a zone of lethal danger, the stabbing points of the enemy front only yards away, numerous projectiles dropping from above. Such aggression as he did display was largely bravado, since his main preoccupation was not to kill the enemy, not even to fight with him, but simply to stay alive. Virtually everything he did in the nightmare of close-quarters confrontation was defensive in intent. General Marshall's study of American soldiers in the Second World War found that only about a quarter of the men in the front-line actually used their weapons against the enemy. Analysis of musketry in earlier wars consistently shows that battlefield performance was a third or less of the optimum achieved on practice ranges. Pitched battles between opposing Greek hoplites rarely resulted in more than about five per cent casualties for the winning side. It seems irrefutable that the behaviour of most men in close combat throughout history has been overwhelmingly defensive in character.

Why, given all of this, did fighting lines stand at all? What prevented men from giving in to the animal urge to flee from such terrible danger? Probably, in part, the fact that their senses were numbed by shock, tiredness and the alcohol commonly imbibed before battle. Many were in a daze, acting like automatons, mindlessly performing drill-book rituals. Some clung to trusted leaders as saviours who would protect them, and some drew strength from a belief in their own and their comrades' superior courage and training. Others were dragooned into line by fear of punishment and shame if they flunked. Two factors seem to have been of overriding importance, however: the social psychology of small groups of fighters; and the depth – or 'weight' – of the opposing lines. Marshall's study is again highly instructive.

> Whenever one surveys the forces of the battlefield, it is to see that fear is general among men, but to observe further that men are commonly loath that their fear will be expressed in specific acts which their comrades will recognise as cowardice. The majority are unwilling to take extraordinary risks and do not aspire to a hero's role, but they are equally unwilling that they should be considered the least worthy among those present. . . . When a soldier is . . . known to the men who are around him, he . . . has reason to fear losing the one thing he is likely to value more highly than life – his reputation as a man among other men.
>
> (quoted in Keegan 1978, 71-2)

This imperative was probably especially strong in the ancient world, where men who fought side-by-side in the line, like the Jewish militiamen on the Temple Mount, would be relatives, neighbours and villagers who lived out their entire lives together, or at least long-service professionals, like the Roman legionaries, who might fight alongside the same men for a decade or more. Small–group cohesion was not simply about the avoidance of shame; if the group placed binding moral obligations on its members, in return it offered them protection. An isolated man was hunted prey; a knot of men with locked shields and weapons ready was a hedgehog.

The group, no less than the individual, was preoccupied with survival, however, and the group might foster a collective decision to retreat, even flee, as often as to stand, let alone charge. What tied each small group of comrades into its place in the line and kept it from retreating? It was the 'weight' given by hundreds of such groups formed up in depth. Here, for example, is the Greek historian and former general Polybius describing the Macedonian pike phalanx.

> . . . we can easily picture the nature and the tremendous power of a charge by the whole of the phalanx, when it advances 16 deep with levelled pikes. Of these 16 ranks, those who are stationed further back than the fifth cannot use their pikes to take an active part in the battle. . . . Once the charge is launched, these rear ranks, by the sheer pressure of their bodily weight, greatly increase its momentum and *make it impossible for the foremost ranks to face about* [my emphasis].
>
> (*Histories*, 18.30)

Roman legionaries probably formed up eight ranks deep. Of these only the front two ranks could have struck blows directly at the enemy. The remaining six were limited to overhead discharges of javelins and to providing the weight necessary to prevent the men in greatest danger from retreating. Behind them stood the junior officers – four per century to cover a width of ten files – stationed not only where they could observe and direct the action, but also in a position to prevent the line giving ground or leaking men to the rear. Crudely, then, depth of formation – 'weight' – made the line solid because it trapped the men most endangered behind a great press of their own comrades who remained relatively safe. In the final analysis, close-order confrontations – assuming neither side broke and ran at the first onset – tended to become protracted because the best chance the men in the front-line had of surviving lay in sticking with their mates in a defensive huddle facing the enemy – not in hurling themselves at them, nor in turning their backs on them. The classic combat poise of ancient heavy infantry was to be standing tight-packed, sheltered by shields, bodies and debris, ready with projecting spears or drawn swords, facing an enemy line in similar poise a few yards distant.

These considerations allow us to reconstruct something of the human reality of the battle on the Temple Mount. The Roman assault column must have been massed in great depth, for it had to pass the narrow gap formed by the demolished walls of the Antonia. Probably it extended the line on either flank as it passed out onto the Temple concourse. We do not know exactly where the Jewish line formed to receive it, but given that the total width of the concourse was only 300m, we have to assume a battle fought on a considerably narrower front than this. The legionaries are likely to have been spaced at intervals of less than a metre, so the total number of men in direct contact with the enemy – those in the front two ranks – may have been only 300 or so. If the first line was formed eight deep, then it might have contained some 1,200 men, and if the total assault column did in fact comprise about 7,200, then it would have been backed up in no less than five lines behind the first (each of which might have formed one of Josephus' '1,000-strong cohorts'). The front-line fighting would have involved a steady stream of javelins discharged overhead by the rear ranks, and, if auxiliary archers were included in the assault column, overhead shooting by them at somewhat longer ranges. There would also have been periodic 'pushes', perhaps along the whole front, or by parts of the line only, each time resulting in a flare-up of furious hand-to-hand fighting. These frantic clashes would exhaust the combatants after a few minutes at the most, and either the assailants would recoil to recover, or their opponents would be forced to give ground a little. Thus the Romans, in Josephus' account, 'were loudly cheered at every advance, and urged to stand fast at every retreat', though 'in the main the battle was stationary, the ebb and flow very slight and sudden.' Crucial to the duration of the fight was the narrowness of the front, the weight of men behind, and the almost limitless supply of fresh men to replace those in the front-line. We must imagine senior officers in the rear organising reliefs for one part of the line after another through the long morning's fighting.

Why did the Romans fail to break through? In arms, armour and training they were the Jews' superiors. Close-order confrontation, without room to dodge, to evade, to manoeuvre, was the Roman not the Jewish way. But on such a narrow front probably less than five per cent of the Roman assault force could engage the enemy directly at any one time. The Jews, holding an outer line across the concourse and also positioned above on the northern and western colonnades, could deploy more of their men effectively, both in front-line confrontation and in massed missile-shooting. The Romans were probably under fire from the colonnade rooftops, and, in so far as their pushes were successful in driving back the Jewish line and advancing their own further out onto the concourse, their flanks would have become more exposed to enfilade fire. Having failed to achieve a breakthrough at the start of the battle – either by stealing through the sentry-posts in the darkness, or by charging and scattering an unsteady line – they found themselves stuck in a tactical impasse. The Roman commander therefore called off the assault at noon.

To avoid a recurrence of this impasse, Titus had to widen the front of future attacks. So the Romans spent another week levelling the remains of the Antonia Fortress and began constructing four platforms against the north-west corner of the Temple Mount and the colonnades either side of it. Thus they were again reduced by the resilience of the defence to gruelling navvy work, including on this occasion fetching timber from up to 12 miles away. Moreover, it was now high summer and they were probably forced to labour in full armour, for Jewish missile shooting and sorties were relentless, and there was continual skirmishing between the front-lines on the Temple Mount, the Romans massed near the ruins of the Antonia, the Jews on the northern side of the Inner Court of the Temple. The defence remained, in fact, surprisingly active. There was a raid to seize horses that Roman cavalrymen out looking for firewood or fodder were in the habit of leaving to graze freely near the walls. There was a large-scale attack on the Roman outposts on the Mount of Olives, perhaps as some sort of diversion, perhaps in an unsuccessful attempt to break through the wall of circumvallation and ease the blockade (the Jews' intentions are unclear in Josephus' account). The rebels also endeavoured to strengthen their defences on the Temple Mount, destroying a large section of the northern and western colonnades where these joined with the ruins of the Antonia, thus inter-posing a gap of 10m or more between their own and the Roman positions. A few days after this, moreover, on 27 July, they set a successful trap for the Romans working on a platform being built against the western colonnade.

Though the northern extent of this colonnade had now been destroyed, the Roman platform was being raised against the surviving section near the broken end. At this point the Jews secretly filled the spaces between the rafters and the ceiling below with a flammable mixture of dry wood, bitumen and pitch. They then made a show of withdrawing from this part of the colonnade. Many of the Romans working on the platform below sensed an opportunity and ran forwards with ladders to mount an immediate assault by escalade. Hundreds quickly reached the top of the undefended wall and climbed out onto the roof of the colonnade. At that point the Jews ignited their fire-trap and engulfed their enemies in flames.

> Encircled by the blaze, some flung themselves down into the city behind them, some into the thick of the foe. Many, in the hope of escaping with their lives, jumped down among their own men and broke their legs. Most, for all their haste, were too slow for the fire, though a few cheated the flames with their own daggers. . . . Some retired to the wide colonnade wall and got clear of the fire, but here they were trapped by the Jews and, after long holding out in the face of many injuries, finally perished to a man.
>
> (Josephus, *JW*, 6.181-5)

The whole of the colonnade from the north-west corner down as far as the western gate had now been destroyed, and the Jews completed the job by cutting away the burnt wreckage. Given that Roman platforms continued to rise on the far side of the wall, the Jews' purpose was probably to deny their enemies use of the colonnade rooftop when they broke in. Josephus' account is obscure at this point, however, for he reports the Romans also firing colonnades, but leaves it unclear when, where and why. He also reports a succession of Roman assaults, but again the sequence, location and strategy are unclear. What follows is a possible reconstruction, but it achieves what seems to be a more plausible narrative only by assuming faulty memory and some inaccuracy on Josephus' part.

With some at least of the platforms complete, Titus ordered a new assault on the Temple Mount to begin. For several days in early August, the battering rams pounded at the walls, including a specially constructed giant ram, while small parties of men attempted to lever out stones from the base of the wall with crowbars. The rams made no impression at all: the huge size of the blocks, the close-bonded construction, and the thickness of the masonry ensured that. The crowbar men did a little better, prising free with tremendous effort some of the facing stones, but there was such a thickness of stone behind that this had no effect on the stability of the structure. Titus abandoned the attempt to breach the walls and instead ordered an attempt to climb over them. The height of the platforms meant that assault by escalade was now possible, but it remained, as always, a strategy unlikely to succeed against a strong garrison and almost certain to result in heavy casualties. The present occasion was no exception. Some of the ladders, weighed down by heavy infantry, were pushed sideways and toppled over. Heavy covering fire from Roman missile-shooters outside the walls kept most of the Jews away from the battlements, however, and instead they waited under cover until men came off the tops of the ladders onto the walkways. 'The Jews were in no hurry to stop them, but when they climbed up they were violently assailed: some were pushed backwards and sent headlong; others clashed with the defenders and were killed; many, as they stepped off the ladders, were unable to get behind their shields before they were run through with swords . . .' The assault by escalade thus also failed. Titus now ordered fire to be used against the gates and the colonnades, and for 24 hours the Romans laboured to feed the flames and maximise destruction. The entire length of the northern colonnade was burnt out right up to the north-east corner of the Temple Mount, where the ground drops away precipitously into the Kidron Valley. The fires were then deliberately extinguished and the engineers sent forward to clear away the debris and prepare a path for further assaults.

The Jewish position on the outer walls of the Mount was now untenable. With the colonnades burnt out, they could man the narrow walkways with only a single line of men, and these would have no way of retreating if things went badly, for behind them was a sharp drop. At the extremities of the line, moreover, they would be vulnerable to enfilade from Roman artillery and archers massed in the ruins of the Antonia, and if the Romans stormed forwards *en masse* from this position, they could soon find themselves under fire from the rear as well. So the attempt to hold the outer wall was abandoned and the Jewish line was reformed across the middle of the Sanctuary. The left was anchored on the western gate, which was linked with the Upper City by a bridge spanning the Tyropoeon Valley, and defended by a tower that John of Gischala had built during the factional struggle. The right rested on the eastern colonnade of the Sanctuary. The centre of the line ran through the Temple and the Inner Court. If the entire Temple Mount was a gigantic fortification, then the Outer Court, part of which the Romans now held, was like an outer bailey, while the Inner Court, still held by the Jews, formed an inner bailey, and the Temple itself a great bastion or keep within this. A chest-high balustrade ran around the outside of the Inner Court (marking the point beyond which Gentiles were not permitted to pass), and inside this was a high, stepped, rectangular podium surmounted by a massive stone wall. There were four gateways on both the north and south sides, and a ninth of special grandeur, the Eastern Gate, in the centre of the east side, aligned with the entrance to the Temple itself. Chambers and colonnades ran around the inside of the wall, so there were wide fighting-platforms at rooftop level, which was raised perhaps 20m or more above the surrounding Sanctuary concourse. The eastern half of the interior formed the Court of Women. The western half was elevated above this on a second podium and separated from it by another massive wall. Beyond the Corinthian Gate which passed through the middle of this wall was the narrow Court of the Israelites, and beyond this, and clearly visible from it over a knee-high balustrade, was the Court of the Priests. Here, behind the blood-spattered altar, raised up on a third podium, stood the towering edifice of the Temple itself, some 45m high, the whole front façade gleaming with white marble and gold in the summer sunshine. A covered entrance porch gave access to a pair of enormous golden gates, and beyond these, concealed behind curtains, was first a Holy Place where sacred objects were stored, and then, at the furthest recess of the entire Temple complex, the Holy of Holies, a bare undeco-rated room entered only once a year by the high priest.

The Temple was the religious, political and military heart of the Jewish cause, and it was in defence of this great citadel that the rebels now massed. As the Romans deployed ever-larger forces in the Outer Court, as its blackened northern rim gradually filled with them, the Jews, starving and exhausted, fell back from the open spaces of the concourse and took station on the rooftops of the Inner Court and Temple. Even so, they retained sufficient vigour still to mount aggressive sorties. Early on 9 August they sallied forth in strength from the Eastern Gate. The Romans facing them, though surprised and outnumbered, held their ground behind locked shields, and Titus ordered cavalry counter-attacks into the Jewish mass. A confused battle of alternating rushes and retreats continued for three hours. Then, unable to make any impression on the Roman line and threatened with imminent defeat, the Jews withdrew to the Inner Court. The following day, too, the Jews attacked the Romans holding the Outer Court, but on this occasion a minor incident during a successful Roman counter-attack brought sudden disaster upon the rebels. Outside the Inner Court, a Roman soldier snatched up a blazing piece of wood, climbed onto a comrade's back, and hurled the firebrand through the open window of one of the chambers. With the Inner Court full of highly flammable timbers and textiles, and the whole place bone-dry in the summer heat, fire took hold immediately and soon shooting flames and thick black smoke could be seen rising around the Temple. Inside there was pandemonium. Both piety and military necessity made this a desperate emergency for the rebels, who were threatened with the loss of their religion's holiest place, along with its sacred texts and treasures, and also with the fortress which was now the lynchpin of their defensive line. But how could they, all at once, fight the flames, save themselves from incineration, and keep the Romans out? Their enemies gave them no respite. The Roman line surged forwards, apparently without orders, the legionaries perhaps sensing that this unex-pected moment might be the final consummation of more than three months' toil and sacrifice. Somehow, in the chaos and confusion, because hundreds of Jews were rushing in to help fight the flames, because those whose task it was to guard the gates were distracted, somehow the Romans broke into the Temple. Tossing firebrands, hurling javelins, hacking with swords, the legionaries were suddenly within the Inner Court. Pandemonium now became panic.

Titus was probably already on the scene, though Josephus' account of his role is highly suspect. The Flavian court historian has him arguing at a council of war before the attack on the Temple against its destruction, and now we are told he was in the midst of the mayhem attempting to restrain his soldiery and save this 'ornament for an empire'. On this occasion we have other testimony against which to measure Josephus' veracity. The fifth-century *Chronicle* of Sulpicius Severus, a Christian history from the time of Adam, preserves a different version of the meeting, one perhaps derived from Tacitus. In this version, though opinion was indeed divided, Titus was among those arguing for the destruction of the city, and the reason given, if we discount the Christian gloss, sounds convincing: it was 'a prime necessity in order to wipe out more completely the religion of the Jews and the Christians'. The beating heart of Judaism was to be ripped out.

Now the initiative of the soldiers was bringing this about more quickly than anyone had expected. As new fires broke out in the Temple complex and the Jews lost the battle to quench the flames, and with the Romans among them, crazy to kill and killing all they could reach, those of John's and Eleazar's men who could, fought their way through to the southern gateways and fled across the Outer Court. Inside, among those who could not get out, there was only sporadic resistance. Some priests tore up the golden spikes which kept birds off the roof of the Temple and hurled them down at the Romans – until they were forced back by the flames. Some cast themselves into the inferno. Others clung desperately to the rooftops (and were executed when they eventually came down). But of concerted resistance there was none, and most of those trapped died like cattle in an abattoir.

> While the Temple burnt, looting went on right and left, and all who were caught were put to the sword. There was no pity for age, no regard for rank; little children and old men, laymen and priests alike were butchered. Every class was held in the iron embrace of war, whether they defended themselves or cried for mercy. Through the roar of the flames as they swept relentlessly on could be heard the groans of the fallen. Such was the height of the hill and vastness of the blazing edifice that the entire city seemed to be on fire, while no noise could be imagined more shattering and horrifying. There was the war-cry of the Roman legions as they converged; the yells of the partisans encircled with fire and sword; the panic flight into the arms of the enemy of the people cut off above, and their shrieks as the end approached. The cries from the hill were answered from the crowded streets, and now many who were wasted with hunger and beyond speech, when they saw the Temple in flames, found strength to moan and wail.
>
> (Josephus, *JW*, 6.271-4)

74 *An engraving of the sack of Jerusalem in AD 70. Though a melodramatic image by a Victorian book-illustrator, it still perhaps conveys something of the terrible reality*

The fall of Jerusalem

11 August to 7 September AD 70

Jerusalem had refused repeated demands for surrender. Now it was being taken by force, and the 'law of war' ordained that it should suffer the sack – massacre, enslavement, looting and destruction (**74**). The siege was transformed into a battle of annihilation. In a space of less than a square mile, many tens of thousands of people found themselves trapped in a murderous moral vacuum without rules or norms. For a month, more or less, Roman soldiers had open season on Jews in the city. 'I have looked upon evils,' said the aged King Priam, foretelling of his own and his family's fate at the fall of Troy,

> and seen my sons destroyed and my daughters dragged away captive and chambers of marriage wrecked and innocent children taken and dashed to the ground in the hatefulness of war, and the wives of my sons dragged off by the accursed hands of the Achaians. And myself last of all, my dogs in front of my doorway will rip me raw, after some man with stroke of the sharp bronze spear, or with spearcast, has torn life out of my body . . . when an old man is dead and down, and the dogs mutilate the grey head and the grey beard and the parts that are secret, this, for all sad mortality, is the sight most pitiful.
>
> (Homer, *The Iliad*, 22.60-75)

What made soldiers – some soldiers – behave like this? Sieges were a form of total war in which entire cities became battlegrounds. All the conventional boundaries broke down – those between soldiers and civilians, men and women, public arenas and private spaces. The lines between combatants and non-combatants, 'legitimate' and 'illegitimate' targets, became blurred. The enemy comprised not just the fighters in the front-line, but the people who supported them with food, shelter, medical care, encouragement, sometimes even an active hand in the fighting; they, after all, were the people in whose cause the fighters fought. The enemy – a whole city of people – was dehumanised by war propaganda and 'barrack-room' culture. If Josephus, a fellow Jew, can condemn the rebels as 'the dregs of society', as 'bandits', 'criminals' and 'murderers', as people who have terrorised decent citizens, profaned the holy places, and given power to 'tyrants', it is not difficult to imagine how the foreign soldiers of an imperial power might further demonise them also as 'fuzzy-wuzzies', 'gooks' and 'rag-heads'. When the tensions of prolonged pitched-battle break, dammed-up fear can be transformed in an instant into a frenzy of hatred and bloodlust. Men at that moment and for some time after experience an irresistible urge to hack and stab at the exposed backs of fleeing enemies. How much more must this have been so after months of siege, especially when there was such imbalance between defenders and attackers, the former concealed, protected and elevated by mighty walls? The besieged seem to cheat, to take fewer risks, to refuse to 'fight like men' out in the open. The frenzy of the legionaries at the sack of Jerusalem is not hard to understand. Hating the enemy, greedy for plunder, and crazed by months of battle, even had their generals ordered them not to sack the city, it is unlikely they could have been restrained. Roman soldiers – who made and unmade emperors – often ran amok. In any case – notwithstanding Josephus' plea of innocence on his patron's behalf – Titus and his generals are unlikely to have taken much trouble to spare the city. There was political value in the example about to be set.

There was madness, too, on the Jewish side, though in this case the innocent madness of the doomed. As hunger, exhaustion and defeat eroded the morale of the militias, the millenarian spirit among the people took on increasingly mystical forms. Where men failed, God would have to fill in. A forlorn-hope messiah had persuaded many that it was now, at this eleventh hour, that a sign of deliverance would be given if the people went up to the Temple. A crowd of men, women and children, all of them apparently unarmed, massed on the roof of one of the outer colonnades on the day of the Temple's destruction. It is possible that the biblical *Book of Revelation* preserves a fragmentary record of the prophecy that inspired them, for it declares that while the Outer Court might fall to the heathens, God's heavenly forces would intervene before the Temple itself could be violated.

> 'Come and measure the temple of God and the altar and those who worship there, but do not measure the court outside the temple; leave that out, for it is given over to the nations, and they will trample over the holy city for 42 months.' . . . the beast that comes up from the bottomless pit will make war on them and conquer them and kill them . . . Then the

seventh angel blew his trumpet, and there were loud voices in heaven saying, 'The kingdom of the world has become the kingdom of the Lord and of his Messiah, and he will reign forever and ever.' . . . Then God's temple in heaven was opened, and the ark of the covenant was seen within his temple; and there were flashes of lightning, rumblings, peals of thunder, an earthquake, and heavy hail.

(11 *passim*)

If the dream was something like this, the little congregation of mystics had chosen the best and the worst of moments to try to live it. The scene before them was indeed apocalyptic: the Sanctuary a blackened shell filled with pagan soldiers; the Temple billowing flame and smoke; the roars of warriors mixing with the screams of priests and pilgrims; the concourse strewn with bodies and the debris of battle; fugitives scattered across it pursued by enemy horse and foot. Soon the soldiers saw them, a huddled crowd of perhaps a few hundred standing firm together when all about them was chaos and panic – a bizarre and tragic encounter between professional killers on the rampage and deluded mystics waiting for a sign. 'Carried away by their fury, the soldiers fired the colonnade from below, and, as a result, some flung themselves out of the blaze to their deaths, others perished in the flames, and of that vast number there escaped not one.'

This, it seems, had been the last organised body of Jews on the Temple Mount – by one of history's ironies, after such bloody struggle, a party of civilians. The conquerors could now celebrate their victory. The Temple was plundered of its wealth – a huge quantity of money, the accumulated tithes and offerings of millions of pious Jews; great heaps of gold, cloth and other precious things, some of it Temple furniture, much of it that had been held in store; and some of the riches also of the Jerusalem aristocracy, brought here for safe-keeping in troubled times. 'So laden with plunder was every single soldier that all over Syria the value of gold was reduced by half.' (Perhaps, though, the Romans did not get it all. Some believe that the mysterious copper scroll discovered in the Qumran caves lists the hiding-places to which Temple treasures were borne.) Titus himself was in the midst of the soldiers, and now, as the Roman standards were brought forward, he became the focus of a great and cheering host, the men still blackened, sweating and blood-spattered from the recent battle. An ox, a sheep and a pig were sacrificed before the Eastern Gate – a pagan profanation – and the Mount echoed with the noise as thousands of Roman soldiers roared their traditional acclamation of a victorious chief: *Imperator! Imperator! Imperator!*

Still, though, it was not quite over. Simon's men remained firmly ensconced in the Upper City, and most of John's men seem to have escaped the fall of the Temple Mount to join them there. There were still many thousands of rebel fighters in the city – albeit much weakened physically and morally – and they held strong defensive positions, including the great Royal Palace on the highest peak. It seemed inconceivable that they could win, but they might cost the Romans dear if they fought to the bitter end. Both sides had an interest now in a parley, and the opposing leaders met to negotiate on the Viaduct, a great bridge spanning the Tyropoeon Valley between the Western Gate of the Sanctuary and the Gymnasium on the eastern slope of the Upper City. John and Simon sought permission to pass through the Roman cordon with their women and children and depart into the Wilderness. To this Titus would not agree; his offer was slavery instead of execution. To have agreed to less would have made his victory incomplete and risked giving heavy reinforcement to the guerrilla struggle in the south. He had the main rebel army before him and he was determined that it should not escape.

> Titus, furious that men no better than prisoners should put forward demands as if they had defeated him, ordered it to be announced that it was no longer any use their deserting or hoping for terms, as he would spare no one. They must fight to the last ditch and save themselves any way they could. From now on he would insist on all his rights as victor. Then he gave his men leave to burn and sack the city.
>
> (Josephus, *JW*, 6.352-3)

The war resumed the following day. The Romans fired much of the Lower City, and in two days it was cleared of rebels, the latter evacuating with whatever movable property they could carry for the greater safety of the high ground to the west. John and Simon turned the Royal Palace into a new citadel for the defenders. This fortification was no less formidable than the Temple Mount. Built of massive Herodian masonry, it was protected on its more vulnerable northern side by the Hippicus, Phasael and Mariamme Towers, while to the west the ground dropped away steeply into the Hinnom Valley, and to the east the approach up a more gentle slope was obstructed by the defences built during the factional struggle and by a thick carpet of buildings terraced into the hillside (**16, 64, 71** & **colour plate 21**). The rebels, moreover, were making use of the vast network of rock-cut drains and cisterns that ran beneath the city (**75**). Here they could duck and weave, moving around unseen, escaping when the enemy was too strong, striking unexpectedly when opportunity offered. The city underground was a natural habitat to veteran guerrilla fighters like the Jews. Here, too, they could lie low for days, perhaps weeks, supported by caches of food and weapons, awaiting a chance to flee southwards if the battle for the city was lost. There was still some cause for hope, then: the Romans might yet be held at the Royal Palace; its capture might at least cost them dear in sweat and blood; and at worst, rather than certain death or enslavement if they fell into Roman hands, there was a chance of escape in the honeycomb of tunnels and portals below ground. To stiffen the resolve of their followers further, Simon and John ordered the public execution of two Roman prisoners. One was killed and then dragged symbolically around the city. The other was about to be beheaded when he gave his captors the slip and escaped to the Roman lines (at which point he was dismissed from the army in disgrace for having been taken prisoner in the first place). The Jewish leaders' purpose was to redraw the line of hatred separating the two sides, confirming to each that the struggle remained a war to the death, without hope of mercy; their own men would fight harder for knowing that the Romans would not

75 *Steps down into one of the numerous underground cisterns, water-channels and sewers with which Jerusalem was riddled in the first century AD – providing havens for fugitive fighters after the fall of the city*

spare them. The revolutionary terror also continued its work. When five Idumaean leaders were found to have been secretly negotiating surrender with Titus, Simon had them arrested and executed.

The Romans were left with no choice but to begin again the tedious work of building platforms. The elevated position and high walls of the Royal Palace and the thousands of rebels actively engaged in its defence left them no alternative: the fortification could not be stormed directly. The four legions were set to work in the Hinnom Valley on 20 August, and over the following two-and-a-half weeks they constructed serviceable platforms against the western wall of the Palace. In the meantime, the allied and auxiliary troops worked on the opposite side of the Upper City, constructing platforms near the Viaduct, the Gymnasium, and Simon's Tower. As the work proceeded, the war of attrition continued. Though Jewish sorties were now few and ineffective, the work was slowed by missile shooting and the need for protection. But the defenders were weakening all the time. The blockade was slowly starving the city to death, and though the fighters still got what food there was, it was not enough and they showed the symptoms of their 'creeping famine'. Physical and moral exhaustion were making them enervated and apathetic. More now – despite the terror and the uncertain reception – were being driven to desert. The Roman policy aimed to encourage defection and was less severe than Titus had threatened; not all were enslaved. When a group of aristocrats, including kinsmen of the former client-king of Adiabene, surrendered, they were detained and later sent to Rome as hostages. Citizens of Jerusalem who came over were judged by a military assize and set free if deemed 'respectable'; property, no doubt, was the principle attribute of those pardoned. Many bribed their way to freedom. A priest called Jesus negotiated safe passage by smuggling out a hoard of Temple treasure – lampstands, tables, basins and cups, all of them gold, high-priestly vestments encrusted with jewels, and much else. The former Temple treasurer bought his escape with priestly tunics and girdles, purple and scarlet cloth, and cinnamon, cassia and other spices used in making incense. Others who defected – activists and militiamen, pilgrims and refugees from outside the city, perhaps any of the poor who had nothing to trade but their bodies – these were enslaved. But even this terrible fate may have seemed attractive at this late hour beside the horrors awaiting those who remained in the Upper City: starvation and pestilence, to be followed by massacre, mutilation and gang-rape when the end came.

That end came swiftly. On 7 September the platforms against the Royal Palace were finished and the rams were brought forward. Some of the rebels abandoned the threatened wall without a fight, and the fire of those who remained was quickly suppressed by the weight of incoming Roman shot. The crews of the rams were soon working unmolested and sections of the western wall were brought down that very day. Roman legionaries then found themselves storming through undefended breaches. The morale and discipline of the garrison had finally collapsed. All co-ordinated military action had ceased. Each small group of men was now shifting for itself, seeking an avenue of escape and a bolt-hole. The rebel leaders and their immediate followers had taken refuge in the three northern towers, but even these were abandoned without a fight – with an army to defend them, they were immensely strong fortifications, but with an army disintegrating all around them, they were a trap. The leaders and other small groups of fighters scattered across the city, seeking ways through the Roman cordon. Most failed and, if not cut down when they ran into parties of soldiers, sought temporary refuge in the gloom of the sewers.

A few moments of terror had transformed the revolutionary army into a stampeding crowd. History is driven by war and revolution, by the collective action of large masses, and it turns on whether men and women chose to stand and fight as a block, or scatter, each for himself, like chaff in the wind. All war is really the war of nerves: the struggle is not so much to kill as to demonstrate the power to kill, a superior power to kill, and to master one's own fears while bringing those of the enemy to breaking-point. Most men who die in combat, die, after all, not in the fighting-line but in the rout. It is fear of death, not death itself, that wins battles and turns history. So the Jewish Revolution against Rome ended, to all intents and purposes, when, on 7 September, the morale of the militiamen, who had struggled so hard for so long, suddenly collapsed and turned them from fighting force into panic-stricken mob.

Why had it happened? A better question would be: why had it not happened before? 'Crowds are implicit in armies,' argues John Keegan. 'Inside every army is a crowd struggling to get out, and the strongest fear with which every commander lives . . . is that of his army reverting to a crowd . . .' The suffering of the Jewish people

257

since AD 67, and especially of the Jews besieged in Jerusalem between late April and early September AD 70, was comparable with that suffered by any people in any war. Tens of thousands had died by the sword, tens of thousands more from hunger and disease, and a good many had been deliberately tortured to death by their enemies. Tens of thousands were now slaves, and other tens of thousands refugees. The survivors trapped in Jerusalem were racked by hunger, fear and grief. Though the revolutionary militias had long since shed the half-hearted, the weak-willed and the cowardly, so that only hardened veterans now remained, all men have their breaking-point. What had sustained the struggle until this moment was revolutionary hope. Because the privation, sacrifice and danger might yet yield apocalyptic victory; because the suffering might redeem the people in God's eyes and win back his favour; because the holy prophecies foretold of 'terrible carnage and great tribulation for the Israelites in the battle of destruction against the sons of darkness'; for these reasons, men had been able to endure. It was hope that had kept emaciated and exhausted men in the line until now. When the last wall was breached and still no sign came from heaven, hope died, the militias dissolved, and the revolution was over.

Masters of the city, their standards raised on the highest towers amid cheers and acclamations, the soldiers now set about the business of the sack with grim relish.

> They poured onto the streets sword in hand, cut down without mercy all who came within reach, and burnt the houses of any who took refuge indoors, occupants and all. Many they raided, and as they entered in search of plunder, they found whole families dead and the rooms full of the victims of starvation. Horrified by the sight, they emerged empty-handed. Pity for those who had died in this way was matched by no such feeling for the living: they ran every man through whom they met and blocked the narrow streets with corpses, deluging the whole city with gore, so that many of the fires were quenched by the blood of the slain. At dusk the slaughter ceased, but in the night the fire gained the mastery . . .
>
> (Josephus, *JW*, 6.403-7)

In 1970, during excavations in the Jewish Quarter of Old Jerusalem, the remains of a house burnt down in the sack of the city in AD 70 were uncovered. At ground-floor level the 'Burnt House' had comprised a small courtyard, five rooms and a ritual bath. The upper walls had collapsed, the stones changing colour in the inferno, and beneath the debris was buried a layer of earth, ash, soot, charred wood, stone vessels, potsherds, broken glass, and iron nails. Many objects had been violently scattered about and smashed before being scorched by fire. The plastered walls were black with soot, and excavators digging the site found that they too became blackened by soot. There was a scattering of coins across the floor, some of the Roman procurators, but more of the revolutionary regime, with issues of 'Year 2' (AD 67), 'Year 3' (AD 68) and 'Year 4' (AD 69). There was no doubt about the date of destruction. Nor the violence. An iron-headed spear had been left leaning in the corner of one room. And a human arm, with hand outstretched as if grasping at a step, was found near the kitchen doorway.

8 The black terror

. . . Mighty men have pitched their camps against me, and have encompassed me with all their weapons of war. They have let fly arrows against which there is no cure, and the flame of (their) javelins is like a consuming fire among the trees. The clamour of their shouting is like the bellowing of many waters, like a storm of destruction devouring a multitude of men; as their waves rear up, Naught and Vanity spout upward to the stars.

(*The Thanksgiving Hymns*, 7, DSS, Qumran)

A carnival of reaction

Rome, spring AD 71

Rome was the greatest city in the Mediterranean, and a triumph was its greatest pageant. Hundreds of thousands were on the streets and the city was wearing festive colours. The spectacle was eagerly awaited. There would be tableaux and models reconstructing the recent war, glittering heaps of plundered treasure, a march of victorious soldiers, a chance to see 'the royals' in all their finery, including the all-conquering prince himself. Perhaps still more fascinating would be the sight of some of the demonic rebels, 700 of them shuffling past in chains, among them the monstrous John of Gischala and Simon bar Giora. The main worry was to get a good view, and then not lose one's place.

The day had begun with a great assembly of soldiers, formed up by centuries and cohorts under their officers. They were received by the senators and equestrians of Rome, and by Vespasian and Titus, who wore crimson robes and bay-leaf crowns and were seated on ivory thrones set upon a dais. After silencing the thunderous cheers, Vespasian said a prayer and made a short speech, after which the soldiers were dismissed to the breakfast feast traditional on a day of triumph. The emperor donned triumphal robes, sacrificed to the gods, and then joined the main procession as it formed up around mid-morning. Later that day, as the procession wound its way through the city, heading for the Sacred Way which ran through the Forum and up to the Capitoline Hill, the waiting crowds were not disappointed (**4**). The tableaux and models were presented on immense moving stages, some of them three or four storeys high, which wobbled their way precariously through the streets. Behind gold and ivory frames and rich curtains were to be seen carefully crafted scenes from the recent war:

76 *A bronze* sestertius *depicting a palm tree flanked by a victorious Roman emperor and a female personification of Judaea in mourning. The coin is inscribed 'Judaea Captured' and 'By order of the Senate'. Huge numbers of these victory coins were issued in gold, silver and bronze up until AD 81*

. . . a smiling countryside laid waste; whole units of the enemy put to the sword; men in flight and men led off to captivity; walls of enormous size thrown down by engines; great strongholds stormed; cities whose battlements were lined with defenders utterly overwhelmed; an army streaming inside the ramparts, the whole place reeking of slaughter, those unable to resist raising their hands in supplication; temples set on fire and torn down over the heads of their occupants; and after utter desolation and misery, rivers flowing not over tilled fields supplying drink to men and animals, but through a countryside still blazing on every side.

(Josephus, *JW*, 7. 143–5)

The treasures on display were also dazzling – quite in excess of those normally seen in a Roman triumph. There was not only the plunder taken from the Temple and the sack of the Upper City at the moment of their capture. There was also that extorted from captives afterwards by torture and threats, and more that had been found in weeks of trawling through the ruins of the city looking for buried hoards. 'Of the city's great wealth,' reports Josephus of events weeks after the siege, 'quantities were still being found among the ruins. Much of this was dug up by the Romans, but still more came into their hands as a result of information from the prisoners – gold and silver and the most valuable articles of other kinds, which in view of the incalculable chances of war the owners had stowed underground.' Rome was fuelled by the spoils of war. They were the means by which the state rewarded its soldiers, enriched its ruling class, and paid for peace at home with 'bread and circuses'. The soldiers had in fact already had their cut of the Jerusalem plunder. Before leaving the city, Titus had organised a magnificent victory celebration in the Roman camp. Standing on a dais and flanked by his staff, he had first delivered a speech of thanks and praise, promising 'honours and distinctions' to all those 'who in the course of the war had performed any outstanding exploit'. As their names were read out and they came forward, 'he put golden crowns on their heads, gave them gold torques, miniature gold spears and standards made of silver, and promoted every man to higher rank; in addition, from the spoils, he assigned to them silver, gold, garments and any amount of other booty'. Afterwards a great number of bullocks had been sacrificed and consumed by the troops in a victory feast. More had been expended in a grand tour of the East in the autumn of AD 70, when Titus had put on lavish shows to celebrate the end of the war (and the birthdays of his father and brother) at Caesarea Maritima, Caesarea Philippi, Berytus, Antioch, Alexandria, and many other cities. But the treasure was vast and the best of it had been kept back for the Roman triumph the following year. Great masses of gold, silver, ivory, gemstones, tapestries, every imaginable precious object, passed through the streets of Rome that day, 'more like a flowing river than a procession'. Most of the spoils were heaped up indiscriminately, but a few items were singled out for special display. There was the golden shewbread table from the Temple, and the golden seven-branched candlestick, the *menorah*, and, most poignant of all in this pagan pageant, the Torah, the Jewish Book of the Law, which appeared last of all in the parade of spoils (**77**). Behind this came images of Victory fashioned in gold and ivory, and behind these the victorious masters of the world, Vespasian and Titus in triumphal robes and riding chariots, Domitian magnificently attired and on horseback.

Also in the procession were the conquered: 700 former Jewish fighters picked out for the triumph 'for their exceptional stature and physique' and because they were 'the tallest and handsomest of the youngsters'. There was no glory in defeating weak men; it was important that the enemy should appear formidable. Any such blemishes as they had were covered over 'under the elaborate and beautiful garments' in which they had been dressed for the day. They had to be perfect, or at least seem to be perfect, for these men, like everything else in the procession, were, in a sense, offerings to the ghastly war-gods of the Roman state. They had been chosen six months before from among the tens of thousands taken in the great round-ups and manhunts after the fall of Jerusalem. Every man who showed himself in the days and weeks after 7 September had either been killed or taken prisoner. The ground itself had been torn up to ferret out men hiding in sewers and cisterns (**78**). Many in fact had been found already dead, some by one another's hands, some by starvation. 'So foul a stench of human flesh greeted those who charged in that many turned back at once,' recalls Josephus, 'but others were so avaricious that they pushed on, climbing over the piles of corpses, for many valuables were found in the passages and all scruples were silenced by the prospect of gain.'

Some of the prisoners had been killed immediately – any who threatened resistance, most who were found underground, and others who were too old and infirm to interest the slave dealers. But 'men in their prime who might be useful' had been herded into the Inner Court of the Temple to be guarded by an imperial freedman until each man's case came before the Roman officer appointed to decide their fate. Many had perished during this wait, killed by their guards, who refused them food and water. Of those who had finally come before the officer, all who had 'taken part in sedition and terrorism' were executed. Then those judged fit to grace the triumph

77 *A relief sculpture from the Arch of Titus in the Roman Forum (erected AD 81) depicting the Jewish War triumph of AD 71. Garlanded servants are shown carrying booty from the Temple in Jerusalem – the seven-branched candlestick (or* menorah), *the shewbread table, silver trumpets, and a chalice. Other figures carry wooden placards, presumably naming cities captured, peoples defeated, and leaders either slain in battle or displayed as prisoners in the procession*

were imprisoned pending transhipment to Rome. All the rest who were under 17 were sold as slaves. Those over 17 were divided into two groups. Some were sent in chains to the imperial mines and quarries in Egypt to spend the rest of their lives at heavy labour under the lash. The others were reserved for the arena.

To celebrate the victory, there were shows in many eastern cities, and later there would be shows in Rome and elsewhere. The bloody games were regular events, but extra shows could always be put on for a special occasion. Indeed, so popular and frequent were the games in the early empire that spectacle had become highly inflationary: the crowds were too familiar with the genre, too sated with 'special effects', to be easily impressed. The patrons – the imperial family, successful generals, senior politicians – were compelled to send ever larger numbers of men and beasts into the arena to participate in ever more elaborate and gory displays. In the early second century there were almost 3,000 men a year going into the arena in Rome alone. Some – those formally condemned to death as 'criminals' – were burnt alive, hammered onto crosses, or exposed to be eaten by wild beasts. Others were simply released into the arena to be hunted down by either animals or gladiators. Many were themselves trained as gladiators and would appear either in the beast-hunt or in individual duels with other gladiators. The gladiator combats were the most popular part of the show. Dressed up in the imagined costumes of subjugated enemies and trained in the presumed fighting methods of 'noble savages', the victims acted out, for the entertainment of the mob, a macabre pantomime of Roman military power. Perhaps this was the ultimate fate of the 700 Jewish men who had been 'specially selected'.

78 *Engraving of the Well of Siloam in the south-east corner of Jerusalem. The underground parts of the city provided refuges and escape-routes for many rebels after their defeat*

Also displayed were the two Jewish leaders, John of Gischala and Simon bar Giora. (We have no information about the fate of Eleazar the Zealot.) John's morale appears to have collapsed in the closing stages of the siege, and he had been taken captive when the food supply in his underground hiding-place ran out and he was forced to give himself up. Simon had remained energetic to the very end, and the Romans had taken time to find him. With a small group of trusted friends, a team of tunnellers, and a good supply of food, he had made his way down the length of a sewer-pipe and set about digging his way to safety. Though the little party of revolutionaries worked hard, the distance had been too great and the food had run out before the rock could be dug away. Even then, when every resource seemed exhausted, Simon still attempted a ruse. Using the tunnel system beneath the Temple Mount, he had suddenly appeared amid the ruins of the Temple dressed in several short white tunics and a crimson cape. The Romans had been shocked but not sufficiently panicked to enable Simon to prosecute his plan – whatever it was. He had been arrested, put in chains, and sent to Titus in Caesarea. Simon had been the greatest of the revolutionary leaders, and now the Romans reserved for him the greatest humiliation. John had been a man of some wealth and rank, his radical affiliation somewhat tainted by opportunism and self-interested scheming, and this may have had something to do with the Roman decision to spare him execution and condemn him instead to life imprisonment. Not so Simon. Though our only source for Simon bar Giora's career is poisoned by class hatred, there is little in the factual record that tells against him. Clearly he was not a 'tyrant', or men would not have followed him. Clearly, too, he was not a 'murderer', since the few executions he ordered occurred in the direst of military crises. He was a charismatic and dynamic popular leader, a man sprung from the villages of ancient Palestine and able to embody a fighting people's highest aspirations because he was driven not by the small-mindedness of private interests but by a collective vision of the world transformed. Rome may have recognised something of itself in John, but in Simon it saw only the rage of the oppressed.

The procession finished at the Temple of Jupiter on the Capitoline Hill. Now was the time for the supreme sacrifice to the blood-drenched god of thunder. The black terror of Jupiter had claimed already tens of thousands, but the greatest death was always reserved for this moment. The chained body of Simon bar Giora was pulled to the ground and dragged across the Forum. The scourges of his tormentors tore off ribbons of flesh as he passed, and then, at the place reserved by tradition for public execution, the life was squeezed out of him by slow strangulation. When the news was announced that the enemy commander-in-chief was dead, the Capitol and the Forum resounded to cheers, the holy sacrifices were performed, and the citizens of Rome settled down to sumptuous feasting.

There would be many more celebrations of victory and imperial power in the years to come. The procession that day had passed the site of Nero's Palace. The grotesque 35m-tall colossus of the former tyrant had been modified into an image of the Sun, and the area around it had been transformed into a vast building site. Using the spoils of war – looted bullion and gangs of slave-labourers – Vespasian's engineers were constructing the greatest of all amphitheatres. It would be ten years in the building, and when finished it would extend 188m on its long axis, 156m on its short one, and 52m from ground level to the top of the outer wall. Raised up on a honeycomb of arcades and barrel-vaults would be seating for tens of thousands of spectators ranged around an elliptical arena. Vespasian did not live to see it finished. The inaugural games of AD 80 were hosted by his son and successor. According to his biographer, Titus provided for the occasion 'a most lavish gladiatorial show', including 'a sea-fight on the old artificial lake', and 'a wild-beast hunt in which 5,000 animals of different sorts died in a single day'. The following year – after Titus' premature and suspicious death – his younger brother and successor, Domitian, inaugurated a new monument. It was built on a narrow neck of high ground between the Forum and the Colosseum, such that it could be seen from both of them and would provide a link, as it were, between the ancient heart of Roman power and the 'bread and circuses' of Flavian patronage. This monument was the Arch of Titus. Two panels of marble relief-sculpture were placed facing each other on either side of the passageway: they depicted scenes from the triumph of AD 71, one showing the golden treasures from the Temple carried aloft, the other Titus the conqueror in his four-horse chariot. On the vaulted ceiling above was placed another image of Titus, his time with Jupiter in the guise of an eagle, his escort on the journey to heaven. The Lord of Darkness had come to claim one of his own: Titus, butcher of the Jews, was now a god of Rome.

Flickers of defiance

Masada, near the Dead Sea, spring AD 73 or 74
The rock of Masada is a most forbidding battleground. The plateau at the top, which is 600m north-south and 300m east-west at the widest point, is almost entirely encircled by cliffs (**79, 80 & colour plate 22**). Along part of the eastern side there is a 400m sheer drop, and from this direction the only way up is by a precipitous, winding, single-lane track, known to Josephus, because of its distinctive appearance when viewed from a distance, as 'the Snake'. The western ascent is much easier, it being only 75m from ground level to the summit, but again there is only one route up. Someone attacking the rock in antiquity faced the enormous additional problem that the site had been heavily fortified: a perimeter wall 1,300m long ran around almost the entire rim of the summit. The wall stood about 5m high and was strengthened by the addition of numerous towers. There was a huge supply of arms in the fortress (Josephus says enough for 10,000 men, though this is undoubtedly exaggeration, and much of the original stock must have been taken for use elsewhere). There were also huge reserves of food and water. When seized by rebels at the beginning of the war, the storerooms constructed by King Herod the Great – Masada was one of his many refuges – were found to be full of perfectly preserved foodstuffs: according to Josephus they included corn, wine, oil, pulses and dates; though figs, which keep especially well, are likely too (**colour plate 23**). The

79 *Engraving by the early nineteenth-century English artist Tipping showing the rock of Masada viewed from the north-west. The three terraces of Herod's hanging-palace are clearly depicted on the peak, though the Roman siege-ramp to the right of the picture appears steeper and more precipitous than in reality, and the height of the rock overall has been considerably exaggerated*

many coins and inscribed potsherds found on the site may attest to some sort of rationing system. As for water, Herod had constructed huge cisterns and a system of dams and aqueducts to fill them; excavators working on the site in 1963-5 witnessed winter flash-floods in the nearby wadis and concluded that when the Herodian system was working the cisterns could have been filled in a few hours. The situation of the prospective attacker, by contrast, was unenviable. For most of the year Masada is surrounded by a sun-parched wasteland of rock and sand largely devoid of life. Any besieging army would have to haul all its food and water across miles of desert track. Little wonder, then, that it was here that the revolutionaries of AD 66 made their final stand.

They were led by Eleazar ben Yair, one of the old revolutionary family which had included Hezekiah, the bandit-chief destroyed by Herod in 48-47 BC, his son Judas, organiser of the anti-Roman tax revolt of AD 6 and probable founder of the Zealot movement, and Judas' son Menahem, a prominent Zealot leader in Jerusalem in the summer of AD 66. With Eleazar were 960 followers, called by Josephus 'Sicarians', though elsewhere he describes the Masada group as 'Zealots', and it seems that the two terms were used pretty well interchangeably. There appears to have been a real split, though, between the Jerusalem group which established itself on the Temple Mount under Eleazar ben Simon in November AD 66 (and was later absorbed into John of Gischala's command), and the Masada group, which kept out of the city after their expulsion from it in September of that year. With the subsequent death of Menahem – hunted down by government forces – the leadership seems to have passed to his kinsman, Eleazar ben Yair, and a strategy of social banditry and rural guerrilla warfare was followed thereafter. The Masada group was, for instance, one of many with which Simon bar Giora had dealings during his campaigns in southern Judaea and Idumaea in AD 67-9. Josephus implies a disagreement about strategy: Simon, it seems, 'failed to persuade them to attempt anything more ambitious than plundering expeditions and raids around Masada, since they were used to their fortress and dared not venture far from their lair.' Several years later, little had changed: the Masada Zealots were still in arms against Rome, still supporting themselves by raiding, and still restricting their operations to the area immediately around the fortress. Were they, then, by AD 73, nothing more than local bandits?

Three things argue against this characterisation: first, the existence of several known centres of resistance and the large numbers involved in each case; second, written evidence for the radicalism of the participants; and third, the scale of the Roman military response. The impression we get is of a continuing rural insurgency in southern Palestine in the two or three years after the fall of Jerusalem. The region was largely wasteland and Roman campaigns here in AD 68 and possibly 69 had been limited and inconclusive; numerous groups of revolutionaries and bandits had continued to operate, many choosing, in classic guerrilla style, to remain at large rather than risk becoming trapped in a city under siege. After September AD 70 these bands were reinforced by a trickle of veteran fighters who had succeeded in escaping from Jerusalem. The fugitives, according to Josephus, helped to establish at

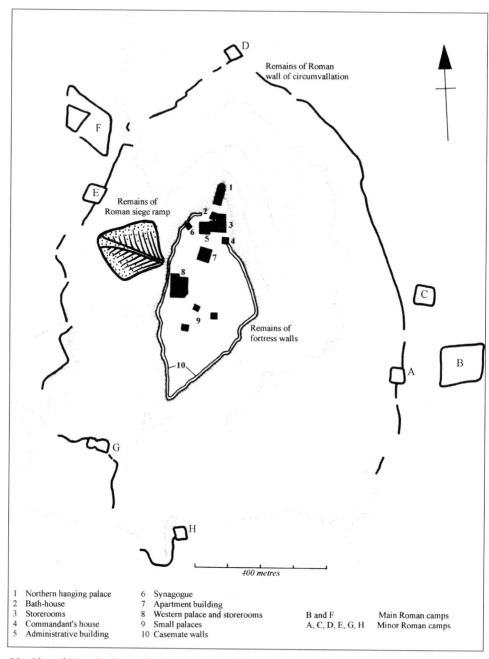

Remains of Roman
wall of circumvallation

Remains of
Roman siege ramp

Remains of
fortress walls

400 metres

1	Northern hanging palace	6	Synagogue
2	Bath-house	7	Apartment building
3	Storerooms	8	Western palace and storerooms
4	Commandant's house	9	Small palaces
5	Administrative building	10	Casemate walls

B and F — Main Roman camps
A, C, D, E, G, H — Minor Roman camps

80 *Plan of Masada showing both fortress and the Roman siege works*

81 *Within the thickness of the casemate walls around the fortress, the Zealots built partitions to create small domestic units suitably subdivided*

least one major new base – in addition, that is, to Herodium, Machaerus and Masada – at a place called 'the Forest of Jardes'. The strategy of the southern guerrillas appears to have been highly defensive. Their aim was to maintain themselves as resistance groups by keeping to the Wilderness and avoiding contact with Roman troops: they were in for the long haul. At Masada the Zealots lived a simple communal life in family groups. The archaeological evidence of their occupation contrasts sharply with that of the Herodian palaces on the site. Many of the 110 rooms of the casemate wall had been partitioned to create more efficient domestic units (**81**). Here were found cupboards and niches cut into the walls; ovens, stoves and bundles of faggots beside soot-blackened walls; ceramic jars and cooking pots, and mugs and bowls made of soft stone; clay oil-lamps; fragments of cloth from bags and tunics; palm-frond mats and baskets of the sort you see in eastern markets today; leather sandals, also little changed; eating and toilet utensils of wood, bone, ivory and bronze; and buckles, brooches and rings. Other families had lived in parts of the old palaces, and yet others, perhaps the latest arrivals, had been accommodated in simple shelters of mud; again there was abundant evidence for daily life. Excavators also found two ritual baths (*mikve*), each comprising the necessary three pools, one for holding pure rainwater, one for washing hands and feet before immersion, and one for the actual cleansing process. Further testimony to Zealot piety was provided by the discovery of a synagogue and, both in this building and in parts of the casemate wall, fragments of holy text. One of these fragments was of supreme importance in identifying the defenders of Masada as politico-religious revolutionaries, not mere bandits.

Buried beneath two metres of rubble in one of the casemate rooms was a layer of occupation debris – vessels, cloth, leather, mats, baskets – and, in one corner, a scatter of 17 silver shekels representing all five years of the revolt. Close to the shekels excavators began to find scrolls. When read in the laboratory in the form of infra-red photos, they were found to include some fragments from the *Book of Psalms*, one from the *Book of Leviticus*, and another which included the words 'Song of the holocaust of the sixth Sabbath on the ninth of the second month'. The sixth Sabbath could fall on the ninth of the second month only on the basis of the special calendar used by the Essenes of Qumran – and in fact the sectarian text from which the extract came, *Songs for the Holocaust of the Sabbath*, was already known among the Dead Sea Scrolls. This discovery – given the general evidence on the site for their piety – seems to tie the Masada Zealots into a wider radical network. Josephus confirms this when, at the end of his history, he places the defenders of Masada firmly in the context of the Jewish revolt as a whole. After describing the banditry of the Sicarians, he continues:

> The public and private life of the whole nation was corrupt. People were so determined to outdo each other in impiety towards God and injustice towards neighbours, the upper classes ill-using the masses, the masses striving to overthrow the upper classes. One group was bent on domination, the other on violence and robbing the rich. First to begin this lawlessness and this barbarity to kinsmen were the Sicarians, who left no word unspoken, no deed untried, to insult and destroy the objects of their foul plots.
>
> (*JW*, 7.260-2)

He continues with a denunciation of John of Gischala and Simon bar Giora, and then returns to the Sicarians to discuss their last stand at Masada. Josephus sees these people, then, as the hardcore revolutionaries, the ones who began the struggle years before the mass uprising, and who now continued to the bitter end after all others had been defeated.

The Romans certainly took the continuing insurgency in the south seriously. If the rebels' short-term strategy was simply to survive, their long-term hopes must have hinged on a new upsurge of mass struggle. The fear was that the Zealot guerrillas could spark such an upsurge. Palestine was destined to remain disturbed for the next 60 years, with a minor revolt in AD 117 and a major one under Simon bar Kochba in AD 132-6 (which, though we lack the primary sources, may well have been on an even bigger scale than that of AD 66-73). The Roman strategy, therefore, was to continue the methodical and ruthless destruction of resistance that had characterised their conduct of the war in AD 67-70. They were at first preoccupied with Jerusalem. As the hunt for fugitive rebels continued in and around the city, Titus ordered all the walls to be levelled except for the Hippicus, Phasael and Mariamme Towers and a stretch on the western side, which were retained as a fortification for the Roman garrison. When he demobilised his army, returning the Fifth, Twelfth and Fifteen Legions to other stations in the East, he ordered the Tenth, supported by some auxiliary units, to remain. Vespasian then imposed a victor's peace on the country: the Temple was not to be rebuilt, the high priesthood and Sanhedrin were abolished, and Temple tax was now to be paid to Capitoline Jupiter (effectively the Roman treasury); and most Jewish land became imperial property, many Jewish aristocrats losing their estates, and the bulk of the peasantry becoming tenants of the emperor. There was little attempt to rebuild the Jewish aristocracy as a client élite, and none at all to win 'hearts and minds' more widely. Palestine was to be plundered for the benefit of the Roman ruling class, not only in war but also in peace. Since these terms gave the rebels in the south no incentive to lay down their arms, the *Pax Romana* would have to be enforced here, as in the north, by blood and iron.

The dates of the Roman campaigns in the south are uncertain. Herodium, Machaerus and the Forest of Jardes may have fallen in AD 71, 72 or 73, Masada in 73 or 74 (**60**). What is clear is the sequence: the Romans conducted a systematic counter-insurgency campaign, working steadily outwards from Jerusalem, suppressing the rebel bases nearest to it first. Herodium, which is in southern Judaea about ten miles south of Jerusalem on the edge of the desert, fell at an early stage. The rebels were ensconced in the palace-fortress which Herod the Great had built at the top of a steep-sided artificial cone (**colour plate 8**). From this, had they resisted strongly, they could only have been evicted with great difficulty, since access was limited to an underground passageway leading up from the bottom of the hill, the summit was protected by a high casemate wall and four projecting towers, and there were extensive cisterns and storerooms in the thickness of the cone. Fortunately for Lucilius Bassus, the Roman commander, the defenders submitted quickly. Why, and on what terms, we are not told.

Bassus then led his army across the Jordan and into southern Peraea to reduce another formidable fortress. Machaerus, a few miles east of the Dead Sea, had been built by the Hasmonaean kings as a border defence against Nabataean Arabia, but it had later been rebuilt as another palace-fortress by Herod the Great. It is a flat-topped rocky eminence in barren uplands, well protected by ravines and steep slopes, and the Jewish kings had strengthened it further with walls and towers around the summit. Bassus set about constructing a ramp on the western approach to the fortress, and the Jews countered with vigorous daily sorties. Some of the Jews operating beyond the walls appear to have become careless, and a particularly energetic young fighter called Eleazar, who had played a leading role in the sorties, was suddenly swooped upon and captured by a Roman soldier. Bassus ordered that an example be made and the terrible ritual of death by crucifixion began. The captive was stripped and scourged in sight of the walls, and then a cross was erected. At this point the resistance of the defenders suddenly collapsed. Josephus reports that the Jews were 'distressed by the young man's agony', that his cause had many advocates inside the

82 *A view of Roman siege camp G from the top of Masada. Visible in the picture are the wall of circumvallation continuing either side of the camp, the walls of the camp itself, the main road through the camp, and the tent lines on either side of this*

fortress since 'he came of an eminent and very numerous family', and that he appealed to the defenders 'not to stand by while he suffered the most pitiable of deaths' but instead 'to save their own lives by submitting to the might and fortune of Rome, by which all others had now been crushed.' More likely Eleazar's prospective fate was the catalyst of a capitulationist mood already well established. Convinced that defeat was a matter of time, the defenders took the opportunity to surrender on terms and avoid the appalling death with which they were being threatened. Bassus agreed to let them all go.

The Roman general may have wanted to end the siege quickly because of the news that rebels were massing in his rear. Josephus reports a forced march to the Forest of Jardes (whose location is uncertain), where 'many who had escaped from the sieges of Jerusalem and Machaerus had collected', including a militia commander who had made his way through the Jerusalem sewers and slipped unnoticed through the Roman lines. Bassus threw a cavalry cordon around the forest to prevent anyone escaping and then set his infantry to work cutting down the trees. As their fastness was steadily reduced, the Jews attempted to break out by launching a series of attacks on the Roman lines. Each of these was thrown back, and, after prolonged fighting, the entire force was wiped out. Judging by the fact that only 12 Romans were killed in the action, the Jews had probably numbered only a few hundred at the most.

Bassus did not live to complete the suppression of the insurgency; he died in office and was replaced by Flavius Silva, 'who, seeing the rest of the country reduced to impotence and only one fortress still holding out, marched against it with all available forces'. So it was, in the winter of AD 72/3 or 73/4, that a Roman force of perhaps 15,000 men appeared at Masada – the Tenth Legion, various auxiliary units, the usual civilian ancillaries, and numerous Jewish slave-labourers to ferry food and water across the desert. Having pacified and garrisoned the surrounding region, ensuring that all the rebels were bottled up on the rock, Silva set about establishing a blockade around it. He built eight camps for his troops and a wall of circumvallation over three miles in circumference. Two of the camps were 'vexillation' camps, each capable of accommodating half a legion, and these were set just behind the Roman wall opposite the two approaches to the fortress, B on the east, F on the west (**colour plate 24**). The other six camps were for auxiliaries: C and E were 'milliary' (able to hold about 1,000 men each), the others 'quingenary' (about 500 men each) (**82**). The auxiliary camps were carefully placed to cover the main approaches, possible escape-routes, and, in the case of Camp H, to permit observation into Masada from above. Altogether there was accommodation for about 9,000 men; presumably the slaves slept in the open or in crude shelters outside the camps. The interior space of the camps was divided up into regular tent lines (one per century of 80 men), with separate cells for each eight-man section (or *contubernium*). These cells were formed of dry-stone walls with benches for sitting and sleeping, across the top of which, supported on poles, leather tents were spread. The wall of circumvallation, which continued in places even along the tops of vertical cliffs, was almost 2m thick, and was reinforced on the eastern side, where a breakout would have been more feasible, by 15 towers set at 70-90m intervals. Silva was leaving nothing to chance. Masada was the last stronghold of the rebels. None was to be allowed to escape to resume the struggle elsewhere. This was to be the final battle.

But how to get at them? The rebels were well supplied with food and water, and could probably survive an indefinite blockade. Masada would have to be stormed, and that could only be done by creating an assault ramp by which to approach it. In only one place did this seem remotely possible, and even here the engineering work demanded was daunting. Beyond the western gate of the fortress there was a ridge of high ground – Josephus calls it 'the White Cliff' – and Silva ordered his men to build a huge ramp of earth and timber on top of this, eventually raising its height by some 30m (**83**). At the upper end of the ramp, nearest to the fortress walls, they then constructed a level fighting-platform, and onto this they hauled their engines, including a massive iron-plated tower almost 30m tall filled with stone-throwers and bolt-shooters to clear the enemy battlements of defenders, and a huge ram which quickly smashed through a section of the wall. Excavators found the area near the top of the ramp littered with hundreds of stone balls the size of grapefruits, and a sizeable section of the wall at this point is missing.

The Zealots, however, had not been idle. Though Josephus does not say this, they must have contested the Roman operations. More than a dozen huge round boulders were found unused in various casemate rooms at strategic points along the perimeter:

83 *A view of the remains of the Roman siege ramp at Masada looking west from the Roman position*

evidence of at least one of the defensive measures employed. What our source does record is that, while the Romans were battering down the main wall, the defenders were busy constructing a new one behind it. This, moreover, was designed to resist ramming. Battering had the effect of shattering and dislodging stone, but the new wall was a timber-framed structure filled with earth, and 'the blows of the engines falling on yielding earth, the concussion shook the rampart together and made it more solid'. The disadvantage of such a structure, however, was the vulnerability of its timbers to fire, and Silva ordered his men to direct volleys of firebrands at the wall. The flames quickly took hold. Though a contrary wind briefly threatened to drive the fire back onto the Roman engines and consume them, it suddenly changed direction again and 'flung the flames against the wall, turning it into one solid blazing mass'. By the end of the day's fighting, the Jews' second wall had been destroyed, a wide breach into the fortress opened, and a Roman heavy infantry assault the following morning was a certainty. The Romans kept watch that night with unusual vigilance, lest any of the Jews attempted a getaway.

The Zealots, however, neither attempted to leave in the night, nor to defend the fortress the following morning. When the Romans attacked, storming fully armed over the gangplanks between platform and rampart, they found no enemy in the breach and the compound beyond eerily empty and silent. The Zealots had gone. The bewildered legionaries shouted out in the hope that their enemies would show themselves. None did, save for two women and five children who shortly afterwards appeared from their place of hiding in a water-channel. They were the sole survivors of a Zealot community of 960 people. One of the two women told the story of Masada's last hours to Roman interrogators – this story was entered in the official Roman military records, and these were consulted by Josephus when we wrote his history of the war – and so the knowledge of what happened has come down to us. Though there has been some doubt cast on the truth of the story – and in particular on whether all or any of the human remains found on the site in the 1963-5 excavations were in fact those of the defenders – there seems little reason to doubt the basic factual record. At the very least the archaeology can do nothing to refute the written testimony, and there is no reason to assume the latter to be a concoction. Josephus had access to reliable contemporary sources, the Hellenistic tradition of historical writing did not sanction wholesale fabrication, and the event described, while it may be exceptional, is certainly not incredible. The story goes that Eleazar ben Yair persuaded his followers to enter into a suicide pact rather than allow themselves to fall into Roman hands. The men first killed their wives and children. They then made a huge bonfire of their belongings. Next they drew lots, and ten men were selected to kill their companions, each of whom lay down next to his wife and children and offered his throat to be cut. Then the ten drew lots, and one man was selected to kill the other nine before finally killing himself. And this, apparently, was how the Romans found them: rows of bodies lying in their family groups, 960 men, women and children altogether.

Josephus cannot know what Eleazar said to his followers on the terrible night of 15 April AD 73 or 74 to persuade them to end their lives, but the words the historian attributes to him are based on intimate knowledge of the revolutionaries and no doubt reflect something of the ideology that inspired them. Josephus has him remind the Zealots of the fate of defeated rebels: wives raped, children enslaved, possessions robbed, their own lives in the hands of vengeful enemies. He argues that the alternative is for them to die as free men whose immortal souls will enjoy eternal rest in the presence of God. But he speaks also of God's disfavour towards their fellow countrymen, whose holy city he chose not to protect, and also towards themselves, whose near impregnable fortress he has not allowed to save them.

> Long ago we resolved to serve neither the Romans nor anyone but God, who alone is the true and righteous Lord of men. Now the time has come that bids us prove our determination with deeds. At such a time we must not disgrace ourselves. Hitherto we have never submitted to slavery, even when that brought no danger with it. We must not choose slavery now. To fall alive into the hands of the Romans will mean the end of everything. We were the first to revolt, and we shall be the last to break off the struggle. I think it is God who has given us the privilege to choose to die nobly and as free men, unlike others who were taken unawares by their defeat. In our case we know that daybreak will end our resistance, but we are still free at this moment to choose an honourable death with our loved ones. This our enemies cannot prevent, however much they may pray to take us alive.
>
> (*JW*, 7.323-6)

Conclusion

Revolutions change history. The Jewish Revolution would obviously have done so if the Jews had won. Is it true, then, as some have argued, that this was never a possibility? Between 13 and 7 BC the Romans conquered all of Germany as far as the River Elbe. In AD 9, when the provincial governor attempted to tax the new territory, the Germans rose in revolt, destroyed three legions at the battle of the Teutoburg Forest, and threw the Romans out. Henceforward most of Germany remained outside the empire. Rome, then, was not invincible. But was successful revolt a possibility for the Palestinian Jews in AD 66-70? Peace had been made with Parthia only in AD 63, and this dangerous enemy had in the past penetrated deeply into Roman territory and inflicted punishing defeats on the legions. In AD 60 or 61 the Boudiccan rebels had almost driven the Romans from Britain, in AD 68-9 Rome was consumed by civil war, and in AD 70 there was a major revolt of Germans and Gauls in the Rhineland. Had the timing and course of events been only a little different, or had other threats, whether internal revolt or foreign invasion, developed, the Flavian restoration of empire might have gone differently. The military resilience of the Jews, moreover, testifies to the potential threat to imperial power posed by even geographically localised rebellion. With probably never more than 50,000 or so men under arms – and these mainly farmers' sons fighting as lightly equipped irregulars – the Jews forced the Romans to fight a long, hard, bloody struggle. It is far too easy for historians who know the future to condemn those who appear to fight for doomed causes. In fact, the course of history is not predetermined; it is never the case that what happens has to happen because 'there is no alternative'; human beings make their own history, and alternative futures are always possible. If defeat for the Jews in AD 70 was the most likely outcome, it was never a certain one, and the revolutionaries were right to fight.

Failed revolutions also change history. The full historical impact of the Jewish Revolution of AD 66-73 is impossible to estimate, for, with the passage of time, its implications escalate into an incalculable myriad. The three great Mediterranean religions of the last 2,000 years – Judaism, Christianity and Islam – have been profoundly affected by it. The defeat of apocalyptic hope and the physical destruction of the Judaeo-Christian sect cleared the way for the Pauline Christians to denationalise Jesus, cauterise his revolutionary message, and repackage him as a saviour-god dispensing opiate. The Jewish disaster cleared the field also for conservative Pharisees (or 'rabbis' as they came increasingly to be called), men like Johanan ben Zakkai of Jamnia, to recast Judaism as a religion of accommodation, conformity and obedience. And centuries later, how could Islam, that explosive resurgence of semitic monotheism, have swept across the East so easily if the old versions of the cult had not been emasculated by priests and rabbis? For Pauline Christianity and rabbinical Judaism both reflected the collapse of revolutionary hope, the destruction of revolutionary organisation, and the persecution of revolutionary cadre; they were, in essence, an escape from these terrible worldly realities into a spiritualised never-never land.

Others, though, fought on. The Romans could not extirpate the Jewish revolutionary tradition entirely, and it survived in many of the empire's dark recesses. Some Zealots escaped to Alexandria in Egypt and attempted to build a new base in the large Jewish ghetto. They were rounded up and handed over to the Romans by the Jewish *dunatoi*. They then astonished their captors by continuing to spit defiance at them even as they were tortured to death, all of them refusing to the end to acknowledge the Roman emperor as their master. The government's spiteful response was to order the demolition of the temple of the Egyptian Jews at Onias. Cyrene also was disturbed. A Zealot fugitive called Jonathan, a weaver by trade, 'persuaded a number of men of the poorer classes to listen to him, and he led them out into the desert promising to show them signs and portents.' Again it was the local Jewish *dunatoi* who initiated repressive action. They informed the Roman governor of the disturbance and a military force was dispatched to disperse the millenarians. Jonathan himself escaped at first, but he was later hunted down, taken in chains to Rome, and there tortured and burnt alive.

At that point Josephus concludes his history, and it is worth spelling out what, unwittingly perhaps, he teaches us. From him we learn – and the lesson is confirmed by the gospels and the scrolls – that the great events of history recorded elsewhere are but the culmination of long molecular processes deep in the social structure. The social bandits, the radical sects, the messiahs, the apocalyptic hopes of the revolutionaries, and the peasant vision of a holy Jubilee: all these ingredients of the great popular movement of AD 66 were decades in the making. So, though we do not have a source like Josephus for this period, we must imagine that, beneath the police gaze of the Roman state, an underground current of Zealotism carried on in the villages and ghettoes of the Jews after the disaster of AD 70. New books of apocalyptic literature certainly appeared – *Revelation*, *2 Esdras*, *2 Baruch* – and there were further insurrections – in AD 115-17 in the cities of the Diaspora, in Cyrene, Egypt and Cyprus, and then in AD 132-6 in Palestine itself. This last was the revolt of Simon bar Kochba, the new Jewish Messiah, known as 'Son of the Star', recognised and supported as such by the greatest Jewish sage of the time, the radical rabbi Akiba. The rebels seized back the holy city of Jerusalem, appointed a new high priest, and restored Temple ritual. They issued coins which they inscribed 'Year One of the Redemption of Israel', and they rebuilt the walls of the city. Exiles returned, volunteers arrived from the Diaspora, the countryside around the holy city filled with an invisible army of rural guerrillas, and the cave complexes and desert fortresses of AD 66-73 were again defended by Jewish freedom-fighters. It took the Romans four long years and eight legions to crush the revolt. It is another story, of course, and one whose details are probably lost forever – saving some spectacular new discovery in the Judaean Wilderness. But enough is known to convey a message of hope: it is that even in the darkest days of defeat, no matter how brutally men and women are subjugated, as long as there is evil in the world, there will be Essenes, Zealots and flickers of defiance; and as long as that is so, there will sometimes be mighty conflagrations when the Sons of Righteousness shine forth and there is the light of a possible sunrise.

Chronology

N.B. Rulers and ruling authorities are shown in italics. All dates are AD unless indicated otherwise.

Date	Emperors and events in Roman Empire	Ruling authorities in Palestine	Events in Palestine
c.1000–965 BC		*? King David.*	? United Israelite kingdom.
c.965–930 BC		*? King Solomon.*	? Construction of First Temple.
c.926–722 BC		*Kings of Israel.*	Northern kingdom of Israel; fall of kingdom to Assyrians.
c.926–587 BC		*Kings of Judah.*	Southern kingdom of Judah; fall of kingdom to Babylonians.
c.587–537 BC		*Kings of Babylon.*	Babylonian Captivity; ends with Return from Exile.
c.550–300 BC			Most books of *The Old Testament* written.
537–332 BC		*Kings of Persia.*	
c.516 BC			Completion of Second Temple.
332 BC			Conquest by Alexander the Great.
323–200 BC		*Ptolemies of Egypt.*	
c.250/200 BC – AD 66			Dead Sea Scrolls written.
200–164 BC		*Seleucids of Syria.*	
175–164 BC		*King Antiochus Epiphanes IV.*	
167–142 BC			Maccabaean Revolt after Seleucids attempt to replace cult of Yahweh with cult of Zeus.
164–37 BC		*Hasmonaean kings.*	
164–161 BC		*Judas Maccabaeus* king.	
161–142 BC		*Jonathan Maccabaeus* king (and high priest from 153-152)	?Formation of Essene sect.
142–134 BC		*Simon Maccabaeus* king.	
134–104 BC		*John Hyrcanus I* king.	
104–103 BC		*Aristobulus I* king.	
103–76 BC		*Alexander Jannaeus* king and high priest.	
76–67 BC		*Alexandra Salome* regent; *John Hyrcanus II* high priest.	
66–63 BC	Pompey's eastern campaigns.	*Aristobulus II* king and high priest.	
63 BC			Pompey's capture of Jerusalem and violation of Temple.
63–40 BC		*John Hyrcanus II* high priest.	Sustained conflict and occasional civil war between pro- and anti-Roman Hasmonaean factions.
59 BC			Governor of Asia attempts to stop payments of Temple tithe.
59–49 BC	*First Triumvirate.*		
53 BC			Crassus plunders Temple for Parthian War.
49–30 BC	Civil wars.		
48–47 BC			Herod defeats bandit-chief Hezekiah.
42–31 BC	*Second Triumvirate.*		
40–37 BC		*Antigonus* king and high priest.	Parthian-backed government in Palestine; civil war.
38–37 BC			Herod defeats bandits at Mount Arbel.
37–4 BC		*Herod the Great* king	Roman-backed government restored in Palestine; bloody purge of pro-Hasmonaeans. Five successive land grants eventually make Herod greatest Jewish king since Solomon.
30 BC–AD 14	*Augustus* emperor.		
12 BC			Inaugural Caesar's Games at opening of new city and harbour at Caesarea.

Date	Emperors and events in Roman Empire	Ruling authorities in in Palestine	Events in Palestine
4 BC			Riots in Jerusalem against display of eagle on Temple; death of Herod the Great; mass struggles across Judaea; Temple looted by Roman troops; Herodian succession imposed.
4 BC – AD 6		*Archelaus* ethnarch of Judaea.	
4 BC – AD 34		*Philip* tetrarch of Golan region.	
4 BC – AD 39		*Herod Antipas* tetrarch of Galilee and Peraea.	
6-8		*Coponius* prefect of Judaea.	Client-state of Judaea dissolved and Roman province created; Judas the Galilean leads abortive tax strike; Roman authorities seek control of Temple.
9-12		*Marcus Ambivius* prefect of Judaea.	
12-15		*Annius Rufus* prefect of Judaea.	
14-37	*Tiberius* emperor.		
15-26		*Valerius Gratus* prefect of Judaea.	
19	Expulsion of Jews from Rome.		
26-36		*Pontius Pilate* prefect of Judaea.	Civil disobedience against display of Roman military standards in Jerusalem; use of Temple treasure to pay for aqueduct; erection of imperial shields in Jerusalem; messianic disturbance in Samaria.
c.30-36			Mission of Jesus of Nazareth.
37		*Marullus* prefect of Judaea.	
37-41	*Caligula* emperor.	*Herennius Capito* prefect of Judaea.	Attempt to erect statue of Caligula-Jupiter in Temple; Judaea on brink of war.
37-44		*Herod Agrippa I* king of Golan region.	
41-54	*Claudius* emperor.		
41-44		*Herod Agrippa I* king of all Palestine	Herodian client-kingdom of Palestine restored.
c.44-46		*Cuspius Fadus* procurator.	Disturbances across Palestine as direct Roman rule reimposed.
c.46-48		*Tiberius Alexander* procurator.	Famine and abortive Zealot revolt.
48	Expulsion of Jews from Rome.		
48-52		*Ventidius Cumanus* procurator.	Offensive behaviour by soldiers leads to protests and riots; communal violence between Jews and Samaritans.
50-93		*Herod Agrippa II* king of Golan region and later parts of Galilee and Peraea (from 53 and 54).	
52-60		*Marcus Antonius Felix* procurator.	Romans suppress bandits and millenarians; Sicarian terrorists assassinate leading public figures.
c.52-58	St Paul's three missionary journeys.		
53	Parthian invasion of Armenia; Tiridates installed as king.		
54-68	*Nero* emperor.		
55	Corbulo appointed Roman commander in Armenian War.		
58			Arrest and detention of St Paul.
58-60	Corbulo invades Armenia; Tiridates overthrown; Tigranes installed as king.		
59			Citizenship riots in Caesarea.
60-61	Boudiccan Revolt in Britain.		
60-62		*Porcius Festus* procurator.	Increasing disorder due to bandits, terrorists and rioters; St Paul sent to Rome for trial.
61	Disturbances in Rome at mass execution of 400 slaves.		
61-62	Vologases' invasion of Armenia; Tigranes overthrown; Tiridates reinstated as king; Roman defeat at Rhandeia.		

Date	Emperors and events in Roman Empire	Ruling authorities in in Palestine	Events in Palestine
62	'Turning point' in Nero's reign: Burrus dies and Seneca retires; Nero divorces Octavia, marries Poppaea, and appoints Tigellinus Praetorian Prefect.		Sanhedrin executes Judaeo-Christian leader St James (after earlier execution of St Stephen).
62-64		*Clodius Albinus* procurator.	Further increases in disorder; Sicarians win release of political prisoners. Conflict between Herod Agrippa and high priests; faction-fighting among high priests.
63	Corbulo invades Armenia; truce agreed at Rhandeia; Tiridates agrees to give homage to Nero.		
64	Nero performs in games at Naples. Great fire at Rome; work starts on 'Golden House'; persecution of Christians; ? martyrdoms of St Peter and St Paul.		
64-66		*Gessius Florus* procurator.	
65	Nero performs in Neronian Games in Rome. Conspiracy of Piso.		Jewish leaders appeal to Govenor of Syria against Procurator of Judaea.
66	Tiridates' visit to Rome. Nero performs in games at Actium.		
mid-May 66			Anti-semitic riots in Caesarea. Florus enters Jerusalem in force; demands arrest of anti-Roman militants; Upper Market massacre; second massacre at gates of Jerusalem; defeat of Roman troops in street-fighting; Florus abandons Jerusalem to the rebels.
late May or early June – mid-Nov 66		*Eleazar ben Ananias* leads first aristocratic government.	Herod Agrippa II appeals for order at meeting in Gymnasium in Jerusalem; later flees; first aristocratic government formed.
early Aug – early Sept 66			Attempted Herodian coup in Jerusalem; Menaham's Zealots join fighting; Herodians defeated and surrender; Herodian leader Ananias caught and executed.
Sept-Oct 66			Consolidation of first aristocratic government; destruction of Zealot faction; wave of communal violence and pogroms; fall of Joppa for first time.
mid – late Oct 66			Cestius Gallus invades Palestine; attack on Zebulon; battle of Gibeon; Romans defeated in attack on Jerusalem.
early Nov 66			Battle of Beth-Horon.
mid-Nov 66 – winter 67/68		*Ananus ben Ananus* leads second aristocratic government.	Second aristocratic government formed; radicals and militias marginalised; Eleazar and Zealots confined to Temple Mount; Simon bar Giora driven out; Josephus appointed military governor of Galilee.
winter 66/67			Troops raised and strong-points strengthened in Galilee; conflict between aristocrats and radicals; defeat of radicals in Tiberias; fall of Sepphoris.
early 67 – early 68	Nero's tour of Greece; emperor performs in all major games. Vespasian appointed to Judaean command.		Guerrilla campaigns by Simon bar Giora in Judaea and Idumaea.
? early spring 67			Abortive Jewish attacks on Ascalon.
spring 67			Vespasian's first invasion of Galilee.
mid-May – early June 67			Siege of Jotapata; fall of Japha; fall of Mount Gerizim; fall of Jotapata; capture of Josephus.
? mid-summer 67			Fall of Joppa for second time.
early Sept 67			Vespasian's second invasion of Galilee; fall of Tiberias and Tarichaeae.
late Sept – late Oct			Siege and fall of Gamala.
early autumn 67			Fall of Mount Tabor.
? late autumn 67			Fall of Gischala, Jamnia and Azotus.
winter 67/68		*John of Gischala* dominant in first radical government.	Overthrow of second aristocratic government by Zealot, Galilean and Idumaean militias.

Date	Emperors and events in Roman Empire	Ruling authorities in in Palestine	Events in Palestine
spring – early summer 68	Revolt of Vindex in Rhineland and Galba in Spain.		Romans invade Peraea, Judaea and Idumaea; fall of Gadara, Bethennabris, Emmaus, Jericho and Qumran. Continuing guerrilla campaigns by Simon bar Giora in Judaea and Idumaea.
mid-summer 68	Fall of Nero. *Galba* emperor.		
Jan 69	Fall of *Galba*; Otho and Vitellius both elevated. *Otho* emperor.		
spring – early summer 69			Romans invade Idumaea and Judaea; fall of Hebron. Simon bar Giora defeats Zealots and Idumaean conservatives in south.
April 69	First battle of Cremona; fall of Otho. *Vitellius* emperor.	*Simon bar Giora* dominant in second radical government.	Overthrow of first radical government by alliance of high priests and Simon bar Giora's southern bandit army.
July 69	Elevation of Vespasian.		
Dec 69	Flavians capture Rome after second battle of Cremona; fall of Vitellius.		
69–79	*Vespasian* emperor.		
69–70	Revolt of Rhineland auxiliaries and Gallic chieftains.		
c.70	? Mark's gospel written in Rome.		
c.70–100	? Matthew's gospel written in Alexandria; ? Luke's gospel written in Antioch.		
April 70			Titus invades Judaea and begins siege of Jerusalem.
early – mid-May 70			Capture of Third and Second Walls of Jerusalem.
late May 70			Romans construct ramps against Antonia Fortress and First Wall; these destroyed by Jewish mines and fire.
June 70			Romans establish blockade and begin mass crucifixions; new ramps constructed against Antonia Fortress.
July – mid-Aug 70			Romans attack and capture Antonia Fortress and Temple Mount in heavy and protracted fighting; Temple destroyed by fire.
mid-Aug – early Sept 70			Romans attack and capture Upper City and Royal Palace; Jerusalem sacked and fugitives hunted down.
autumn 70			Titus tours East and hosts victory games.
spring 71	Vespasian and Titus celebrate Jewish War triumph; execution of Simon bar Giora.		
71 – 73 or 74			Continuing guerrilla warfare in south; Roman mopping up operations; fall of Herodium, Machaerus, Forest of Jardes, and Masada.
? 70s	Zealot disturbances in Alexandria and Cyrene.		Jamnia rabbinical academy founded by Johanan ben Zakkai.
c.79	Publication of 'Jewish War' by Josephus.		
79–81	*Titus* emperor.		
80	Inaugural Colosseum games.		
81–96	*Domitian* emperor.		
81	Arch of Titus completed.		
c.93–94	Publication of 'Jewish Antiquities' by Josephus.		
c.95	Publication of 'My Life' by Josephus.		
96–98	*Nerva* emperor.		
98–117	*Trajan* emperor.		
c.100	? John's gospel written in Ephesus.		
115–117	Jewish revolt in Cyrene, Egypt and Cyprus.		Disturbances inspired by Diaspora revolt.
117–138	*Hadrian* emperor.		
132–136			Revolt of Simon bar Kochba and Akiba.

Bibliographical references

This bibliography includes not only works bearing directly on the Jewish War, but also studies of other events with which the Jewish War can be usefully compared. It is not, however, a comprehensive bibliography of all relevant material. Its purpose is to suggest further reading, and, especially in the absence of text references, to indicate my sources.

Abbreviations

Deut.	*The Book of Deuteronomy*
DSS	Dead Sea Scrolls
JA	*Jewish Antiquities*
JW	*The Jewish War*
Lev.	*The Book of Leviticus*
Num.	*The Book of Numbers*

Primary sources

N.B. I have credited the translations I relied upon in brackets.

The Holy Bible (the King James and the New Revised Standard versions).
Homer, *The Iliad* (trans. Richmond Lattimore, University of Chicago).
Josephus, *My Life* (trans. W. Whiston, Hendrickson Publishers).
Josephus, *Jewish Antiquities* (trans. W. Whiston, Hendrickson Publishers).
Josephus, *The Jewish War* (trans. W. Whiston, Hendrickson Publishers, and trans. G.A. Williamson, Penguin).
Juvenal, *Satires* (trans. P. Green, Penguin).
Petronius, *The Satyricon* (trans. J. Lindsay, Paul Elek Ltd).
Philo, *Every Good Man is Free* (trans. F.H. Colson, Loeb).
Pliny the Elder, *Natural History* (trans. J.F. Healy, Penguin).
Polybius, *The Rise of the Roman Empire* (trans. I. Scott-Kilvert, Penguin).
Suetonius, *The Twelve Caesars* (trans. R. Graves, Penguin).
Tacitus, *The Annals* (trans. M. Grant, Penguin).
Tacitus, *The Histories* (trans. K. Wellesley, Penguin).
Vegetius, *Epitome of Military Science* (trans. N.P. Miller, Liverpool UP).
Virgil, *The Aeneid* (trans. W.F. Jackson Knight, Penguin).

Secondary sources

N.B. I have cited the editions actually used, so many publication dates are not the original ones.

Anderson, J.G.C., 1952, 'The eastern frontier from Tiberius to Nero', in *The Cambridge Ancient History, Vol. X, The Augustan Empire, 44 BC – AD 70* (Cambridge, CUP), 743-80.
Applebaum, S., 1971, 'The Zealots: the case for revaluation', in *The Journal of Roman Studies*, 61, 155-70.
Avigad, N., 1976, *Archaeological Discoveries in the Jewish Quarter of Jerusalem, Second Temple period* (Jerusalem, Israel Museum).
Avigad, N., 1984, *Discovering Jerusalem* (Oxford, Blackwell).
Balsdon, J.P.V.D., 1979, *Romans and Aliens* (London, Duckworth).
Barker, P., 1980, *Wargames Rules, 3000 BC to 1485 AD* (Goring-by-Sea, Wargames Research Group).
Bishop, M.C.& Coulston, J.C., 1989, *Roman Military Equipment* (Aylesbury, Shire).
Brailsford, H.N., 1983, *The Levellers and the English Revolution* (Nottingham, Spokesman).
Campbell, J., 1996, *Deciphering the Dead Sea Scrolls* (London, Fontana).
Carcopino, J., 1956, *Daily Life in Ancient Rome, the people and the city at the height of the Empire* (Harmondsworth, Penguin).
Cheesman, G.L., 1914, *The Auxilia of the Roman Imperial Army* (Oxford, Clarendon).
Cohn, N., 1970, *The Pursuit of the Millennium, revolutionary millenarians and mystical anarchists of the Middle Ages* (London, Paladin).
Connolly, P., 1975, *The Roman Army* (London, Macdonald).

Connolly, P., 1983, *Living in the Time of Jesus of Nazareth* (Oxford, OUP).

Connolly, P., 1988, *Greece and Rome at War* (London, Macdonald).

Connolly, P., 1988, *Tiberius Claudius Maximus the Infantryman* (Oxford, OUP).

Connolly, P., 1988, *Tiberius Claudius Maximus the Cavalryman* (Oxford, OUP).

Countryman, E., 1987, *The American Revolution* (Harmondsworth, Penguin).

de Ste Croix, G.E.M., 1981, *The Class Struggle in the Ancient Greek World* (London, Duckworth).

Dupont-Sommer, A., 1952, *The Dead Sea Scrolls, a preliminary survey* (Oxford, Blackwell).

Dupont-Sommer, A., 1955 (2nd ed.), *The Jewish Sect of Qumran and the Essenes, new studies on the Dead Sea Scrolls* (London, Vallentine, Mitchell & Co.).

Embleton, R. & Graham, F., 1984, *Hadrian's Wall in the Days of the Romans* (Newcastle, Frank Graham).

Engels, F., 1965, *The Peasant War in Germany* (Moscow, Progress).

Fiensy, D.A., 1991, *The Social History of Palestine in the Herodian Period* (Lampeter, Edwin Mellen Press).

Finegan, J., 1992 (revised ed.), *The Archaeology of the New Testament, the life of Jesus and the beginning of the early Church* (Princeton, PUP).

Finley, M.I., 1992, *The Ancient Economy* (Harmondsworth, Penguin).

Fiorato, V., Boylston, A. & Knüsel, C., 2001, *Blood Red Roses, the archaeology of a mass grave from the battle of Towton, AD 1461* (Oxford, Oxbow).

Freyne, S., 1980, *Galilee from Alexander the Great to Hadrian, 323 BCE to 135 CE* (Wilmington and Notre Dame, Michael Glazier and University of Notre Dame).

Furneaux, R., 1972, *The Roman Siege of Jerusalem* (New York, David McKay).

Gichon, M., 1986, 'Aspects of a Roman army in war according to the *Bellum Iudaicum* of Josephus', in Freeman, P. & Kennedy, D. (eds), *The Defence of the Roman and Byzantine East* (British Archaeological Reports Int. Series 297(i)), 287-310.

Gilliver, C.M., 1999, *The Roman Art of War* (Stroud, Tempus).

Goldsworthy, A., 2000, *Roman Warfare* (London, Cassell).

Goldsworthy, A., 2001, *Cannae* (London, Cassell).

Goodman, M., 1982, 'The first Jewish revolt: social conflict and the problem of debt', in *The Journal of Jewish Studies*, 33, 417-27.

Goodman, M., 1987, *The Ruling Class of Judaea, the origins of the Jewish revolt against Rome, AD 66-70* (Cambridge, CUP).

Gracey, M.H., 1986, 'The armies of the Judaean client-kings', in Freeman, P. & Kennedy, D. (eds), *The Defence of the Roman and Byzantine East* (British Archaeological Reports Int. Series 297(i)), 311-23.

Grant, M., 1970, *Nero* (London, Weidenfeld & Nicolson).

Grant, M., 1971, *Herod the Great* (New York, American Heritage Press).

Grant, M., 1976, *Cities of Vesuvius, Pompeii and Herculaneum* (Harmondsworth, Penguin).

Grant, M., 1997, *The History of Ancient Israel* (London, Phoenix).

Grant, M., 1999, *The Jews in the Roman World* (London, Phoenix).

Griffen, M.T., 1987, *Nero, the end of a dynasty* (London, Batsford).

Guérin, D., 1977, *Class Struggle in the First French Republic, bourgeois and bras nus, 1793-1795* (London, Pluto).

Hanson, V.D., 1989, *The Western Way of War, infantry battle in Classical Greece* (London, Hodder & Stoughton).

Hanson, V.D., 1999, *The Wars of the Ancient Greeks* (London, Cassell).

Harman, C., 1999, *A People's History of the World* (London, Bookmarks).

Harris, R.L., 1995, *Exploring the World of the Bible Lands* (London, Thames & Hudson).

Hill, C., 1955, *The English Revolution, 1640, an essay* (London, Lawrence & Wishart).

Hill, C., 1961, *A Century of Revolution, 1603-1714* (London, Nelson).

Hill, C., 1972, *God's Englishman, Oliver Cromwell and the English Revolution* (Harmondsworth, Penguin).

Hill, C., 1984, *The World Turned Upside Down* (Harmondsworth, Penguin).

Hobsbawm, E.J., 1972, *Bandits* (Harmondsworth, Penguin).

Horsley, R.A., 1979, 'Josephus and the Bandits', in *The Journal for the Study of Judaism*, 10, 37-63.

Hughes, B.P., 1997, *Firepower, weapons effectiveness on the battlefield, 1630-1850* (Staplehurst, Spellmount).

Jackson, R., 1988, *Doctors and Diseases in the Roman Empire* (London, British Museum Press).

Jones, A.H.M., 1998, *The Greek City, from Alexander to Justinian* (Oxford, OUP).

Jones, P. & Sidwell, K., 1997, *The World of Rome, an introduction to Roman culture* (Cambridge, CUP).

Kamm, A., 1999, *The Israelites, an introduction* (London, Routledge).

Keegan, J., 1978, *The Face of Battle, a study of Agincourt, Waterloo and the Somme* (Harmondsworth, Penguin).

Keegan, J. & Holmes, R., 1985, *Soldiers, a history of men in battle* (London, Guild Publishing).

Kern, P.B., 1999, *Ancient Siege Warfare* (London, Souvenir Press).

Lane Fox, R., 1991, *The Unauthorized Version, truth and fiction in the Bible* (London, Viking).

Lefebvre, G., 1962, *The French Revolution, Volume 1, from its origins to 1793* (New York, Columbia University Press).

Lefebvre, G., 1964, *The French Revolution, Volume 2, from 1793 to 1799* (New York, Columbia University Press).

Lepper, F. & Frere, S., *Trajan's Column, a new edition of the Cichorius plates, introduction, commentary and notes* (Gloucester, Alan Sutton).

Leon, A., 1970 (2nd ed.), *The Jewish Question, a Marxist interpretation* (New York, Pathfinder).

Lewis, N. & Reinhold, M., 1966, *Roman Civilization, Sourcebook II, The Empire* (New York, Harper & Row).

Maccoby, H., 1973, *Revolution in Judaea, Jesus and the Jewish resistance* (London, Ocean).

Maiuri, A., 1977, *Herculaneum* (Rome, Istituto Poligrafico Dello Stato).

Manning, B., 1978, *The English People and the English Revolution* (Harmondsworth, Penguin).

Manning, B., 1992, *1649: the Crisis of the English Revolution* (London, Bookmarks).

Marsden, E.W., 1999, *Greek and Roman artillery, historical development* (Oxford, OUP).

Mathiez, M., 1964, *The French Revolution* (New York, Grosset & Dunlap).

Meshorer, Y., 1982, *Ancient Jewish Coinage* (New York, Amphora Books).

Murphy-O'Connor, J., 1998 (4th ed.), *The Holy Land, an Oxford archaeological guide from earliest times to 1700* (Oxford, OUP).

Netzer, E., 1999, *Herodium, an archaeological guide* (Jerusalem, Herodium Expedition).

Parker, H.M.D., 1958, *The Roman Legions* (Cambridge, W. Heffer & Sons).

Pearlman, M., 1999 (6th ed.), *The Dead Sea Scrolls in the Shrine of the Book* (Jerusalem, Israel Museum).

Porter, J.R., 1995, *The Illustrated Guide to the Bible* (London, BCA).

Price, J.J., 1992, *Jerusalem under Siege, the collapse of the Jewish state, 66-70 CE* (Leiden, Brill).

Rajak, T., 1983, *Josephus, the historian and his society* (London, Duckworth).

Reed, J., 1983, *Insurgent Mexico* (Harmondsworth, Penguin).

Richardson, P., 1999, *Herod, King of the Jews and Friend of the Romans* (Edinburgh, T & T Clark).

Roman, Y., 1997, *Masada, king's stronghold, Zealots' refuge* (Jerusalem, Israel National Parks).

Rose, J., 1999, 'Jesus: history's most famous missing person', in *International Socialism*, 85, 73-85.

Rose, J., 2000, 'Old Zion, redemption and truth, hostages to fortune for the new Israelites: a study of Zionist ideology, three Zionists and ancient Jewish history', unpublished University of Southampton MA dissertation.

Rudé, G., 1967, *The Crowd in the French Revolution* (Oxford, OUP).

Rudé, G., 1988, *The French Revolution* (London, Weidenfeld & Nicolson).

Sabin, P., 2000, 'The face of Roman battle', in *The Journal of Roman Studies*, 90, 1-17.

Scullard, H.H., 1959, *From the Gracchi to Nero, a history of Rome from 133 BC to AD 68* (London, Methuen).

Shanin, T. (ed.), 1971, *Peasants and Peasant Societies, selected readings* (Harmondsworth, Penguin).

Soboul, A., 1980, *The Sans-culottes, the popular movement and the revolutionary government, 1793-1794* (Princeton, PUP).

Soboul, A., 1989, *The French Revolution, 1787-1799, from the storming of the Bastille to Napoleon* (London, Unwin Hyman).

Thompson, E.P., 1980, *The Making of the English Working Class* (Harmondsworth, Penguin).

Trotsky, L., 1967, *The History of the Russian Revolution* (London, Sphere).

Vamosh, M.F., 1996, *Caesarea, queen of the coast* (Ramat Gan, Israel National Parks Authority).

Vermes, G., 1998 (complete ed.), *The Complete Dead Sea Scrolls in English* (Harmondsworth, Penguin).

Warmington, B.H., 1969, *Nero, reality and legend* (London, Chatto & Windus).

Watson, G.R., 1985, *The Roman Soldier* (London, Thames & Hudson).

Webster, G., 1969, *The Roman Imperial Army* (London, Adam & Charles Black).

Williams, D., 1996, *The Reach of Rome, a history of the Roman imperial frontier, 1st-5th centuries AD* (London, Constable).

Wilson, I., 1985, *Jesus: the evidence* (London, Pan).

Yadin, Y., 1966, *Masada, Herod's fortress and the Zealots' last stand* (London, Weidenfeld & Nicolson).

Yadin, Y., 1971, *Bar-Kokhba, the rediscovery of the legendary hero of the last Jewish revolt against imperial Rome* (London, Weidenfeld & Nicolson).

Index

This index is designed as an aid to general reading rather than formal scholarship. So that readers can find explanations easily, I have ignored passing references and included only substantive ones.